GOLDEN SUMMERS
HEIDELBERG AND BEYOND

Jane Clark and Bridget Whitelaw

Managed by the International Cultural Corporation of Australia Limited
Organized by the National Gallery of Victoria
Indemnified by the Australian Government through the
Department of Arts, Heritage and Environment

National Gallery of Victoria   30 October 1985 – 27 January 1986
Sponsored by *The Age*
Art Gallery of New South Wales   21 February – 20 April 1986
Sponsored by *The Sydney Morning Herald*
Art Gallery of South Australia   9 May – 29 June 1986
Sponsored by *The South Australian Gas Company*
with assistance from
Advertiser Newspapers Limited
Art Gallery of Western Australia   30 July – 14 September 1986
Sponsored by *The Western Mail*

THE AGE

The Sydney Morning Herald

 GAS
South Australian Gas Company

ADVERTISER NEWSPAPERS
LIMITED

The Western Mail

Published by the International Cultural Corporation of Australia
Limited 1985

National Library of Australia Cataloguing-in-Publication entry

Clark, Jane, 1955–
  Golden summers

  Rev. ed.

  Bibliography.
  ISBN 0 642 09855 7.

  1. Painting, Australian – Exhibitions. 2. Impressionism (Art) –
  Australian – Exhibitions. I. Whitelaw, Bridget, 1950 –. II.
  International Cultural Corporation of Australia. III. National Gallery
  of Victoria. IV. Title.

759.994' 074' 0994

Editor: Judith Ryan
Designer: Kathy Richards
Typesetter: Impact Graphics Pty Ltd

First edition 1985: printed by Color Offset (Aust.) Pty Ltd

Revised edition 1986: printed by Griffin Press Limited

Cover illustration (detail)
Arthur Streeton (1867–1943)
Golden Summer, Eaglemont, 1889
Oil on canvas
81.3 × 152.6 cm
Signed, dated and inscribed l.l.: Pastoral/Arthur Streeton/1889
Inscribed l.r.: Eaglemont
Collection of William J. Hughes, Perth
Reproduced by courtesy of Mrs Oliver Streeton

FOREWORD

After managing many famous exhibitions, none has given the International Cultural Corporation of Australia Limited more pride and pleasure than *Golden Summers*. We are delighted to be associated with that group of artists whom Australians hold dearest to their hearts – the painters of the Heidelberg School and their associates. After nearly a hundred years, their impressions of the Australian landscape – city and bush – still stir our sense of locality and identity. This remarkable exhibition will probably keep our sentiment for these paintings alive for years to come. And by bringing together for the first time a comprehensive collection of over 150 of the artists' works, the National Gallery of Victoria lets us see with great clarity how convincingly important is the work of the school.

The Corporation acknowledges with admiration the initiative of the National Gallery of Victoria in curating this project. As the managers of *Golden Summers* we are, as always, indebted to the Directors and staff of each Gallery associated with the exhibition for their co-operation and for lending so many important works from their public collections. We especially wish to thank the many private lenders who have so generously provided their paintings and so actively helped in the complex arrangements of bringing them from homes all over Australia to the walls of the exhibiting Galleries. I hope they will have great satisfaction in knowing that their individual gestures to this exhibition will allow thousands of Australians to see these paintings for the first time.

Exhibitions are dependent on sponsorship. The Corporation, having managed some twenty sponsored exhibitions, continues to be encouraged by the readiness of Australian companies to support the arts. *Golden Summers* has the benefit of informed and sympathetic sponsors whose help is gratefully acknowledged.

Behind all the visible managerial activity of this exhibition lies the unseen and crucial assistance of the Australian Government, the Minister for Arts, Heritage and Environment the Honourable Barry Cohen, and a team of devoted and tireless public servants who administer the details of the indemnity without which it would be difficult indeed to bring exhibitions like *Golden Summers* to the Australian people.

Golden Summers: Heidelberg and beyond is of historic importance in our exhibition calendar. The International Cultural Corporation is proud to manage it and hopes it will delight and stimulate its audiences.

James B. Leslie, A.O., M.C.
Chairman
International Cultural Corporation of Australia Limited

ACKNOWLEDGEMENTS OF THE INTERNATIONAL CULTURAL CORPORATION OF AUSTRALIA LIMITED

LENDERS TO THE EXHIBITION

Mr Charles John Altson
Art Gallery of New South Wales
Art Gallery of South Australia
Art Galler of Western Australia
Mr Max Atkinson
Australian National Gallery
Ballarat Fine Art Gallery
Benalla Art Gallery
Box Hill City Concil
Mr Joseph Brown
Carrick Hill
Mr M.J.M. Carter
Castlemaine Art Gallery and Historical Museum
Dixson Galleries, State Library of New South Wales
Elders IXL Collection
The Ellison Collection
Ewing Gallery, University of Melbourne
Mr James O. Fairfax
Mrs Margaret Fink
Mr Larry Patrick Foley
Geelong Art Gallery
Sir Andrew and Lady Grimwade
Mr Neville Healy
Mr Alan Hickinbotham
The Robert Holmes à Court Collection
Mr William J. Hughes
Mrs Robin Kelly
LaTrobe Collection, State Library of Victoria
Mr Frank McDonald
National Gallery of Victoria
National Gallery of Australia
New England Regional Art Museum
Shepparton Art Gallery
Dr Donald R. Sheumack
Mr Craig W. Thomas
Warrnambool Art Gallery
Mr David R.C. Waterhouse
Those private collectors who wish to remain anonymous

ORGANIZING GALLERY

NATIONAL GALLERY OF VICTORIA
Patrick McCaughey – Director
Jane Clark – Myer Curator of Special Exhibitions
Bridget Whitelaw – Curator of 19th Century Australian Art

Catalogue
Judith Ryan – Editor
Kathy Richards – Graphic Designer

EXHIBITING GALLERIES

ART GALLERY OF NEW SOUTH WALES
Edmund Capon – Director

ART GALLERY OF SOUTH AUSTRALIA
Daniel Thomas – Director

ART GALLERY OF WESTERN AUSTRALIA
Frank Ellis – Director

MANAGEMENT

INTERNATIONAL CULTURAL CORPORATION OF AUSTRALIA LIMITED

Board of Directors
James Leslie – Chairman
Norman Baker – Deputy Chairman
Jean Battersby
Franco Belgiorno-Nettis
Edmund Capon
Michael Darling
Robert Edwards
Ann Lewis
John Lockhart
Patrick McCaughey
Alan McGregor
Storry Walton – Executive Director

Project Team
Carol Henry
Lisa Purser
Svetlana Karovich

INDEMNITY

The Australian Government through the Department of Arts, Heritage and Environment

PUBLICITY AND ADVERTISING

Clemenger Harvie Pty Ltd

SPONSORSHIP

The Age – Melbourne
The Sydney Morning Herald – Sydney
The South Australian Gas Company with assistance from *Advertiser Newspapers Limited* – Adelaide
The Western Mail – Perth

PHOTOGRAPHY

Photography on this mammoth project has been shared by a number of photographers who are gratefully acknowledged, of necessity alphabetically: Brian Bird, Robert Colvin, Kerry Dundas, Barry Ford, Victor France Photographics, McKenzie Gray Photography, Grant Handcock, Henry Jolles, Sue McNab, Clayton McWhinney, Dennis Russell, Helen Skuse, Brian Stevenson, John Storey, Greg Weight, Ann Williams, Greg Woodward and Milton Wordley & Associates. Other photographs have been generously provided by courtesy of the lenders who are listed in the Acknowledgements.

VALUERS

We are indebted to the following individuals who have provided their services in an honorary capacity: Mr Joseph Brown, Art Consultant, 74 Caroline Street, South Yarra, Victoria; Chris Deutscher of Deutscher Fine Art, 68 Drummond Street, Carlton, Victoria; and Sue Hewitt, Australian Representative for Christie's, 298 New South Head Road, Double Bay, New South Wales.

ACKNOWLEDGEMENTS

This catalogue is the result of more than two years full-time exploration of one of the most interesting and exciting chapters in Australian art history. Contemporary critical opinion in the form of newspaper reviews and exhibition catalogues has been sought wherever possible in an attempt to avoid the highly tendentious 'mythologizing' of the subject which characterizes so much early 20th century writing. In fact, the useful art historical label 'The Heidelberg School' was first used by a local journalist generalizing about an exhibition of Streeton's and Withers's work 'done chiefly in this attractive suburb, where, with others of like inclination, they have established a summer congregation for out-of-door painting' (*The Australasian Critic*, 1 July 1891). These painters – along with contemporaries including Tom Roberts, Charles Conder, Julian Ashton, E. Phillips Fox and John Longstaff – were, as one English writer put it, 'the pace-makers' of late 19th century Australian art, 'pointing the way which will lead the Australian school to success' (*The Magazine of Art*, 1898). Melbourne newspapers, *The Age, The Argus* and, above all, the racy weekly *Table Talk*, are especially informative; *The Sydney Morning Herald, Daily Telegraph, Illustrated Sydney News* and numerous illustrated journals will also be found cited in footnotes throughout the catalogue. The exhibition is arranged geographically and chronologically to reflect the artists' strong feelings for particular localities and their own place in history.

Information about each work is provided in the following order: title and date (any attributed dates are in square parentheses), medium, dimensions (height before width), exact inscriptions, present whereabouts. The original titles given by the artists when their paintings were first exhibited are used wherever possible; any subsequent changes of title over the years are then cited in the later documentation of that work. Provenance is documented as fully as possible. Although the 'Exhibitions' listings attempt to record only the period up to c.1900, many important later exhibitions with published catalogues are documented in the 'Literature' section of each entry. It is hoped that these records will be useful for further research.

This first concerted exposition of the work of the Heidelberg School is built upon foundations of much recent scholarship, both published and unpublished. Initially conceived as a National Gallery of Victoria 'internal' exhibition and now to be seen in four states across the country, it has also proved a constantly expanding team effort. Acknowledgements are accordingly numerous and wide-ranging. First I must thank the Director, Patrick McCaughey, for initiating the project and for his unflagging enthusiasm; secondly Bridget Whitelaw, Curator of 19th Century Australian Art, who shared the work with me for some eighteen months. Many colleagues here have rendered special assistance and support: Deputy Directors Nancy Staub and Kenneth Hood (to whose brilliant inspiration we owe the exhibition's evocative title); Curators Robert Lindsay, Jan Minchin, Terence Lane, Irena Zdanowicz, Geoffrey Edwards; Kathy Taylor, our willing and efficient volunteer research assistant in the Australian Department; the Conservation and Framing team, led by Tom Dixon and John Payne; as well as Jennie Moloney, Danny McOwen, Gordon Morrison and Garth McLean; the Gallery Library and Photographic, Exhibitions, Education, Installation and Secretarial staff. Judy Ryan, the Gallery's Editor, and Kathy Richards, Graphic Designer, have worked fantastically hard. Casey Newman and Judy Shelverton typed the manuscript for publication with total efficiency and enthusiasm. I would like to thank colleagues from many participating Galleries: especially Barry Pearce and Deborah Edwards in Sydney, Daniel Thomas, Ron Radford and Jane Hylton in Adelaide, Christopher Johnson and Bruce Adams in Perth. Many librarians at the State Libraries of Victoria, New South Wales and South Australia and the National Library of Australia have assisted with research. All private lenders and many descendants of the artists have also been unfailingly generous with their time and knowledge. And listed below are other individuals to whom I am much indebted in different ways. I can only thank you all sincerely and alphabetically: Roderick Anderson, Rob Andrew, Leigh Astbury, Mr Joseph Brown, Graeme Davison, Chris Deutscher, Lauraine Diggins, Christine Downer, Michael Dunn, Paul and Jon Dwyer, Dinah Dysart, Mary Eagle, Miss Renée Erdos, Pam Francis, Ann Galbally, Doug Hall, Victoria Hammond, David Hansen, Charles Hewitt, Sue Hewitt, Noel Hutchinson, David Jaffé, Henry Jolles, John Jones, Frances Lindsay, Alan Lloyd, Pamela Luhrs, Helen Maxwell, Mrs Joshua McClelland, Diane Macleod, Mr Alan McCulloch, Frank McDonald, Jack McLean, Peter Naish, Juliet Peers, John Perry, Peter Perry, Mrs Margaret Phillips, Margaret Rich, Kathie Robb, Ann Roberts, Margaret Rose, Leo Rounds, Jessie Serle, Peyton Skipwith, Amanda Stephens, Simon Storey, Graeme Sturgeon, Louise Sweetland, Mrs Celia Taylor, Helen Topliss, Gerard Vaughan, Mrs Helen Vellacott, Mrs Aimée Wilkins and Dick Wynveen.

The stunning appearance of the exhibition here in Melbourne is due to Peter Corrigan of Edmond and Corrigan, Architecture and Urban Design, for the architectural space; HBR Display Industries Pty Ltd; David McCabe Design Pty Ltd and Alison Fincher for the display; graphics for all venues were designed by Sue Alnutt. Its management since June 1985 has been undertaken by the International Cultural Corporation of Australia Limited; Svetlana Karovich in particular has given me much willing support, based here in Melbourne. Finally I am most grateful to the Myer family and The Myer Foundation for so very generously sponsoring my part in this exciting project.

Jane Clark
Myer Curator of Special Exhibitions
National Gallery of Victoria

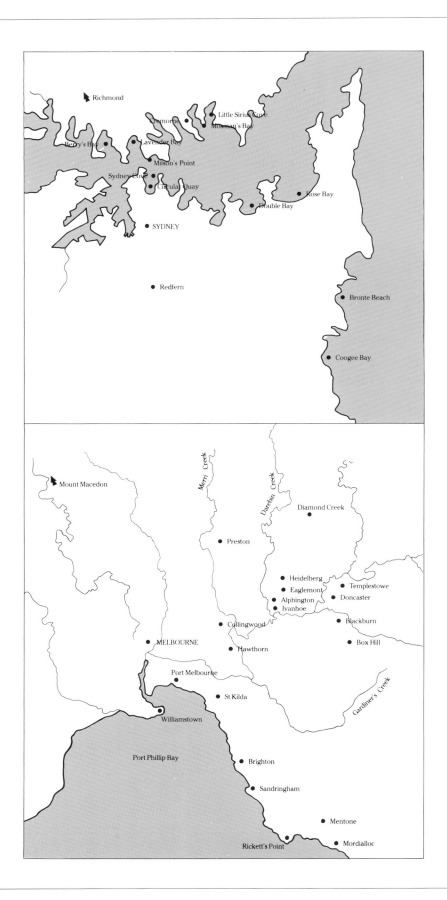

Sydney

Richmond

Little Sirius Cove
Cremorne
Mosman's Bay
Berry's Bay
Lavender Bay
Milson's Point
Sydney Cove
Circular Quay
Rose Bay
Double Bay
SYDNEY

Redfern
Bronte Beach

Coogee Bay

Melbourne

Merri Creek
Darebin Creek
Mount Macedon

Diamond Creek

Preston

Heidelberg
Eaglemont
Templestowe
Alphington
Doncaster
Ivanhoe
Blackburn
Collingwood

MELBOURNE
Box Hill
Hawthorn
Gardiner's Creek

Port Melbourne

St Kilda

Williamstown

Port Phillip Bay
Brighton

Sandringham

Mentone
Rickett's Point
Mordialloc

CONTENTS

PREFACE

Golden Summers : Heidelberg and beyond covers the most celebrated period in the history of Australian art: those years from 1885 until shortly after the turn of the century which were dominated by Tom Roberts, Arthur Streeton, Charles Conder and Fred McCubbin. Popularly known as the Heidelberg School, they ranged far beyond their own initial forays into the bush around Melbourne. They painted Sydney Harbour, ventured up the Hawkesbury River and also depicted Australia's emerging cities, pastoral industries and rapidly disappearing pioneering past. They delighted in its beaches and in leisured moments of Australian society taking its ease. They loved both the zenith landscape with the baking sun at high noon and a luminescent moment of moonrise. Above all they believed that the task for the Australian artist was to paint Australian realities. After the grave and splendid vision of colonial masters, painters of the Heidelberg School turned for inspiration to the grit of daily Australian experience. They won for themselves, their contemporaries and for future generations a rich and stirring poetry from the spectacle of a landscape being transformed into a country which bore its own distinctive identity.

It is exactly one hundred years since Tom Roberts returned to Australia to marshall together the nascent forces of Australian art and generate the artistic and philosophic impetus which gave rise to the Heidelberg School. Now is just the right moment to survey this school in depth. The exhibition *Golden Summers* brings together the school's leading masters and their less well-known contemporaries as they have never been seen before. Not even the artists themselves would have had such an opportunity to see the development of the school in an exhibition of this magnitude.

It has been made possible through a number of quite distinct factors. The National Gallery of Victoria as organizing Gallery has had willing and generous support from its sister institutions – the Art Galleries of New South Wales, South Australia and Western Australia – and co-operation from the Australian National Gallery. Likewise Regional Galleries have responded to many heavy requests for loans, depriving themselves of principal works for an extended period. Private collectors have also been exceptionally generous and the exhibition has not been refused a single significant request for a loan. The depth of the lenders' generosity can be gauged by their willingness to let the exhibition be seen in four different venues, thus giving it a national dimension.

The exhibition has been generously sponsored in each of the states and the eagerness of these separate sponsors to enter into a co-operative sponsorship arrangement has been both timely and deeply gratifying. Each has played a vital and constructive role in ensuring the exhibition's success.

Golden Summers has been curated by Jane Clark, Myer Curator of Special Exhibitions at the National Gallery of Victoria, and Bridget Whitelaw, Curator of Nineteenth Century Australian Art at the National Gallery of Victoria. It has been a long haul for them both, especially Miss Clark who has taken on a substantial part of the authorship of this catalogue. They have established new standards of scholarship in regard to the period and subsequent work is indebted to their findings.

Lastly, the International Cultural Corporation of Australia Limited has been its usual willing and efficient partner with the exhibiting Galleries in the management of this exhibition. The Department of Arts, Heritage and Environment has played a conspicuous part in arranging the Australian Government indemnity without which the exhibition would not have been possible. To both parties the National Gallery of Victoria extends a heartfelt sense of gratitude for their understanding, patience and energetic response to many demands placed upon them.

Patrick McCaughey
Director
National Gallery of Victoria

INTRODUCTION

Ann Galbally

Go in prophet style and tackle our stuff for love.

– John Peter Russell to Tom Roberts, Paris, February 1885

During the later 19th century, nationalistic feeling in a number of Western countries often crystallized through the discovery, recording and celebration of particular regions, such as Brittany in France, Cornwall in England and, in Australia, areas around Melbourne and then Sydney Harbour. Characteristic rural landscapes and their particular ways of life were painted by artists who both wished to disassociate themselves from what they felt was the 'artificial' and 'unhealthy' life of the city and try to recover the 'naturalness' and 'purity' of a life and a countryside uncontaminated by industry and commerce.[1]

The artists who created this vision were of course products of the cities and had usually undergone a lengthy and vigorous academic training there. But they wished to be freed from adhering to a social/artistic system in which art was seen as merely a product to be made and marketed while they followed a prescribed urban existence with social lionization and wealth as their ultimate reward. In opposition to this system, artistic radicals in the 19th century were very often social radicals as well – Gustave Courbet, James Abbott McNeill Whistler and Paul Gauguin were the most prominent examples. In the mercurial social system of Australia and particularly of Melbourne in the later 19th century, class and social divisions were more flexible than in the old world but there were artists such as Charles Conder, the young Arthur Streeton and Tom Roberts – when it suited him – who were natural bohemians, living outside the accepted social system, celebrating the life of 'art for art's sake' yet also able to participate in society at the highest levels when they chose to.

These threads come together to form Australia's most attractive cultural myth, that of the 'Heidelberg School' which supposedly existed at Heidelberg, then a rural suburb of Melbourne, for a decade or so c.1888–1900 but which actually took place in two stages and with two sets of actors – Box Hill and Eaglemont c.1885-90; and then the 'Charterisville' estate at Heidelberg.[2] The popular view of the Heidelberg School is that Streeton, McCubbin, Roberts, Conder and Withers were the first artists to see and paint the 'real' Australian landscape while those who had gone before them – Glover, von Guérard, Martens and Chevalier – were lesser artists because they had only been able to paint the landscape 'through European eyes'. It was an interpretation of art history born of the first world war: in its aftermath, when Australian art history first began to

be written, writers were tempted to look across the chasm created by the war at the period that had gone before and to see the decades of the 1880s and 1890s as a golden age – a time of pure, unsullied Australian nationalism.

Writing before the war had ended and anxious to give the newly-aroused nationalism a history and heroic context, the artist Lionel Lindsay chose Streeton as his protagonist and in *Art in Australia* 2, 1917, hailed him as the 'discoverer' of Australian landscape. Streeton, who had returned from London to settle in Australia in the 1920s, began to write his memoirs and willingly corroborated Lindsay's view of the primacy of the Heidelberg School in the development of Australian art. William Moore, who had long been collecting material for his pioneering *The Story of Australian Art*, began writing in the 1920s in the same climate and his important history (based largely on accounts given to him by the artists involved) further legitimized this interpretation of a 'national' school.[3] Later, as Australians became more interested in modern French painting, the artists of the Heidelberg School were further invested with the mantle of 'French Impressionism', thus guaranteeing them a role as artistic revolutionaries as well as protagonists of local nationalism.

This typecasting was popular enough to dominate all aesthetic and historical discussion of the art of the period until the 1970s. Recent art – historical research into the facts of these artists' lives and analysis of their *oeuvre* has undone such well-accepted but oversimplified generalities and replaced them with a much more varied picture. The artists of the Heidelberg School did not invariably paint pastoral Australia under a midday sun with a bright 'impressionist' palette. As will be discovered in this exhibition, they also liked painting city street scenes in the rain or at dusk; or portraits of their friends and interesting public figures; late afternoon into twilight effects over the Yarra valley or youths illicitly 'skinny-dipping' in the Yarra or Port Phillip Bay.

The knowledge of French Impressionist techniques was minimal amongst this group in the 1880s. It grew with the return and subsequent teaching of Emanuel Phillips Fox and Tudor St George Tucker in the 1890s – but at no stage was Impressionism practised in Australia in the 19th century as it was practised by Monet and Renoir in the 1870s.[4] Rather, the overseas models for artistic revolution for Streeton, Roberts, McCubbin, Conder and their cohorts were the *plein air* French artists of the 1860s and 1870s, Jean François Millet and his follower Jules Bastien-Lepage, and their subsequent English interpreters George Clausen, Stanhope Alexander Forbes and Henry La Thangue. Technically the idiosyncratic 'square brush technique' found in Roberts, the early Streeton and Conder was derived from French art via the Cornish Newlyn School artists; as was the 'tone and value' so prized by Roberts and especially McCubbin in the 1880s and 1890s when they aimed to create an atmospheric envelope in which their 'real' men and women could be seen to live and move in 'natural' surroundings.

This exhibition offers us a most welcome opportunity to see an extensive collection of Australian art of the late 19th and early 20th centuries. We are being given a chance to re-consider the art of Streeton, Roberts, McCubbin, Fox and others as an achievement going beyond the limitations of 'blue and gold' pastoral painting; to enjoy the diversity of their work, their feeling for place and atmosphere and their urban-based sensitivity to and nostalgia for Australian pioneering history.

[1] As Stanhope Forbes wrote, 'Under the spell of the genius Jean François Millet, and the more recent, and then living, Jules Bastien-Lepage, most of us young students were turning our backs on the great cities, forsaking the studios with their unvarying north light, to set up our easels in country districts where we could pose our models and attack our work in sunshine or in shadow, under the open sky'. *The Annual Report of the Royal Cornwall Polytechnic Society for 1900*, Falmouth, 1901, quoted in Fox & Greenacre 1979, p.16.
[2] For a well documented account of the camps see Topliss 1984.
[3] Published in two volumes in 1934 by Angus and Robertson.
[4] For a detailed discussion of the reception of French Impressionism in Australia see Zubans 1970, pp.53-72; and her forthcoming monograph on E.P. Fox.

BIOGRAPHIES OF THE ARTISTS

Jane Clark

Group of students from the National Gallery School, Melbourne, c.1887
From left, back row: John Longstaff, John Llewelyn Jones, Alexander Colquhoun, E. Phillips Fox, Frederick McCubbin
Middle row: Tudor St George Tucker, Julian Gibbs, David Davies, Fred Williams.
Seated, front: Aby Altson
LaTrobe Collection, State Library of Victoria

LOUIS ABRAHAMS 1852-1903
Painter, etcher and businessman

Louis Abrahams, from a photograph album, 'Centennial International Exhibition, Victorian Court', 1888
Photograph: LaTrobe Collection, State Library of Victoria

Abrahams was born in London in 1852; and arrived in Melbourne at the age of eight. In 1871-72 and again 1879-84 he studied at the Gallery School. On 7 October 1880 he signed the students' petition to the trustees for 'higher instruction'; and on 3 November 1881 led the request for reforms at the School, along with other progressive students. His nickname was 'The Don'. In 1882 he founded, with McCubbin and four other male students, a 'Life-Club' for drawing from the nude model. He joined the Buonarotti Society in 1883; and established the first *plein air* painting camp at Box Hill with McCubbin and Roberts in 1885. He exhibited with the Australian Artists' Association in 1886 and 1887 (both etchings and paintings). In March 1888 he married Miss Golda Figa Brasch in Sydney; and on his return to Melbourne took a studio in the new Grosvenor Chambers, Collins Street. From 1889 onwards he often audited the Victorian Artists' Society accounts. He joined weekend expeditions to Heidelberg whenever possible; but was unable to devote much time to painting because of

increasing responsibility in his father's firm, B. Sniders and Abrahams, Cigar Manufacturers, Drury Lane off Lonsdale Street. He obtained large numbers of cigar-box lids for fellow artists to use in painting '9 by 5' impressions. He exhibited with the Victorian Artists' Society in 1890. The same year, the McCubbins' first son was christened Louis in Abrahams's honour. Abrahams reciprocated by naming his own son Frederick. He often entertained other painters at his 'regular mansion' in Kew and his family purchased important pictures by various Heidelberg School friends (several of which are included in the present exhibition). During the 1890s, however, he became increasingly depressed, writing to Roberts in Sydney, for example, about his 'lost' artistic career (1892). He visited London in 1897; and he purchased one of the first motor cars in Victoria. His health declined and, tragically, in 1903 he shot himself dead in the cellar of his factory.

McCulloch 1984, p.11; Topliss 1984, p.72; information from the artist's family

ABY A. ALTSON c.1867-c.1949
Painter and illustrator

Aby Altson, portrait drawing by Arthur Buckland, 1894
Photograph: State Library of Victoria (see also National Gallery student group photograph)

Altson was born at Middlesborough-on Tees, Yorkshire, probably in 1867[1], son o Isaac Altson, merchant. He was brought to Melbourne by his brother Barnett Hyman Altson in September 1883 and was employed at his uncle's leather and saddlery business. From 1885 he studied

drawing two nights per week at the Gallery's School of Design. In 1886 he also joined the painting classes; and enrolled full time in the School of Painting under Folingsby 1887-90, winning prizes each year. Local critics called him 'a most promising pupil of the future great Australian school'. Early in 1889 he joined Streeton camping at Eaglemont, where his nickname was 'Farmer'. His father and other members of his family came to Melbourne, c.1889. In 1890 he was awarded the second National Gallery of Victoria travelling scholarship for *Flood Sufferings*; and on 4 March 1891 he sailed for Paris. There he studied at the Académie Julian, principally under Gustave Courtois and the Naturalist Pascal-Adolphe-Jean Dagnan-Bouveret; also enrolled in the private ateliers of history painter Jean-Paul Laurens and Colarossi where, he wrote to Roberts, he was known as 'Aby Farmer Captain Starlight Native-Bear'. In 1892 he received a gold medal at the Salon for a painting entitled *Echo*; also exhibiting a portrait of Bertram Mackennal's daughter, Henrietta. He changed the spelling of his name to 'Abbey' at this time. In 1893 he painted *The Golden Age* as his third travelling scholarship picture, making the nude studies on a remote island off the south-west coast of France. He exhibited this painting at the Salon of 1893 (*mention honorable*), at the Royal Academy in 1894 and sent it to Melbourne in 1895. He moved to London in January 1894; later studio addresses include St John's Wood in 1896 and Kensington 1897-98. He married in England; worked as an illustrator for *The Westminster Magazine* and exhibited with the Royal Society of British Artists. Through the agency of London dealers he painted numerous portraits of Indian maharajas, notably Ranga Singh of Nawanaga, travelling frequently between England and India. His English wife died in 1924. Altson then lived in India from September 1924 until 1927. He migrated to America in 1937 and established himself with dealers on New York's 5th Avenue; mainly producing glamorous female portraits and glossy historical costume story-pieces. He died in the U.S.A., c.1949-50.

Table Talk, 19 April 1887, pp.1-2; 16 November 1888; 14 November 1890, p.17; 1 December 1899, p.7; Jope-Slade 1895, pp.389ff.; McCulloch 1984, p.24

[1] Altson's year of birth was given variously as 1867, 1868 and 1869 in biographical accounts during the 1880s and 1890s. After the artist's death, Mr Alan McCulloch corresponded with members of his family who thought Altson was born in 1864. It is possible that

he told people in Melbourne he was younger than his real age (for example that he was only twenty-three when he won the travelling scholarship) in order to appear more of a 'youthful prodigy'. Streeton certainly did this on some occasions.

(JULIAN) HOWARD ASHTON 1877-1964
Artist and journalist

Howard Ashton, 1923, from a photograph in Sydney Ure Smith's collection of sketches, etchings, etc.
Photograph: Dixson Galleries, State Library of New South Wales

Howard Ashton was born 9 August 1877 in Islington, London, the eldest son of Julian Rossi Ashton. He emigrated with his parents, reaching Australia aboard the *Cuzco*, April 1878; and arriving in Melbourne 18 June. In 1883 the family moved to Sydney. He was 'brought up in a Bohemian home'; attended Bondi Public School and Sydney Boys' High School. From 1896 to 1903 he studied at his father's Academy Julien. In 1897 he began to exhibit with the Society of Artists. His *Through Sunny Meadows* was purchased by the Art Gallery of New South Wales in 1898. From 1904 he concentrated on journalism and art criticism rather than painting. In Melbourne 1908-16 he worked mainly for *The Argus*. He became increasingly reactionary with age: opposing the modern movement as 'artistic Bolshevism'. He served as president of the Royal Art Society of New South Wales 1940-45; and died at home in Sydney in 1964.

Art in Australia, 1919; Katherine Harper, in *A.D.B.*, vol.7, 1979

JULIAN ROSSI ASHTON 1851-1942
Painter, illustrator, teacher and writer

Julian Ashton, in *The Illustrated Sydney News*, 14 November 1889
Photograph: State Library of South Australia

Julian Ashton was born 27 January 1851 at Addlestone in Surrey, England; son of an amateur painter (d.1866) and a daughter of the Florentine Count Rossi. In 1866 he began work as a draughtsman in the engineers' office of the Great Eastern Railway Co. He then enrolled at the West London School of Art in 1868, whilst working as an illustrator; and, from 1873, designing metalwork for church furnishings with Heart, Son, Peard and Co. He also studied painting in Paris at the Académie Julian, c.1874; exhibiting work at the Royal Academy and with the Society of British Artists. Offered a contract with *The Illustrated Australian News*, he arrived in Melbourne (via Portland) in June 1878, with his wife and young son. He exhibited pictures painted in England; and his artist-brother, George Rossi Ashton, joined him from South Africa in 1879. Ashton befriended Louis Buvelot, painted his portrait and encouraged *plein air* landscape painting by local artists. He transferred to work for a rival newspaper, *The Australasian Sketcher*; then in 1883 he moved to Sydney and travelled widely as a staff artist of *The Picturesque Atlas of Australasia*. From 1884 he painted on the Hawkesbury River with A.J. Daplyn; and there became the central figure of a *plein air* painting group which included Conder, Fullwood, Frank Mahony and Nerli. In 1885 he was appointed director of classes run by the Art Society of New South Wales, with Daplyn as the paid instructor. He served as president of the Art Society 1886-92; and began to take private pupils. In January 1888 he wrote an article enti-

tled 'Art in Australia and its possibilities' for *The Daily Telegraph*. As a trustee of the Art Gallery of New South Wales, from 1889 to 1899, he proposed and carried a resolution that 'not less than £500 annually be spent by the trustees on the purchase of Australian works of art'. Revisiting Melbourne in 1890, he initiated the purchase of Streeton's *'Still glides the stream and shall for ever glide'* for the Sydney Gallery. The following year he won a commission to paint the first large-scale mural work in Australia: sixteen pictures for the Marble Bar of Adam's Hotel in Sydney. From 1892 to 1896 he taught at the Art Society's school. In 1893 he learned etching from Livingston Hopkins; with whom he established an artists' camp at Balmoral, visited by Streeton, Roberts, Fullwood and others. He exhibited with the newly formed Society of Artists in 1895; and in 1896 he opened his own 'Academy Julien' in Beaumont Chambers, 88 King Street, which soon became Sydney's leading art school. He was chairman of the Society of Artists in 1897-98, and again 1907-21. In 1898 he helped to organize the Grafton Galleries Exhibition of Australian Art in London. In 1907 he moved his Academy to new premises as the Sydney Art School. Ashton fought for recognition of Australian art and artists all his life. He was awarded the first Society of Artists medal in 1924 and a C.B.E. 'for services to art' in 1930. At the age of ninety he published his autobiography; and he died a year later on 30 April 1942 at Bondi.

Illustrated Sydney News, 14 November 1889, p.20; *The Julian Ashton Book*, Art in Australia, Ure Smith, Sydney, 1920; Ashton 1941; Katherine Harper, in *A.D.B.*, vol.7, 1979; Dysart 1981

RUPERT CHARLES WULSTEN BUNNY 1864-1947
Painter and occasional illustrator

Bunny was born 29 September 1864 at St Kilda, Melbourne; third son of Judge Bunny of the Victorian County Court, the first Mayor of St Kilda. He was educated at Alma Road Grammar School and in Hobart at Hutchins School 1870-79; and toured Europe with his family 1874-75. He was very musical and also took private art lessons from the Melbourne painter William Ford (c.1820-c.86). In 1880 he enrolled at Melbourne University, first in Civil Engineering and then Architecture, but only for a few months. Deciding on a career as an artist, he joined the Gallery's

Rupert Bunny, self-portrait drawing, c.1894
Photograph: State Library of Victoria

School of Design in 1881, under Oswald Rose Campbell. Within a year was allowed to proceed to the Painting School as well, where he made very rapid progress; and later wrote that he never had to unlearn anything that Folingsby had taught him there. In 1883 he entered Folingsby's first Gallery School painting competition. Also that year he was nominated by Longstaff as a member of the Buonarotti Society in both the 'musical' and 'artistic' categories. Early in 1884 he sailed for Europe with his father; they were in Naples by March. He spent eighteen months in London at Calderon's Art School. He met the English *plein air* painters Thomas Cooper Gotch (who had visited Australia in 1883) and Henry Scott Tuke; and they introduced him to Jean-Paul Laurens, a leading French academic history painter. Bunny then studied in Paris, 1886-88, at Laurens's atelier – where 'the strongest men from all countries flock . . . to *pousser* their studies further'. He also worked briefly under Pierre-Paul-Léon Glaize and Jean-Joseph Constant. From 1888 he exhibited at the Old Salon (*mention honorable* 1890 and bronze medal 1900). In 1892 he began exhibiting at the Royal Academy; Alfred Felton presented his *Sea Idyll* to the National Gallery of Victoria. He met Dame Nellie Melba, MacKennal, Longstaff, Altson and many other expatriate Australians. He married a French woman in 1902; and several examples of his work were purchased by the French government. He visited and held exhibitions in Melbourne and Sydney in 1911; again in 1923 and 1928. After his wife's death in 1933 he returned to live permanently in Australia. He began to compose music; exhibited regularly and came to be regarded as a forerunner of modernism. He died at home in South Yarra on 24 May 1947.

Jope-Slade 1895, pp.389ff.; David Thomas 1970; David Thomas, in *A.D.B.*, vol.7, 1979

ABRAM LOUIS BUVELOT 1814-88
Painter, photographer and teacher

Abram Louis Buvelot, portrait drawing by Tom Roberts, 1886
Art Gallery of New South Wales

Buvelot was born 3 March 1814 at Morgues, Vaud, Switzerland. He attended art school at Lausanne; then c.1834 studied in Paris with Camille Flers. In 1835 he travelled to Brazil where his uncle had a coffee plantation. In October 1840 he moved to Rio and established himself as a professional painter, lithographer and photographer; patronized by Emperor Dom Pedro II. He married Marie-Félicité Lalouette. The earliest known published review of his work (Rio 1844) commended truthful effects of light, topographical and atmospheric realism and the attractiveness of his subjects – qualities which remained to the end of his long career. Early in 1852 he returned to Switzerland, working chiefly as a photographer. He visited Calcutta in December 1854. Then from August 1855 to September 1864 he was drawing master at a new experimental industrial school at La Chaux-de-Fonds, Neuchâtel. In November 1864 he sailed from Liverpool; his first wife having died, he was accompanied by Caroline-Julie Beguin – a fellow teacher at La Chaux-de-Fonds. They disembarked in Melbourne February 1865; bought a portrait photography studio in Bourke Street; and moved to 88 LaTrobe Street East in 1866, where Buvelot resumed painting. In 1873 they moved to George Street, Fitzroy. Buvelot exhibited landscapes in Melbourne from 1866 to 1882 and was 'discovered' by *The Argus* critic James Smith. His work was revolutionary for its un-English style; with 'a general freedom to which we are unaccustomed'; 'with so little labour achieves such remarkable results'. *Winter Morning near Heidelberg* and *Summer Afternoon, Templestowe* were among the first Australian paintings purchased for the National Gallery of Victoria. By 1869, when he taught drawing at the Carlton School of Design, he was considered the colony's leading landscapist. Most of his students hoped he would become head of the new Gallery School in 1870; he had applied for the instructorship without fee, but was still passed over in favour of Eugen von Guérard. The young Heidelberg School artists considered Buvelot the 'father of Australian landscape painting'. He encouraged sketching and watercolour painting *en plein air*; although his own full-scale canvases, and all his generation's, were completed in the studio. Most of his subjects were found in the environs of Melbourne: at Heidelberg, Templestowe, Dromana, Lilydale and Mount Macedon. His failing eyesight and crippled hands forced him to give up painting c.1884. When he died four years later a monument was erected at the Kew Cemetery by public subscription. James Smith and George Folingsby mounted a large retrospective exhibition of his work in July 1888, which was opened by the Governor and Lady Loch.

Jocelyn Gray, in *A.D.B.*, vol.3, 1969; Miss Gray's M.A. thesis, University of Melbourne, remains the only extensive study of Buvelot's career; Daniel Thomas 1976; Whitelaw 1976

THOMAS CLARK 1814?-83
Painter, illustrator and teacher

Clark was born in London, probably in 1814; son of an artist. He is said to have been director of the Nottingham School of Arts before appointment, in 1843, as anatomical draughtsman at King's College, London. From 1846 to 1851 he was headmaster at the Government School of Design and drawing master at King

Edward's School in Birmingham. He probably visited Russia. Clark emigrated to Victoria with his family c.1852; joined the Victorian Society of Fine Arts and exhibited from 1857 along with Eugen von Guérard, Nicholas Chevalier and William Strutt; and taught in the Society's art classes. As instructor of figure drawing at the Carlton School of Design 1868-70, he introduced 'drawing from the living model' and 'outdoor sketching'. He later continued this association as a judge of the annual student competitions, as did Buvelot. In 1870 he was appointed first drawing master at the National Gallery of Victoria, under von Guérard. His large history painting *Ulysses and Diomed capturing the horses of Rhesus, King of Thrace* hung at the School and was very popular with students. He resigned due to ill health in October 1876 but remained in contact with young art students. Roberts and McCubbin were especially fond of Clark, McCubbin describing him as 'a venerable old gentleman with a head the counterpart of the bust of Socrates'; he encouraged Roberts to study in London and Paris. He died in Melbourne, 21 April 1883.

Table Talk, 9 January 1891; *Tatler*, 21 May 1898, p.18, photograph no.9; Ann Galbally, in *A.D.B.*, vol.3, 1969; Daniel Thomas 1976, p.33

CHARLES EDWARD CONDER 1868-1909
Painter, occasional decorator and illustrator

Conder was born 24 October 1868 in London, son of a railway engineer. He spent three years in India as a small child but was educated in England, at boarding school in Eastbourne 1877-83. He then studied art for a year, until his deeply religious father sent him to Australia in an effort to drive ideas of an artistic career out of his system. He arrived in Sydney on 13 June 1884, aboard s.s. *Windsor Castle*; and worked for eight months with his uncle, William Jacomb Conder, a surveyor in the New South Wales Lands Department, spending two years in country survey camps 1885-87. In 1886 he began night classes under A.J. Daplyn at the Art Society of New South Wales and won a three guinea prize that year for the best painting from nature. In 1887 he joined *The Illustrated Sydney News*, continuing art studies with his uncle's consent and encouragement. He met Tom Roberts, visiting Sydney in the summer of 1887-88; also met Girolamo Nerli. He joined Julian Ashton and others painting on the Hawkesbury River at Richmond;

Charles Conder, cabinet-portrait photograph of 1886
LaTrobe Collection, State Library of Victoria

exhibited with the Art Society in 1888 when his *Departure of the Orient* was purchased by the Art Gallery of New South Wales. Conder then moved to Melbourne and joined the Box Hill camp in spring of 1888. He attended evening drawing classes at the Gallery School under McCubbin; during the day he conducted his own studio in Melbourne Chambers teaching young ladies to paint! He spent the summer of 1888-89 at Eaglemont – known to his friends as 'K'. He exhibited with the Victorian Artists' Society; and organized with Roberts and Streeton the 9 by 5 Impression Exhibition in August 1889, for which he designed the allegorical catalogue cover. His father is said to have visited that year and brought him the latest in Aesthetic studio décor and accoutrements. Conder spent most of the following summer at Eaglemont once again; and moved to a new Melbourne studio, in Gordon Chambers with Streeton and Richardson as neighbours. He then decided to return to Europe: sailing 26 April 1890 on the s.s. *Austral*, via Ceylon, Italy and England. Conder was the only Australian-trained artist to enter wholeheartedly into the spirit of bohemian Paris: by August 1890 he was living in Montmartre; studying intermittently at the Académie Julian; then at Cormon's atelier (probably on John Peter Russell's advice) where he met Toulouse-Lautrec. He saw Altson, Phil May, George Walton and other antipodean artist friends. He shared a studio and exhibited jointly with

the English artist William Rothenstein from 1891 (Conder's work was praised by Degas and Pissarro). He visited Algeria to convalesce from the effects of his dissolute Parisian life. Moving to London in 1893, he joined the New English Art Club where Walter Sickert nicknamed him 'The Strange Bird'. He began painting in watercolour on silk fans; met Aubrey Beardsley and contributed illustrations to *The Yellow Book*. In 1895 he produced six decorative panels for Samuel Bing's *La Maison de l'Art Nouveau*. He now lived alternately in London, Paris and Dieppe, meeting Oscar Wilde in 1896. He learned lithography in 1899 and produced the *Balzac* set. In Paris, December 1901, he married Stella Maris Belford. The following year in London he briefly renewed his friendship with Streeton. He visited Spain and Algeciras during 1905 but shortly afterwards was incapacitated by his final illness. He died comparatively young at Virginia Water, near Windsor, 9 April 1909.

Gibson 1914; Rothenstein 1938; Hoff 1960 and 1972; Hoff, in *A.D.B.*, vol.3, 1969

HERBERT JAMES DALY 1865-c.1929
Surveyor and draughtsman, mining engineer, journalist, and painter

Herbert Daly, photograph in *The Cyclopedia of Victoria*, 1903
State Library of Victoria

Daly was born in 1865 at Riversdale, Ballinasloe, County Galway, Ireland; the son of William Dawson Daly, Esq., landed proprietor. Educated in London at Christ's Hospital and Charter House School, he then served some years in the Royal Navy. Arriving in Australia in 1881, he was engaged for four years as draughtsman and surveyor's assistant in the New South Wales Survey Department – at the same time as Conder. In 1885 he 'joined the Melbourne Press, gathering his first journalistic experience on *Table Talk*'. In 1887 he went to Western Australia for a year and took out the first miner's right issued for the Yilgarn goldfields. 'He was a really high class mining scout with a pretty good eye for untested gold mines', one contemporary remembered. On 9 June 1888 he married at St Paul's Church, Kyneton, Miss Katherine Emily (Kitty) Mitchell of 'Barfold', daughter of the late William H.F. Mitchell. In the same year he entered the Victorian Department of Mines; and also enrolled at the Gallery School for drawing classes under McCubbin, 1888 to mid-1890. He exhibited one work in the 9 by 5 Impression Exhibition of August 1889. In May 1892 he submitted a painting to the Victorian Artists' Society which was not accepted for exhibition. During 1895 and 1896 he travelled widely in Australia as a reporter, illustrator and special mining editor for *The Argus*. In September 1896 he became manager of Hannan's mining company at Kalgoorlie, Western Australia. He travelled to South Africa and England in mid-1897, joined Consolidated Mines Selection Co. Ltd and returned to open their Melbourne office in 1898; he also maintained a large private consultancy practice. Daly was director of North Broken Hill Silver Mining Co. and the Jubilee Gold Mining Co. at Ballarat 1900-08. He revisited Europe on several occasions; took lessons from Emanuel Phillips Fox (probably in Paris); and painted in Cornwall, the South of France and Algeria. He exhibited thirty paintings in Melbourne, September 1912: fruits of his 'many artistic forages under eastern skies... His brush never fails him when sunlight is concerned' (*The Argus*, 10 September 1912, p.9). He contributed 'about twenty sketches and studies of French landscape, painted somewhat after the manner of the late E.P. Fox', to a group exhibition at the Fine Arts Society, Melbourne, November 1916, along with Ethel Carrick Fox, Ina Gregory, Violet Teague, Alexander Colquhoun and others. At the Athenaeum Gallery, Melbourne, in 1918 he exhibited work to aid the Red Cross. He exhibited with the Australian Art Association in 1920; and in Paris 1927. Daly was first and foremost a successful mining engineer; secondly an amateur artist working mainly in watercolour, a friend and pupil of the Heidelberg School painters. In later years he owned a house at Mount Macedon – 'Ardruda'; he died in Ireland c.1929.

Table Talk, 24 July, 1896, p.2; J. Smith (ed.), *The Cyclopedia of Victoria*, 1903, I, p.390; G. Blainey (ed.), *If I remember rightly: the memoirs of W.S. Robinson 1876-1963*, Cheshire, Melbourne, 1967, pp.38f.; also information kindly supplied by G.H. O'D. Crowther, Esq., Lou Klepac and Mrs Helen Vellacott

ALFRED JAMES DAPLYN 1844-1926
Painter, teacher and writer

Alfred J. Daplyn, in *The Illustrated Sydney News*, 28 November 1889
State Library of South Australia

Daplyn was born in London in 1844. He studied in Paris at the Ecole des Beaux-Arts under Jean-Léon Gérôme; then became one of Carolus-Duran's first pupils, along with R.A.M. Stevenson and W.H. Low. These artists spent vacations sketching *en plein air* at Fontainebleau, in Brittany and Finisterre; and Daplyn is said to have met Corot. He visited Italy; briefly returned to London; travelled to America and then to Australia. He arrived in Melbourne 1882; and exhibited with the Victorian Academy of Arts 1882-84. In 1883 he joined the Art Society of New South Wales, although still resident in Melbourne. He probably went to Sydney later that same year. (On 15 February 1884 he was recorded as a 'visitor' to the Buonarotti Society in Melbourne; that is, not a local.) Daplyn painted at Richmond on the Hawkesbury River with Julian Ashton, Conder, Fullwood and others, camping there for some weeks during 1884. From 1885 to 1892 he was the first salaried painting instructor at the Art Society under the directorship of Ashton; his

pupils included Conder and Sydney Long. He was elected a council member of the Art Society in 1895; served as honorary secretary from 1898 to 1913; and established the Daplyn Art Scholarship. His handbook for artists, based on the experience of his own career, was published as *Landscape Painting from Nature in Australia* by W.C. Penfold and Co., Sydney, 1902 and two subsequent editions. He was back in London 1913-19; but sent out work for exhibition in Sydney. He returned to Australia in 1920 and exhibited again with the Art Society of New South Wales for a further three years. He died in London in 1926.

Illustrated Sydney News, 28 November 1889, p.23; *Table Talk*, 1 May 1891, p.6; McCulloch 1984, p.266

DAVID DAVIES 1864-1939
Painter

Davies was born 21 May 1864; son of a miner, Thomas Davies of Ballarat West, Victoria. He first studied art at the local school of design under J.F. Martell and Thomas Price; and exhibited student works before leaving Ballarat in August 1886. Arriving in Melbourne, he enrolled at the Gallery School; spent three months in the School of Design under McCubbin, then transferred to the Painting School under Folingsby from 1887 to 1890. In November 1888 he won the student landscape prize with *A Hot Day*. He returned to Ballarat for six months from December 1888. Two years later he left for Paris, on the proceeds of sale of his *Under the Burden and Heat of the Day* (Ballarat Fine Art Gallery). From 1891 he studied at the Académie Julian under Jean-Paul Laurens, along with Aby Altson. In December that year he married Miss Janet Sophia Davies, formerly a fellow student in Melbourne and now studying drawing at Colarossi's atelier (she was also the sister of Charles Davies, part-owner of the 'Mount Eagle' estate); Altson and Rupert Bunny were witnesses at their marriage. Davies spent most of 1892 at the St Ives *plein air* painters' colony in Cornwall; he probably also visited Venice that year. He returned to Australia for four years from Easter 1893: living at Templestowe, where he painted his famous 'moonrise' series, and in 1896 at Cheltenham. His *Moonrise* of 1894 was purchased by the National Gallery of Victoria. A younger contemporary, Clewin Harcourt, wrote, 'It is my belief that we don't give sufficient credit to Dave Davies who helped considerably to form the Australian style of the early days. He saw beauty and character in the parched grass and shimmering heated air of midsummer and rendered it with truth and delicacy of tone. Davies was a charming & kindly fellow, always ready to help us youngsters in our difficulties'.[1] In 1897 he took his family back to Europe: by 1898 they were living in Cornwall, at Lelant on the River Hayle. He was in London in 1905; in North Wales 1906-08. He exhibited at the Royal Academy, the New English Art Club and in Paris at the new Salon. In 1908 he settled at Dieppe. He exhibited a few paintings in Sydney and Melbourne 1911-12: and in May 1926 held his only major exhibition in Australia. In 1932 he moved back to Cornwall once again where he died, at Looe, in March 1939.

Table Talk, 16 November 1888, p.14; MacDonald 1920; Candice Bruce, in *A.D.B.*, vol.8, 1981; Sparks 1984

[1] Letter of 4 November 1955. LaTrobe Collection, State Library of Victoria. Hoff Conder MS 9678.

For portrait, see Gallery School student group photograph

ROGER EYKYN FALLS active 1880s-90s
Coffee planter and painter

Falls was born in Bournemouth, Hampshire, England, the son of a doctor and nephew of Roger Eykyn Falls, M.P. for Windsor. His initial painting activities as a self-taught amateur were temporarily interrupted when he embarked upon a coffee-planting career in Ceylon. Subsequently, however, he spent six months in France where 'he met some French artists, who took a great interest in him and helped him considerably'. After an interlude of eighteen months in South Africa he arrived in Victoria and enrolled in the Gallery's drawing classes in 1886. Falls combined his artistic interests with considerable involvement in Melbourne society: in 1887, for example, he painted several pictures whilst a guest of Lord and Lady Brassey aboard their cruising yacht *Sunbeam*. In 1888 he submitted a painting entitled *By the Sea* for the Centennial Exhibition. In May 1889 he exhibited with the Victorian Artists' Society; and in August that year showed four pictures in the famous 9 by 5 Impression Exhibition. His work was catalogued in a *Sale of Australian Pictures* by many major local artists, auctioned at Garraway's Rooms by Messrs Shevill and Co. in October 1889. By February 1890 he occupied a most 'artistically' furnished studio in Provident Buildings, 453 Collins Street West. He was planning to resume his art studies in Europe in the near future and eventually to settle in Australia. Presumably he departed shortly afterwards; but it would appear that he never returned.

Table Talk, 7 February 1890, p.5

GEORGE FREDERICK FOLINGSBY 1828-91
Painter and teacher

Folingsby was born 23 August 1828 in Wicklow, Ireland. He went to Canada at the age of eighteen; then to New York where he studied drawing whilst working as a black-and-white illustrator for *The New York Lantern*, *Harper's Magazine* and *Cassell's Illustrated Magazine of Art* of which he became pictorial editor. He then accompanied a wealthy uncle travelling through Greece and much of Europe. He settled in Munich in 1852, studying drawing at the Academy for two years; followed by six months in Paris at Thomas Couture's atelier. He returned to Munich for a further five years 'among the disciples' of Carl Theodor von Piloty, director of the Academy, whose students were 'trained to accuracy and severity of drawing; antique sculpture had been rightly used as a means to a certain ideal rendering of nature – a somewhat ultra-academic training' (*The Portfolio*, 1878, p.72). Piloty (1826-86) was famous for 'choice of subjects noble in thought', his most celebrated being *Galileo in Prison*. Folingsby remained in Munich for almost twenty-five years; exhibiting successfully in London, Belfast, Vienna, Philadelphia and elsewhere, and occasionally revisiting Paris. His painting of *Bunyan in Prison* was one of the National Gallery of Victoria's first acquisitions, in 1864. In 1878 the Melbourne trustees commissioned another historical subject, *The First Meeting of Henry VIII and Anne Boleyn*; and, as he had heard there was an opening for a portrait painter in Melbourne, he decided to emigrate. He arrived in July 1879 and opened a studio in Market Buildings, Flinders Lane. His first commissions were portraits of David Mitchell (father of the future Dame Nellie Melba) and Sir Redmond Barry, president of the Gallery trustees. In April 1882 he succeeded Eugen von Guérard as head of the National Gallery of Victoria and 'Master of the School of Painting'. His arrival had a 'magical effect' amongst the students, who were eager for higher instruction in art along traditional academic lines. 'He changed the whole plan on which art education had formerly been carried on' (*Table Talk*, 9 January 1891, p.11). He also brought to Australia his large art collection, which included some old master works and sketches by leading contemporary French and British academic painters such as Paul Delaroche and Sir William Quiller Orchardson. Folingsby lived at 'Leonie', Lisson Grove, Hawthorn, with his wife Clara, also a painter, and daughter, Grace. Unfortunately his relationship with the Victorian Artists' Society deteriorated with his advancing years:

> With all his good qualities and geniality to his friends, Mr Folingsby was a man of strong personality, as all great artists are, and did not like his opinions contradicted. There is no doubt that if he had been more tolerant of the Victorian artists – still speaking of them as a body – he would have been recognised as the Sir Frederick Leighton of this part of the world.

In 1889 his health began to fail; and he died of 'dropsy of the liver' at Kew in January 1891.

Table Talk, 4 October 1888, p.4; 9 January 1891, p.11; Astbury 1978; Ruth Zubans in *A.D.B.*, vol.4, 1972

EMANUEL PHILLIPS FOX 1865-1915
Painter and teacher

E. Phillips Fox, photograph in *Art and Architecture*, 1908
State Library of Victoria (see also National Gallery student group photograph)

Emanuel Phillips Fox was born 12 March 1865 at Fitzroy, Victoria, the son of a photographer, Alexander Fox. He took early drawing lessons from a Mr Carter; and enrolled at the Gallery School in 1878 under O.R. Campbell and von Guérard (his sister, Caroline, was already there). Although he matriculated to the University of Melbourne at the age of fifteen, he decided instead to continue with artistic training. On 7 October 1880 he signed the students' request to the trustees for 'higher instruction'. He qualified as a drawing teacher and taught at various suburban schools of design whilst pursuing his own studies as a painter. He painted around Melbourne and in Gippsland, winning student prizes for landscape in 1884 and 1886. In February 1887 he departed for Paris, sponsored by younger brothers and friends. He studied first at the Académie Julian under Tony Robert-Fleury; then early in 1889 passed rigorous entrance examinations for the Ecole des Beaux-Arts, where he studied under William-Adolphe Bouguereau and Jean-Léon Gérôme and won first prize in the latter's class. At the same time he took lessons from the American expatriate painter, Thomas Alexander Harrison (1853-1930), who had a considerable reputation for 'impressionist' style and had worked closely with the late Jules Bastien-Lepage. Fox joined excursions to Brittany and other popular *plein air* painting spots; he also visited Madrid. In 1890 he exhibited at both the Old Salon and the new Salon des artistes français. He stayed briefly with the *plein air* painters' colony at St Ives, Cornwall before returning to Melbourne in 1891. Here, with Tudor St George Tucker, he opened the Melbourne Art School in Cromwell Building, Bourke Street, opposite the Post Office; and also a summer school at 'Charterisville' in Heidelberg, advertising the teaching methods as 'based on the French system'. During the 1890s he shipped paintings back to Europe for exhibition and at the new Salon of 1894 he became the first Australian-born artist to receive a gold medal. In 1900-01 he was awarded a commission, jointly with John Longstaff, to produce Australian historical paintings for the National Gallery of Victoria under the terms of the Gilbee Bequest. Rather extraordinarily, these pictures stipulated that the pictures had to be painted in England; so Fox duly departed in March 1901 to paint *The Landing of Captain Cook at Botany Bay*. By 1904 he was living in Paris. In 1905 he married an English artist, Ethel Carrick; they toured Italy and Spain together, 1906-07 and in 1908 visited and exhibited work in Melbourne. Also in 1908, Fox became an *associé* of the

Société Nationale des Beaux-Arts; and in 1910 the first Australian elected a full *sociétaire*. In 1912 he was elected a member of the International Society of Painters, Sculptors and Gravers, London; and visited Spain and Algeria. Returning to Australia in 1913, he was much admired by the younger generation of local artists for the bright colours of his French-influenced paintings. The following year he visited Tahiti where he was particularly impressed by Gauguin's work; and he died in Melbourne on 8 October 1915.

Table Talk, 23 January 1891, pp.7f.; 9 December 1892; *Age*, 22 October 1832, p.5; Souter 1908, pp.88ff.; Fox 1969; Zubans, Ph.D. thesis, University of Melbourne, 1979

FLORENCE ADA FULLER 1867-1946
Painter and teacher

Florence Fuller, in *The Illustrated Sydney News*, 1 August 1891
Photograph: Mitchell Library, State Library of New South Wales

Florence Fuller was born at Port Elizabeth, South Africa in 1867; daughter of John Fuller; cousin of Sir Matthew Davies, Victorian M.L.A.; and niece of the artist Robert Dowling. She was brought to Melbourne as a child. She studied painting and drawing at the Gallery School in 1883 and 1888. In 1886 she opened a studio in the city, where she received some instruction from a neighbouring tenant, Monsieur de Crouée of Paris. She became a protégée of Lady Loch — wife of the Governor and herself an amateur painter — whose portrait by Dowling she had completed in 1887; Lady Loch tried to per-

suade her to go to Europe to study. She painted portraits, anecdotal genre, flowers, fruit and landscape subjects; exhibited with the Australian Artists' Association 1886-87; with the Victorian Academy of Arts; with the Victorian Artists' Society 1888-90, 1892-93, 1896, 1900-06; and the Yarra Sculptors' Society. In March 1891 she held a private exhibition at her teaching studio in Pine Street, Malvern. In November the following year she travelled to the Cape of Good Hope to convalesce after a long illness. She then lived and worked in England and France from 1894 to 1904. In January 1896 she sent works out to Melbourne for exhibition in Jane Sutherland's Grosvenor Chambers studio; very well reviewed by local critics. She exhibited at the Royal Academy in 1897 and 1904; also at Manchester and the Paris Salon; and regularly sent work to the Victorian Artists' Society in Melbourne. In 1904 she moved to Perth. From 1908 to 1911 she lived in India at the headquarters of the Theosophical Society; then revisited England in 1911. During the 1920s she painted in Sydney until she became mentally ill; she died at Gladesville, New South Wales, on 17 July 1946.

Table Talk, 6 March 1891, p.5; *Illustrated Sydney News*, 9 May 1891, p.10; 1 August 1891, p.8; McCulloch 1984, p.389

ALBERT HENRY FULLWOOD 1863-1930
Painter and illustrator

A. Henry Fullwood, as he generally called himself, was born 15 March 1863, son of a jeweller in Birmingham, England. He began to study art at the Birmingham School of Art. Arriving in Sydney 14 December 1883 aboard the *Rialto*, he worked first as a staff artist for *The Picturesque Atlas of Australasia* for about five years; also produced black-and-white drawings for *The Bulletin*, *The Australian Town and Country Journal* and numerous other illustrated publications. He shared a studio with Frank P. Mahony; practised etching with the American illustrator Livingston Hopkins ('Hop' of *The Bulletin*). He joined Ashton, Daplyn, Conder, Nerli and others on painting excursions to Griffith's farm at Richmond. Fullwood much admired Streeton's work, which he saw for the first time at the Art Society of New South Wales exhibition of September 1890. He painted with Streeton and Roberts at Sirius Cove, where his nickname was 'Uncle Remus'; and in 1895 helped to establish the new Society of Artists. Five years later he held an auction of his work and departed for the U.S.A. In

A. Henry Fullwood, in *The Illustrated Sydney News*, 28 November 1889
Photograph: State Library of South Australia

1901 he went to London, exhibiting there at the Royal Academy and in Paris at the Salon; and illustrating freelance for *The Graphic*. During the first world war he joined Streeton and Roberts working at Wandsworth Hospital; and in 1918 became an official war artist. He returned to Australia in 1920 and died at Waverley, Sydney, on October 1930.

Illustrated Sydney News, 28 November 1889, p.23; Anne Gray, *A. Henry Fullwood, War Paintings*, Australian War Memorial, Canberra, 1983; Dinah Dysart, *A. Henry Fullwood in Australia*, S.H. Ervin Museum and Art Gallery, Sydney, 1984

INA (GEORGINA ALICE) GREGORY 1874-1964
Painter

Ina Gregory was born 18 October 1874 and grew up at 'Rosedale', Inkerman Street, St Kilda. She and an elder sister, Ada, commenced drawing lessons in their 'teens and in the 1890s studied under Fox and Tucker at the Melbourne Art School and at 'Charterisville'. She appears in Fox's *Art Students*. In 1893 and 1895 she received prizes for life drawing. She also studied drawing at the Gallery School in 1893-94, possibly earlier, and won a student prize there in 1898. She exhibited with the Victorian Artists' Society in 1898 and for a number of years after 1900: portraits, landscape and genre. In 1905 she produced book illustrations with Violet Teague, a close friend from both the Gallery and the Melbourne Art School. She also became friendly with Ethel Carrick Fox and Jane Price. In 1907 she contributed to the First Australian Exhibition of Women's Work at the Melbourne Exhibition Building. An unpublished manuscript novel (now lost) about student life at 'Charterisville', usually attributed to Ina Gregory, was probably the work of Ada. The two sisters lived together until Ada's death in 1935. The family also had a country property, 'Maroondah', at Healesville. Ina became a Rosecrucian and member of the Theosophical Society; and implicitly believed in fairies. In old age she moved to Oakleigh to stay with a Mrs Jessica Lavery. She died in 1964.

Moore 1934, I, pp.79ff.; Topliss 1984, p.74; information kindly supplied by Mrs Robin Kelly and descendants of the artist

JOHANN JOSEPH EUGEN VON GUERARD 1811-1901
Painter and teacher

Eugen von Guérard, photograph, c.1870
LaTrobe Collection, State Library of Victoria

Eugen von Guérard was born 17 November 1811 in Vienna; son of a German miniature painter, Bernhard von Guérard (1771-1836), employed by the Emperor of Austria. From 1826 father and son toured Italy, then stayed – working and studying – in Rome for two years 1830-32. After his father's death, the younger von Guérard studied landscape painting for five years c.1839-44 at the Dusseldorf Academy, then one of the main art teaching centres in Europe. He travelled in Germany, the Netherlands, Switzerland, France and, in his own words, 'had a good many occasions to see the finest works of art and to form his taste and expression'. He moved to London in 1852; but in August that year decided to try his luck on the Victorian goldfields, arriving at Geelong, 24 December 1852, aboard the emigrant sailing ship *Windemere*. He made many sketches of the mining districts around Ballarat until 1854, when he resumed his career as a landscape painter in Melbourne, and married Fräulein Louise Arnz, a native of Dusseldorf. Within a year he received his first commission to paint a rich settler's homestead and he began to travel extensively; at the same time collecting material, in the form of numerous small and highly detailed drawings, for more romantic landscape subjects. He visited the Western District of Victoria, Cape Otway, the Grampians, Gippsland, Cape Schank, Tasmania, South Australia, the Australian Alps, the Blue Mountains and Sydney. His album of lithographs, *Eugene von Guérard's Australian Landscapes*, was published in 1867 and awarded a prize at the Intercolonial Exhibition. By the 1860s von Guérard was recognized as one of Victoria's foremost landscape artists, exhibiting regularly in Melbourne and at various international expositions in Europe and America. In 1870 he was appointed first 'Instructor of Painting and Master of the School of Art' and, in an honorary capacity, 'Curator of Pictures, Works of Art, Prints and Photographs' at the Melbourne Gallery; his *Mount Kosciusko* was purchased for the collection. Also that year, he received the Cross of the Order of Franz Josef, forwarded by the Emperor of Austria to the Governor of Victoria. His output diminished and the subsequent summer sketching tours were to Tasmania in 1875 and New Zealand 1876. Although well liked by most students, he was evidently an uninspiring teacher. According to one young member of the Victorian Academy of Arts, writing to *The Daily Telegraph* (29 November 1871), he did 'nothing more than impart to five or six young ladies and gentlemen a boarding school acquaintance with the pencil which just enables them to make the feeblest of feeble copies'. In 1881 he resigned from the Gallery; in January 1882 he departed with his wife for Italy via Suez and settled, semi-retired, in Dusseldorf. In 1891, their daughter Victoria having married an Englishman, the von Guérards moved to London. Nicholas Chevalier, who had also been in Melbourne 1855-68, became a close friend. Von Guérard died in London on 17 April 1901.

Smith 1975, pp.113f., 145f., 162ff.; Daniel Thomas 1976, pp.45f.; Whitelaw 1976; Candice Bruce, *Eugen von Guérard*, A.G.D.C. and Australian National Gallery, Canberra, 1980; Candice Bruce, Edward Comstock & Frank McDonald, *Eugen von Guérard 1811-1901: a German Romantic in the Antipodes*, Alistair Taylor, Martinborough, New Zealand, 1982

TOM (THOMAS) HUMPHREY 1858-1922
Painter and photographer

Humphrey, born 1858 in Aberdeen, Scotland, came to Australia in 1869. He attended the Gallery School from 1878 to 1883 whilst working as photographer and shop manager for Johnstone, O'Shannassy and Falk. He signed students' requests to the trustees for 'higher instruction' and reforms at the School, and was one of the first members of the Buonarotti Society in 1883. He joined weekend painting expeditions with McCubbin and especially with fellow Scots, John Mather and John Ford Paterson; painted at Box Hill, Olinda and elsewhere. He exhibited with the Victorian Academy of Arts in 1885 and 1887; with the Australian Artists' Association in 1887; and the Victorian Artists' Society from 1888 to 1913. His half-sister from Aberdeen, Miss Lizzie Deans, married Paterson's younger brother, Hugh, on 21 October 1889. In 1890, working full-time as a professional photographer, Humphrey set up his own business as T. Humphrey and Co. He continued to paint whenever possible: at 'Charterisville' with Fox and Tucker, for example, and whilst staying with the McCubbins at Blackburn in 1894. Roberts later described his work as an 'expression of the intimate and tender spirit of the Bush in its quiet moods'. The National Gallery of Victoria purchased his *Under a Summer Sun* in 1895. In 1899 he married Miss Alice Mills; but within three years he developed symptoms of tuberculosis. Having sold his first photograhy establishment, the couple opened jointly the Alice Mills Studio, c.1903, in Altson's Building at the corner of Collins and Elizabeth Streets, Melbourne. Humphrey continued to paint, chiefly at various bayside beaches and at home in Armadale, until his death in 1922.

Hall 1979; Topliss 1984, p.75; information from the artist's daughter, the late Dr Molly True

For portrait, see sketch painted by Tucker in this catalogue

(SIR) JOHN LONGSTAFF 1862-1941
Painter

John Longstaff, portrait drawing by Phil May, 1894
Photograph: State Library of Victoria (see also National Gallery student group photograph)

Longstaff was born 10 March 1862 at Clunes, Victoria; the son of Ralph Longstaff, storekeeper. He was educated at the Clunes State School and a boarding school at Miners Rest. In 1880 he came to work in Melbourne; entered the Gallery School in 1882 and was joined by his sister, Polly, in Melbourne the following year. He was a founding member of the Buonarotti Society in 1883. At the Gallery School, 1882-87, he became a favourite pupil of Folingsby; and painted his teacher's portrait, c.1886. In 1887 he won the first travelling scholarship with *Breaking the News*. That same year he married a Miss Rosa Crocker and, after a grand farewell by the Buonarotti Society, the couple left for Paris in September aboard the *Valetta*. Longstaff then enrolled at Fernand Cormon's atelier in 1888 on the advice of John Peter Russell; and later also studied at Colarossi's, along with Altson and Davies. He met Rodin; and in 1889 he visited the Russells at Belle-Ile. He also met Toulouse-Lautrec, Louis Anquetin, Conder – newly arrived from Australia in 1890 – and William Rothenstein. In fulfilment of the terms of his scholarship, he sent home to the National Gallery of Victoria full-size copies of Titian's *Entombment of Christ* (Louvre, Paris) and Velasquez's *Aesopus* (Prado, Madrid). He also acted as a purchasing adviser in London and Paris for both the Sydney and Melbourne Galleries. He exhibited in the Paris Salon of 1890; and was awarded a *mention honorable* in 1891 for *Mother and her child* (now in the National Gallery of Victoria). He showed his third (original) scholarship picture, *The Sirens*, in the Salon of 1892 and at the Royal Academy in 1894 before shipping it home to Melbourne. In July 1895 he revisited Australia himself, welcomed very enthusiastically by the Victorian Artists' Society; and received a number of portrait commissions. At first he stayed in a hotel at Heidelberg; but soon moved his family to a cottage at Brighton – where McCubbin and Colquhoun were also living. Together with Fox, he was selected by the Gallery trustees to paint an Australian historical picture for the Gilbee Bequest. He therefore sailed for England in 1901, finally completing the vast *Arrival of Burke, Wills and King at the deserted camp at Cooper's Creek, Sunday Evening, 21st April 1861* in 1907. By 1906 he had a fashionable residence in St John's Wood and a 'magnificent studio' in nearby Carlton Hill. He exhibited regularly in London and was an official war artist with the A.I.F. in France, 1918-19. After his return to Australia in 1921, he held numerous official positions with art societies in both Melbourne and Sydney. He was knighted in 1928, awarded the medal of the Advance Australia Association in 1933; and served as a trustee of the National Gallery of Victoria from 1927 until his death in 1941.

Argus 29 June 1895, p.4; Jope-Slade 1895, p.390; Murdoch 1948; Timms 1975; Leigh Astbury, in *A.D.B.*, forthcoming

ARTHUR JOSE DE SOUZA LOUREIRO 1853-1932
Painter, teacher, occasional wood carver and decorative painter

Arthur (Artur) Loureiro was born 11 February 1853 at Oporto in Portugal, son of Dr Francisco Loureiro. He began drawing lessons at night school in Oporto; and

Arthur Loureiro, in *The Illustrated Sydney News*, 1 August 1891
Photograph: Mitchell Library, State Library of New South Wales

learned painting from Antonio José da Costa (1840-1929). His formal training commenced at the Escola Pintura do Porto under João António Correia (1822-96), a former pupil of Vernet, Delaroche and Ingres in Paris. In 1873 Loureiro entered the Academia Portuense in Lisbon. He applied for that Academy's travelling scholarship to Rome in 1875; and, the competition being cancelled, he was privately sponsored instead by one of the examiners, Delfim Guimarães, afterwards Conde de Almedina, to study in Lisbon, Madrid, Florence and Rome 1876-79. He also visited England and Germany at this time. Returning to Lisbon in 1879, he won the government travelling scholarship for landscape painters to study in Paris for three years. In 1880 he entered the Ecole des Beaux-Arts in the atelier of Alexandre Cabanel – the former school of Benjamin Constant and Jules Bastien-Lepage, whom he reputedly met. He joined the expatriate Portuguese group, 'The Lion Club', on their *plein air* excursions into the country around Paris. He exhibited annually at the Paris Salons of 1880-82: both portraits and subject paintings. On 5 September 1881 in Surrey, England, he married Miss Marie Thérèse Huybers of Hobart, who had been completing her education in Europe; one of her sisters was the Australian novelist 'Tasma'; another had an affair in Paris with the Symbolist poet, Joris Karl Huysmans, later married Gustave Courbet's sculptor nephew and became art critic for *The Age* in Melbourne. Loureiro's only son, Vasco, was born in Surrey in 1882. That year he first exhibited in London; and the family then moved to a cottage at Brolles in the

forest of Fontainebleau. However, due to poor health, Loureiro was unable to fulfil the terms of his Portuguese travelling scholarship; and 'advised to proceed to a sunny country', he chose his wife's native land, 'the bright sky, the warm sun and the pure Australian air in which we breathe champagne. . . to pursue his work out of door'. Arriving in Melbourne early in 1885, he was 'discovered' by *The Argus* critic James Smith, painting in the Fitzroy Gardens; his *plein air* style was immediately praised by local reviewers. He opened a 'School of Design' in his city studio; by mid-1886 he had moved to share premises with the Italians G.P. Nerli and Ugo Catani in Nicholson's Chambers, Swanston Street. He was a founder member of the Australian Artists' Association in 1886 and was elected to its first council with Roberts, McCubbin, Ashton and others. In 1887 he opened a second studio at home in Denmark Street, Kew. He exhibited regularly with the Australian Artists' Association, the Victorian Artists' Society; and at the Centennial Exhibition of 1888 — submitting in addition eighty-three paintings by his pupils. His work was wide ranging in both style and subject matter. In 1890 he built a new house and large teaching studio in Stawell Street, Kew, designed by fashionable architect Francis Smart in the Aesthetic 'Queen Anne' style – 'his artistic nest, a red brick mansion, yclept Cabana'. The same year he was appointed head of the art department at the Presbyterian Ladies' College, East Melbourne; he also taught at Genazzano, where his eldest Australian-born daughter, Fauvette, was educated. In 1891 he was proposed by James Smith to succeed Folingsby as director of the National Gallery of Victoria and master of the Art School but declined on grounds of ill health. His Landseer-like painting of a St Bernard dog, *Baron*, was purchased by the Gallery in 1895. He exhibited with the Yarra Sculptors' Society and at the Grafton Galleries, London in 1898; his large Australian historical work *The Death of Burke* (1892) was awarded a gold medal in London. *The Vision of St Stanislaus*, awarded a bronze medal at the Paris Exposition Universelle of 1900, was purchased by the Gallery the following year. Loureiro revisited Europe for a holiday in 1901 and decided to remain there. Having settled his affairs in Australia 1902-04, he returned permanently to Portugal. He opened a select private painting school in the Palácio de Cristal, Oporto; remarried, his Australian wife having died March 1907; painted and exhibited increasingly conventional portraits and landscapes. He was knighted in the Order of Santiago in 1932 for his services to Portuguese art; and later that year died

suddenly whilst on his annual *plein air* painting holiday at Gerez.

Table Talk, 19 October 1888, pp.3f.; *Illustrated Sydney News*, 1 August 1891, p.6; Braz Burity, *Catalogo da exposição de pintura de Arthur Loureiro*, Sociedade Nacional des Belas-Artes de Lisboa, 1920; *Pintores da Escola do Porto Séc. XIX e XX nas colecções do Museu Nacional de Soares dos Reis*, Fundação Calouste Gulbenkian, Lisbon, 1983, nos 27ff.; Clark 1985

(SIR) EDGAR BERTRAM MACKENNAL
R.A. 1863-1931
Sculptor

Bertram Mackennal, portrait drawing by Aby Altson, 1894
Photograph: State Library of Victoria

Born 12 June 1863 in Melbourne, Bertram Mackennal was the son of architectural sculptor John Simpson Mackennal (1832-1901). He dropped his first Christian name as a boy, although his father always called him 'Edgar'. He first studied art with his father; then at the Gallery's School of Design, 1878-82, under Campbell. He also attended classes at the Victorian Academy of Arts. Fellow students called him 'Mr Sunny'. In 1881 a visiting English sculptor, Marshall Wood, gave him some instruction and offered him work as a studio assistant in London. Mackennal therefore left Melbourne in 1882, only to find that Wood had died suddenly only four days earlier. Advised by another leading London sculptor, William Hamo Thornycroft, and encouraged by Tom Roberts and C.D. Richardson with whom he was sharing a studio, he enrolled at the Royal Academy Schools on 4 December 1883; but soon felt he was wasting time, allowed only to draw from casts as he had already done for years in Australia. He visited Rome, with letters of introduction to artists such as Elihu Vedder from John Peter Russell; then worked in Paris, again with introductions and some financial assistance from Russell. In 1884 he married Agnes Eliza Spooner, who had also been a student at the Royal Academy. He met Alfred Gilbert; and wrote that Rodin 'was the most marvellous modeller in the world and the greatest searcher after truth. He was the first man whose work made me understand that art is not Nature, but something grander and superimposed on nature'. In 1886 he exhibited at the Royal Academy whilst working as head of the modelling and design departments of the Coalport Potteries in Shropshire, producing 'figures, cups and other china articles'. The following year he won a competition, open only to Australian artists, for sculptural decorations on the façade of Parliament House, Melbourne. He therefore returned home early in 1888, opening a studio in Swanston Street, opposite the Gallery and Public Library. There, Streeton recalled, 'on the last Friday evening of each month he entertained at his bohemian supper table favourite guests, but only two or three at a time because of his small apartment'. In 1891 he received a 'consolation' prize from the Gallery trustees for a sculpture, *The Triumph of Truth*, which was never commissioned (despite an uproar in the local press). He left for Paris in March the same year with funds contributed by 'a group of Melbourne gentlemen', and 'a cartload of letters of introduction to eminent men in Europe' from the famous French actress Sara Bernhardt, then visiting Melbourne. He met Altson, Longstaff, Bunny and other expatriate artists; exhibited at the Salon of 1892; worked in Edinburgh during 1893; set up a studio in St John's Wood 1894. His *Circe*, awarded a *mention honorable* in the Salon of 1893, was widely publicized a year later at the Royal Academy in London. Mackennal's reputation was made. Many prestigious commissions followed. In 1899, for example, Dame Nellie Melba sat for a marble bust of herself which she presented to the National Gallery of Victoria. He briefly revisited Australia the following year; and *Circe* was purchased by Herr Carl Pinschoff, a leading patron of the Heidelberg School artists. In London his work was

purchased for the Tate Gallery. Mackennal was the first colonial elected an Associate of the Royal Academy (in 1909) and a full Royal Academician (1922); and the first Australian artist to be knighted, in 1921. Five years later he visited and exhibited in Australia once again. He died at Torquay in Devon on 11 October 1931.

Table Talk, 8 March 1889, p.5; 17 January 1890, p.8; Jope-Slade 1895, pp.390ff.; Sturgeon 1978, pp.59ff.; Scarlett 1980

FREDERICK McCUBBIN 1855-1917
Painter and teacher

McCubbin was a baker's son, born in West Melbourne on 25 February 1855. Evidently his mother encouraged his 'fondness for drawing'; and 'the worthy pastor' of the local church lent him Cunningham's *Lives of the Most Eminent British Painters* to read and a set of landscape prints to copy. From 1867 to 1870 he attended evening classes at the Artisans School of Design in Carlton, along with Abrahams and Richardson. He ceased formal education in 1869; and spent a year working as a solicitor's clerk until he was caught constructing model theatres during office hours. He met Buvelot and much admired his landscape style. He sketched regularly around the inner suburbs. From 1871 was apprenticed for five years as a coach painter with Stevenson and Elliot's; also in 1871 he enrolled at the Gallery School where he remained a student for fifteen years. He studied drawing under Thomas Clark; and Campbell from 1876. From c.1875 he was able to attend daytime painting classes as well, at first von Guérard's; then 1882-86 under Folingsby. He was also influenced by Julian and George Rossi Ashton. Although his father's death in 1876 meant increased responsibility in the family business, McCubbin was able to exhibit that year with the Victorian Academy of Arts. In October 1880 he signed the students' petition to the trustees for 'higher instruction' at the Gallery; and then the letter requesting life classes and other reforms. He told Mrs Roberts that his 'forte' was figure drawing. In 1882 he founded, with Abrahams and four others, a new 'Life-Club' for drawing the nude – paying for their own models and supported by Folingsby. In 1883 he received the £30 first prize for 'the best studies in colour and drawing'. In 1884 he won a major student prize for *Home Again*; and also did some commercial black-and-white work for illustrated papers at this time. McCubbin was an

enthusiastic member of the Buonarotti Society from its inception; his student nickname was 'the Prof'. (According to friend and fellow student, Alexander Colquhoun, 'He was an extensive and discriminating reader, particularly in the direction of biography and higher fiction, and it was his common habit to memorise what he had read and deliver it to the first receptive friend he came across in the form of a brief but glowing epitome'.) In 1885, with Roberts and Abrahams, he established the first Box Hill camp – he painted *Lost* there in 1886. In November 1886, he was elected to the committee of the Australian Artists' Association; and that year he was appointed drawing master at the Gallery School (a post he held – very well loved by his students – until his death in 1917). He probably sold the family bakery about this time. During the summer of 1886-87 he and Roberts met Streeton painting at Beaumaris. He contributed to the great Centennial Exhibition of 1888. In March 1889 he married Miss Anne Moriarty (they had met at an artists' picnic at Blackburn in 1884) and moved to Auburn; the Gallery students gave them 'a very handsome marble clock and mantel ornaments as a wedding gift'. In August 1889 he produced five paintings for the 9 by 5 Impression Exhibition; that year he also painted *Down on his Luck*, first of his large-scale 'pioneering history' subjects. In 1890 he named his first born son Louis, after Abrahams. He took Julian Ashton to see the 1890 Victorian Artists' Society and, as a result of this visit, Streeton's *Still glides the stream...* was purchased for the Art Gallery of New South Wales. During the 1890s, McCubbin remained in Melbourne – tied by teaching duties and his growing family of 'little Profs' – when most of the other Heidelberg School artists left for Sydney or Europe. He borrowed Loureiro's large house and studio at Kew during summer holidays when the Loureiro family moved to Healesville. From 1891 his title at the Gallery was 'Master of the School of Design and Instructor of Painting', under the new director Lindsay Bernard Hall. He exhibited regularly with the Victorian Artists' Society; was elected president in 1893 and again for three subsequent terms (1902-04, 1908-09, 1911-12); he also sent paintings to Sydney for exhibition. In 1895 he moved from Blackburn to Brighton. In 1900 he visited Tasmania; then stayed briefly in Carlton before moving the family to 'Fontainebleau' at Mount Macedon – *The Pioneer* was painted there 1903-05. In 1907 McCubbin made his first and only journey to Europe, sailing on 21 May 1907 aboard s.s. *Heinrich*. Meeting up with Roberts in London, he was most impressed by J.M.W. Turner's paintings, which he had admired since boyhood in reproduction. The influence of Turner was manifest in the higher key and looser handling of McCubbin's late style. He died at South Yarra in 1917.

MacDonald 1916; Colquhoun n.d. [1919]; Galbally 1981

See drawing by John Sommers, 1876, and self-portrait of 1886 in this catalogue

JOHN MATHER 1848-1916
Painter, etcher and teacher

John Mather, photograph in *Table Talk*, 25 January 1900
State Library of Victoria

Mather was born in October 1848 at Hamilton, Lanarkshire, Scotland. He sketched from early childhood; living on the Duke of Hamilton's estate, he was allowed to study work in that great picture collection. He began formal art training under the Glasgow watercolourist Thomas Fairbairn (1820-84); exhibited at the Royal Institute of Fine Arts, Glasgow, c.1868, and pursued his studies at the Edinburgh National Gallery School. He worked in various parts of Scotland and England; then in Paris, chiefly as a decorator. Suffering from asthma he decided to emigrate to 'sunny Australia'. He arrived in Melbourne 1877-78. Although continuing to accept some decorative commissions (for example, he worked on the dome of the Melbourne Exhibition Building), he hoped to become a full-time professional painter. He enrolled at the Gallery School under Folingsby in 1882. He admired Buvelot; and joined *plein air* landscape painting

expeditions around Melbourne with McCubbin, Withers and others. He helped Abrahams with etchings at the Box Hill camp. Mather exhibited with the Victorian Academy of Arts and Art Society of New South Wales; and was elected as a founding committee member of the Australian Artists' Association in Melbourne in 1886. He took a studio at 'Koombahla', Healesville in 1888; also painted in the parks and gardens of Melbourne, at bayside beaches, on the Yarra at Launching Place, and later in New South Wales, Tasmania, Western Australia and New Zealand. Evidently he became a popular teacher: one weekend afternoon at Eaglemont he addressed a group of eighty artists, art students and their friends. From 1891 he conducted painting classes at his city studio in Austral Buildings, Collins Street. In 1893 he became the first artist trustee at the National Gallery of Victoria, a position he held until his death. His *Autumn in the Fitzroy Gardens* was acquired by the Gallery in 1894: one of a number of Heidelberg School landscapes purchased that year. He exhibited regularly in Melbourne and Sydney, served as president of the Victorian Artists' Society 1893-1901 and later for two further terms. From 1905 to 1916 he was a member of the Felton Bequests Committee. In 1912 he became a foundation member of the Australian Art Association. He died in 1916.

Table Talk, 2 November 1888, p.3; 21 January 1900, p.5; McCulloch 1984, p.778

GIROLAMO PIERI BALLATI NERLI 1860-1926
Painter and teacher

Nerli was born in Siena, Italy, on 12 February 1860, properly called Girolamo Ballati Nerli Pieri Pecci. His father was an Italian nobleman, Ferdinando Ballati Nerli Pieri Pecci; his mother, Henrietta, was the daughter of Ann, Baroness Hamilton of Sweden and an Englishman, Thomas Medwin, an authority on Byron and Shelley. Young Nerli enrolled at the Accademia di Belle Arti in Florence, probably in the late 1870s, studying under the history painters Antonio Ciseri and Giovanni Muzzioli. He was also influenced by more progressive ideas such as those of the romantically bohemian *Scapigliati* group; and especially the *Macchiaioli*, pioneers of *plein air* painting in Italy, so-called because of the *macchie*, or spots, of bright colour which characterize their work. In 1879 he may have seen examples of true French Impressionism at first hand: two

Girolamo Nerli, photograph, 1896
Hocken Library, Dunedin, New Zealand

paintings by Camille Pissarro which were exhibited with the Societa Promotrice di Belle Arti in Florence. Nerli himself received a medal for work exhibited in Milan. Late in 1885 he arrived in Melbourne with fellow Italian painter, Ugo Catani; having sailed from Marseilles aboard the *Calédonian*, via Madagascar, Mauritius and Bourbon. The two Italians had brought with them oil sketches and studies by various contemporary artist friends, which they displayed in their city studio; from May 1886 they shared premises with Arthur Loureiro. Nerli moved to Sydney towards the end of 1886. He met Conder and painted with Julian Ashton's circle. The critic James Green wrote later that 'Nerli's mastery of both the human form and the most difficult color problems, his excellence in composition and his fine ability in drawing, with not a little of the poetry of Arno and the *chic* and *abandon* of Paris in his nature, made ample amends for any spice of affectation in his work, and helped to level up the painting of the colony to a higher standard'. In October or November 1889 he travelled to New Zealand, accompanying a New South Wales loan collection of pictures for exhibition in Dunedin. He exhibited in Sydney in September 1890; and possibly visited Western Australia at this time. In August 1892 he sailed to Apia in Samoa where he met and painted several portraits of Robert Louis Stevenson. He saw Stevenson again in Sydney in December that year. By June 1893 he had returned to Dunedin, taking private pupils and exhibiting with the Otago Art Society. He was a joint founder of the Otago Art Academy in February 1894; appointed 'Teacher of Painting' at the state-run Dunedin School of Art in February 1895;

and became very popular with his students. In October 1896 he suddenly left Dunedin and by April the following year was a working member of the Auckland Society of Arts. On 5 March 1898 he married a Miss Marie Cecilia Josephine Barron in Christchurch. By December 1898 he was in Perth, exhibiting with the West Australian Art Society. He exhibited in Brisbane 1899; in Sydney 1899 and 1900; and in Melbourne c.1900-02. Nerli and his wife returned to Europe: they were in London during the first world war. Later he settled at Nervi, near Genoa, where he died at the 'Villa Durallo' on 24 June 1926.

Australasian Art Review, 1 June 1899, p.24; by far the most reliable account of Nerli's life is Entwisle 1984, pp.103ff.

JOHN FORD PATERSON 1851-1912
Painter

John Ford Paterson, in *The Illustrated Sydney News,* 27 June 1890
Photograph: State Library of Victoria

Born at Dundee, Scotland in March 1851, Paterson trained as an artist for five years at the Royal Scottish Academy in Edinburgh; he first exhibited there in 1869. In 1871 he migrated to Australia with other members of his family, including an elder brother Charles Stewart Paterson (1843-1917) and younger Hugh (b.1856), both painter-decorators, businessmen and patrons of their Heidelberg School friends. In 1875 John Ford Paterson revisited Scotland, studying landscape painting with G.W. Johnson and meeting Scottish *plein airists* - members of the group known as the Glasgow Boys – such as William McTaggart, James Guthrie and James

Lawson Wingate. Returning to settle permanently in Melbourne in 1884, with 'a resolute determination to make his influence felt', he renewed his friendship with Buvelot. Local Scots compatriots included Humphrey and Mather. He was a committee member of the 'breakaway' Australian Artists' Association in 1886 and a founding member of the Victorian Artists' Society two years later. (By 1892 Streeton called him 'one of the faithful properties of the Gallery, Eastern Hill'; and he was its president 1901-02). In 1889 he opened a new studio in Cramond House, Queensberry Street, Carlton; reputed as the best-lighted in Melbourne and decorated with Moorish vases, Egyptian artefacts and suits of 'medieval' armour. By 1890 he also had a country property at Berwick. He revisited Britain in 1892. Paterson's work was generally very well received, especially in English exhibitions of antipodean art. Although he turned to poultry farming near Ringwood as times grew harder in the 90s, by the end of the century his major *Fernshaw – A Bush Symphony* had been purchased for the National Gallery of Victoria. He died suddenly at home in Carlton on 1 July 1912.

R.A.M. Stevenson, 'Art in Australia', *The Magazine of Art*, 1886, pp.397ff.; *Table Talk*, 26 October 1888, p.3, 30 August 1889, p.5, 25 July 1901, pp.16f.; *Illustrated Australian News*, 1 July 1896, p.3; Marjorie J.Tipping in *A.D.B.*, vol.5, 1974; McCulloch 1984, p.880; Watkins 1984

CHARLES DOUGLAS RICHARDSON 1853-1932
Painter, sculptor and teacher

Charles Douglas Richardson was born in 1853 in Islington, London; son of an academic portrait and figure painter, John Richardson (1818-62). The family emigrated to Portland in 1858 when Richardson was a small child. After they moved to Melbourne in 1860 he attended Scotch College where Henricus L. van den Houten (1801-79) was drawing master; also took lessons from Thomas Wright (1830-86). He was then apprenticed to Messrs de Gruchy and Leigh, lithographers. In c.1870 he enrolled at the Artisans School of Design, Carlton, with Roberts and McCubbin; was appointed junior master and secretary of the students' club; studied anatomy at the Melbourne Hospital and University of Melbourne; drew from plaster casts and copied paintings at the National Gallery

Charles Douglas Richardson, in *The Illustrated Sydney News*, 27 June 1890
Photograph: State Library of Victoria

before its School was established. He attended the Gallery's School of Design 1871-73 and 1878-81, under Clark and then Campbell, where his fellows included Roberts, McCubbin, Abrahams and Mackennal. In 1873 he won a student prize there for drawing. He established a life drawing club with Roberts and McCubbin, paying their own models, until the practice was forbidden and the group disbanded by Campbell. With Roberts he initiated the students' requests to trustees for reforms at the School in October 1880. He had joined the Victorian Academy of Arts in 1876; in 1878 he was elected to the committee and helped in all capacities including the life class. In 1880 he exhibited with the Art Society of New South Wales; and was represented at both the 1879 and 1880 International Exhibitions in Sydney and Melbourne. Like Mackennal, he was advised by the British sculptor, Marshall Wood, to study overseas. He left for London in 1881 and is said to have shared a studio there with Roberts and Mackennal. On 7 March 1882 he entered the Royal Academy Schools where his nickname was 'The Bushranger'. He made a painting tour to Cornwall and visited France and Italy. In the annual student competitions he won the second Armitage Prize for a Design in Monochrome in 1883 and the first Armitage Prize plus first prize for sculptural modelling in 1884; he exhibited at the annual Academy exhibitions of 1885 and 1888. Richardson returned to Melbourne in 1889. Various works painted in England were much praised by local critics. He contributed twenty-five items to the 9 by 5 Impression

Exhibition in August 1889, including sketches in wax. He taught life classes at the Victorian Artists' Society from 1890; took a studio in Gordon Chambers, Flinders Street, with Conder and Streeton as neighbours. He exhibited regularly with the Victorian Artists' Society – paintings, sculpture and designs for architectural decoration. He became a foundation member and president of the Yarra Sculptors' Society in 1898. He executed decorations for *The Age* building in 1899, the monument to the Golden Jubilee of Discovery of Gold at Bendigo 1903-06 and numerous other public sculptural commissions. In 1914 he married Margaret Baskerville, a fellow student from the Gallery School; they lived and had studios in Church Street, Middle Brighton. Richardson was president of the Victorian Artists' Society 1917-24 and 1925-30. In latter years he became increasingly fascinated by religious and mystic philosophies. He died in Melbourne in 1932.

Table Talk, 5 April 1889, p.6; *Illustrated Sydney News*, 27 June 1890, p.13; Ernest S. Smellie, 'An Australian Artist: Mr C.D. Richardson', *The Magazine of Art*, 1900, pp.467ff.; Ernest Fysh, *Memoir of C.D. Richardson, Sculptor and Painter*, Melbourne, 1933; Scarlett 1980, pp.554ff.; Peers 1985; Margaret Rose, *Margaret Baskerville and Charles Douglas Richardson*, forthcoming

TOM (THOMAS WILLIAM) ROBERTS 1856-1931
Painter, photographer, occasional teacher and writer

Tom Roberts was born 9 March 1856 at Dorchester, England; son of Richard Roberts, editor of the *Dorset County Chronicle* (d.1868), and Matilda Agnes Cela Roberts. He was educated at the local Dorchester grammar school until 1869, when he emigrated with his widowed mother, brother and sister to join relatives already living in Melbourne. In 1873 he attended the East Collingwood School of Design where he was awarded a prize for landscape (judged by Buvelot and von Guérard). He seems to have attended the Carlton School briefly in 1874; but also that year enrolled at the Gallery School whilst working as a photographer's assistant in Collingwood and then at Stewart's photography studio in Bourke Street East. He led regular sketching expeditions with McCubbin and others; and established an independent life drawing group with McCubbin and Richardson, paying their own model. He also studied anatomy with Richardson at the Melbourne Hospital and University of Melbourne. In October 1876, on Thomas Clark's retirement, he applied unsuccessfully for the position of master of the Gallery School of Design; in his letter of application he stated that he would introduce a life class. Roberts initiated several students' requests to trustees for reforms at the School. In his efforts to raise money to study in England he drew for local illustrated journals and sold a copy of Edwin Long's popular historical costume piece *A Question of Propriety* (in the National Gallery of Victoria). He departed aboard s.s. *Garonne* in 1881. On 6 December that year he enrolled in the Royal Academy Antique Schools, officially recommended by Edwin Long; contemporaries included Maurice W. Greiffenhagen, Robert Anning Bell, Harry Bates, C.D. Richardson, Bertram Mackennal and George Walton. In the summer of 1883 he toured Spain with Australians John Peter Russell, Percy Russell and Dr William Maloney; met Spanish art students Loreano Barrau and Ramon Casas. He visited Italy in 1884; and Paris c.1884-85. Thomas Clark had advised him to go to the Académie Julian; which he did, very briefly, working under Barrau's master Jean-Léon Gérôme. Roberts left England on 4 March 1885 on the s.s. *Lusitania*; arriving in Melbourne 18 April, 'primed with whatever was the latest in art'. He was soon employed by Barrie and Brown, photographers, arranging poses and lighting. He produced drawings for *The Picturesque Atlas* and *The Australasian Sketcher*; camped at Box Hill with McCubbin and Abrahams. Roberts's overseas experience, his energy and ambition had a somewhat catalytic effect on the professional 'art life' of Melbourne. During 1886 he joined the Buonarotti Society; became a foundation member of the Australian Artists' Association, breaking away from the conservative Victorian Academy; and met his future wife, Lillie Williamson. He spent the summer of 1886-87 at Mentone with McCubbin and Abrahams; met Streeton at Beaumaris. Early in 1888 he visited Sydney and there met Conder. In April 1888 he moved into the new purpose-built studios, Grosvenor Chambers, Collins Street East – 'a habitation for high art in Melbourne' – along with Abrahams, George Walton, J.C. Waite, the sculptor Percival Ball and, later, Misses Jane Sutherland, Clara Southern and Jane Price. He instigated artistic *conversaziones*. He contributed to the Centennial Exhibition of 1888. He probably began work on *Shearing the Rams* late that year; then joined Streeton and Conder at the Eaglemont camp – his Heidelberg School nickname was 'Bulldog'. In August 1889 he organized the 9 by 5 Impression Exhibition, in which he showed sixty-two paintings; this was probably inspired by his memory of Whistler's 'Notes' – 'Harmonies' – 'Nocturnes' exhibition in London in 1884. He revisited 'Brocklesby' station to continue work on *Shearing the Rams* over the summer months of 1889-90; the painting was completed by May 1890. Roberts followed Streeton to Sydney in 1891 and founded Curlew Camp on Little Sirius Cove. From 1892 he also maintained a city studio at various different addresses over the years. He sailed north to Queensland and the Torres Strait Islands in 1892; travelled extensively in New South Wales to paint *The Break Away*, 1891, *Shearing at Newstead*, 1894, *Bailed Up*, 1895; and also painted many portraits. He was a foundation member and became first president of the Society of Artists in 1895. In April 1896 he married, moved to Balmain and was 'much in Society'. He held art classes with Streeton at Vickery Chambers; exhibited regularly in Sydney and Melbourne; wrote numerous articles and letters to newspaper editors. In 1901 he was commissioned to paint a large representation of the opening of Australia's first Federal Parliament in Melbourne. Finally completing the work in London in 1903, he entered what he felt was a 'black period' in his career, finding inspiration very difficult and experiencing some eye trouble. He travelled in Europe again, to Brussels in 1903, Holland 1906, Italy 1913-14; also around Britain. He exhibited at the Royal Academy, the New English Art Club, the Paris Salon and elsewhere. In London he met numerous expatriate Australians and organized social reunions. During the first world war he enlisted as an orderly at the Third London General Hospital, Wandsworth, along with Streeton, Fullwood, George Coates and more than twenty members of the Chelsea Arts Club – which was then full of Australians. On 12 December 1919 he sailed for Melbourne aboard the *Orvieto*. During the following year he painted at Heidelberg, in the Dandenongs at Kallista and Sherbrooke, in Sydney, Tasmania and New Zealand. He returned to London early in 1921, then revisited Italy. Two years later he left England once again, on 6 January 1923 on the *Suevic*; and then settled permanently at Kallista. The first Mrs Roberts died 3 January 1928; in August the artist married an old friend, Miss Jean Boyes of Lochmaben, Tasmania. He became ill in May 1931 and died at Kallista on 14 September.
Croll 1935 and 1946; Spate 1978; Topliss 1985 *For portrait, see 9 by 5 panel painted by Charles Conder*

H. CONSTANCE ROTH 1861 – ??
Painter, decorator and teacher

Madame Roth, in *The Illustrated Sydney News*,
14 November 1889
Photograph: State Library of South Australia

Born 14 May 1861 in Derbyshire,
England, Miss H. Constance Jones studied
at the Derby branch of the South Kensington
Art School; then in London at
Heatherley's and the British Museum
antique classes. She worked as manager
of a decorative firm in Glasgow. In 1884
she married Felix Roth and accompanied
him first to Melbourne, then to Sydney
(her uncle was Dr William Henry Cutts of
Collins Street, Melbourne). She soon
became a popular art teacher, known professionally
as Madame Constance Roth. In
1886 she exhibited with the Australian
Artists' Association in Melbourne and the
Art Society of New South Wales. She contributed
to *The Picturesque Atlas of Australasia*.
The artistic *salon* which she
conducted was a focus for painters, actors
and musicians; Roberts and Conder first
became acquainted there, early in 1888.
Madame Roth revisited Melbourne in
1888; and travelled to Tasmania 1889.
One of her decorative painted panels was
purchased by the Art Gallery of New
South Wales in 1890. By 1892 she had 'left
the colony'. In 1894 she exhibited *A hunt
for breakfast on an Australian lagoon* at
the Royal Academy in London (no.958);
and she visited South Africa the following
year. Her subsequent career is apparently
undocumented.

Table Talk, 11 July 1890, p.5; 26 April
1895, p.2; *Illustrated Sydney News*, 14
November 1889, p.20

JOHN PETER RUSSELL 1858-1930
Painter

John Peter Russell, self-portrait painted in 1886,
Musée Rodin, Paris
Photograph by courtesy of Ann Galbally

Russell was born 16 June 1858 at
Darlinghurst, Sydney; son of the owner of
a successful engineering company. He
was educated at Boulburn School, Garroorigang.
In 1874-75 he travelled to Fiji,
Tahiti, China and Japan, where he
acquired some Japanese woodblock
prints. In 1876 he was sent to England for
three years as 'gentleman' apprentice to
Robey and Co. in Lincoln; and he qualified
as an engineer (long afterwards he was
able to cast the keel of his own yacht at
Belle-Ile). His earliest known paintings are
dated 1879. Russell visited Sydney briefly
in 1880. The death of his father that year
made him financially independent; and
returning to London, he enrolled at the
Slade Art School on 5 January 1881 studying
under Alphonse Legros (1837-1911).
He revisited Sydney in 1882-83, exhibiting
twice with the Art Society of New
South Wales; and yet again later in 1883
after his Spanish walking tour with
Roberts, Maloney and his architect-brother.
In 1885 he visited the *plein air*
painting centres in Cornwall. He then
entered the Paris atelier of Fernand-Anne
Piestre, called Cormon for three years
1885-88. His Paris friends included Mackennal,
Harry Bates, George Walton, and
progressive French artists such as Louis
Anquetin, Emile Bernard, Armand Guillaumin,
Henri de Toulouse-Lautrec, Vincent
van Gogh and Auguste Rodin. He
painted van Gogh's portrait in 1886. In
1888 he married Marianna Antoinetta
Mattiocco, an Italian model from Rodin's
studio, and moved to Belle-Ile off the coast
of Brittanny; their house at Belle-Ile was

known as *Le Château Anglais*, or 'English
Castle'. There he met the great French
Impressionist, Claude Monet (1840-1926);
and entertained Longstaff, MacKennal
and other Australians. When his wife died
in 1908 he sold the *Château* and left the
island. In 1912 he married Caroline de
Witt Merrill, an American singer. During
1914 he worked at Portofino in Italy and
in London. He revisited Paris in 1920; then
sailed for Sydney and New Zealand 1921-
22. Returning permanently to Sydney in
1923, he built a studio at Watson's Bay. In
1924 his offer to present his own collection
of Impressionist and Post-Impressionist
paintings to the Art Gallery of New
South Wales was declined. He died in Sydney
on 22 April 1930.

Galbally 1977

JOHN E. SOMMERS, SENIOR active c.1870-c.1910
Painter and teacher

Sommers studied at the Gallery's School
of Design under Clark and Campbell 1872-
79. He drew McCubbin's portrait in 1876.
By about 1881 he was employed at Castlemaine
by the Education Department. He
contributed prolifically to Victorian Artists'
Society exhibitions – landscapes and
portraits in oil and watercolour – until his
resignation in 1898. His subsequent
career is not securely documented.

CLARA SOUTHERN 1861-1940
Painter and occasional teacher

Clara Southern was born at Kyneton, Victoria
in 1861. She began her art training as
a pupil of Madame Mouchette, painter,
schoolmistress and founder of the Alliance
Française in Victoria; and later took
lessons from Walter Withers. From 1883
to 1887 she studied at the Gallery School
where she was nicknamed 'Panther' for
her lithe beauty. She was admitted to the
Buonarotti Society on 23 January 1886.
From mid-1888 she shared a teaching studio
in fashionable Grosvenor Chambers
with Jane Sutherland; their neighbours
included Tom Roberts, George Walton
and Jane R. Price. Miss Southern regularly
joined weekend painting excursions to
the Eaglemont artists' camp at Heidelberg.
After her marriage to John Flinn,
she moved to 'Blythe Bank' at Warrandyte
c.1908; and started an artists' community
there which later included Louis McCubbin,
Penleigh Boyd, Harold Herbert,

Clara Southern, photograph in *The Bulletin*, 29 May 1929
State Library of South Australia

Charles Wheeler and Frank Crozier. She died at Warrandyte in 1940.

Burke 1980, pp.29ff.; Topliss 1984, p.77; McCulloch 1984, p.1139

(SIR) ARTHUR ERNEST STREETON 1867-1943
Painter, occasional teacher and art critic

Arthur Streeton was born at Mount Duneed, near Geelong, Victoria on 8 April 1867; son of a school teacher. The family moved to Melbourne in 1874 and Arthur attended Punt Road State School. In 1880 he was employed as a junior clerk by Rolfe and Co., Bourke Street, importers of rum, brandy and spirits; then in White's Soft Goods. From 1882 to 1888 he attended night classes at the Gallery's School of Design under Campbell and McCubbin and he enrolled very briefly in Folingsby's painting classes. He joined regular students' *plein air* painting excursions to Heidelberg, Oakleigh, Alphington and 'some days as far as Templestowe and Diamond Creek'. In 1886 he acquired the book *Talks about Art* by the American painter William Morris Hunt (1824-79), a great admirer of the *plein airist* Barbizon School – especially Corot and Millet – who also espoused some aspects of French Impressionism. From 1886 to 1888 Streeton was apprenticed as a lithographer with George Troedel and Co., Collins Street East. McCubbin and Roberts asked him to join the Box Hill camp after finding him painting on the beach at Beaumaris. His nickname was 'Smike', from Dickens's novel *Nicholas Nickleby*, presumably because of his slight physique. He was invited as a 'visitor' to the Buonarotti Society's farewell party for Longstaff on 23 August 1887. Late in the following year Streeton founded the Heidelberg artists' camp at Eaglemont: he was given 'artistic possession' of the old estate by Charles Davies, Esq. – elder brother of a Gallery School student and future brother-in-law of David Davies. He painted *Golden Summer, Eaglemont* there in 1889. In August that year he contributed forty works to the 9 by 5 Impression Exhibition. He occupied a city studio in Gordon Chambers, with Conder and Richardson, until mid-1890 when he moved to Sydney on the proceeds of sale of his *Still glides the stream* to the Art Gallery of New South Wales. Conder took *Golden Summer* to Europe in 1890. Streeton then divided his time between Sydney Harbour and painting grounds further inland, especially the 'heroic' landscape of the Blue Mountains. He revisited Melbourne in 1891, working and exhibiting in Roberts's studio whilst the latter was painting *The Break Away* at Corowa. The critic Sidney Dickinson coined the term 'Heidelberg School' in a review of Streeton's work (*The Australasian Critic*, 1 July 1891, p.240). 'Mr Streeton's pictures are very typical of Australian scenery', he wrote, '. . . boldly and vigorously painted, broad in effect, and with striking contrasts and robust harmonies of colour . . . Truth to local colour is one of Mr Streeton's strong merits – he sees it readily and describes it with admirable positiveness'. During 1892 Streeton lived mainly in Richmond, Victoria, and often painted at Heidelberg. *Golden Summer* was hung 'on the line' at the Paris Salon, awarded a *mention honorable* and purchased by an English collector. In August 1895 Streeton visited Adelaide. Back in Sydney, he and Roberts lived at Curlew Camp, Little Sirius Cove; they shared a teaching studio in Vickery Chambers from 1896. In December 1896 Streeton held a one-man-show and art union in Melbourne, his 'Sydney Sunshine Exhibition'; and the National Gallery of Victoria purchased *The purple noon's transparent might* on John Mather's recommendation. In 1897 Professor Marshall-Hall dedicated his *Hymn to Sydney* to this 'poet of the brush'. Streeton left for Europe, spending five months in Cairo and Italy *en route*. He settled in Chelsea 1899; and met Conder, now in a very worrying state of health. He exhibited at the Royal Academy in 1900; visited Paris the following year; and welcomed Roberts to London in 1903. He visited Melbourne in 1906 and held a very successful show there in 1907. He also exhibited work in Sydney before returning to London in November. Having married a Canadian violinist, Miss Nora Clench, he spent his honeymoon in Venice in 1908. He sent paintings for exhibition in Paris and America and received considerable critical recognition. In 1914 he revisited Australia. He served with the R.A.M.C. during the first world war and then as an official war artist in 1918. From 1919 to 1922 he spent a further four years in Australia. He then visited Canada and London before returning to live permanently in the hills outside Melbourne at Olinda. From 1929 he was art critic for *The Argus*; he published *The Arthur Streeton Catalogue* in 1935 and did much to revive public interest in the art of the Heidelberg School. He was knighted 1937. Streeton died at Olinda in September 1943.

Illustrated Sydney News, 27 June 1890, p.13; Croll 1946; Galbally 1979, and M.A. thesis, University of Melbourne, 1967

See portrait painted by Tom Roberts in 1891

JANE SUTHERLAND 1855-1928
Painter and teacher

Born 1855 in Scotland, Miss Sutherland was one of a large, very liberal artistic and musical family; her father George (1829-85) was a painter, engraver and carver of ships' figureheads. They arrived in Australia 1864 and Melbourne in 1870. Jane attended the Gallery School from 1871 to 1885 and received a student prize in 1883. She joined sketching 'jaunts into the bush' at Alphington, Templestowe, Diamond Creek; and painted at Box Hill with Roberts, McCubbin, Streeton, Abrahams and others. She was one of the first women allowed to join the Buonarotti Society – elected 24 July 1884. From mid-1888 she shared a studio with Clara Southern in Grosvenor Chambers, described by *Table Talk* as 'fitted up so attractively and prettily that it is the cosiest of artistic works' (2 August 1888, p.7). Their neighbour, Jane Price, later recalled that 'every now and then Tom Roberts would give an evening and we would lend him our two rooms to make it more spacious'. Jane Sutherland was probably the best known and most professional of the women painters associated with the Heidelberg School: 'one of the busiest lady artists in Melbourne', according to *Table Talk*, 'as, in addition to her painting, she has several pupils, whom she receives individually or in classes, giving close attention to drawing as the absolutely necessary groundwork'. Even so, she seems never to have taken her work as seriously as her male contemporaries. Although both she and Clara Southern produced 'impressions' at the time of the 9 by 5 exhibition in August 1889, these were 'not for public exhibition'. Her highest recorded asking price for a painting was evidently £21 in 1903, whilst Roberts and McCubbin asked hundreds of guineas for some of theirs. She exhibited with the Victorian Academy of Arts from 1878, the Australian Artists' Association and the Victorian Artists' Society for many years; and in 1900 was elected to the council of the Victorian Artists' Society. After suffering a mild stroke c.1904, she worked on a small scale and often in pastel rather than oils. She probably ceased painting c.1911 and she died in 1928.

Burke 1980, pp.28f.; Lindsay & Rosewarne 1977; McCulloch 1984, pp.1167f.; Topliss 1984

TUDOR ST GEORGE TUCKER 1862-1906
Painter and teacher

Tucker was born in London in 1862, son of a British cavalry officer in the Indian army. He was educated in philosophy and music as well as painting; and came to Melbourne for health reasons in 1881. Attending the Gallery School from 1883 to 1887, he won first prize for drawing two years in succession; he also gave drawing lessons himself at this time. He joined *plein air* painting excursions with Streeton, McCubbin, Fox, Humphrey and others; and became an early member of the Buonarotti Society. One fellow student later recalled that Tucker 'came out from England at the height of Oscar Wilde's "aesthetic craze". He was aged about 20 years at the time, and he used to saunter down "The Block" with a lily or a sunflower in his hand, and with his hair combed out in beautiful fair curls. One young woman made a great flopping sunhat, with an immense sunflower embroidered across the top, for him to wear when playing tennis'. He departed to study in Europe in May 1887, aboard the *Orizaba*. In Paris from 1887 to 1892, he first attended the Académie Julian under Bouguereau and then studied with Fox at the Ecole des Beaux-Arts under Gérôme and Tony Robert-Fleury. Conder wrote home to Melbourne in 1890 that Tucker and Fox were considered the leading Aus-

tralian artists in Paris. Tucker won a students' gold medal c.1892. He exhibited at the Old Salon in Paris and the Royal Academy in London. In 1892 he returned to Melbourne and established himself in Folingsby's former studio, Market Buildings, Flinders Lane. With Fox as partner, he conducted the very successful Melbourne Art School in the city and at 'Charterisville' from 1893: run on 'the principle of the Académie Julian in Paris'. They took it in turns to be in charge a month at a time. One of the students there, Ina Gregory, described Tucker as 'a tall slender man with refined sensitive features, the dark blue eyes being a striking feature. He had soft golden-brown hair and I remember his slightly sauntering graceful walk as he approached to give us lessons'. During 1894 he made weekend excursions to the McCubbins' at Blackburn with Humphrey and other artist friends. He returned to London in 1899 and died there in 1906.

Table Talk, 26 August 1892, p.6; Moore 1934, I, pp.78f.

See Gallery School student group photograph

GEORGE WALTON 1855-90
Portrait painter

Mr George Walton.

George Walton, newspaper illustration, c.1890 By courtesy of Maxwell Hall, Esq., Newcastle-upon-Tyne

Walton was born at Blenkinsop, near Haltwhistle, Northumberland, England in 1855. He studied first at the Newcastle School of Art under William Cosens Way whilst employed as a clerk in the North-Eastern Railway at Alston and Newcastle-upon-Tyne. He moved to London, and

enrolled at the Royal Academy Schools on 31 December 1878; later became a friend of Tom Roberts there; apparently much encouraged by Lord Leighton, P.R.A. In 1881 he exhibited a portrait at the Royal Scottish Academy; 1882-83 exhibited at the Suffolk Street Gallery. Eleven of his paintings – mainly portraits – were hung in the Royal Academy exhibitions between 1883 and 1888; he also exhibited with the Bewick Club in Newcastle. In 1884 he visited Paris, working there with John Peter Russell, Bertram Mackennal, Harry Bates and Mouat Loudon. He arrived in Melbourne early in 1888; renewed his friendship with Roberts and in April took a studio in Grosvenor Chambers. Walton's portraits were very well reviewed by the critics and he received a number of important commissions: for example, Alderman Benjamin Benjamin, Mayor of Melbourne, and Miss Nellie Stewart. He exhibited with the Victorian Artists' Society, the Art Society of New South Wales and in Hobart. In 1890 he decided to visit England for six months to see his family. He was farewelled by the local artistic fraternity in April, with Conder, at Legal's restaurant; although they did not sail together Walton and Conder met again (and saw Phil May) in Paris later that year. Walton never returned to Australia. Whilst staying with relatives at Appleby, Westmoreland, he died of diabetes on 30 December 1890.

Table Talk, 7 September 1888, p.1; 16 January 1891, p.11; Newcastle-upon-Tyne local press obituary, 17 January 1891, kindly forwarded by Maxwell Hall, Esq.

WALTER HERBERT WITHERS 1854-1914
Painter, illustrator, teacher, occasional decorative painter and designer

Born 22 October 1854 at Aston, Birmingham, England, Withers was the grandson of an artist. He studied in London from 1870 to 1882 at the Royal Academy and South Kensington Schools; visited Paris and made sketching tours in England. Opposed by his father in this choice of career, he arrived in Australia 1 January 1883 to work on the land for eighteen months. He attended life classes only at the Gallery School for three years from 1884, whilst employed as a draughtsman by William Inglis and Co. and Fergusson and Mitchell, lithographic printers. He became a member of the Buonarotti Society. In 1887 he returned to England and married there on 11 October. He studied in Paris 1887-88 at the Académie

Walter Withers, photograph, c.1890
LaTrobe Collection, State Library of Victoria

Julian under Bouguereau and Robert-Fleury; worked as correspondent for the London *Magazine of Music*; met Fox, Tucker and Longstaff. Late in 1888 he sailed for Melbourne with an offer of re-employment from Fergusson to illustrate Edmund Finn's *Chronicles of Early Melbourne*; he travelled via Italy. Living in Walpole Street, Kew, he painted regularly at Eaglemont with the Heidelberg artists especially between October 1889 and June 1890 when his wife was visiting England. He was nicknamed 'The Colonel' for his efficient and organized ways – Roberts actually called him 'The Orderly Colonel'. In September 1890 he took over the south end of the Heidelberg mansion 'Charterisville'. There he painted and taught while his wife gave music lessons; and sub-let the lodges to other artists at 2/6 per week. The critic Sidney Dickinson named him, with Streeton, as a leader of 'the Heidelberg School' (*The Australasian Critic*, 1 July 1891, p.240). Withers opened a city teaching studio in 1891 in the Provident Buildings, Collins Street, with Ugo Catani and George Ashton as neighbours (they combined premises for parties). In 1893 he moved to Creswick, where Percy and Norman Lindsay were amongst the pupils in his *plein air* painting class. He returned to Heidelberg (Cape Street) in 1894; was elected president of the Victorian Artists' Society; and sold *A Bright Winter's Morning* to the National Gallery of Victoria. In 1897 he received the first Wynne Prize, in Sydney, for *The Storm* (Art Gallery of New South Wales); also that year, trying to liven up artistic Melbourne, he revived Roberts's idea of open 'studio days' for the visiting public. In 1900 he was awarded the Wynne Prize again. In 1901 he succeeded Loureiro as art master at the Presbyterian Ladies' College. Two years later he moved permanently to Eltham, where he built a large studio. Withers was a founding member of the Australian Art Association 1912; and a trustee of the National Gallery of Victoria 1912-14. He died at Eltham in 1914.

Table Talk, 22 May 1891, p.4; *The Art and Life of Walter Withers*, Australian Art Books, Melbourne, [c.1925]; Margaret Rich, *Walter Withers: A Survey*, Geelong Art Gallery, 1975; information from John Ness Barkes, Helen Roberts and Tom Silver Fine Art

Frederick McCubbin – 'The Prof' or 'Mr Mac' –
surrounded by his students at the National
Gallery of Victoria, 1893
LaTrobe Collection, State Library of Victoria

THE ART SCHOOLS

Jane Clark

There used to be a sort of legend about that time that Australia would do great things in Art.
Where it sprang from or how goodness only knows.
– Memoir of Frederick McCubbin,
student at the National Gallery School 1871-86

In those days. . . in Melbourne there took form an unostentatious but perceptible art movement, caused by the instinctive drawing together of the younger men for purposes of mutual improvement, and among these in addition to Mr McCubbin were Tom Roberts, C.D. Richardson and, later on, Arthur Streeton and Charles Conder, a combination informal and little noted at the time but which exercised a powerful influence on the art which followed it. . . In the meantime John Longstaff, the winner of the first travelling scholarship, had appeared on the scene and with E.P. Fox and others helped to form a group, which taken altogether may be said to have established an epoch in Australian art.
– Reminiscence of Alexander Colquhoun,
a fellow student 1877-79 and 1882-87

Prior to the opening of the National Gallery's art school in 1870, basic instruction in drawing and painting was most readily obtainable in Victoria at various technical Schools of Design established around Melbourne's inner suburbs and in a number of country towns. 'It is surprising the amount of talent that owes its first encouragement to these schools', recalled Frederick McCubbin in his memoir, 'To enumerate a few only of the talented men that began their training under these conditions, I may mention Charles D. Richardson, sculptor, Mr Tom Roberts, painter and Mr John Longstaff, painter'.[1]

McCubbin himself enrolled at the Artisans School of Design at the Trades Hall in Lygon Street, Carlton which had been opened by the Painters and Paperhangers Society of Victoria in May 1869. He paid two shillings per term to study figure drawing under Thomas Clark; so did his friend Louis Abrahams. Richardson elected in addition to study 'ornament'. Tom Roberts, then living and working in Collingwood, enrolled at the East Collingwood School of Design; but seems also to have attended some sessions at Carlton. In 1873 and 1874 he received prizes in the landscape section of the schools' Annual Competitive Exhibition and Examination. One visiting Frenchman was most impressed by the Schools of Design system – which provided the first public art education in Australia:

These schools teach drawing from busts, life-drawing, geometrical design, mechanical and architectural design, ornamental drawing and copying, etc. The colony allots two shillings and sixpence to each school for every pupil taking an eight-week term. The pupil pays the school from two to five shillings according to the subject taken.[2]

They offered a broader curriculum than either their original English models, or the earlier colonial Mechanics' Institutes. For, although 'chiefly intended for Workmen and their sons and Apprentices' learning to design for industry, they also taught the 'higher' arts of landscape and figure work. This was probably due in part to the inclinations of individual teachers. Thomas Clark, for example, advocated sketching out-of-doors and drawing from the living model at the Carlton school; Abram Louis Buvelot, who also taught there briefly, was regarded as Victoria's foremost landscape artist. At Collingwood, judges of the annual student exhibition included Buvelot and Eugen von Guérard.

In the prosperous aftermath of the goldrush, the fine arts were increasingly regarded as an essential 'civilizing' influence and measure of progress. Victoria's permanent population was growing apace. As McCubbin observed, people were no longer concerned exclusively with 'material success, everybody wanting to get back to the old land with long purses'. On 30 June 1869, the Public Library's ambitious loan exhibition of 'Art Treasures' ended with a 'Grand Closing Concert in aid of a fund to endow a Scholarship for the best pupil of the year in the School of Design'. The Victorian Academy of Arts, newly formed in 1870, provided instruction for its members – both professional and amateur. That same year, however, a new option became available to local art students: in mid-1870 classes commenced at the Public Library and Museum in Swanston Street (its name was officially changed in 1875 to 'Public Library, Museum and National Gallery of Victoria'). Here the School of Design offered drawing classes every day and on two evenings each week: 'of necessity the stepping stone for students wishing to enter the School of Painting'. The latter was open only during the day.[3] Von Guérard was appointed 'Master of the School of Painting'. Clark, appointed drawing master in August, encouraged McCubbin to transfer from the Carlton school; Roberts enrolled in 1874.

Theoretically, the Gallery School followed traditional European academic teaching methods: a progression from outline copying, to three-dimensional drawings of antique sculpture (in the form of plaster casts) and drawings of the human figure, to outdoor sketching and, finally, to original compositions.[4] Serious students, however, soon found the classes far from satisfactory. For one thing, despite protestation from the students and von Guérard, Victorian morality forbade the provision of a live model – a most fundamental requirement for any comprehensive artistic training. Clark was particularly popular – a 'venerable old gentleman with a head the counterpart of the bust of Socrates', according to McCubbin; but he was 'partly paralysed, he could only speak in the faintest whisper and he was that feeble he could hardly hold a crayon – so we youngsters did what we pretty well pleased'.[5] The majority of students considered von Guérard, 'as far as we are capable of judging, . . . a thoroughly efficient Teacher, & a most kind and considerate Master'[6]; but he taught them very little. James Smith, a Gallery trustee and *The Argus* art critic, pointed out:

> Numerous more or less clever, more or less indifferent, copies of certain favourite works were produced from year to year, but this sort of Chinese industry did nothing whatever to promote the artistic education of those who devoted themselves to it. What they did was purely mechanical, and while they not unfrequently succeeded in manufacturing a *fac-simile* of a good picture, it might be that the fabricator was incapable of drawing an object from nature correctly, and was ignorant of proportion, anatomy, linear perspective, the principles of composition, the laws of light and shadow, the contrast, harmony, and reflection of colours, their diminution by distance, and aerial perspective generally. In short many of these copyists set themselves to utter the language of art before they had taken the trouble to acquire its alphabet; and the deplorable daubs which have been exhibited from time to time on the walls of the Victorian Academy of Arts were melancholy illustrations of the evils of a system which was diametrically opposed to all the ordinarily conceived canons of instruction.[7]

'Herr von Guérard had not the power of impressing his genuine talent on his pupils', said *Table Talk*, 'while Mr Thomas Clark had not the physical strength to meet the requirements of his work'.[8] This lack of direction certainly did not worry all the students: the vast majority were women, many of whom regarded the National Gallery as a kind of 'finishing school' – and whose aspirations extended no further than copying Gallery 'treasures' or genteel renderings of flowers and fruit. (Oscar Comettant, visiting in 1886, was given the following enrolment statistics: 112 ladies out of a total of 157 students in the School of Design, and eighteen out of thirty in the School of Painting. These proportions seem to have been relatively constant.)

Such progress as was made at the School – and in fact it was considerable – could be attributed largely to mutual encouragement amongst the students themselves. Richardson recalled 'reading books on art, longing to apply the information gained, and discussing theories of art with the other students – theories of a varied and frequently wild character. The number of questions settled by the students should have revolutionized the art world and made Melbourne the only true art centre'.[9] Many of them joined the artistic-musical-literary Buonarotti Society. Above all, they were almost incurably optimistic. Richardson, Roberts and McCubbin took themselves off to the University and the Melbourne Hospital to study anatomy. Bertram Mackennal's father helped them with 'a little clay modelling and casting of plaster of paris from studies in the school'.[10] They painted out-of-doors in their spare time. And they sat for one another for figure drawing: 'Tom Roberts was the model one day, but the act of gazing at a blank wall for an hour so overcame his feelings that he fainted'.[11] By 1878 they had established a twice-weekly life class at the Gallery, paying their own models, 'where they drew from the nude in a somewhat furtive and conscious fashion, for the public mind had not then been educated up to the point of nice discrimination in such matters'.[12] Unfortunately, Clark had resigned in 1876 because of failing health. (Roberts applied for the position – without success.) His successor, Oswald Rose Campbell (1820-87), whilst a proficient artist and first chairman of the Victorian Academy of Arts, was a totally unsympathetic teacher.

'Well under the new regime', wrote McCubbin, ' . . . began the most dreary and hopeless period of our student days . . . Not an idea nor a hint that could help us in any way'. Of his own training in London Campbell declared, 'I never was taught anything at all in the Academies – very seldom was I spoken to at all'. And he told the Gallery trustees that he considered 'life study unnecessary to figure drawing'! He discontinued Clark's outdoor sketching sessions and brought the debate over live models to a head by suspending Roberts, McCubbin, Richardson and others in July 1879. Roberts and Richardson were the troublemakers according to Campbell; and he wrote, 'if these would be quiet I believe the others would be quite content'. In fact they were increasingly supported by their fellow students, including a number of the women. And the following year both had paintings accepted for the Victorian section of the great International Exhibition. The large display of work by well-known European painters and sculptors in this exhibition undoubtedly aroused a new popular interest in art. (The same event in Sydney brought about the foundation of the Art Gallery of New South Wales.) As word spread of von Guérard's impending retirement, the question of life classes became only one of several causes of student discontent and confrontation. The trustees themselves disapproved of copying as the major part of the syllabus. In October 1880 they received a petition, signed by thirty-six students, requesting 'higher' instruction:

> The fact is that out of the numerous pupils who for years have been benefited by the classes in the galleries – none have distinguished themselves as original painters or professional artists, although many have become very proficient as copyists. We believe that this arises from neither indifference nor lack of ability on the part of the pupils, but that it is caused . . . by the want of earnest and careful teaching of the higher practice of painting. This teaching can be obtained from no other than an accomplished and enthusiastic artist, and it is almost the only substitute we can

enjoy here for those productions of generations of great painters which exist in galleries at home and on the Continent.

This was published in *The Argus* on 7 October 1880; and followed up with specific requests signed by Roberts and Richardson on behalf of both Painting and Design students:

> That an advanced class for study, more especially from the life, be formed under the direction of some artist (a figure painter) of well-known ability, the same gentleman to exercise a general supervision over all the classes, so that they may work together towards one end.[13]

Von Guérard retired at the end of 1881. Roberts and Richardson departed for London and the Royal Academy Schools, carrying references from the trustees commending their 'satisfactory proficiency' and the 'zeal and assiduity' with which they had pursued their studies in Melbourne.[14] In April 1882 the trustees appointed George Frederick Folingsby as 'Director of the National Gallery and Master of the School of Painting'.[15] 'The coming of Folingsby had a magical effect on the students', wrote Colquhoun, 'the number of students at this time was small, and the accommodation limited, yet surely no royal palace ever contained a bigger percentage of hope, fear, pride, envy and ambition'. No comparable training was available in Australia. The new director took personal control of both the School of Design and the School of Painting (although Campbell remained on the staff – under Folingsby's rule – until 1886 when he was replaced by McCubbin). 'By changing the whole plan on which art education had been formerly carried on', said *Table Talk*, 'Mr Folingsby has done more for Australian art than any other artist . . . [He aimed] to take away the colorbox, and substitute the pencil; make the students learn the alphabet of painting'.[16] Sound, conservative academic training was exactly what his serious students most desired. As Colquhoun recalled: 'No sooner was "The Boss" uttered, than Longstaff and Gibbs ceased their wrestling; Fox quietly dropped his cigarette in somebody else's siccatif; and McCubbin, who had been warbling "My Pretty Jane", began setting his palette . . .' The trustees were also delighted:

> He first took students away from copying in the Gallery to original work, and laid the foundation of what may become a school of art of which the subjects are purely Australian. From his own training and practice – which had been devoted almost exclusively to figure-painting – his pupils were naturally led the same way, but landscape was not neglected.[17]

Once again a few students, led by McCubbin and Abrahams, formed an independent 'Life-Club' with a nude model. Folingsby told the trustees, 'I assist with my advice and attend personally the posing of each new model, as nothing can be done in painting without good drawing'.[18] He taught painting according to the methods he had learned himself at the Munich Academy and in Paris under Thomas Couture: blocking in the basic forms first of all with bitumen and vermilion. An academic head study – or *ébauche* – was painted by laying in the outline and shadows with a 'reddish-brown sauce', then progressively lightening tonal areas to produce a sense of form.[19] (Streeton later objected to this procedure and left the School of Painting after less than a year; perhaps largely as a result, he was never confident in depicting the human figure.) Many students, inspired by Buvelot, were especially eager to paint landscape; and Folingsby admired Buvelot's work, even though his own artistic priorities undoubtedly lay elsewhere.

He certainly encouraged oil sketches from nature as an integral part of academic method; but he regarded these sketches only as studies for larger, highly finished works to be produced in the studio at some later date. The students themselves enjoyed open air painting for its own sake:

> At the rear of the Gallery there was a large open space, where the grass grew, trees waved, and even a transient wild flower peeped out. This place was turned into an out of door painting ground and in the days of early summer easels might be seen dotted here and there among the shrubs, masonry and lumber that littered the place. Several men who have since distinguished themselves in more exalted spheres, and who with more stately steps have trod the path of Fame, commenced their 'al fresco' attempts in the Gallery's backyard.[20]

In landscape, more than any other branch of painting, the new generation of local artists used their academic Gallery School training as a foundation for reaction and innovation.

In 1883 Folingsby instituted an annual public exhibition and sale of the students' work, displayed in numerous categories: history, genre, portraiture, still life, and so on. Cash prizes were awarded by various philanthropic citizens as well as the Gallery trustees and presented by the Governor. Most admired by local critics were the increasingly ambitious figure pictures with anecdotal subjects; especially, as one writer remarked, 'if they smell of gumleaves'.[21] McCubbin's *Home Again* – second prize winner in 1884 – was, like Folingsby's own popular paintings, a genre scene with local flavour. Some observers felt that the stylistic influence of the director on his students was *too* strong: a French woman visiting the exhibition of 1886, for example, who remarked, 'It's very nice, but they are all little Folingsbies'.[22] That same year, however, Folingsby initiated the travelling scholarship for study overseas, to be awarded every three years by the trustees.[23] This was of great importance for the subsequent development of 19th century Australian subject painting and the popular appreciation of Australian art. It was also the envy of students in New South Wales.[24] Inevitably, in this proud centenary decade, the scholarship winning pictures were large-scale figure compositions with distinctly 'National' content. Longstaff's *Breaking the News* was the first, in 1887. Another 'Australian disaster', Aby Altson's *Flood Sufferings,* followed in 1890.

Longstaff's claim that the Gallery School was 'the only true representative Australian school of painting' was perhaps exaggerated (*The Age*, 16 September 1886); and neither he nor Altson returned permanently to Australia after studying abroad. Somewhat ironically, the Melbourne trustees actually purchased very few examples of local work. Nevertheless, there is no doubt that the Victorian government's support of art education was one of the most significant influences on Australian painting of the period. Almost all of the major figures represented in the present exhibition enrolled at the Gallery School for at least a part of their student careers. By 1892, when Lindsay Bernard Hall succeeded Folingsby, *The Argus* could declare:

> That school is now past its infancy and giving much promise of great achievements in the future. We have among us men whose work would occupy, and in some cases has occupied, a high position in the best European exhibitions. Men who have become permeated with the individuality of Australian life and Australian landscape, and who after a long, weary and unrequited struggle are still working on,

hoping and looking for some recognition and encouragement from the people and the people's Government.[25]

[1] Galbally (ed.) 1979, p.70.
[2] Oscar Comettant, *Au pays des kangourous et des mines d'or*,
Paris, 1890; tr. Judith Armstrong, *In the Land of Kangaroos
and Goldmines*, Rigby, Adelaide, 1980, p.136.
[3] *Trustees report* 1870, p.89. In 1870 there were thirty-five
students enrolled at the School of Design and only six in the
School of Painting; by 1875 the numbers were 152 and
forty-one respectively. See Frances Lindsay & Lucy Kerley
(comp.), *Von Guérard to Wheeler; the first teachers at the
National Gallery School 1870-1939*, Victorian College of the
Arts Gallery, Melbourne, 1978.
[4] An excellent account of 19th century academic practice and
art instruction is Albert Boime, *The Salon and French Painting
in the Nineteenth Century*, Phaidon, London, 1977.
[5] Galbally (ed.) 1979, pp.69, 72.
[6] Letter to trustees from students in the School of Painting, 2
December 1880. Public Record Office, Melbourne.
[7] *Argus*, 6 November 1883, p.9. The Melbourne Gallery's
stated acquisition policy had always included paintings 'more
immediately required for instruction in drawing'; along with
illustrations of 'history, both sacred and secular, poetry,
domestic life, landscape, portraiture' (*Catalogue...*, 1875,
p.10).
[8] *Table Talk*, 9 January 1891, p.11; see also 4 October 1888,
p.4.
[9] C.D. Richardson, *The V.A.S. A Journal of the Arts Issued by
the Victorian Artists' Society*, 73, 5 February 1918, p.6.
[10] Galbally (ed.) 1979, p.74. Clark had tried to provide some
instruction in sculpture but in 1872 reported to the trustees: 'I
am compelled to discontinue the latter [modelling classes] in
consequence of having the room taken from me for
Exhibition purposes'. Quoted by Sturgeon 1978, p.241.
[11] Moore 1906, p.71.
[12] Colquhoun [1919].
[13] Letter to trustees, 26 October 1880; the students also sent
'specimens of independent work' (P.R.O., Melbourne). These
requests for reform were sympathetically reported by the
press even in Sydney (for example, *The Echo*, 1 November
1880), where some limited public art instruction was offered
only by the New South Wales Academy of Art.
[14] Mr David Muir has been very generous with information
about this period at the Gallery School.
[15] In fact the trustees had already approached Folingsby to
establish a life class and advanced painting classes, 3
November 1880; but he declined, owing to a 'sense of
delicacy' towards the incumbent teachers. Folingsby's salary
was £600; von Guérard and Clark had been appointed at £250
p.a.
[16] *Table Talk*, 4 October 1888, p.4.
[17] *Trustees report* 1890, p.6.
[18] *Trustees report* 1882, p.35. The students first described this
'Life-Club' to Folingsby in a letter of 30 June 1882; there were
about six regular members, paying a subscription of five
shillings per month (P.R.O., Melbourne).
[19] Astbury 1978. As Astbury points out, excessive use of
bitumen could have dire consequences in terms of the future
preservation of paintings, while it is obviously antithetical to
plein airist techniques; nevertheless, Folingsby's
encouragement of its use has become so notorious that the
extent of his positive influence at the School is often ignored.
[20] Colquhoun 1908, pp.5f.
[21] *Melbourne University Review*, 27 September 1884, p.46.
[22] *Age*, 11 October 1886: *'C'est très gentil mais ce sont tous de
petits Folingsby'*.
[23] For Folingsby's original letter to the trustees, see *The Argus*,
11 March 1886. The scholarship was financed from proceeds
invested by the trustees since the special fund raising concert
in June 1869.
[24] In 1882 John Peter Russell, young Sydney artist and friend
of Roberts, who had been studying in London, had initiated a
lengthy exchange of letters in the columns of *The Sydney
Morning Herald* on the deficiencies of art education in New
South Wales (12 August, 19 August, 28 August, etc.); he
recommended Conrad Martens and Abram Louis Buvelot as
examples for local students. Comparison continued to be
made with the Victorian system for many years; for example,
Sydney Morning Herald, 8 February 1890. In 1895 a
deputation of students asked the New South Wales
government for subsidized art education and a travelling
scholarship as in Victoria (*Sydney Morning Herald*, 19
December 1895). The English *Magazine of Art* reported that
whilst the Victorian Gallery trustees sponsored travelling
scholarships, their Sydney counterparts spent far greater
sums on contemporary European (and Australian) paintings
as *exempla* – both with the aim of founding 'a National School
of Australian Art' (May L. Manning, 'Art in Australia', *The
Magazine of Art*, 1895, p.217). As late as 1903 the New South
Wales Art Students' League issued *Art Instruction in New
South Wales. A plea for the establishment of a National Art
School* (State Library of Victoria, Art pamphlets 40, 14).
[25] *Argus*, 24 September 1892, Leader. There were five local
applicants for Folingsby's position: McCubbin, Richardson,
Longstaff, Loureiro and Tennyson Cole (*Table Talk*, 13
February 1891, p.12; and see 13 March p.13). Lindsay Bernard
Hall (1859-1935) trained in London, Munich and Antwerp;
was appointed in March 1892, to become the longest serving
director and head of the Art Schools in the history of the
Gallery.

ABRAM LOUIS BUVELOT
Summer Afternoon, Templestowe, 1866
Oil on canvas
76.2 x 118.8 cm
Signed and dated l.r.: Ls Buvelot. 1866.
National Gallery of Victoria
Purchased 1869

Provenance:
The artist

Exhibitions:
Intercolonial Exhibition Official Catalogue, Melbourne, October 1866, The Fine Arts Gallery, no. 155: 'Summer Afternoon, Templestowe'; *The Exhibition of Art and Art Treasures, Catalogue of Works of Art*, Melbourne Public Library and Museum, March – May 1869, no. 494: 'Summer Afternoon (Victoria) – Trustees of the Melbourne Public Library'; *Ls Buvelot Loan Exhibition Catalogue of Drawings & Paintings*, Melbourne, 10 July 1888, no.44: 'Summer Evening, near Templestowe – Trustees National Gallery'; *Victorian Artists' Society Exhibition of Australian Art Past and Present*, National Gallery of Victoria, Melbourne, August 1893, no.203: 'Summer Evening, near Templestowe 1866 – Lent by Trustees Public Library'

Literature:
Catalogue of the Oil Paintings, Watercolour Drawings and Portraits in the National Gallery of Victoria, Melbourne, 1875 (and later edns), no.18: 'Summer Evening near Templestowe – purchased 1866' (and on p.13 called 'A Summer afternoon at Templestowe'); Captain H. Morin Humphreys (ed.), *Men of the Time in Australia*, Victorian Series, Melbourne, 1878 and 1882, p.26; *Age*, 10 July 1888, p.5; *Australasian Art Review*, 1 November 1899, p.24; MacDonald 1916, pp.85f.; *Argus*, 16 October 1934, p.49; Smith 1971, pp.62f.; Whitelaw 1976, p.26; Gray 1978, p.25; Splatt & Bruce 1981, illus. 10

If I chose an example of this Painter's work, which I think thoroughly characteristic of him, it would be 'Summer Evening at Templestowe [sic]'. How particularly he has caught the feeling of the end of a hot summer's day! The long weary afternoon is passing away, and the feeling of the approaching cool south-easterly breeze is suggested. In the sky a big cumulus cloud, that has built up through the sullen heat of midday looms gloomily. Along the dusty road, one sees tired sheep wandering slowly, searching for the scant herbage left by the withering sun. The old homestead is on the right, and near by the beautifully painted Gum tree. The feeling of closing day, approaching night and rest, the billy fire, and the smoke ascending from the burning Gum branches, typify so much of life along Victorian roads. It is thoroughly Australian.
– Frederick McCubbin, 1916

The first fine landscape painted in Victoria was painted by the pioneer, Louis Buvelot. It was my interest in this picture which caused me to walk from Heidelberg station to Templestowe, and paint a small canvas, later bought by Roberts for one guinea, a welcome price in those days.
– Arthur Streeton, 1934

Buvelot has rightly been called one of the fathers of landscape painting in Australia. Arriving as a mature artist, trained in Europe, he became a pioneer of the *plein air* tradition in this country: 'What the work of Monsieur Corot is to France, that of Monsieur Buvelot is to Australia', declared the foreword to the catalogue of Melbourne's 1875 Intercolonial Exhibition. In 1869 McCubbin, Roberts and Richardson were amongst his drawing pupils at the Artisans School of Design in Carlton. As McCubbin wrote, 'Most of us owe it to him that slowly we were able to see the paintable qualities of that which lay immediately around us'.[1] The emphasis on man's civilizing presence in the peaceful local landscape, the golden light and purple or grey-blue shadows look ahead to the still blonder tonality so characteristic of the Heidelberg School painters. A fine charcoal study for this painting is also in the National Gallery of Victoria.

[1] Galbally (ed.) 1979, p.75.

JOHANN JOSEF EUGEN VON GUÉRARD
Mount Kosciusko seen from the Victorian Border (Mount Hope Ranges), 1866
Oil on canvas
107 x 153 cm
Signed and dated l.r.: J. Eug. von Guérard 1866.
Inscribed on stretcher u.l.: '66.27 August ANF [begun]
National Gallery of Victoria
Purchased 1870

Provenance:
The artist[1]

Exhibitions:
Intercolonial Exhibition Official Catalogue, Melbourne, October 1866, The Fine Arts Gallery no.163: 'Large Picture – Mount Kosciusko, seen from the Victorian Border (Mount Hope Ranges)'; *The Exhibition of Art and Art Treasures, Catalogue of Works of Art*, Melbourne Public Library and Museum, March-May 1869, no.231: 'Mount Kosciusko'

Literature:
Age, 27 October 1866, p.4; 29 October 1892; *Argus*, 25 October 1866, p.7; 2 January 1872, p.4; *Illustrated Melbourne Post*, 22 November 1866, p.374; *Illustrated Australian News*, 27 November 1866, pp.5f.; *Catalogue of the Oil Paintings, Watercolour Drawings and Portraits in the National Gallery of Victoria*, Melbourne, 1875 (and later edns), no.30: 'Kosciusko, seen from the Mt. Hope Ranges, Victoria – purchased 1870'; Captain H. Morin Humphreys (ed.), *Men of the Time in Australia*, Victorian Series, Melbourne 1878 and 1882, pp.74f.; Gleeson, *Colonial Painters 1788-1880*, Lansdowne, Melbourne, 1971, pl.68; Daniel Thomas 1976, no.13; Candice Bruce, *Eugen von Guérard*, A.G.D.C. and Australian National Gallery, Canberra, 1980, p.72; Splatt & Bruce 1981, pl.6; Candice Bruce, Edward Comstock and Frank McDonald, *Eugen von Guérard 1811-1901: a German Romantic in the Antipodes*, Alistair Taylor, Martinborough, New Zealand, 1982, no.109

Mr von Guérard's principal contribution to the collection consists of a view of Mount Kosciusko from the Mount Hope Ranges. The timber in the foreground is treated with greater freedom than he usually employs, although he still continues to crowd an immense deal of not always necessary detail into a limited space, which sometimes tends to break up the attention of the observer. But his scale of colour is so harmonious and well graduated as to give a feeling of unity to each of his works; and in that under notice, the eye is led on from the mountain buttresses, enveloped in a purple haze, to the jagged summits, standing out sharp and clear from the rarer atmosphere which surrounds them, by imperceptible stages, until the mind receives that impression of altitude and remoteness which the artist has designed to produce.
– *The Argus*, 25 October 1866

A comparison of the grandiose *Mount Kosciusko seen from the Victorian Border (Mount Hope Ranges)* with contemporary landscape paintings by Abram Louis Buvelot immediately explains the antipathy felt by the younger generation of Melbourne artists towards von Guérard's style and teaching practice. Roberts, McCubbin and their fellow students sought a freer, more spontaneous interpretation of the Australian landscape. Von Guérard's scientifically precise attitude to his subject matter is clear from the original long and topographically descriptive title of *Mount Kosciusko*; in contrast, for example to Buvelot's 'atmospherically' titled *Summer Afternoon, Templestowe*.

Although both pictures were entirely painted indoors from earlier studies on the spot, the working methods of the two artists likewise point to fundamental differences between them. Buvelot generally chose subjects close to home; making pencil sketches and painting in watercolour *en plein air*, as he encouraged his students to do, to capture changing effects of light and colour at various times of the day. Von Guérard, on the other hand, travelled far and wide in search of romantic and 'sublime' landscapes which dwarf humanity. His expedition to Mount Kosciusko and the Mount Hope Ranges (now called the Youngal Ranges) was in November 1862, accompanying Professor Georg Balthasar von Neumayer on a magnetic survey for the Victorian government. Von Guérard filled small sketchbooks with detailed pencil drawings and descriptive notes; and only commenced the large canvas version of *Mount Kosciusko* years later, in August 1866.

Needless to say, this procedure was not practicable for his students at the Gallery School. His teaching method there was based on his own academic training at Dusseldorf: outline drawing, perspective studies, drawing from statues (the Melbourne trustees would not allow a life class for many years), copying lithographs, then advancing to tightly worked copies of Gallery paintings, and only occasional sketches from nature. James Smith, *The Argus* critic, had promoted the artist's early paintings as 'works of art of so high an order' and 'undeniably Australian' (1 February 1855, p.5). By the time of von Guérard's appointment at the Gallery, however, Smith had come to prefer the freer brushwork and broader handling of Buvelot. He attacked von Guérard as 'our local apostle of that microscopism in pictorial delineation'; and continued:

> His landscapes . . . offer a minutely laborious description of almost every leaf upon the gum trees, and every vein and crevice in the rocks, which would make them delightful illustrations of a treatise on the botanical or geological features of the colony . . . Now that he occupies a position where his example will have more influence than it had before, it is more than ever necessary that just notions should be propagated concerning the principal features and the main tendency of his art.[2]

Von Guérard was justifiably hurt and offended by this criticism and he drafted a reply – in execrable English – which was never actually published.[3] In 1872 Smith wrote that *Mount Kosciusko* was 'a minute and faithful likeness of the place its author

intended to represent. Indeed the photographic accuracy of this artist's pictures is too often insisted upon at the expense of breadth of treatment'.[4] Happily the unpleasantness passed: artist and critic resumed their friendship and corresponded for many years after von Guérard's return to Europe.

---

[1] Purchased after considerable wrangling: von Guérard originally offered it to the trustees in 1869 for £220 but eventually, with some bitterness, accepted their offer of £150.
[2] *Argus*, 13 July 1870, p.7. James Smith (1820-1910) was an outstanding journalist, who contributed much to the cultural life of Melbourne in the second half of the 19th century. He emigrated to Victoria in 1854; joined *The Argus* in 1856 and wrote leading articles, as well as art, literary and dramatic criticism until his retirement in 1896.
[3] Unpublished letter to *The Argus*, July 1870, printed by Smith 1975, pp.166ff.
[4] *Argus*, 2 January 1872, p.4.

FREDERICK McCUBBIN
Sketch from Antony and Cleopatra, 1880
Oil on board
28 x 40 cm
Signed and dated l.r.: F. McCubbin 1880
Private collection, Melbourne

Provenance:
Original owner unknown; Mr Roly Brennan, Melbourne until May 1974; The Joshua McClelland Print Room, Melbourne; Sweeney Reed Galleries until September 1974; private collection, Melbourne

Exhibitions:
The Tenth Exhibition of the Victorian Academy of Arts, Melbourne, April 1880, no.12: 'Sketch from Antony and Cleopatra – £8.8.0'

Literature:
Argus, 3 April 1880, p.9; *Australasian*, 10 April 1880, p.454; Galbally (ed.) 1979, pp.74ff.; Galbally 1981, p.22; Astbury 1985, in press, p.24

We had in connection with our class a sketch club. We exhibited once a month. A word was given which we

endeavoured to illustrate for; our ideas were all for History painting. [S]epia drawings of Bible subjects, then Shakespeare's plays, I think were the two great sources of our inspiration – we were nothing if not ambitious . . . I can still look back upon with some pleasure . . . an historical idea built up from a sky study I had made from a window and the buildings I introduced from photos I copied of ancient Thebes by Capt Abney. The subject was ambitious as usual with our sketch club, Cleopatra sailing down the Cyndus.
– Memoir of Frederick McCubbin

At the Gallery School, wrote Alexander Colquhoun, 'the students fell back to a certain extent on the thought of the old world and showed a tendency to seek inspiration from Shakespeare or the Pagan mythologies'. One of the paintings they most admired was Thomas Clark's large canvas, *Ulysses and Diomed capturing the horses of Rhesus, King of Thrace*, which hung in the classroom.[1] The contemporary academic term for painted sketches of such imaginary or 'ideal' compositions was *esquisse peinte*: that which 'engages the spectator's mind and his eye by its very freedom of treatment and air of sincerity, the boldness of its indications and even its unfinished quality'.[2] As McCubbin explained, his *Sketch from Antony and Cleopatra* was inspired by an earlier 'sky study' of his own and photographs of ancient Egyptian architecture.[3] It also reveals his lifelong admiration for the work of J.M.W. Turner (1775-1851). Two of Tom Roberts's very early sketches in pen, ink and wash for similarly ambitious historical compositions, are preserved in his scrapbook. Some *esquisses peintes* by Roberts are also extant, probably dating from his time at the Royal Academy in London.[4]

---

[1] Galbally (ed.) 1979, p.72; oil on canvas, 109.3 x 193.6 cm, now in the Bendigo Art Gallery.
[2] *Dictionnaire de l'Académie des Beaux-Arts*, Paris, 1858 et seq., V, pp.305f.; quoted by Boime 1971, p.44. Students' sketch competitions had been conducted at the Ecole des Beaux-Arts since 1816.
[3] Sky studies and rapid landscape studies were yet another academic stock-in-trade – usually termed *pochades* in France and England. The photographs which fired McCubbin's imagination were in a book at the Melbourne Public Library: Captain Sir William de Wivesleslie Abney, *Thebes and Its Five Greater Temples*, London, 1876.
[4] MS PX* D310, Mitchell Library, Sydney; see Topliss 1985, nos 10 – 14.

GEORGE FREDERICK FOLINGSBY
Group of oil sketches: drapery study; interior architectural study; sketches for 'Bunyan in Prison' and 'Autumn', [c.1860-80s]
National Gallery of Victoria
Purchased 1891

Literature:
Astbury 1978, pp.45ff.; Astbury 1985, in press, figs 14, 17, 24

Folingsby's painting procedure was absolutely traditional in terms of 19th century academic method, 'the higher work and original composition' which his Melbourne students desired so keenly. Oil sketches occupied a central role in the creative process. Sir Joshua Reynolds, as founding president of the Royal Academy in the 18th century, had recommended that all artists paint rather than draw their sketches. Although Folingsby's completed history painting of *Bunyan in Prison* had been purchased by the Gallery in 1864, he evidently brought with him a number of preparatory studies when he emigrated many years afterwards. The outdoor sketch of a woman picking blackberries was for *Autumn*. The interior study exhibited here can be related to backgrounds in many works painted by Gallery students under Folingsby's direction.

GEORGE FREDERICK FOLINGSBY ▶
Autumn, [c. 1882]
Oil on canvas
96.5 x 61 cm
Signed l.r.: G.F. Folingsby
The Joseph Brown Collection
For exhibition in Melbourne only

Provenance:
Mrs William Rigall, 'Somercotes', Alma Road, St Kilda from the artist's estate, March 1891

Literature:
Catalogue of the Fine Collection of Oil Paintings, Sketches, Artists' Materials, etc. of the late G.F. Folingsby and... Mrs Clara Folingsby, Gemmell, Tuckett and Co., Melbourne, 18 March 1891, no. 4; *Table Talk*, 20 March 1891, p.7; Astbury 1978, pp.48, 56; Daniel Thomas, 1980, no. 49, as 'Woman picking blackberries'; Astbury 1985, in press, p.33, pl.2

Typically Victorian in subject matter and treatment, Folingsby's *Autumn* clearly demonstrates his academic training as a figure painter. An elegantly dressed woman is gathering the fruits of the season; set against a landscape background in fading afternoon light, which also evokes the time of year. Folingsby's skill in depicting drapery and costume details was much admired by his contemporaries. Both *Autumn* and its companion picture, *Spring*, were 'familiar to many through the medium of photogravure'.[1] *Spring* was given the most prominent position at the Victorian Academy of Arts exhibition in 1883 and reproduced as an engraving for the Art Union of Victoria that year.

[1] *Table Talk*, 20 March 1891, p.7. *Spring* is reproduced in colour in McCulloch 1984, pl.37.

▲
LOUIS ABRAHAMS
Lion's head, 1880
Oil on wooden panel
11.5 x 11.7 cm
Signed with monogram and dated l.r.: LA/
1880
The Joseph Brown Collection
For exhibition in Melbourne only

Provenance:
By descent in the Roberts family, to Jean
and Noel Roberts until 1980

Literature:
Joseph Brown Spring Exhibition, 1980,
no.53, illus.

Small oil sketches known as *études* (studies), often executed on panel, were an integral part of traditional academic painting practice: originally intended only as preliminary 'raw material' for more carefully finished large-scale works. During the 19th century such spontaneous sketches came increasingly to be appreciated as self sufficient works of art.[1] Abrahams signed and dated this little panel – as a finished picture – which he evidently presented to his friend Tom Roberts shortly afterwards.

[1] *Dictionnaire de l'Académie des Beaux-Arts,* Paris, 1858 et seq., V, *'Etude'*; quoted by Boime 1971, p.149.

▲
RUPERT CHARLES WULSTEN BUNNY
Cactus, [c.1883]
Oil on canvas
67.5 x 57.1 cm
Signed l.r.: Rupert C.W. Bunny
M.J.M. Carter Collection, Adelaide

> The studies in oils have been made from armour and drapery, musical instruments, vases and jars, fruit and vegetables and still life generally.
> – *The Argus*, 6 November 1883

Bunny's still life of flowering cactus is an exercise in colour, composition and drapery study. It was probably painted towards the end of 1883 when his work was commended by James Smith and Buvelot as judges of the first Gallery School competition; early in the following year Bunny left for Europe. A painting of exactly the same subject by a fellow student, Miss Lucy Walker, is now in the Bendigo Art Gallery.[1] Bunny's version is, however, rather more accomplished, showing early evidence of his love of glowing colours and rich textural effects. The handsome oriental ginger jar was evidently still a studio prop at the School during the 1890s, for it also appears in Lindsay Bernard Hall's *'Do you want a Model, Sir?'*[2]

[1] *Cactus*, signed and dated 1884; possibly exhibited in the student exhibition of December that year; bequeathed to the Bendigo Art Gallery by a Mrs Harriet Brown some time between 1887 and 1891.
[2] Lauraine Diggins, October 1982, no.32; now in a private collection.

JOHN E. SOMMERS, senior ▲
Fred. McCubbin at the age of 21, 1876
Compressed charcoal and pencil on paper
33.5 x 26.2 cm
Inscribed l.l.: 'Fred. McCubbin/at the age
of 21/By John Sommers senior'
National Gallery of Victoria
Presented by Hugh McCubbin 1962

Provenance:
The sitter's family

Sommers attended evening classes with
McCubbin at the Gallery's School of
Design. This drawing dates from 1876,
when their 'dear old instructor' Thomas
Clark resigned and 'under the new regime
[of O.R. Campbell] began the most dreary
and hopeless period of our student days'.
With 'not an idea not a hint that could help
us in any way', wrote McCubbin, some of
the older students set up their own class:
'the one good practice I got was the steady
drawing from Life during the greater part
of that time it was an up hill game, I assure
you'. By c.1881, 'Somers [*sic*] had gone to
teach for the Education department at
Castlemaine'.[1]

[1] Galbally (ed.) 1979, pp.73,76.

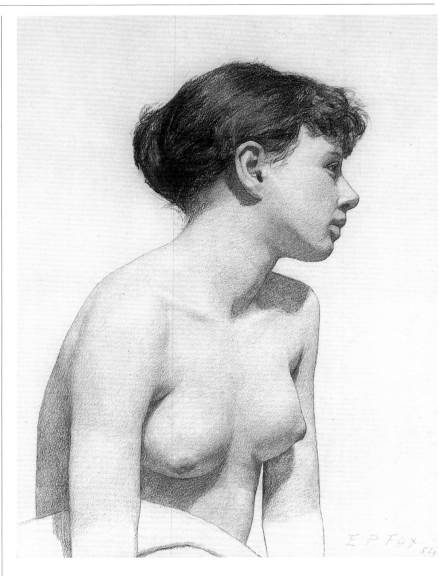

EMANUEL PHILLIPS FOX ▲
Nude study, 1884
Charcoal on paper
48.2 x 35.6 cm
Signed and dated l.r.: E.P. Fox/84
The Joseph Brown Collection
For exhibition in Melbourne only

Literature:
Daniel Thomas 1980, pp.30f.; Astbury
1978a, p.50; Astbury 1985, in press, fig.19

As the Gallery School of Design under
O.R. Campbell offered drawing classes
only from antique casts and clothed
models, this gentle, accomplished study
may have been executed at one of the
'Life-Club' sessions, organized by the students themselves and supported by
Folingsby. (Campbell wrote that he considered 'life study unnecessary to figure
drawing'!) Fox himself taught at various
inner surburban schools of design, for it
was Folingsby's policy to help his students
obtain teaching posts.

DAVID DAVIES
Study of a male nude, [c.1887]
Charcoal and conte on paper
82.6 x 38.3 cm
Signed l.r.: Davi . . . [cut]
Verso: sketch of a man's head
City of Ballarat Fine Art Gallery
Purchased with the Maude Glover Fleay
Trust Fund 1979

Provenance:
Believed to have been given by the artist
to one of his own students, Maude Glover;
to her daughter, Mrs M. Beasy

Literature:
Rich 1984, no.5; Sparks 1984, no.65;
Astbury 1985, in press, p.29

EMANUEL PHILLIPS FOX ▶
Australian landscape, 1884
Oil on canvas
41.5 x 52 cm
Signed and dated l.r.: E.P. Fox 84
Private collection, Adelaide

Provenance:
Christie's, Sydney, 5 October 1971, lot 69

> Among the landscapes, a group by Mr Fox may be singled out for special commendation on account of the originality of treatment, and the nice feeling for form, colour, distance and atmosphere which they denote.
> – *The Argus*, 19 December 1884

Fox regularly contributed landscapes to the student exhibitions, both outdoor sketches from country expeditions and larger paintings worked up in the studio. In 1884, when *The Age* praised his 'brilliant and pure' landscapes, he was awarded the prize in that category (and once again in 1886). In this example the dark brown tonality learned from Folingsby is combined with a broader vision and atmospheric unity closer to Buvelot's. The figures are far more satisfactorily integrated with the landscape than in contemporary student works such as McCubbin's *The Letter* or Longstaff's *Gathering wildflowers*.

CHARLES DOUGLAS RICHARDSON
Two sheets of figure drawings, [1880]
(i) *Seated woman – costume study*
Charcoal heightened with white chalk, on paper
62 x 43.5 cm
Verso: female head and shoulders

(ii) *Seated male nude*
Charcoal on paper
60 x 46.4 cm
Signed and dated l.r.: C. Douglas Richardson/1880
Verso: seated male nude, back view
National Gallery of Victoria
Presented by Miss Fawcett 1959

Literature:
Peers 1985, nos 3-4

Richardson was an ambitious and precocious student: writing 'respectfully' to the Victorian Academy of Arts as early as 1876, 'I beg to state that I am not an "Amateur" and decline to be entered as such in the books of the Academy'. He became junior master and secretary of the students' club at the Carlton School of Design before transferring to the Gallery School. These drawings were executed at the height of the clash with O.R. Campbell when Roberts and Richardson asked the Gallery trustees on behalf of all students: 'That an advanced class for study, more especially from life be formed under the direction of some artist (a figure painter) of well-known ability'.[1] That same year Richardson began conducting the Victorian Academy's life classes, and he wrote:

'Students wishing to join had to submit a drawing from the round to the *Life Class Committee* but a high standard was not insisted upon as the sooner a student was induced to draw from Life the better'.[2] The following year he left for London to study at the Royal Academy.

[1] 26 October 1880, Public Record Office: one of many letters in the long wrangle from 1879 to c.1882.
[2] 20 January 1881. LaTrobe Collection, State Library of Victoria. Academy of Arts, MS 7593.

FREDERICK McCUBBIN ▲
The Letter, 1884
Oil on canvas
68.9 x 51 cm
Signed and dated l.r.: F. McCubbin 18..
[indistinct]
City of Ballarat Fine Art Gallery
Purchased 1946
For exhibition in Melbourne only

Literature:
Hoff 1955, no.4; McCulloch 1969, pl.6;
David Thomas 1969, pp.67f.; Gleeson
1971, pl.22; Radford 1974, no.21; Galbally
1981, pp.54f.; Astbury 1985, in press, p.33,
pl.3

The Letter echoes Folingsby's ladies-in-
landscape compositions both in tonality
and anecdotal implications. Rather tight
handling and strong contrasts between
light and shadow suggest that the canvas
was not painted out-of-doors; David
Thomas has noted that the thicker wrin-
kled paint of the figure is raised above the
rest of the picture surface, indicating that
she was added later. The existence of a
small full-length portrait study of McCubbin's sister Harriet (also an art student)
tends to confirm this, for the two figures
and their dress are almost identical.[1] The
somewhat stage-like setting was probably
worked up from *plein air* landscape
sketches along the Yarra at Darebin. John
Longstaff produced a very similar painting, *Gathering wildflowers* (Bendigo Art
Gallery), at the Gallery School in the same
year.

[1] Also dated 1884; David Thomas 1969,
p.67.

FREDERICK McCUBBIN
Scrapbook, [c.1880s-1917]
National Gallery of Victoria
Presented by Hugh McCubbin 1960

Provenance:
The artist's family

Literature:
Galbally 1981, p.90; Astbury 1981, p.29

Unfortunately it is not known when
McCubbin began compiling this scrapbook but it certainly includes evidence of
his earliest artistic interests. Reproductions of old master paintings range from
the Sistine ceiling, Velasquez and Botticelli
to Titian's *Flora*, a copy of which he had
long admired hanging in a Melbourne
hotel: 'Well no picture I have ever seen
since can ever equal the charms that
picture was to me; ... that divine
work... smiled a welcome and I said
within myself like Douglas of old, Lead on
brave heart I follow'. There are Pre-
Raphaelite works of Millais, Rosetti and
Burne-Jones; landscapes by Corot and
Daubigny; portraits and modern Naturalist subjects by Bastien-Lepage, Dagnan-
Bouveret, George Clausen, Alexander
Harrison, Frank Bramley and so on.
There are numerous black-and-white
illustrations cut from stories in the popular
press; and Nicholas Caire's photograph of
a 'Selector's Hut, Gippsland' as reproduced by the American *Harper's Magazine* in 1890. Various original sketches,
newspaper clippings and reproductions of
Heidelberg School paintings are also
included. (Tom Roberts's scrapbook is in
the Mitchell Library, Sydney: MS
PX*D310.)

FREDERICK McCUBBIN
Home Again, 1884
Oil on canvas
85 x 123 cm
Signed and dated l.r.: F. McCubbin/1884
National Gallery of Victoria
Purchased through The Art Foundation of
Victoria with funds provided by G.J. Coles
Pty Ltd 1981

Provenance:
The Bickley family (members of whom
had travelled from England on the same
ship as the artist's parents in 1853)

Exhibitions:
*Second Annual Exhibition of Paintings by
the Students of the National Gallery under
the direction of G.F. Folingsby, Esq.*,
Melbourne,1884, awarded second prize of
£20

Literature:
Argus, 19 December 1884, p.6; *Age*, 22
December 1884, p.6; Colquhoun [1919];
David Thomas 1969, p.67; Astbury 1978,
p.50; Galbally 1981, pp.26ff.; Jennifer
Phipps, '"Home Again" by Frederick
McCubbin', *Art Bulletin of Victoria* 23,
1982, pp.59ff.; Grassick 1984, pp.346ff.;
Downer & Phipps 1985, no.144,pp.49f.;
Astbury 1985, in press, p.32, pl.1

As Alexander Colquhoun, a fellow student of McCubbin, observed, *Home Again*
marked 'the earliest development of
scholarship pictures. . . [and] its production cost the painter much thought and
strenuous application before he succeeded in satisfying the fastidious
Folingsby'.[1] All the characteristics of
Folingsby's teaching are evident: domestic genre, dramatic storyline, carefully
controlled spotlighting of the protagonists, bitumen under-painting, a grey-
brown palette enlivened with red and purple. The composition foreshadows more
ambitious competition works by Longstaff, Davies, Altson and other Gallery students: an open doorway connects the
detailed interior scene with the world outside – leading, theatrically speaking, off-
stage into the wings. McCubbin has given
his mid-Victorian narrative a strong Australian flavour, prelude to his later more
famous colonial pioneering subjects. A
bearded swagman, bedroll on his shoulder, has suddenly returned to hearth and
home. His wife looks up from her labour;
she is dressed in widow's weeds, a baby at
her feet. She is evidently taking in laundry
to earn a living; the carpet is worn. The
wanderer's arrival is timely indeed.

McCubbin derived this descriptive setting
from sketches of his own family's business
premises in West Melbourne: also seen in
Kitchen at the Old King Street Bakery,
1884 (Art Gallery of South Australia),
*Backyard, King Street, Melbourne with
seated girl*, 1886 (Australian National Gallery) and probably in *Old Stables*, c.1886
(National Gallery of Victoria).

¹ Colquhoun [1919], unpaged.

FREDERICK McCUBBIN
Self portrait, 1886
Oil on canvas
68.2 x 43.2 cm
Signed and dated l.r.: F. McCubbin/1886
Art Gallery of New South Wales
Purchased 1951

Provenance:
Miss Jessie MacKintosh (1893-1957) a
student at the Gallery School in 1908-11
and 1927, and later a pupil of George Bell,
who also trained as a singer and
photographer

Exhibitions:
Probably *Third Annual Exhibition of
Paintings by the Students of the National
Gallery under the direction of Mr.
Folingsby*, Melbourne, 1886, no.64 or
no.65 (two unidentified portraits)

Literature:
Topliss 1984, no.6

'Mr. F. McCubbin seems to be equally at
home in depicting landscape scenery and
portraiture', *The Argus* reported from the
Gallery School's annual exhibition in
1886. 'As Mr. McCubbin is engaged as an
instructor at the Gallery, his pictures are
not exhibited in competition'.[1] This cheerful self-portrait marks the year of McCubbin's appointment as drawing master at
the School of Design after some eighteen
years as an art student. The same year,
1886, he was elected to the committee of
the Australian Artists' Association; and,
financially independent as a professional
painter at last, decided to dispose of the
family business. The portrait vividly testifies to McCubbin's lasting admiration for
his teacher and director, who insisted on
'long practice in drawing from, and a thorough knowledge of, the human figure'.[2] It
is tightly painted in a subdued range of
colours over dark under-painting, exactly
according to Folingsby's instructions 'to
put in the subject first with bitumen and
vermilion'. As a student contemporary
recalled, 'In those days we swore by bitumen mitigated with a little vermilion or
cadmium'.[3] (This traditional academic
procedure was immediately rejected by
Streeton in his brief sojourn at the Gallery
School; and much modified by other local
artists influenced by 'direct painting' practices of the later 19th century.) In fact
McCubbin is standing in exactly the pose
chosen by Folingsby himself, brushes
poised and palette in hand, in a portrait
painted by Longstaff the same year.[4]
Although the younger artist presents himself as a much more lively character: a bit
of a 'masher', with his pink and white
striped shirt, cameo brooch and large
handkerchief. (He was always a great one
for fancy dress!) This is the 'dear Prof' or

'Mr Mac' beloved of his Gallery School
pupils for twenty years. Indeed Miss Jessie
MacKintosh, who acquired the portrait,
was one of them. McCubbin painted at
least five self-portraits later in his career.[5]

[1] *Argus*, 10 March 1886, p.4.
[2] *Annual Report of the Trustees of the
National Gallery of Victoria*, 1882, p.32.
[3] *The Argus*, 10 March 1886, p.4; Croll
1935, p.13; Colquhoun 1908, p.4.

[4] Murdoch 1948, p.51. Longstaff's
portrait of Folingsby is currently held at
the State Library (National Gallery of
Victoria no. 389/1).
[5] c.1900, private collection, Melbourne;
c.1908, Australian National Gallery; 1912,
Art Gallery of South Australia; c.1913,
National Gallery of Victoria; c.1916,
formerly in possession of the McCubbin
family.

JOHN LONGSTAFF
Breaking the News, 1887
Oil on canvas
109.7 x 152.8 cm
Signed and dated l.r.: J.LONGSTAFF.1887.
Art Gallery of Western Australia
Purchased with funds from the Hackett
Bequest 1933

Provenance:
Messrs Clarke and Co. (Alfred E. Clarke
and Robert Elias Wallen), Melbourne,
1887 – (Wallen died 1893); Gemmell,
Tuckett and Co., auctioneers, 1897 – sold
for £100; to J.F. Archibald and William
Macleod, purchased jointly and hung for
many years in their offices at *The Bulletin*,
Sydney, then at Archibald's house;
Macleod later purchased Archibald's
share for £90 and hung the painting at
home, 'Dunvegan', Sydney; to his widow,
1929 – October 1933

Exhibitions:
*Fourth Annual Exhibition of Paintings by
the Students of the National Gallery under
the direction of G.F. Folingsby, Esq.*,
Melbourne, 1887, no.32: 'Breaking the
News – £100.0.0', awarded gold medal
and first annual travelling scholarship;
*Centennial International Exhibition
Official Guide to the Picture Galleries and
Catalogue of Fine Arts*, Melbourne, 1888,
Victorian Loan Collection no.132:
'Breaking the News – Messrs. Clarke and
Wallen', with long comment; *The People's
Palace Exhibition of Loan Collection of
Pictures*, Exhibition Building, Melbourne,
March 1891, no.79: 'Breaking the News –
Messrs. Clarke and Waller [*sic*]'; *Catalogue
of the Diamond Jubilee Loan Exhibition in
the National Gallery, in Commemoration
of the 60th Year of the Reign of her Majesty
Queen Victoria*, Melbourne, June 1897,
no.19: 'Breaking the News – lent by A.E.
Clarke, Esq.'; on loan at the Art Gallery of
New South Wales, May 1898

Literature:
Age, 25 April 1887, p.5; *Argus*, 25 April
1887,p.7; 29 April 1887; 29 June 1895, p.4;
28 May 1898, p.4; *Table Talk*, 29 April
1887, pp.1,8; *Australasian*, 30 April 1887,
p.859; *Australasian Sketcher*, 12 July
1887, pp.99f. and reproduced as a
chromolithograph in the 'Coloured
Supplement'; Moore 1906, p.2; Conor
Macleod, *Macleod of 'The Bulletin'*,
Sydney, 1931, pp.42f.; *West Australian*,
26 September 1933; Moore 1934, I,
pp.221f.; Murdoch 1948, pp.55ff.; *The
Bulletin*, 2 February 1955; Timms 1975,
illus.; Astbury 1978, pp.52, 55; Grassick
1984, pp.347ff.; Astbury 1985, in press,
pp.37f., pl.6

Another lovely day is nearly done;
The miner's wife sets out the humble
fare,
And with her baby waits for one
To fill the vacant chair.

And busying o'er a host of little things
She adds an air of comfort to the
room,
That to her love a feeling brings
Of gladness after gloom.

He's late to-day, but then he's often
late;
It only means a warmer kiss in store;
Right well can she afford to wait—
Hush! steps without the door.

They're more than one – her table's
far too small
For many guests – yet welcome she'd
accord
To dozens, smiling on them all
Across her humble board.

'Come in! Well, Bob; where's *my* man
to-night'
'Outside here, Jennie, but –I've – I've a
fear –
Bear up my girl, we have to fight
A lot of danger here.'

And two great hands are on her shoul-
der laid
With touch like children's on a dying
pet;
And all the dreadful best is made
Of something past regret.

Outside in silence stand his sadden'd
mates;
In truth, methinks, each one of them
may muse
'When my turn comes, to her who
waits
Who'll break the awful news?'

The story now told is of a simple and –
alas! – an often-recurring incident of
everyday life in a mining district. The
scene is the interior of a miner's cottage on the goldfields. Through the
open doorway are to be seen the pop-
pet heads which mark the main shaft
of the mine. The table is laid for the
evening meal. The young wife takes
pride in the neatness of her modest
home, as shown by the little surroundings. We imagine her, with her infant in
her arms, sitting by the fire as she prepares the husband's dinner. Presently
she hears the sound of many footsteps,
and wonderingly listens. Then the
door is opened, and two men enter.
The older of them approaches her with
bowed, uncovered head – a look of
deep concern upon his honest face.
Instantly the dread of what has hap-
pened flashes upon her. She springs

forward, the mute agony of her pallid
face appealing to him to let her know
the worst. His rough, toilworn hands
are gently placed upon her shoulders
to steady her before he breaks the
news which wrecks a life. Through the
open door are indications of the rude
litter on which lies all that remains of
him who was dearer to her than life
itself. In the bent shoulders of his mate,
standing in the doorway, hat in hand,
are shown that instinctive sense of
respect which death and grief inspire.
The bearers outside await his signal to
bring their burden in. This is the
moment the artist has seized for his
pathetic rendering of a touching subject . . .
With 'Breaking the News' Mr. Longstaff has won the gold medal awarded
to the best student of the Victorian
National Gallery. This carries with it a
travelling scholarship of £150 a year,
tenable for three years. The conditions
are that the holder studies in one of the
art-centres of Europe. In each of the
first and second years he contributes to
our National Gallery a copy of an old
master, and in the third year an original picture by himself. Thus the trustees reap the reward of their far-seeing
liberality towards art development.
Mr. Longstaff is Victoria's first travelling student.
– *The Australasian Sketcher*, 12 July
1887

Longstaff painted *Breaking the News* in
one of the ground floor display areas at
the old Melbourne Gallery in Swanston
Street. Alexander Colquhoun, his closest
rival in the 1887 students' competition,
was working at the other end of this
improvized studio: 'With the models of
both in attendance, the place seemed
crowded to suffocation point'.[1] On
Folingsby's advice, Longstaff asked his sister, Polly, to pose for him as the young
wife. The old bearded miner was a retired
Welsh stonemason, 'hoary in locks, but
browned with toil', whom Longstaff had
first seen reading in the Public Library.[2] He
was also assisted by a pair of visiting
actors, Signor and Signora Majeroni, who
advised on dramatic postures and facial
expressions. Folingsby's influence is evident in the compositional arrangement of
the figures across an interior setting. An
open doorway places the incident within a
wider scene, essential to the drama. The
brown tonality is characteristic of Folingsby's painting method. *Breaking the News*
was immediately acclaimed as 'the greatest picture of the year' by critics and public
alike. It was compared most favourably
with popular sentimental Victorian narra-

tive paintings imported from England.[3] At
least one amateur poet was inspired to
'translate' the story into verse. Most significant for the future development of local
figure painting, however, was its strong
appeal to the rising sense of nationalism.
As *The Argus* critic remarked, 'it is ideas
that we want chiefly in Australian art –
something to tell us that the artist is get-
ting into our life and illustrating it'.

[1] Murdoch 1948, p.55. An original sketch
(or sketches) now lost, for *Breaking the
News* was recorded by Moore 1906, p.2,
'in the waiting room of Mr Mackey, the
ophthalmic optician, 108 Elizabeth
Street'; and *Loan Exhibition of Australian
Paintings*, National Gallery of Victoria,
Melbourne, 1925, no.172, lent by G.A.
Rowell, Esq. Colquhoun's painting,
Divided Attention, 1887, is now in the
Bendigo Art Gallery.
[2] The old stonemason, Samuel Thomas of
Fitzroy, had emigrated in 1853;
information from his great grandson Mr
Neil Kirk, August 1982.
[3] In particular *The Mitherless Bairn*, 1855,
by Thomas Faed, acquired by the
National Gallery of Victoria in 1886; and
Sir Luke Fildes's *The Widower*, 1876,
which had been in the Sydney Gallery
since 1883.

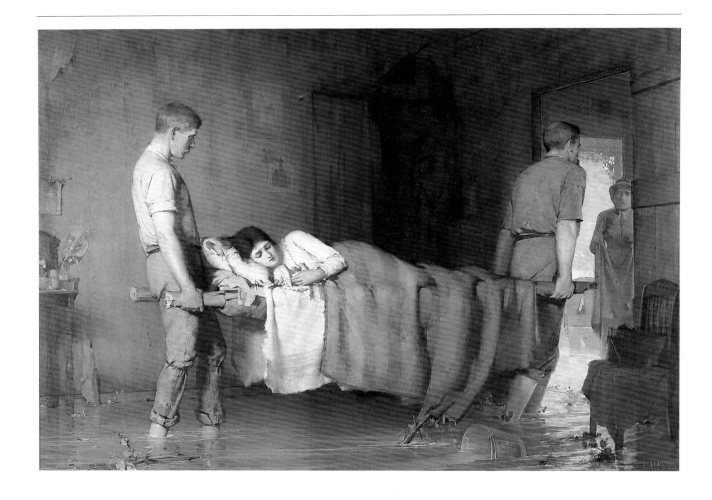

ABY ALTSON
Flood Sufferings, 1890
Oil on canvas
110 x 153.5 cm
Signed and dated l.r.: A. ALTSON 1890
National Gallery of Victoria
Accessioned 1967

Provenance:
John Wagner, of 'Stormont', St Kilda (and later 'Stonnington', Toorak) 1890

Exhibitions:
Seventh Annual Exhibition of Paintings by the Students of the National Gallery under the direction of G.F. Folingsby, Esq., Melbourne, November 1890, no.1: 'Flood Sufferings – £125.0.0'

Literature:
Age, 13 November 1890, p.5; *Argus*, 13 November 1890, p.6; *Daily Telegraph*, 13 November 1890, p.3; *Table Talk*, 14 November 1890, p.17; 21 November 1890, p.8; *Australasian Critic*, 1 December 1890, p.74; Jope-Slade 1895, p.394; Astbury 1978, pp. 51ff.; Grassick 1984, p.350; Downer & Phipps 1985, no.34; Astbury 1985, in press, p.41, pl.8

The picture of the year is undoubtedly Mr Altson's Flood Sufferings... The scene is a farmhouse interior, swamped by the incoming waters, which have flooded the floor half knee-deep. The leafy spoils of the bush mingle with the household lares and penates of the homestead. A delicate young mother and her infant, laid on an impromptu stretcher of gum boughs and covered with blankets, are borne to a place of safety by two stalwart men, while through the open door may be seen an elderly woman holding up her skirts and contemplating the operation with anxiety. The homely realism of the scene is, perhaps, its greatest charm.
– *The Age*, 13 November 1890

Aby Altson 'knew nothing at all about painting when he placed himself under Mr Folingsby'. By 1890, however, he was the Gallery School's star pupil; and with *Flood Sufferings* he carried off, in succession to Longstaff, the second triennial travelling scholarship. There are obvious similarities to Longstaff's *Breaking the News*, in both

conception and execution. This was 'an episode common enough in occurrence but fearfully pathetic in reality', said *Table Talk*. 'The drawing of each figure is excellent, and the painting is strong and consistent. There is a good deal of clever texture work in the picture, and the few accessories are carefully treated so as not to attract attention from the story'. Not long before, a disastrous flood at Bourke had made headline news; and thus, as *The Australasian Critic* remarked, Altson's topical subject 'probably had quite as much effect as its treatment in securing the honour that has been bestowed upon it. A strong prejudice prevails in Australia in favour of pictures describing local incidents or characters – a prejudice which future contestants for the scholarship would do well to bear in mind'. Early the following year Altson sailed for Paris where, as he wrote to Tom Roberts, he was known to fellow students as 'Aby Farmer Captain Starlight Native Bear'!

Rosa Altson (b. 1864) was the artist's first cousin and sister-in-law, and possibly his model for *Flood Sufferings*. Her father was David Altson, merchant and proprietor of a large Melbourne saddlery business. In 1883, visiting England, she and her husband had decided that Aby Altson 'then a lad of 15, should return with [them] to seek his fortune under our sunny skies'. In 1886 Barnett Hyman Altson opened his tobacconist business on the corner of Collins and Elizabeth Streets – 'Altson's Corner': a source of many of the cigar-box panels used by the artist and his friends for their oil sketches and 'impressions' at Heidelberg.

ABY ALTSON
Portrait of Mrs B.H.A., [1889]
Oil on canvas
109.5 x 85 cm
Signed l.l.: Aby Altson
Charles John Altson, Melbourne

Provenance:
Barnett Hyman Altson, the artist's elder brother; by descent

Exhibitions:
Sixth Annual Exhibition of Paintings by the Students of the National Gallery under the direction of G.F. Folingsby, Esq., Melbourne, November 1889, no. 2: 'Portrait of Mrs B.H.A.', awarded first prize for the best portrait

Literature:
Age, 13 November 1889, p.6

DAVID DAVIES ▲
A Hot Day, 1888
Oil on canvas
60.6 x 91.3 cm
Signed and dated l.r.: D. DAVIES. 88.
National Gallery of Victoria
Felton Bequest 1937
Previously known as 'Golden Summer'

Provenance:
Purchased by A.E. Clarke in 1888; subsequent ownership unrecorded; The Fine Art Society, Melbourne 1937

Exhibitions:
Fifth Annual Exhibition of Paintings by the Students of the National Gallery under the Direction of G.F. Folingsby, Esq., Melbourne, 1888, no.13: 'A Hot Day – £42', awarded first prize for landscape

Literature:
Argus, 13 November 1888, p.8; *Herald,* 12 November 1888, p.6; *Daily Telegraph,* 14 November 1888, p.6; *Table Talk,* 16 November 1888, p.14; Astbury 1978, p.54; Astbury 1985, in press, p.41, pl.9

'The prize landscape "A Hot Day", is so thoroughly characteristic of the burning summer time in a lazy country township that it would be singled out anywhere as a purely Australian picture', said *Table Talk*'s review of the 1888 student exhibition. 'Australian' subjects were, of course, at a premium since Longstaff's success with *Breaking the News* the year before; and popular appeal would certainly have been heightened by the experience of severe drought that summer. Anecdotal content – 'the toiling wagoner as he wearily trudges under the broiling sun' – is set into specifically localized landscape: 'The sere and withered foliage and grass... and cloud of dust raised by the horses are all suggestive of midsummer heat' (*The Daily Telegraph*). Davies's broad treatment of the vegetation and distant hills (although criticized by *The Argus* as 'slight and sketchy in workmanship') is based upon true awareness of the modification of local colour in strong sunlight; he has captured the 'glare of the all penetrating light, the feeling of heat in the atmosphere, and the palor of the grey-blue sky'.

TOM ROBERTS ▶
Moorish doorway, Granada, 1883
Oil on canvas
48.3 x 33 cm
Signed l.l: Tom Roberts
Inscribed l.r.: Granada Oct./83
The Joseph Brown Collection
For exhibition in Melbourne only

Provenance:
Probably Dick Roberts, the artist's brother; Molly Roberts, his daughter; Miss B.M. Joske (her daughter)

Literature:
Spate 1978, pp.23f.; Daniel Thomas 1980, no. 37; Topliss 1985, no. 20

Roberts's walking tour of northern France and Spain was made in the company of fellow Australians John Peter Russell, art student in London, his architect brother, Percy Russell, and Dr William Maloney. 'The city of Granada enjoys the happiness of being much the most visited part of Spain', declared *The Magazine of Art* in 1885 (p.447). Indeed the four were following in the steps of Roberts's mentor Edwin Long, Russell's teacher Alphonse Legros, Sir Frederick Leighton P.R.A. and Edouard Manet, amongst other artist tourists. There they met two Spanish art students, Laureano Barau and Ramon Casas, on

TOM ROBERTS ▲
Woman on a balcony, 1884
Oil on academy board
21.7 x 13.1 cm
Inscribed along lower edge: Venezia ap 28.84
Private collection, Melbourne

Provenance:
Dick Roberts (the artist's brother); Mrs Fanny Burchill (his widow); private collection, Melbourne

Exhibitions:
Perhaps included in the *9 by 5 Impression Exhibition*, Melbourne, August 1889, as no. 91: 'Gay Day in Spring, Venice – 2 guineas'

Literature:
Spate 1978, pp.30,66; Topliss 1985, no.45

Roberts visited Italy in the spring of 1884. This charming panel shows little influence of any current 'Impressionist' or 'Whistlerian' ideas he may have picked up in his travels. It provides a glimpse of Venice in sharp focus; the figure quite strongly defined. There is some resemblance to Manet's *Le balcon* which Roberts would certainly have known from reproductions published at the time of the *Exposition posthume Manet* in Paris; (a huge exhibition which his friend Russell visited in January 1884 and Roberts himself might possibly have seen).

holiday from Paris and full of up-to-date ideas about direct *plein air* oil painting. Roberts's own methods were still academic: in fact Maloney relates that he planned to paint a group portrait of his comrades 'in a Posada in Spain, after the beautiful one of the French students in the Melbourne National Gallery [a popular Salon painting of 1862 by Jean Georges Vibert]. This, however, like many other good resolutions, never eventuated'.[1] Nevertheless, his *Moorish doorway* is informal and captures the 'glare' effect of strong sunlight as no other Australian artist had hitherto attempted. Back in London, he exhibited *Basking – A Corner in the Alhambra* at the Royal Academy Summer Exhibition of 1884, no.775.

[1] Croll 1935, p.10.

TOM ROBERTS ▶
Coming South, 1886
Oil on canvas
63.7 x 50.5 cm
Signed and dated l.r.: Tom Roberts 1886
Inscribed l.l. s.s.Lusitania
Verso: Thallon framing label with title very faintly inscribed
National Gallery of Victoria
Presented by Colonel Aubrey Gibson in memory of John and Anne Gibson, settlers (1887) 1967

Provenance:
Dick Roberts, the artist's brother, 1887; Joseph Kendall, 1890s; his son, L.P. Kendall, Canberra; The Joshua McClelland Print Room, Melbourne, 1967; Colonel Aubrey Gibson, Melbourne

Exhibitions:
Roberts's studio, March 1886; *Colonial and Indian Exhibition, Catalogue of the Oil Paintings and Water-colour Drawings in the Victorian Court*, London, 1886, no.19: 'Coming South – Lent by the Artist'

Literature:
Age, 19 January 1886, p.6; *Table Talk*, 22 January 1886, p.11; *Once a Month*, 1 March 1886, pp.264ff.; *Magazine of Art*, 1886, p.400; Spate 1964, p.262; McCulloch 1969, pp.18, 154; Smith 1971, pp.88, 120; Gleeson 1971, pl.28; Finemore 1977, p.23; Spate 1978, pp.50, 73, 78; Splatt & Bruce 1981, p.37; Downer & Phipps 1985, no.172a; Topliss 1985, no.62, p.9; Astbury 1985, in press, pp.101f.

Roberts left London aboard the Orient Line's first mail steamer, s.s. *Lusitania*, in March 1885. True to his academic training, he made sketches during the voyage back to Australia and then completed *Coming South* in his Melbourne studio: hence the sharp definition of forms and patches of clear colour. 'A scene often witnessed on board our steamers on their way out from home, *"Coming South"* was graphically treated, and the grouping of the several figures true to nature', reported *Once a Month*. High tonality, pink and purple tones in the shadows and the random snapshot effect of the composition suggest 'influence of the French School' – as noted by *The Age* – but not of 'true' French Impressionism. (Paintings by Tissot, Manet and Degas and the Thames etchings of Whistler are precedents which come to mind; also Roberts's own experience of photography.) It is 'a very careful and well-drawn work', continued *The Age*. Tilted verticals convey unmista-keably the rocking movement of the ship, with only a glimpse of the sea itself ahead. Roberts probably knew of other painted essays on the theme of emigration. Ford Madox Brown's *The Last of England*, 1855 (Birmingham Museum and Art Gallery), inspired by the artist Thomas Woolner and family's departure to Australia; *An Emigrant's thoughts of Home* (National Gallery of Victoria) was painted by Marshall Claxton in 1859; and Frank Holl produced comparable black-and-white illustrations for *The Graphic* in the 1870s. Although Roberts's version certainly appealed to contemporary sentiment, there is no obvious narrative. As *Table Talk* reported, 'an aged immigrant [is] seemingly lost in thought and gazing blankly at a small boy at her feet. The different expressions on the faces of the passengers engaged in the usual occupations on board ship are given with accurate and true artistic precision . . .'

TOM ROBERTS ▲
Brought back, [c.1883]
Gouache on paper
23.8 x 16.4 cm
Signed l.l.: Tom Roberts
Inscribed verso: ' T /"The Deserter"/by Thomas E. [*sic*] Roberts RBA/(This drawing was exhibited in R.A. 1883)'; and on backing paper 'Exhibited as "Brought Back"'
National Gallery of Victoria
Purchased 1985

Provenance:
Stanley Smith (Marchmont Bookshop), London, 1971; Mr P.E. Butcher, Melbourne

Exhibitions:
The Exhibition of the Royal Academy of Arts, London, 1883, no. 1344: 'Brought back'

Literature:
Topliss 1985, no.778, as 'The Deserter'

A number of wash drawings by Roberts survive from his years at the Royal Academy Schools.[1] A pencil sketch for this particular gouache is preserved in one of his early London sketchbooks.[2] Gouache was often used by artists for drawings intended for reproduction in magazines. Although most accounts of Roberts's career mention that he worked as a black-and-white illustrator for *The Graphic* whilst a student in London, that journal contains no signed examples of his work for the years 1881-85. Perhaps he was employed by *The Graphic* in a technical capacity.[3]

[1] See Topliss 1985, nos 33-36.
[2] This was kindly drawn to my attention by Irena Zdanowicz, National Gallery of Victoria, who is currently researching the subject of *Brought back*; the setting is Trafalgar Square, London. Mitchell Library, Sydney. MS A2481, vol. XIV, Fol.41r; the sketchbook is dated 1882 and inscribed 'Tom Roberts/Student Royal Academy Piccadilly'.
[3] Topliss 1985, p.5.

Minute book of the Buonarotti Society, 1883-87
Castlemaine Art Gallery and Historical Museum

Provenance:
Cherry-Brotherton estate, early 1960s (given to the Gallery)

Literature:
Alexander Colquhoun, 'Mr Frederick McCubbin's long activity in Australian Art', *The Christian Science Monitor*, 29 December 1916; *The Argus, Camera Supplement*, 10 August 1929, p.3; Moore 1934, I, pp.55, 219f.

> To ensure good results in any branch of art, the work done in it must be thorough; to ensure such thoroughness, it is necessary, or at least advisable, to have the stimulus of criticism, sympathy, and friendly rivalry . . .
> It is thought that greater benefit and pleasure will result from the Arts in combination than could possibly be attained by the pursuance of them separately . . . ; and, though, it is not to be expected that in our ranks will be found men, who, like Michael Angelo Buonarotti, unite in one person all the talents of Sculptor, Painter, Poet, Architect, and Musician, we may at least hope that time will show amongst us many who, by their ability and energy in one or the other of the professions the great Tuscan so much loved, have gained also a due share of the world's regard and esteem.
> – G. Rodney Cherry, honorary secretary of the Buonarotti Society

Founded in May 1883 by Cyrus Mason – Victorian Railways employee and earnest amateur painter – the Buonarotti Society met once a fortnight upstairs in the Bourke Street Coffee Palace or at various city hotels – usually Young and Jackson's, the Earl of Zetland, or the New Treasury Club. Members joined as 'artistic', 'musical', 'literary', or in any combination of these three categories. At first, women were only admitted as 'honorary members'; but soon most of the Gallery students had enrolled, and all the leading Heidelberg School painters signed up. 'Visitors' included A.J. Daplyn from Sydney, the society painter Carl Kahler, and reporters from *The Argus*, *The Age* and *The Daily Telegraph*. Drawings and oil sketches were displayed, the fruits of *plein air* excursions to Lilydale, Hanging Rock, Riddell's Creek, and Cheltenham. 'Painting was the first object of the expeditions, but the rough life had a zest all its own which appealed strongly to all', one member recalled. Original poems were recited; for example, Alexander Colquhoun's *'Lines to my Creditors'*. Essays were read on topics such as 'the open air element in Adam Lindsay Gordon's poems', Victor Hugo, Michelangelo's birthday, and the merits of animal locomotion photography. Each meeting concluded with half an hour's life sketching from a 'comrade-victim' to the strains of 'good vocal and instrumental music': McCubbin singing *'My pretty Jane'* or *'I dare not ask a kiss, I dare not beg a smile'*, with original music by Louis Lavater, and Rupert Bunny or John Longstaff on the piano. Roberts was invited to join very shortly after his return to Australia in 1885. Nominated as a member by McCubbin, he proposed almost immediately 'that the Artistic Committee be increased in its power and responsibility'. In fact the 'brothers [and sisters] of the brush' always seem to have been the strongest contingent within the Society; but, rather sadly, initial enthusiasms seem to have dwindled and the Buonarotti quietly faded away after the farewell party for Longstaff and his wife in August 1887.

'PLEIN AIR' PAINTING: THE EARLY ARTISTS' CAMPS AROUND MELBOURNE

Bridget Whitelaw

*Australia being pre-eminently a land of sunshine which allows of painting in the open all
the year round, it is not surprising that those susceptible to art influences should be attracted
to the method practised by the plein airists.*
– Alfred James Daplyn, 1902[1]

The landscape paintings produced by the Heidelberg School at its first *plein air* artists' camps at Box Hill and Mentone were regarded as innovative achievements by the artists and their subsequent critics. These early camps provided both a focus for the expression of artistic fraternity – in which these painters revelled – and an opportunity to develop a *plein air* school of painting, that reflected the local landscape and life of its inhabitants in a boom period of great optimism in the value of all things Australian.

Whilst oil painting *en plein air* had been widespread in Britain and France during the 1870s and 1880s and had already found some favour with Melbourne's artists in the early 1880s, it was unquestionably Tom Roberts's return from Europe which precipitated its development in Melbourne after 1885. The protagonists themselves certainly viewed it in this light; Streeton later commented: 'Some students from the National Gallery were influenced by Roberts to paint landscape directly from nature and with the truthful colour of out of doors instead of painting them indoors upon a bituminous base as was the method of Folingsby'.[2] And Conder wrote to Roberts in 1890, 'if there is any distinct school in Melbourne, I wouldn't say Sydney, its entirely due to you'.[3]

Roberts arrived back in Australia in 1885 with a knowledge of and enthusiasm for the academic Naturalism of the British artists working in the *plein air* colonies such as Newlyn or St Ives in Cornwall and Glasgow in Scotland. These artists were inspired by the style of painters associated with the *plein air* colonies in Brittany and Barbizon, in the Fontainebleau Forest near Paris – in particular, Jules Bastien-Lepage (1848-84) who proved to be something of a cult figure. Bastien-Lepage exhibited works in London in 1882 during Roberts's stay there. His commitment to record his own particular region, Damvilliers in north-eastern France, and his combination of landscape and figure painting appealed to the young *plein air* painters throughout Europe and Australia. His preference for placing a figure in the landscape with a high horizon line, a device he used consistently, was adopted by his admirers. Roberts also returned with great enthusiasm for the art of the Anglo-American James McNeill Whistler whose small tonal sketches depicting atmospheric effects, with broadly applied brush-strokes of thin liquid paint, he had observed in London. These sources, encountered abroad, were the major influences on Roberts's art and hence the development of *plein air* painting in Melbourne.

The small 'impression' done *en plein air* was emphasized by Roberts's contemporaries as his most innovative introduction to the Melbourne art scene. Akin to Whistler's sketches in their concern with the tonal effects of atmosphere and light, 'The impressions brought out by Roberts had the fresh air, true-tone in values idea which was in conflict with the academic training at the National Art School under Folingsby'.[4] The application of the term 'impression' by Streeton, Roberts and their contemporaries to these oil sketches and the critics' use of the adjective 'impressionist' to describe their earliest landscapes has often resulted in the correlation of these works with those of the French Impressionists. The sketches, however, reveal little of the style that we associate with the bright palette and broken brushstroke of Impressionism. In fact, both visual and documentary evidence suggest that Roberts's contact with this French movement was minimal. His concept of impressionism was closer to that of the French artists described as the *juste milieu* who blended aspects of academic and impressionist practice: 'They deliberately chose the informal technique of the independents (impressionists) either painting parts of the picture crudely or attenuating and blending the contours of the forms into each other. At the same time, the complete freedom of the Impressionists negated what they considered solid draughtsmanship and they either gave to their forms a carefully drawn underlying structure or adopted for their subject matter classical and Christian themes'.[5]

The complexity of the problem appears to reside in a semantic confusion resulting from the widespread and indiscriminate use of the term by the British, French and Australian critics and artists of the 1880s. British writers from the early 80s described Whistler as an 'Impressionist'.[6] Emile Zola, who acknowledged the achievements of the French Impressionists in their portrayal of contemporary themes but praised an artist such as Bastien-Lepage more highly, used the term in relation to the latter's style of academic Naturalism: 'He is carried along by his temperament and the open air does the rest. His superiority over the Impressionists rests precisely in this ability to realize his "impressions"'.[7] By 1887 a critic in *The Artist* commented that 'Impressionism in some form or another is becoming the central idea in a very large proportion of modern picture production. The desire to paint effects rather than subjects is rapidly spreading and bids fair to grow into the chief motive of our art'.[8]

The term 'impressionist' was generally applied vaguely, in both Britain and Australia, to a work which the critic regarded as either unfinished or as departing too far from academic convention. It began to be used by some people solely in a pejorative sense; as Sickert commented, 'a very cultured writer will use the word Impressionism sometimes with a sneer, will touch it as it were with the end of his lips much as a lady might use the word Socialist in a drawing room'.[9] Roberts's *A Summer Morning Tiff* was termed a 'composition which shows the influence of the Impressionists and its peculiar merit will be recognized more fully by artists than by the general public'.[10] Streeton's *Midday at Mentone* was described 'as not so much a picture as an impression of nature rapidly transferred to the canvas by a free use of the thumbnail and palette knife, as auxiliary to the brush, and he has succeeded in producing a highly effective result; with which however we hope he will not rest satisfied nor with the method employed, good as it may be, quantum valeat'.[11] Contrary to this critic's expectations, it was precisely such 'impressions' which satisfied the young Melbourne painters – who had little in common with Impressionist practice but combined academic elements with the tonal harmonies of Whistler's liquid sketches.

Although Roberts's return was a major catalyst, the influx of foreign artists such as Arthur Loureiro, Julian Ashton, John Ford Paterson and Alfred James Daplyn also imparted a knowledge of European *plein air* work. Indeed one critic of the day noted: 'The number of foreign artists who are settling in Melbourne is steadily increasing and their residence here cannot fail to make an impression on the art history of the colony, because if they have studied in European schools sufficiently to become masters of the style they adopt their example to Australians is decidedly stimulative'.[12] Paterson, for example, had been a friend of James Guthrie, one of the Glasgow *plein airists*, and Loureiro and Daplyn had painted at Fontainebleau. Loureiro brought to Melbourne in 1885 several *plein air* figure paintings, including *The Forest at Fontainebleau* painted at Brolles in 1882. And a decade later it was noted that 'Sénor A. Loureiro, a native of Oporto who had studied in Rome and Paris and exhibited at the *Salon*, had arrived and was exercising the influence of that freshness of feeling which always comes of outdoor work and study'.[13] Julian Ashton, recently arrived from London, was painting *en plein air* in Melbourne in the early 1880s and indeed claimed his *Evening, Merri Creek* of 1882 to be the first landscape painted in oils, wholly out-of-doors. However, other artists made similar claims; for example McCubbin stated, 'I painted I think the first picture that was ever painted in this part of the world entirely out-of-doors'.[14]

Finally, the considerable influence of Abram Louis Buvelot should be acknowledged. Although Buvelot never finished his oil paintings *en plein air*, his art was derived from the *intimiste* approach of the Barbizon School. His interest in developing a familiarity with an intimate section of landscape, such as his successive visits to Coleraine to record specific details, was one shared by artists like Roberts and McCubbin. The latter recognized their debt to him saying, 'Roberts and I had an immense reverence for the work he did but we had no chance of knowing him, he perhaps being the only man at that time who could give us a hint of all the beauties that were under our very eyes... But most of us owe it to him that slowly we were able to see the paintable qualities of that which lay immediately around us. The exquisite beauty of our lovely skies, the glorious colour and form of our green trees...'[15] A similar reverence is paid to the early Barbizon artists, Jean-Baptiste Camille Corot (1796-1875) and Jean François Millet (1814-75), when mentioned by Roberts, Conder and Streeton in their letter on Impressionism.[16]

McCubbin, Roberts and Abrahams were inspired by this wide range of European models when they set up their first *plein air* painting camp at Box Hill in the summer of 1885. Earlier they had painted closer to the city, for example at Darebin Creek, but now they chose to camp further out. Although the opening of the railway line in 1882 had made the district more accessible and much of the land was under cultivation by 1885, Box Hill still provided areas of natural bush comparatively close to the city, such as the section of David Houston's property where they camped. One visitor, Madame Nancy Elmhurst Goode, described the site: 'In the vicinity of the Homestead belonging to the Houstons was a patch of wild bush, tall young saplings with the sun glistening on their leaves and streamers of bark swaying, groups of tea-tree, dogwood and tall dry grasses'.[17] The Box Hill camp was recalled with great nostalgia by the artists; notably Streeton, although not associated with the group until the following summer, who wrote to McCubbin from London in 1901:

> I close my eyes and see again the... black wattles and ti tree down by the creek, the Houstons cabin, the messmate tree and its mistletoe and horehound patch beneath, the run for trains on Sunday night and Prof far up ahead, mopping his brow near Jack Ganges' – the flush over the Dandenongs and the quiet and grey valley beyond White Horse Road toward Macedon.[18]

Roberts's *The Artists' Camp* celebrates the success of this first *plein air* camp. A testimony to the friendship of the three artists, the painting depicts McCubbin, nicknamed 'The Prof', and Abrahams, called 'The Don', very much at ease in their bush environment grilling chops over the fire. Roberts, known as 'Bulldog', recalled such occasions:

> The evening after work – the chops perfect from the fire of gum twigs – the 'good night' of the jackies as the soft darkness fell – then talks around the fire, the 'Prof' philosophic – we forgot everything but the peace of it.[19]

His *Mentone* – an elegant portrayal of holiday-makers engrossed in the pleasures of sailing – was painted during the summer of 1886-1887 when he was renting a cottage at Mentone with McCubbin and Abrahams. There they first encountered Streeton, as Roberts recollected: 'He was standing out on the wet rocks, painting there, and I saw that his work was full of light and air. We asked him to join us and that was the beginning of a long and delightful association'.[20] They probably chose Mentone for their *plein air* painting camp that summer because of its relative seclusion – in contrast to nearby Brighton Beach which was a crowded resort in season. Until 1887 the railway only extended as far as Brighton, which contributed to its much greater popularity:

Along that beach which stretches away to the south, what crowds of people swarm on a Sunday afternoon in summer. The trains carry forth the teeming thousands of the city to breathe an hour or two the fresh sea breeze, to kick up the yellow sands, and gather such shells as the rippling wavelets may have cast up since the last host came down on the previous Sunday...The fond father and mother bring down the coming generation,with supplies of biscuits and sweetmeats to beguile the journey till they get out upon the beach, where they will dig or wade or climb.[21]

For Roberts and his artist friends, bathing on the more secluded beaches further south of the city would have been one of the delights of their Mentone summer camp. Streeton fondly remembered the time spent there:

I close my eyes and see again the soft red sandy road, the velvety green of the ti tree tops – the sweet salt air about the beach during the rosy afterglow at Sandringham – the... march home – the long draughts of milk, the mulberry tree and the puce coloured walls and the flies...[22]

A familiarity with nature – prerequisite for *plein air* painting – was developed in the paintings by Roberts and McCubbin completed at both Box Hill and Mentone. They abandoned the panoramas chosen by earlier artists, such as von Guérard, in favour of a close-focus view painted under an even light according to the system of related values which created smooth transitions of tones. Daplyn, who emigrated to Australia in 1881 and became a friend of Julian Ashton on *plein air* painting excursions around Sydney, outlined such methods: 'Now the artist makes his studio in the open air. The subject far from embracing miles of country is likely to be the corner of the field, his aim not so much to call forth feelings of awe and rapture, by displaying nature in her grander mood, but to translate for our benefit the beauty that lies in familiar things'.[23] He also advised that the student 'when choosing a subject should half close the eyes, or shut one of them, which has nearly the same effect. The landscape will now become simplified, the grand masses more prominent and the thousand and one details which distract the attention eliminated'.[24] And furthermore, Daplyn recommended leaving black and brown in the studio for, 'Nature has no use for strong colours being so to speak a kaleidoscope of coloured greys'.[25]

It was this doctrine of relative values that Roberts is traditionally held to have taught his friends: 'Frederick McCubbin had just before Roberts' return painted a picture of Melbourne Gaol in the sunlight from the Library gardens. He showed it to his friend. "Yes", commented Roberts, "you have the drawing and colour but you've got no values, and he proceeded to explain this new thing to Frederick McCubbin'.[26] Such a harmony of tonal values is demonstrated by McCubbin's *Lost* and Roberts's *A Summer Morning Tiff*, which also include the close-up views of specific grasses and blue gum saplings native to Box Hill, characteristic of the foregrounds of many contemporary works. These practices were in keeping with the naturalist landscapes of Bastien-Lepage and the British *plein airists*, and with Ashton's firm views, published locally in 1888, on the importance of painting 'with grace and beauty the simple themes that everyday life will furnish'.[27] Ashton went on to praise the sensitivity of the true art lover who has watched the opalescent tints of the morning; 'the glow of sunset has touched him with its glory and sadness'. This poetic interest in twilight and dawn found favour with Roberts and McCubbin in 1887 but was developed more fully in the landscape painting of the 1890s. One of the 'simple themes' of 'everyday life'

depicted by artists at their Box Hill camp was that of rural workers in their own environment – McCubbin's *Winter evening, Hawthorn* and Roberts's *Wood Splitters* are examples for which there were some precedents in local art, notably Ashton's images of the selector at work, published in *The Australasian Sketcher*.[28]

European visitors to Melbourne in the 80s found it 'a really astonishing city with broad streets full of handsome shops and crowded with bustling well dressed people'.[29] This mood of civic pride was reflected in the paintings of the city by many artists. Their energies may have been directed toward landscape painting; nevertheless they derived their existence from Melbourne and its wealthier residents. Paintings of streets, wharfs, parks and inhabitants formed an important component of their art. Although the young artists camped in bush locations at weekends and during the summer, their earning occupations and their studios were located in the city. Their pictures of Melbourne were both celebrations of its progress and prosperity and descriptions of its everyday life. Streeton's *Between the Lights–Princes Bridge*, a view of the newly constructed bridge, and McCubbin's *Melbourne in 1888*, depicting the industry of the inner city wharfs, were exhibited together in 1888 – the year of the Centennial Exhibition which marked the climax of the Melbourne's boom period.

The early works of the Heidelberg School were often approached by critics with caution:

How curious it is by the way, that some of our best artists Messrs. Tom Roberts, McCubbin and Streeton are all a little touched with the mania which afflicts the French impressionists, looking at nature as though through a glass darkly neither recognising her definition of form nor her positive colours. Mr. Mather on the other hand looks her straight in the face, so to speak, and presents her with the bright apparel she loves to wear especially in the lucid atmosphere of Australia. I do not write this in disparagement of the work of the three gentlemen... I admire their landscapes in spite of what I regard as their incompleteness; just as I admire those of the latter because of their completeness.[30]

Nevertheless, as early as 1888, a critic like Frederick Broomfield was able to point to the development of a distinctively Australian school of art. He found

eloquent albeit silent attestation to the fact that Australian art was receiving every year more and more attention. The predominant element this year was distinctly local. The majority of the canvases were covered with scenes from the Australian bush, incidents of Australian life and glimpses of the Australian coast. A few years ago there would have been perhaps half a dozen pictures in the entire collection which would have owed their origin to the inspiration of the country in which they were painted... Today the visitor is agreeably assured that the sentiment of this new Southern world is beginning to find artistic expression and that the penumbra of a genuinely Australian School of Art is veritably visible, presaging we know not what excellence in the future.[31]

[1] Daplyn 1902, p.vi; for an account of this *plein air* exponent, teacher and writer, see biography in this catalogue.
[2] Croll 1935, p.16.
[3] Letter from Conder to Roberts, 2 August 1890. Mitchell Library, Sydney. Roberts correspondence MS A2480.
[4] Streeton, quoted by Croll 1935, p.13.

[5] Boime 1971, p.16.
[6] *Artist*, 1 May 1883, IV, pp.69f.
[7] Quoted by Weisberg 1980, p.188.
[8] *Artist*, August 1887, III, p.258
[9] Walter Sickert, 'The Language of Art', *A Free House!*, 1947, p.92f.
[10] *Argus*, 7 September 1886, p.7.
[11] *Argus*, 2 April 1887, p.12.
[12] *Table Talk*, 21 December 1888, p.3.
[13] *Australasian Art Review*, 1 November 1889, p.25.
[14] Galbally (ed.) 1979,p.75.
[15] ibid., p.75.
[16] *Argus*, 3 September 1889. Works by Corot and Millet were included in Centennial Exhibition of 1888.
[17] Mme Elmhurst Goode's recollection of camp, quoted by Croll 1935, pp.23f.
[18] Letter from Streeton to McCubbin, 8 April 1901. LaTrobe Collection, State Library of Victoria. McCubbin papers MS988/ 4.
[19] Quoted by Moore 1934, I, p.70.
[20] Croll 1935, p.71. McCubbin would have known Streeton from the Gallery School; he introduced him to Roberts at Rickett's Point, Mentone; MacDonald 1916, p.57.
[21] Sutherland 1888, p.562; and see Bate 1962.
[22] Letter from Streeton in London to McCubbin, 8 April 1901. LaTrobe Collection, State Library of Victoria. McCubbin papers MS8525 988/4.
[23] Daplyn, op. cit., p.v.
[24] ibid., p.14.
[25] Daplyn, op. cit., p.21.
[26] MacDonald 1916, p.57.
[27] Ashton, 'An Aim for Australian Art', *Centennial Magazine*, I, 1888, pp.31f.
[28] For example, 'The Selector at Work', in *The Australasian Sketcher*, 15 July 1882.
[29] Francis Adams, *Australian Essays*, 1885, quoted in 'Marvellous Melbourne, A Study of Nineteenth Century Urban Growth', in *The Australian City*, Deakin University, 1978, p.239.
[30] *Table Talk*, 27 April 1888, p.2.
[31] Fred. J. Broomfield, 'Art and Artists in Victoria', *Centennial Magazine*. I, 1888, p.883.

ARTHUR LOUREIRO ▶
The Forest at Fontainebleau, 1882
Oil on canvas
99 x 64.1 cm
Inscribed l.l.: ARTHUR–LOUREIRO–/
BROLLES-1882-
The Ewing Collection, University of
Melbourne

Provenance:
Probably Charles Raymond Staples, Kew,
from c.1885 until October 1891; Samuel E.
Ewing

Literature:
Table Talk, 19 October 1888, p.4; Jennifer
Phipps et al., *The Ewing Collection*,
University of Melbourne, 1981, no.12;
Clark 1985, p.95

Loureiro brought this picture with him to
Australia late in 1884. It provides evidence of the kind of European *plein air*
landscape paintings known in Melbourne
prior to Roberts's return from abroad the
following year. As the critic James Green
later noted:

> Senor A. Loureiro, a native of Oporto,
> who had studied in Rome and Paris
> and exhibited at the *Salon*, had
> arrived, and was exercising the influ-
> ence of that freshness of feeling which
> always comes of outdoor work and
> study, even in the handling of the fig-
> ure.[1]

Loureiro and his Australian-born wife had
lived and worked at Brolles in the forest of
Fontainebleau, not far from Paris, for
much of 1882. Fontainebleau was 'the
great *al-fresco* school of art of modern
France', according to Robert Louis
Stevenson; earlier the painting ground of
Millet, Corot, Diaz, Rousseau and other
famous Barbizon pioneers of *plein air* oil
painting practice.[2] Loureiro met the
Newlyn *plein airist* Thomas Gotch at Fontainebleau; and probably also Henry Scott
Tuke. Arriving in Melbourne, he was 'discovered by Buvelot and Mr James Smith
painting in the Fitzroy Gardens. It was
through their criticism that he came
before the Melbourne public'.[3]

[1] *Australasian Art Review*, 1 November
1899, p.25.
[2] *Magazine of Art*, 1884, p.253.
[3] *Table Talk*, 19 October 1888, p.4.

J.C.

JULIAN ASHTON ▲
Evening – Merri Creek, 1882
Oil on canvas
91.5 x 122 cm
Signed and dated l.l.: J.R. ASHTON/OCT 1882
Verso, on paper label: 'The Merry Creek The first landscape painted out-of-doors in Australia'
Art Gallery of New South Wales
Presented by Howard Ashton 1942

Provenance:
By descent in the artist's family

Literature:
The Julian Ashton Book, Art and Australia, 1920, pl.XVII; Ashton 1941, p.28; Dysart 1982, no.11
Reproduced by permission Julian Ashton Art School

> During the five years I was in Melbourne my time was so taken up with illustration that I had little leisure for painting. Besides the water colours of the Yarra I had done a fairly large canvas of Merri Creek which I think is the first picture painted entirely out of doors in the Commonwealth. Up to that time the artists Von Guerard and Chevalier did careful drawings in the open, and in the studio turned them into dull uninspiring pictures. I had but lately come from France with all the enthusiasm of the *plein airists* who denounced any picture that was not painted out of doors.
> – Julian Ashton, 1941

Having recently arrived from overseas to take up employment as illustrator with *The Illustrated Australian News*, Julian Ashton was a keen advocate of *plein air* painting. By 1880, according to his own account, he was painting with Abram Louis Buvelot, whom he termed 'the only painter who could be called an artist'. The influence of Buvelot and the Barbizon School is reflected in the rich green tones of *Merri Creek*. Ashton himself claimed to have influenced the younger Melbourne artists prior to his departure for Sydney in 1883:

> When I first came to Melbourne from England I used to find the Art Student of those days struggling with compositions in the grand classical style – Hercules and Orpheus, Nymphs pursued by Satyrs etc. I told them in suitably strong language that they were fools. That they had beautiful subjects all around them that they were neglecting, and I used to take McCubbin who was then driving a baker's cart, out to Heidelberg and help him paint landscape in those faraway days.[1]

Although Ann Galbally has questioned whether he did take McCubbin out to Heidelberg prior to 1883, his encouragement of artists to paint local scenery *en plein air* is evident.

[1] Julian Ashton to Baldwin Spencer, 25 January 1918. Mitchell Library, Sydney MS 875. Ashton's brother, George, also influenced McCubbin; see *Table Talk*, 3 May 1889, p.4.

CHARLES CONDER ▲
Stockyard near Jamberoo, 1886
Oil on cardboard
22.7 x 28.8 cm
Signed l.l.: Charles Conder
Inscribed l.r.: Stockyard/near Jamberoo Charles Conder/2 Dec. 1886
Inscribed verso: 'By Charles Conder painted 2 Dec. 1886 when Conder was 18 years 5 weeks old'
Dixson Gallery, State Library of New South Wales
Presented by Sir William Dixson 1951

Literature:
Hoff 1960, no.1, pl.2; Hoff 1972, no.C4

Conder's earliest signed and dated oil painting reflects the influence of Julian Ashton, whose drawing classes he attended at the Art Society School in Sydney. In 1886 he was awarded the three guinea prize for 'the best painting from nature'. Conder was also studying under the *plein airist* Alfred James Daplyn at this time.

LOUIS ABRAHAMS ▶
Camp, Box Hill, [c.1886]
Watercolour on paper
17.2 x 24.7 cm (sight)
Inscribed and signed l.l.: Camp Box Hill/
Don
Private collection, Melbourne

Provenance:
By descent in the artist's family to his
niece, Mrs Alice Phipps, Melbourne; her
son, Mr James N. Marks, Melbourne

Literature:
McCulloch 1969, pl.54; Topliss 1984, no.40

Louis Abrahams, nicknamed 'the Don',
painted at the Box Hill camp with Roberts
and McCubbin. This watercolour vividly
depicts the *plein airist* method of painting,
making his 'studio in the open air'[1]: an
artist, possibly Roberts, is shown at work
on a large canvas which is propped up
against a tree.

[1] Daplyn 1902, p.10.

TOM ROBERTS ▲
A quiet day on Darebin Creek, 1885
Oil on wood panel
26.4 x 34.8 cm
Signed and dated l.r.: Tom Roberts.85
Inscribed verso: 'A quiet day on Darebin
Creek/... Roberts.../ ...Ea Mel-
bourne/e-[a]fter the exhibition to Mrs/
[Wh]itelaw-Woronson Rd, St John's
Wood/ [L]ondon... to her order/Tom
Roberts'
Australian National Gallery
Purchased 1969

Provenance:
Mrs William Whitelaw, London; Wade,
New South Wales; Artamon Galleries,
Sydney 1969

Exhibitions:
In Roberts's studio, March 1886; *Colonial
and Indian Exhibition Catalogue of the Oil
Paintings and Water-Colour Drawings of
the Victorian Court*, London, 1886, no.9:
'Darebin Creek – Lent by the Artist'

Literature:
Age, 19 January 1886, p.6; *Once a Month*,
1 March 1886, p.265; Terry Ingram,
Financial Review, 7 September 1972;
McCulloch 1969, pl.4; Spate 1978, p.42;
Topliss 1985, no.49

Soon after his return from Europe,
Roberts organized painting trips with his
friends to areas of natural bush along the
Yarra River near Studley Park, close to the
city, such as Gardiner's Creek, Merri
Creek and Darebin Creek. Here he shows
a fellow artist at work, painting *en plein
air*. Such expeditions had already
occurred prior to Roberts's studies in
Europe; as McCubbin recalled:

> One Saturday afternoon Tom Roberts
> invited me to go sketching in Studley
> Park, he lived near the corner of Smith
> and Johnston St Collingwood. There
> was [*sic*] no trams in those days – just
> the old bus to the corner and a tramp of
> half an hour to the park. And there for
> the first time I got awakened to the
> beauties of Australian landscape. I
> remember that happy afternoon as a
> delightful memory. Mrs. Roberts
> Tom's mother said to me Well and
> what is your forte, my sons is Land-
> scape I said figure drawing. Well we
> had a splendid day and got wet
> through on the way back in a thunder
> storm.[1]

Roberts's choice of relatively dark and
close tones links this work stylistically
with the tradition of the *plein air* Barbizon
School in France, exemplified by Abram
Louis Buvelot and Julian Ashton in Melbourne.

[1] Galbally (ed.) 1979, p.74.

TOM ROBERTS ▶
The Artists' Camp, [c.1886]
Oil on canvas
46.1 x 60.9 cm
Signed l.l.: Tom Roberts.
National Gallery of Victoria
Felton Bequest 1943

Provenance:
Original owner unknown; Mrs Grace
Cook, Glen Iris, until 1943

Exhibitions:
*First Annual Exhibition of the Australian
Artists' Association*, Buxton's Gallery,
Melbourne, September 1886, no.34: 'The
Artists' Camp', illus.

Literature:
Argus, 7 September 1886, p.7; Hoff 1951,
p.127; McCulloch 1969, pl.74; Gleeson
1971, pl.29; Smith 1971, p.73; Finemore
1977, p.25; Galbally 1978, p.61; Burn
1980, pp.83, 94; Splatt & Bruce 1981,
pl.15; Topliss 1984, pp.20f.; Topliss 1985,
no.63; Astbury 1985, in press, pp.103, 167

The Artists' Camp commemorates the site
of David Houston's paddock at Box Hill
where Roberts, McCubbin and Abrahams
pitched camp late in 1885 to paint *en plein
air*. The selected location was only three
quarters of a mile from the Box Hill railway station and provided an area of natural bush to paint. The reasons for choosing
this site are unknown and no record exists
of a first meeting between the artists and
Mr Houston. It has been suggested that Dr
L.L. Smith, a local landowner and a patron
of Roberts, might have introduced them.[1]
Box Hill was no longer virgin bush by
1885. The arrival of the railway line in

1882 had increased its accessibility and considerable areas were under cultivation, however it still provided patches of natural vegetation comparatively close to the city. Roberts's biographer, R.H. Croll, claimed that the artist had worked there during the 1870s; and certainly there is a sense of nostalgia in Roberts's later description of the camp:

> Happy Box-Hill – the barked roof of the old people, Houstens [sic] – the land sylvan as it ever was – tea-tree along the creek – young blue gums over the flat bit alongside, and on the rise, our tent. The evenings after work – the chops perfect from the fire of gum-twigs – the 'good-night' of the jackies as the soft darkness fell – then talks round the fire, the 'Prof' (McCubbin) philosophic – we forgot everything, but the peace of it.[2]

His painting of the 'Prof' with Abrahams, nicknamed the 'Don', grilling chops, celebrates the friendship of the three young artists and their close familiarity with the bush. Such intimacy with nature was a prerequisite for *plein air* painting, according to the English exponent Stanhope Forbes, whom Roberts admired:

> It was a breath of fresh air in the tired atmosphere of the studios, and painters began to see that it needed more than an occasional visit to the country to get at the heart of its mysteries; that he who wished to solve them must live amongst the scenes he sought to render, and become thoroughly familiarised with every aspect of nature. Not only for the landscape painter . . . ; but equally for him who desired to study humanity in relation to its surroundings, was it essential that he should closely study every changing mood of out door life.[3]

The painting when first exhibited in 1886 was among those criticized by the press:

> It is interesting to watch the general leaning of our young artists and art students towards the French methods of landscape painting; their avoidance of too much definition of form and their disposition to secure striking effects by colour laid on in broad masses.[4]

Although in the context of Roberts's subsequent landscapes it is scarcely radical, the selection of a close-up view of the artists and tent and the absence of any panoramic vistas contrast with most previous Australian landscape conventions. Roberts's interest in the *plein air* painting of Bastien-Lepage and his followers is reflected in his choice of close tonal values, in the composition with its focus on the figures within a comparatively shallow space; and in the devices of tall thin trees fringing the composition, background 'screen' of vegetation and foreground details of specific flora – such as the gum sapling which became a motif of the Heidelberg School.

[1] Topliss 1984, p.21.
[2] Quoted by Moore 1934, I, p.70.
[3] Quoted by Fox & Greenacre 1979, p.16.
[4] *Argus*, 7 September 1886, p.7.

TOM ROBERTS ▶
A Summer Morning Tiff, 1886
Oil on canvas (on board)
76.3 x 51 cm
Signed l.l.: Tom Roberts
City of Ballarat Fine Art Gallery
Martha Pinkerton Bequest Fund 1943
For exhibition in Melbourne only

Provenance:
David Cook, at least 1888-93; subsequent
ownership unrecorded

Exhibitions:
*First Annual Exhibition of the Australian
Artists' Association*, Buxton's Gallery,
Melbourne, September 1886, no.30: 'A
Summer Morning Tiff'; *Centennial
International Exhibition, Official Guide to
the Picture Galleries and Catalogue of Fine
Arts*, Melbourne, 1888, Victorian Artists
Gallery, no.91: 'A Tiff – The property of
David Cook, Esq.'; *Victorian Artists'
Society Exhibition of Australian Art Past
and Present*, National Gallery of Victoria,
Melbourne, August 1893, no.23: 'A
Summer Morning Tiff 1888 [sic] – Lent by
David Cook'

Literature:
Argus, 7 September 1886, p.7; *Art
Journal*, London, January 1887, p.31;
Croll 1935, p.31; *Ballarat Fine Art Public
Gallery Association Bulletin*, 1946, p.2;
Hoff 1951, p.127; McCulloch 1969, pp.22,
154; Smith 1971, p.74; Gleeson 1971,
pl.30; Radford 1974, no.31; Hughes 1977,
p.57; Spate 1978, pp.45, 49-52; Burn 1980,
p.94; Splatt & Bruce 1981, p.30, pl.2;
Topliss 1985, no.66; Astbury 1985, in
press, pp.33f., pl.4

Mr Tom Roberts, a purely Australian
painter, sends 'A Summer Morning
Tiff', high and consistent in key, not
more than sufficiently realistic and telling its story directly and well.
– *The Art Journal*, January 1887

Only a word at the splitter's track, –
A thoughtless blunder.
She is fair and haughty, and answers
back,
So they part asunder
With a jerk he loosens the fastening
rein, –
And she turns her back with a fine
disdain.
Ah me! sigh the saplings, in sad refrain,
As she passes under.

Both the title of this painting and these
accompanying lines of verse, printed in
the 1886 exhibition catalogue, attest to
Roberts's interest in the narrative aspects
of the subject. The painting has striking
similarities with one entitled *A Tiff* by
Frank Cox, an English artist, which was
exhibited at the Royal Academy in 1878
and later published as an engraving.[1] A
letter written by Roberts to Lillie Williamson (his future wife) on 5 April 1886 states:
'McCubbin's sister [Harriet, also a student
at the Gallery School] stands for us in sunlight among some exquisite young white
firm saplings. She is a little downcast – up
the hill a youth in some state about to let
his horse through the slip panel – title not
yet decided – "a tiff" has been done before
– suppose "another tiff"'.[2] Nancy Elmhurst
Goode's recollection of work on *The Reconciliation*, [c.1887], a sequel to *A Summer Morning Tiff*, gives an interesting
account of the *plein air* camp and
Roberts's methods of painting such
scenes.[3] *The Reconciliation* (Castlemaine
Art Gallery and Historical Museum) is,
however, more academic and conventional than the earlier work. *A Summer
Morning Tiff* was one of Roberts's first
attempts to depict the specific qualities of
a 'familiar corner of nature' – Box Hill. It
includes the blue gum saplings known as
'boxwood' or 'red gum', native to Box Hill,
featured in the front of the canvas. It
reveals a development away from the
tonal contrasts Roberts employed earlier,
for example in *A quiet day on Darebin
Creek*, towards a system of related tonal
values where the colours were mixed on
the palette and applied as a final tone to
the canvas. James Smith considered that
'*Summer Morning Tiff* shows the influence of the Impressionists . . . their avoidance of too much definition of form and
their disposition to secure striking effects
by colour laid on in broad masses . . .' In
fact, the influence of Bastien-Lepage is
most clearly evident in this work: in the

study of tonal values, the raised horizon
line and the placement of the figure in the
landscape.

---

[1] LaTrobe Collection, State Library of
Victoria. Hoff Conder MS 9678.
Engraving and contemporary description
of *A Tiff* by Frank E. Cox:
Tis an oft-repeated scene of a well-
known drama that we have before us
here. A passing cloud is crossing the
summer sky, and but for its presence
all would be bright and happy. They
had met at the old trusting-place – the
gate at the turning of the lane – and
were conversing together, when some
unfortunate circumstance caused this
temporary storm. They need,
however, only glance at the spaniel to
receive sufficient reproof for their
folly. He is wondering in his canine
mind why his mistress has departed
thus hurriedly, and why she is not
accompanied, as usual by the young
squire. Duty and affection both call
upon him to follow his mistress; but he
did not understand the hasty word
which had caused the quarrel, and he
cannot comprehend all this 'to-do:' it
seems to him unreasonable, and
moreover he feels himself defrauded
of his customary evening walk, and he
does not like it. But we note that the
young man is looking round, half
repentant, to watch his beloved
depart; hoping that she will turn
towards him ere she disappears: and
glancing at her face, we see that
mingled with the pout of offended
dignity there is a look of sorrowful
penitence and a readiness to forgive
and forget. Both feel the truth of the
well-worn proverb, *Amantium irae
amoris integratio est*, and the old dog
will not be disappointed of his walk
after all. 'A Tiff' was exhibited at the
Royal Academy in 1878.
[2] Letter quoted by Topliss 1985.
[3] Quoted by Croll 1935, pp.23f.

FREDERICK McCUBBIN
Lost, 1886
Oil on canvas
115.8 x 73.7 cm
Signed l.l.: F. McCubbin/1886
Dated l.r.: 1886
Inscribed verso: 'McCubbin V.A.S.'
National Gallery of Victoria
Felton Bequest 1940

Provenance:
Professor Henry Laurie, Melbourne; by descent in the Laurie family; purchased from Mrs Eunice E. Laurie as 'Lost in the Bush' or 'The Lost Child'

Exhibitions:
Illustrated Catalogue of the Australian Artists' Association Summer Exhibition, Buxton's Gallery, Melbourne, March 1887, no.30: 'Lost – £52.10.0', illus.; *Centennial International Exhibition Official Guide to the Picture Galleries and Catalogue of Fine Arts*, Melbourne, 1888, Victorian Artists Gallery no.28: 'Lost – The property of Prof. Laurie'; *Victorian Artists' Society Exhibition of Australian Art Past and Present*, National Gallery of Victoria, Melbourne, August 1893, no.157: 'Lost – Lent by Mrs Laurie'

Literature:
Argus, 5 March 1887, p.14; *Australasian Supplement*, 19 March.1887; MacDonald 1916, p.58; *Catalogue of Paintings by the Late Frederick McCubbin*, Victorian Artists' Society Galleries, September-October 1921, no.59: 'Lost in the Bush – Lent by Courtesy of Dr H. Laurie'; Moore 1934, I, p.126; Hoff 1951, p.127; Hoff 1955, no.5; Gleeson 1969, pl.12; McCulloch 1969, pl.9; David Thomas 1969, pp.66ff.; Gleeson 1971, pl.18; Spate 1978, p.85; Astbury 1981, p.40; Galbally 1981, p.75, pl.13; Splatt & Bruce 1981, pl.16; Astbury 1985, in press, pl.27, pp.158ff.

Lost is one of McCubbin's earliest works to depict 'romantic' rather than literal aspects of pioneering life in Australia. It combines local history with the sentiment of Victorian narrative art; and with the style of much contemporary European Naturalist *plein air* work. It is his first known painting on the theme of the lost child: a sequel, entitled *Found* and exhibited in 1892, is known from photographs and his *Lost* of 1907 is now in the National Gallery of Victoria. Compositionally it is related to *Gathering Mistletoe*, also painted in 1886 (collection of Dorothy Mathews). The theme of children lost in the bush had a long literary and artistic tradition in Australia by this date. Henry Kingsley had immortalized it in *The Recollections of Geoffrey Hamlyn*, London, 1859. In 1864 distressing accounts of the three Duff children rescued after nine days in the bush received considerable media coverage. *The Illustrated Melbourne Post* of 22 September 1864 included an illustration by Nicholas Chevalier entitled 'Lost in the Bush'. William Strutt exhibited *The Little Wanderers* or *The Lost Track* at the Royal Academy, London, in 1865; and a contemporary literary version was *The Australian Babes in the Wood* of 1866. Samuel Thomas Gill's sketch of the Duff children, included in his *Australian Sketchbook*, was still widely circulated later in the 19th century. During the 1880s there were frequent references to children lost in the bush and the popular pantomime *Babes in the Wood* remained regular Christmas entertainment; McCubbin recalled seeing performances as a child. As late as 1901 the popular appeal of the theme continued, with publication of Henry Lawson's story 'The Babies in the Bush' in *Joe Wilson and His Mates*. *Lost* may well have been inspired by an almost contemporary incident which received extensive publicity in May 1885: when Clara Crosbie was found alive after three weeks lost in the bush near Lilydale. *The Australasian Sketcher* of 25 June 1885 included an illustration of her recovery.

Julian Ashton claimed to have suggested to McCubbin that he paint the life about him in the early 80s; and he later wrote that 'true historical painting consists in reproducing the scenes which lie around. . . ' (*The Centennial Magazine*, August 1889, p.31). In McCubbin's *Lost* the fate of the little girl is left ambiguous. As *The Argus* critic remarked, she simply 'constitutes the forlorn centre of a grove of saplings and an undergrowth of withered grass and scrub'. The influence of Roberts's theories of tonal values and enthusiasm for *plein air* painting are evident in the placement of the child's figure against a dense bush background with just a glimpse of blue-grey sky. The delicate tracery of branches and grasses in the foreground serves to heighten the feeling of isolation. Foreground details of foliage and flowers in sharp focus – a favourite compositional device in European Naturalist landscape – were also very commonly employed in black-and-white illustrations for journals of the day.

TOM ROBERTS
Twilight at Healesville, [c.1886]
Oil on cedar panel
35.3 x 24.7 cm
Inscribed verso: 'Twilight at Healesville by Tom Roberts. Given by artist to me in 19?1 Marcus Bryant'
Max Atkinson, Hobart

Provenance:
The artist to Marcus Bryant; Christie's, Sydney, October 1973, lot 423; Mr Neil Batt; private collection, Hobart

Literature:
Topliss 1985, no.88

This preliminary sketch of a man splitting wood is one of a number which Roberts painted in preparation for *Wood Splitters* and *End to a Career – an Old Scrub Cutter* of 1888. The sketch thus forms an essential part of the established process of picture-making to which Roberts had been exposed during his years at the Royal Academy. The poetic rendering of the twilight and smoke and the muted range of colours rapidly applied, points to the influence of Whistler and some English *plein airists*.

TOM ROBERTS
Wood Splitters, [c.1886]
Oil on canvas
61 x 91.8 cm
Signed l.l.: TOM ROBERTS
City of Ballarat Fine Art Gallery
Gift of the estate of J.R. Hartley 1961

Provenance:
George Lush (Director of the Kauri Timber Co.) March 1891; in his estate sale as 'Clearing', sold for 20 guineas (*The Age*, 2 September 1932); J.R. Hartley until 1961

Exhibitions:
The People's Palace Exhibition of Loan Collection of Pictures, Exhibition Building, Melbourne, March 1891, no.45: 'Wood Splitters – lent by George Lush, Esq.'

Literature:
Inson & Ward 1971, p.28; Spate 1978, pp.48, 85, 151; Topliss 1985, no.87; Astbury 1985, in press, pl.16, pp.103f.

While the choice of subject owes much to similar scenes of rural activity by French and English schools of direct *plein air* painting, Roberts's method of working through numerous preparatory sketches and his use of conventional poses for the workers reveals an acceptance of aspects of academic practice. The figure on the right with axe raised appeared with only slight modification in his subsequent painting on the theme *End to a Career – an Old Scrub-Cutter* which was exhibited in 1888. Works depicting the life of the selector had appeared earlier in Australian art. For example, S.T. Gill's *Timber Splitters* was included in the Victorian Jubilee Exhibition of 1884 and the selector's existence appeared frequently as the subject of illustrations in the black-and-white press. Roberts's painting was innovative, however, for its sympathetic portrayal of the rural worker in harmony with his environment. It was probably executed at Box Hill, much of which had been cleared in the 1870s but where timber splitting still occurred in some areas. Ron Radford has suggested that the title should be 'The Charcoal Burners', as this is what the men appear to be preparing for. The painting has also been previously titled 'The Splitters'.

FREDERICK McCUBBIN
Winter evening, Hawthorn, 1886
Oil on canvas
51 x 76 cm
Signed and dated l.r.: F.McCubbin/1886
Castlemaine Art Gallery and Historical
Museum
Gift of J.T. Tweddle 1926

Provenance:
Probably in *Australian Pictures Collected
by the late Louis Abrahams*, Decoration
Co., Melbourne, 15 August 1919, lot 19:
'Winter Evening at Hawthorn'; J.T.
Tweddle 1926

Exhibitions:
Probably *Illustrated Catalogue of the
Australian Artists' Association Summer
Exhibition*, Buxton's Gallery, Melbourne,
March 1887, no.36: 'Heath Paddock,
Hawthorn – £21'

Literature:
Argus, 5 March 1887, p.14; *Australasian
Supplement*, 19 March 1887; Splatt &
Bruce 1981, p.29, pl.17

> I remember as if it were yesterday
> standing one evening a long time ago,
> watching the sunset glowing in the
> trees... and it was largely through
> Buvelot that I realised the beauty of
> the scene.
> – Frederick McCubbin, 1916

Winter evening, Hawthorn was painted in
1886 when McCubbin was living in Hawthorn, a suburb close enough to Melbourne to provide a distant view of the
metropolis whilst still incorporating areas
of rusticity such as this. It is among his
earliest treatments of the rural worker as a
natural component of the landscape, in
the tradition of Jean François Millet. It was
probably exhibited in 1887 as *Heath Paddock, Hawthorn*, described in *The Argus*
as 'a clever bit of nature near Hawthorn'.

JOHN MATHER
By the Sea, 1886
Also known as 'Picnic Point,
near Brighton'
Oil on canvas
40.8 x 76.2 cm
Signed l.l.: J. Mather 3.86
City of Ballarat Fine Art Gallery
Gift of James Oddie 1886

Provenance:
The artist to James Oddie; presented to
the Ballarat Fine Art Gallery, July 1886

Exhibitions:
*The Seventh Annual Exhibition of the Art
Society of New South Wales*, Sydney, April
1886, no.34: 'By the Sea – £31.10.0', illus.

Literature:
J.H. Powell, *Descriptive Catalogue Ballarat*, March 1891, Oddie Collection
no.15, as 'Picnic Point, near Brighton';
Radford 1974, no.24; Topliss 1984, no.99

> Mr Mather looks Nature straight in the
> face, so to speak, and presents her in
> the bright apparel she loves to wear,
> especially in the lucid atmosphere of
> Australia.
> – *Table Talk*, 27 April 1888

Mather's *By the Sea* prefigures Roberts's
painting of Mentone completed in the following year. The subject was a popular
one and a view of Brighton beach from
almost the same vantage point by Daplyn
was also included in the Seventh Annual
Exhibition of the Art Society of New South
Wales in 1886. Mather's picture is more
conventional and panoramic in its scope
than Roberts's version and reveals closer
affinities with the seascapes of Buvelot
with whom he was associated. Later
depictions of Brighton beach by Mather,
completed in a higher key, are indebted to
the influence of Roberts, Streeton and
Conder with whom he was associated at
Eaglemont.

TOM ROBERTS ▲
The Sunny South, [c.1887]
Oil on canvas
30.8 x 61.4 cm
National Gallery of Victoria
Felton Bequest 1940

Provenance:
Original owner unknown, probably
Professor Henry Laurie; Mrs Eunice E.
Laurie, Melbourne 1940

Exhibitions:
*Catalogue of the Australian Artists'
Association Summer Exhibition*, Buxton's
Gallery, Melbourne, March 1887, no.9:
'The Sunny South – £21', illus.; probably
*Victorian Artists' Society Exhibition of
Australian Art Past and Present*, National
Gallery of Victoria, Melbourne, August
1893, no.128: 'Summer 1888 – Lent by
Mrs Laurie'

Literature:
Argus, 5 March 1887, p.14; McCulloch
1969, pp.30,154; Smith 1971, p.99;
Gleeson 1971, pl.32; Finemore 1977, p.25;
Spate 1978, pp.50f., pl.11; Splatt & Bruce
1981, pl.28; Topliss 1985, no.85

> Mr Tom Roberts's versatile and indus-
> trious pencil has produced . . . 'The
> Sunny South', representing some bath-
> ers, who are about to emerge from the
> shadows of the ti-tree to plunge into
> the sunshine and the sea.
> – *The Argus*, 5 March 1887

The Sunny South is probably one of the
earliest Australian paintings of the nude in
landscape and a celebration of the pleasures of the artists' camp at Mentone in the
summer of 1886-87. Swimming in the
open, in the Yarra River or the sea, was
common practice in the mid-19th century
undertaken primarily for the purpose of
washing.[1] By-laws were later passed to
regulate sea bathing, by dividing the foreshore into segregated areas and stipulat-
ing specific hours allowable for each sex.
In 1887 men were prohibited from bathing in the open between eight o'clock in
the morning and seven in the evening;
whilst the law remained until 1911, its
enforcement was not strictly policed. The
term 'Sunny South', a tribute to Australia
as a land of health and prosperity, appears
to have been in common usage by 1887;

for example, a book about Australia entitled *Glimpses of the Sunny South* by H. Carmichael was published that year in London.[2]

[1] Bate 1962, p.808. See also Geoffrey Dutton, *Sun, Sea, Surf and Sand – the Myth of the Beach*, Oxford University Press, Melbourne, 1985.
[2] Helen Topliss also notes that a melodrama called 'Sunny South' had played in Melbourne in 1883. Topliss 1985, p.13.

TOM ROBERTS ▲
Mentone, 1887
Oil on canvas (mounted on board)
50.8 x 76.5 cm
Signed and dated l.r.: TOM ROBERTS. 87
l.l.: MENTONE
National Gallery of Victoria
Purchased with the assistance of a special grant from the Government of Victoria 1979

Provenance:
Original owner probably B. Sniders, St Kilda (partner in the Abrahams family tobacco business); late 1920s, Mr F.W. Thompson, Kew; to his son, H.W.L. Thompson, until 1970; Jack Manton, Melbourne

Exhibitions:
Probably *Illustrated Catalogue of the Australian Artists' Association Summer Exhibition*, Buxton's Gallery, Melbourne, March 1887, no.23: 'Slumbering Sea, Mentone – £31.10.0'; *Victorian Artists' Society Exhibition of Australian Art Past and Present*, National Gallery of Victoria, Melbourne, August 1893, no.158: 'Mentone – Lent by B. Sniders, Esq.'

Literature:
Argus, 5 March 1887, p.14; Gleeson 1969, pl.15; Gleeson 1971, pl.31, p.94; Radford 1974, no.31; Spate 1978, pl.10; McCaughey 1979, p.40, p.112; Splatt & Bruce 1981, pl.26; Topliss 1985, no.79

Roberts's *Mentone* shows a group of people at ease with their environment. It is probably the painting described by *The Argus* in 1887 as 'a broadly painted coast scene full of light and warmth and colour'. This sense of intimacy is rather different from most earlier Australian beach scenes, such as John Mather's more traditional *By the Sea* of 1886. As the theme of a boating party was popular in contemporary European art, some recent writers have focused on the painting's links with French Impressionist works of similar subjects. Roberts's interests were, however, more closely allied to the European *plein air* tradition – a concern to depict the specific effects of light and the characteristics of the locale – than the French Impressionists' painterly analysis of light for its own sake.

FREDERICK McCUBBIN ▲
Moyes Bay, Beaumaris, 1887
Oil on canvas
58.6 x 91.6 cm
Signed l.r.: F. McCubbin
Art Gallery of Western Australia
Acquired through the Great Australian
Paintings Appeal with funds presented by
the Swan Brewery Co. Ltd 1978

Provenance:
Theodore Fink, Melbourne; Mrs Nina
Sheppard, Melbourne, by 1955; Mrs G.M.
Chartres, Melbourne; The Joshua
McClelland Print Room, Melbourne, June
1978

Exhibitions:
*Australian Artists' Association, Winter
Exhibition Catalogue*, Buxton's Gallery,
Melbourne, September 1887, no.33: 'The
Shore – £25', illustrated with caption
'Moyes Bay, Beaumaris'; *Centennial
International Exhibition Official Guide to
the Picture Galleries and Catalogue of Fine
Arts*, Victorian Artists Gallery no.18:
'Beach at Mentone – The property of
Theo. Fink, Esq.'

Literature:
Argus, 7 October 1887, p.5; *Herald*, 26
September 1921; Hoff 1955, no.7; Radford
1974, no.22; *Art and Australia*, September
1978, p.14; *Financial Review*, 15 June
1978; Galbally 1981, p.55, pl.8; Pearce
1983, no.14

There is a breezy out-of-door feeling
about Mr. McCubbin's *The Shore*
[alternative title], the tone of the picture strikes us as not warm enough for
the season indicated by the attire of the
figures. Although the work is impressionist in its general character, the
execution of the broken rock, shingle,
herbage, and pools of water in the foreground betokens attention to detail.
– *The Argus*, 7 October 1887

This delightfully informal *plein air* beach
scene was painted during the summer of
1887 when McCubbin shared a cottage at
Mentone with Roberts, Abrahams and
Streeton. McCubbin later recalled the
influences on his work during that summer, when Roberts taught him to see
'glorious colour'. The bright light and subject matter of this scene are certainly comparable with Roberts's *Mentone*, painted
at the same time. McCubbin's view is more
intimate, with just a hint of sentiment. The
focus of his painting is an elegant woman
watching over the activities of a small
child with a toy sailing boat.

JANE SUTHERLAND ▲
Obstruction, 1887
Oil on canvas
41 x 31 cm
City of Ballarat Fine Art Gallery
L.J. Wilson Bequest Fund 1976

Provenance:
A. Maclean, Esq. 1890; subsequent
ownership unknown

Australian Artists' Association, Winter Exhibition, Melbourne, October 1887, no.32: 'Obstruction – £10.10.0', illus.; *Exhibition of Works of Victorian Artists and a Loan Collection of Pictures*, Exhibition Trustees and Victorian Artists' Society, Exhibition Building, Melbourne, December 1890, no.126: 'Obstruction, Near Box Hill – Contributed by A.Maclean, Esq.'

Literature:

Argus, 7 October 1887, p.9; Lindsay & Rosewarne 1977, no.3; Splatt & Bruce 1981, pl.66

> Miss Jane Sutherland's 'Obstruction' is an improvement on her previous work. The progress of a small state-scholar to school has been barred by an aggressive cow on the other side of the fence, and the child is uncertain whether to advance or retire. The group of trees in the centre of the picture, and the little girl's figure, are very nicely treated.
> – *The Argus*, 7 October 1887

Obstruction was painted at the artists' Box Hill camp. Jane Sutherland had studied with McCubbin at the Gallery School and shared his interest in portraying children in the landscape. This was a popular theme favoured by many 19th century women artists – Berthe Morisot and Mary Cassatt in France, for example – and one which Jane Sutherland pursued in her paintings of the 1890s.

TOM ROBERTS ▲
'Evening, when the quiet east flushes faintly at the sun's last look', [1887-88]
Oil on canvas
51 x 76.6 cm
Signed l.l.: TOM ROBERTS
National Gallery of Victoria
W.H. Short Bequest 1944

Provenance:

Probably Louis Abrahams until *Australian Pictures collected by the late Louis Abrahams*, Decoration Co., Melbourne, 15 August 1919, lot 8: 'Landscape' [18 guineas], described in *The Herald* as 'a charming moonrise landscape which belongs to the Box Hill period'; subsequent ownership unrecorded; acquired by the National Gallery of Victoria as 'Landscape – twilight'

Exhibitions:

Victorian Artists' Society Catalogue of Autumn Exhibition, 'Grosvenor' Gallery, National Gallery of Victoria, Melbourne, May 1888, no.5: '"Evening, when the quiet east flushes faintly at the sun's last look" – £30'; probably *Victorian Artists' Society Exhibition of Australian Art Past and Present*, National Gallery of Victoria, August 1893, no.30: 'The After Glow 1887 – Lent by L. Abrahams'

Literature:

Age, 30 April 1888, p.6; *Argus*, 30 April 1888, p.11; 16 August 1919; *Herald*, 12 August 1919; Finemore 1977, p.40; Spate 1978, pp.12, 50, 54ff., pl.13; Splatt & Bruce 1981, pl.38; Topliss 1985, no.81

> His 'Evening, when the quiet east flushes faintly at the sun's last look' represents the full moon rising in a sky of warm pink over a landscape of considerable extent, which has apparently been parched by a hot summer.
> – *The Argus*, 30 April 1888

In this work the harmony of muted pinks is primarily the result of careful observation of changing light rather than a calculated aesthetic attitude. As Streeton wrote: 'Before 1886 we were all rather attracted by the conventional aspect of the brilliant colour of the western sky at sunset. Roberts was the first to point out the exquisite and delicate variation in colour and tone of the eastern sky at sunset, and the rosy flush of the afterglow, our nearest approach to twilight in the northern hemisphere'.[1] *Evening, when the quiet east flushes faintly at the sun's last look* was included in the first exhibition of the Victorian Artists' Society, in May 1888, with other twilight scenes by McCubbin, Walter Withers, John Ford Paterson and Streeton (*Settler's Camp*, for example). Many contemporary paintings bore similarly long poetic titles: such as Paterson's *'Light Thickens, and the Crow makes Wing to the Distant Wood'* of 1887 (from Shakespeare's *Macbeth*, II,ii,45) and Withers's *Declining Rays* which was accompanied by lines from Shelley.

[1] Quoted by Croll 1935, p.16.

TOM HUMPHREY
The Way to School, [1888]
Oil on canvas
101 x 60.5 cm
Signed l.l.: Tom Humphrey
Warrnambool Art Gallery
Purchased 1889

Provenance:
The artist

Exhibitions:
Victorian Artists' Society Winter Exhibition, 'Grosvenor Gallery', National Gallery of Victoria, Melbourne, May 1889, no.55: 'The Way to School – £31.10.0', illus.

Literature:
Argus, 15 May 1889, p.9; Hall 1979, no.2; Splatt & Bruce 1981, pp.101,105; Topliss 1984, no.43
Previously known as 'Springtime'

Although Humphrey was still working as a photographer in the city during the later 1880s, he probably joined the group at Box Hill whenever he had a free weekend: according to *The Argus*, he was 'a clever member of the little coterie of young artists'. His schoolgirl carrying her lunch basket is very like the child in Jane Sutherland's *Obstruction* and his sundappled path leading through tall grass and gum saplings echoes Roberts's *Summer Morning Tiff*, painted at Box Hill in a previous summer. *The Way to School*, one of Humphrey's finest works, was amongst the first Australian purchases by the Warrnambool Gallery.

ARTHUR STREETON
Settler's Camp, 1888
Oil on canvas
86.5 x 112.5 cm
Signed and dated l.r.: Arthur Streeton/88
The Robert Holmes à Court Collection

Provenance:

Charles Raymond Staples, Melbourne, 1888, probably until October 1891; private collection, New South Wales; until Leonard Joel, Melbourne, 24 July 1985, lot 100; Robert Holmes à Court, Perth

Exhibitions:

Victorian Artists' Society, Catalogue of Autumn Exhibition, 'Grosvenor Gallery', National Gallery of Victoria, Melbourne, April 1888, no.16: 'Settler's Camp – £52.10.0', illus.; *Centennial International Exhibition, Official Guide to the Picture Galleries and Catalogue of Fine Arts*, Melbourne, 1888, Victorian Artists Gallery no.3: 'Settler's Camp – The property of C.R. Staples, Esq.'

Literature:

Table Talk, 27 April 1888, p.2; *Argus*, 30 April 1888, p.11; 10 May 1888, p.8; *Age*, 30 April 1888, p.6; Moore 1934, I, p.71; Streeton 1935, no.37; Croll 1946, p.4; Galbally 1979, no.14, pp.11, 14; Astbury 1985, in press, pp.132f.
Reproduced by courtesy of Mrs Oliver Streeton

> Mr Arthur Streeton's 'Settler's Camp'... is a poetical interpretation of a prosaic passage in the daily life of one of the pioneers of agricultural settlement. A free selector, who has pitched his tent on the outskirts of a forest, in Gippsland, let us say, has just lit the fire for his evening meal, and through a narrow vista the light of the departing day looks in and almost transfigures the homely surroundings of the lonely and self-reliant man.
> – *The Argus*, 30 April 1888

During the 1880s, images of selectors clearing the land – 'the pioneers of agricultural settlement' – and the vicissitudes of bush life became staple copy for the black-and-white illustrated press. On 25 November 1885, for example, *The Illustrated Australian News* presented a page of 'Incidents in the life of a Selector'. Local photographers also documented this rapidly passing phase of Australian history: such as Nicholas Caire, in his collection of *Gippsland Scenery*. Many painters essayed the theme. Julian Ashton and Alfred Daplyn both exhibited 'pioneer' subjects; and conventionally picturesque camps, homesteads and settlers were produced by J.A. Turner, Henricus van den Houten, J.H. Carse and numerous other illustrative artists.[1] Streeton himself had painted *Australian December, Selector's First Crop* in 1887. His *Settler's Camp*, however, painted in the centenary year of 1888, differs from these precedents in its close-up focus on prosaic reality – as *The Argus* critic observed. A writer in *Table Talk* admired the 'deep screen of dark gum trees' forming a backdrop for the solitary figure. Comparison with the small engraved reproduction in the Victorian

NO.	TITLE.	NAME.	PRICE.
16	Settler's Camp... ...	... *A. Streeton* ...	52 10 0

No. 16.   A. STREETON.

Engraving in *Victorian Artists' Society Catalogue of Autumn Exhibition*, April 1888, no.16
State Library of Victoria

Artists' Society exhibition catalogue of April 1888 shows that Streeton originally intended to include another figure, seated outside the tent. (The drawings for these catalogue illustrations were presumably made in the artists' studios some weeks before the exhibition.) Examination of the finished canvas suggests that he began to paint in the second 'settler', but changed his mind. Perhaps he was running short of time, for this was his largest and most ambitious painting to date! More probably he realized that by focusing on a single foreground figure – 'the lonely and self-reliant man' – in the silent darkening bush, he could strengthen the dramatic and romantic elements of his theme. Roberts's *End to a Career – an Old Scrub Cutter*, painted and exhibited at the same time, also showed an old bushman alone but, in this case, hard at work.

Although *The Argus* critic suggested Gippsland in eastern Victoria, as the setting of *Settler's Camp*, Streeton was actually working at Box Hill with Roberts, McCubbin and Louis Abrahams during 1888. (Many contemporary pioneering images, including Caire's photographs, were indeed set in the forests of Gippsland.) In fact the romantically twilit *Settler's Camp* was almost certainly painted in Streeton's studio rather than *en plein air* – daylight being a prerequisite for painting out-of-doors. At the Victorian Artists' Society exhibition it was hung together with and compared very favourably with similar crepuscular woodland landscapes by John Ford Paterson and McCubbin.[2] Its sale to Charles

Raymond Staples, real estate magnate and soon 'the largest speculator on the Stock Exchange of Melbourne', enabled Streeton to leave his apprenticeship with Troedel and Co. and thus devote himself full-time to painting.

[1] See Astbury 1985, in press, especially pp.132ff.
[2] *Argus*, 30 April 1888, p.11. Paterson's *Entrance to the Bush* showed 'a cart track in a dense forest, where the undergrowth is enveloped in gloom, and the dying light of day is just visible through the tall shafts of the columnar trees'. In McCubbin's *Twilight* 'the radiance of the sunset is rapidly fading out of the western sky facing the spectator; and the whole landscape is filled with a sentiment of stillness, seclusion and repose'.

J.C.

FANNY H. BARBOUR
'Jottings', 1887-88
LaTrobe Collection, State Library of Victoria MS 8746
Presented by Mrs L.D. Bayer 1970

Miss Fanny Barbour's illustrated 'Jottings' provide a delightfully personal glimpse of colonial life in the 1880s. The diary begins on 13 July 1887 in Bundaberg, Queensland, where twenty-two year old Fanny is staying with her elder sister and brother-in-law (the local bank manager). Four months later she is back in East Melbourne. She takes painting lessons from Loureiro and visits his young Tasmanian wife in Kew; joins picnics and sketching excursions to Heidelberg, Brighton, Sandringham and Daylesford; visits Government House; admires McCubbin's work at the Australian Artists' Association ('I don't think Tom Robarts [sic] has improved... McCubbin said one of Streeton's was the best in the room, didn't like it'); reviews the European pictures imported for the Earl of Buckinghamshire's 'Grosvenor Gallery' exhibition; and recalls nostalgically her country childhood at 'Gundowring'. Later she meets Charles Conder, who draws a cheerful picnic group at Mount Macedon in her pocket sketchbook (now in a private collection). Other friends include the artists Arthur and Emma Minnie Boyd, the Springthorpes, A'Becketts and the Ritchies of 'Blythvale'; and other families who actively supported the Heidelberg artists at this time. In 1889 Fanny and her mother each purchased one picture at the 9 by 5 Impression Exhibition.

J.C.

MARVELLOUS MELBOURNE

Jane Clark

It is a long way from the slopes of Mount Helicon to the valley of the Yarra Yarra, and there are such obvious differences between the Vale of Tempe and Pegleg Gully that it might have been thought hopeless to expect the Muses to round the Cape and visit Australia. But, fortunately, there are clear proofs that it is not hopeless . . .

– *The Melbourne University Review*, 24 December 1885

By the time of Australia's centenary decade 'refinements and culture, progress and prosperity' were visible everywhere.[1] The Centennial Exhibition opened in Melbourne with great pomp and pageantry on 1 August 1888. Displays covered thirty-three acres: including the country's largest assemblage of fine art to date – English, Continental and Australian. Within a week more than eighty thousand citizens had filed through the Exhibition Building.

The National Gallery of Victoria was also a 'popular resort of the city', as a writer for *The Argus* witnessed one Saturday afternoon:

> Dense crowds of people might be seen gathering on every hand, all armed with catalogues and eagerly discussing the prospects of Australian art . . . Indeed the popularity of art may be described as second only to that of football and negro minstrelsy, and well above cricket, or even land sales.[2]

Business was booming. Colonial society was more sophisticated than ever before. Collections of contemporary paintings were shipped out by London dealers hoping to persuade the wealthy squatters to invest their fortunes in art. The Anglo-Australian Society's exhibition in October 1885 even included an *avant-garde* work by Whistler, *A Note in Blue and Green* – which was, however, not appreciated by the Melbourne critics.[3] A number of more conventional pictures were acquired by various regional galleries from the Earl of Buckinghamshire's 'Grosvenor Gallery' show two years later.

Foreign artists in person were also attracted by the boom economy, many finding employment as illustrators for *The Picturesque Atlas of Australasia* and similar centenary publications. John Mather told *Table Talk* that the colony's leading portraitists were Messrs Walton, Roberts, Loureiro and Folingsby – all academically trained in Europe and now receiving the most prestigious local commissions. Loureiro, who had studied in Oporto, Lisbon, Rome, Paris and London, also painted decorative schemes for the drawing rooms and ball-rooms of various mansions newly erected in 'marvellous Melbourne'. The Governor, Sir Henry Loch, went so far as to declare:

> Victoria is the Italy of these Southern Seas, and, like Venice of old is destined to become the Nursing Mother of the Arts as well as the Mistress of Commerce. It is simply impossible to overestimate the importance of the influence exercised by art in refining and elevating the tastes of a young and thriving community like our own.[4]

Above all, there was a new sense of artistic *camaraderie* amongst the local 'brothers of the brush'. Tom Roberts was one of the 'expert advisers' on the design of Grosvenor Chambers – purpose-built artists' studios opened at the fashionable top end of Collins Street early in 1888; his neighbours there soon included Walton, Louis Abrahams, Phil May, the Misses Sutherland, Southern and Price and the sculptor Percival Ball.[5] Roberts initiated a series of *conversazioni* at which 'the latest French and other art journals were inspected, singing and artistic conversation indulged in'.[6] In 1886 he had been a founding member of the Australian Artists' Association: made up of professional (and predominantly *plein air*) painters breaking away from the Victorian Academy of Arts which, they felt, was dominated by amateurs and laymen (one contemporary called it the 'showroom of a "pot boiler" manufactory'). When the two rival art societies were eventually reconciled and amalgamated in 1888 as the Victorian Artists' Society, Roberts was elected first president.[7]

Roberts encouraged his fellow artists to woo potential buyers by raising their own social profile. In Sydney he told the artist D.H. Souter:

> There is no occasion, dear boy, for an artist to be a boor. A man may be able to paint decently well and also know how to comport himself in good society. Besides, you don't as a rule sell your stuff to people who rent cottages at seventeen and six a week: Business, my dear boy, business.[8]

In April 1889 members of the Victorian Artists' Society decided

Cartoon of 'Overgrown Melbourne', in *Truth*,
29 March 1884
LaTrobe Collection, State Library of Victoria

to hold a 'Studio Wednesday' – 'following the London custom of throwing open the studio to visitors on a certain day for the inspection of pictures prior to the public exhibition. . . All the Studios looked bright and attractive, but Grosvenor Chambers was especially *en fete*'.[9] Roberts attended Government House receptions; his friend Roger Falls painted pictures whilst cruising Port Phillip Bay aboard Lord Brassey's private yacht. In 1889 Roberts became secretary of the 'Arts and Letters' section of the Australian Association for Advancement of Science whose membership included some of Melbourne's leading intellectual figures.[10] When he organized the thoroughly successful 9 by 5 Impression Exhibition, together with Streeton, Conder, Richardson and McCubbin in August that year, the spicy aura of controversy was as necessary a public drawcard as the fashionable gallery decor. Some of the local artists might be beginning to look askance at the enthusiastic young group who had made their headquarters at Heidelberg; but, as *Table Talk* remarked, they already had 'champions among men [and women] with intellectual gifts of the highest kind'.[11]

[1] H.T. Burgess, *The Year Book of Australia*, 1888; quoted by Astbury 1981, p.26. See also Maya V. Tucker, 'Centennial Celebrations 1888', *Australia 1888* 7, April 1981, pp.11ff.
[2] 'Animated Canvas', *The Argus*, 5 May 1888 (by 'Daemon').
[3] *Argus*, 26 October 1885, p.7. Whistler was evidently persuaded to contribute to this exhibition by his expatriate Australian 'disciple', Mortimer Menpes. These exhibitions were invaluable visual experience for local artists, such as Streeton and McCubbin, who had never left Australia; some overseas dealers were nevertheless accused – probably with some justification – of swamping 'the colonial markets with the sweepings of the English Studios'.
[4] 'Art Culture in Victoria', *Table Talk*, 18 March 1886, p.9.
[5] *Table Talk*, 27 April 1888, p.12.
[6] *Table Talk*, 22 June 1888, p.9.
[7] A first meeting of the 'breakaway' group was evidently held in August 1885, in the studio which Loureiro shared with Nerli and Catani (*Australasian Art Review*, 1 December 1899, p.23). They met at Buxton's Art Gallery to discuss an exhibition (*Argus*, 2 June 1886, p.7); the inaugural 'A.A.A.' exhibition was opened by the Governor in September 1886. See also *The Argus*, 12 March 1888, p.11 and 14 March 1888, p.5. These 'institutional reforms' were probably largely inspired by similar moves by European artists; for example, the reorganization of the French Salon in 1881 and foundation of the New English Art Club in 1886.
[8] Quoted by Croll 1935, pp.40f.
[9] *Table Talk*, 26 April 1889, p.5.
[10] *Table Talk*, 26 December 1889; see also 7 June 1889, p.5. Conder's uncle was one of the council members (*Melbourne University Review*, 31 August 1888, p.91).
[11] *Table Talk*, 23 August 1889, p.4.

JOHN PETER RUSSELL ▲
Portrait of Dr William Maloney, 1887
Oil on canvas
48.5 x 37 cm
Signed, dated and inscribed along lower
edge: AMITIE   WILL   MALONEY
MEDICUS/J P RUSSELL PICTOR/JULY
1887/PARIS
Verso: oil sketch
National Gallery of Victoria
Purchased 1943
For exhibition in Melbourne only

Provenance:
Miss A. Hardenack, Melbourne 1943

Literature:
Gleeson 1971, pl.72; Galbally 1977, no.59,
pp.11, 41, pl.xv; Smith 1977, pl.86

Russell probably met Maloney for the first
time in London, where both were students: Russell at the Slade Art School and
'the little Doctor' studying medicine.[1] During the summer of 1883 they joined Tom
Roberts and Russell's architect brother for
a walking tour in Spain.

It was proposed that the artists should
make sketches, Maloney recalled, 'Mr
Percy Russell should study the architecture and advise on it, and that I should do
the literary work'. This wonderful portrait
was painted later in Paris; during the period of Russell's greatest personal and artistic development. For three years at
Cormon's *atelier* he was known as 'a big
Australian who had become notable
among art students in Paris by his athletic
prowess in a boxing club he had formed'.[2]
He came into contact with some of the
most progressive figures in French art –
van Gogh, Rodin, Bernard, Anquetin and
Monet. Gradually he began to work more
freely and to heighten the colour of his
paintings. Dr Maloney's bright pink and

white shirt is lit from above, with blue
shadows amongst the folds of fabric. The
light causes greenish shadows about his
eyes; and emphasizes his almost truculent
pose, with arms folded nonchalantly
across the back of a chair. In the background, a bronze-coloured scroll decorated with oriental characters shows
Russell's awareness of the growing fashion for Japanese art and its influence on
contemporary French painting. Maloney
probably took the portrait with him when
he left Paris; its inscription was borne out
by a lifelong friendship between artist and
sitter. He returned to Australia and, in
1890, founded the Maloney Medical Institute in Elizabeth Street and entered politics as M.L.A. for West Melbourne. Russell
wrote to Tom Roberts from Paris: 'Say T R,
Will Maloney is honest, with a surprising
youthful honesty and will do heaps of
good for Australian politics. Can't you
keep him from going off his head? impreg-
nate him with some of that hard common
sense of yours'.[3] In 1897 Russell sent out to
Australia a large painting of his wife at
Belle-Ile, inscribed 'To Friend Will Maloney...' And the friendship was resumed
with all its old intimacy when the artist
finally returned home himself and settled
in Sydney in the 1920s.[4]

[1] Maloney arrived in 1880. Russell
enrolled at the Slade on 5 January 1881.
[2] Hartrick 1939, p.39. The earliest known
portrait from Russell's years in Paris is a
profile head of Maloney dated 1885, see
Galbally 1977, nos 30-2.
[3] c. 1891. Printed in Galbally 1977, p.95.
[4] Galbally, op.cit., p.11.

◀TOM ROBERTS
Mrs. L.A. Abrahams, 1888
Oil on canvas
40.8 x 35.9 cm
Signed and dated l.l.: Tom Roberts 1888
National Gallery of Victoria
Purchased 1946

Provenance:
Mr and Mrs Louis Abrahams; probably in
*Australian Pictures Collected by the late
Louis Abrahams*, Decoration Co., Mel-
bourne, 15 August 1919, lot 9: 'Tom
Roberts – Interior with Figure'; subse-
quent ownership unrecorded

Exhibitions:
*Victorian Artists' Society Catalogue of
Spring Exhibition*, Melbourne, November
1888, no.31: 'Mrs. L.A. Abrahams';
probably *Victorian Artists' Society
Exhibition of Australian Art Past and
Present*, National Gallery of Victoria,
Melbourne, August 1893, no.167: 'Portrait
– Tom Roberts – Lent by L. Abrahams,
Esq.'

Literature:
Age, 16 November 1888, p.8; Finemore
1977, pp.44ff., pl.XII; Spate 1978, p.115,
pl.31; Galbally 1980, p.131; Lane 1984,
p.11; Downer & Phipps 1985, no.174;
Topliss 1985, no.111

By 1888 *Table Talk* considered it was
'especially as a portrait painter that Mr
Roberts has made his name' (31 August,
p.2). This delightful small portrait may
have been a wedding present, for Roberts
had been a witness at the marriage of
Golda Figa Brasch and Louis Abrahams,
'cigar manufacturer of Carlton', in Sydney
on 21 March that year; Abrahams was
also, of course, a fellow artist. Mrs Abrahams liked to accompany her husband on
excursions to Heidelberg and later she
also exhibited as an amateur painter.[1]
Here she is probably seated in a mezzanine room in the recently opened Grosvenor Chambers in Collins Street, where
both Roberts and Abrahams had 'studios
with ante-rooms attached' in 1888.[2] Her
elegant figure makes a subtle study of
dark tones on dark, clearly influenced by
Roberts's admiration of Whistler. The setting is thoroughly and fashionably Aesthetic: a Japanese fan and a paper lantern
hang over the door, from which Whistlerian 'artistic muslin drapery' has been
pulled aside; the oriental cane chair, tray
and cloth, the ebonized 'Old English'
table, the fur rug and Ali Baba jar full of
pampas grass are all prerequisites of an
1880s Aesthetic décor. Roberts was a
prime mover in popularizing the style in
Melbourne and this may well be his own
studio ante-room 'beautifully decorated
with flowers', where afternoon tea was

served to visitors 'in dainty little cups, together with the crispest of crisp biscuits'.[3] Not long after Mrs Abrahams's sitting, Roberts held one of his much publicized 'Studio Wednesday' open days there:

> Mr Roberts' studio – which is one of the best in Melbourne – was most picturesquely arranged. . . [with] cunningly placed draperies in rich soft tones, broken here and there by bunches of dry reeds and grasses. Some kind friends had sent a profusion of lovely flowers. . . and as these were clustered together in great masses, and kept away from the paintings they lit up the room without impairing the colouring of the pictures, and so produced a most charming effect.[4]

[1] First Australian Exhibition of Women's Work, Exhibition Building, Melbourne, 1907, Non-competitive Exhibits, pp.183ff.
[2] Table Talk, 21 April 1888, p.12.
[3] Table Talk, 27 April 1888, p.2. Roberts's studio is also described in Melbourne Punch, 6 May 1889, p.300.
[4] Table Talk, 26 April 1889, p.5.

TOM ROBERTS ▶
Madame Pfund, [1887]
Oil on canvas
142 x 98.5 cm
National Gallery of Victoria
Purchased 1948

Provenance:
Madame Pfund; Dr Robert Loosli (her nephew); Miss Kathleen E. Loosli (his daughter)

Exhibitions:
Australian Artists' Association Winter Exhibition, Melbourne, October 1887, no.46: 'Madame Pfund', illus.

Literature:
Table Talk, 23 September 1887, p.11; 14 October 1887, p.11; Age, 27 September 1887, p.6; Argus, 7 October 1887, p.9; Illustrated Sydney News, 1 August 1891, p.6; Spate 1978, p.107; Topliss 1985, no.92

> The verisimilitude of Tom Roberts's portrait of a lady will be immediately recognised by numbers of young persons of her own sex, whose minds and characters she has assisted to form, while the fine technique of the work will be not less appreciated and admired.
> – The Argus, 7 October 1887

Madame Elise Pfund, née Tschaggeny (1833-1921), had come to Melbourne from Switzerland in September 1863 accompanying Lady Darling, wife of the newly appointed Governor; she married James Pfund, Victorian Government Architect, that same year. In 1867 she established 'Oberwyl', an elegant school for young ladies, in Burnett Street, St Kilda; on her retirement eighteen years later she was succeeded by a Miss Hatchell-Brown and the French artist Madame Mouchette. As a prominent figure in Melbourne's social and professional life, Madame Pfund became an important patron of the Heidelberg School painters. She joined the Australian Artists' Association in 1887, and her fellow-countryman Louis Buvelot was a good friend. In 1889 she purchased works by Roberts, Streeton and Conder from their 9 by 5 Impression Exhibition. Roberts also painted a portrait of her husband, in 1888, inscribed 'to Mrs Pfund on the 25th Anniversary of her Marriage'.

GEORGE WALTON ▲
Priscilla, 1886
Oil on canvas
48 x 40.3 cm
Signed and dated l.l.: Geo. Walton/1886
Verso: label (torn) 'Priscilla St John's Wood
N.W...'
National Gallery of Victoria
Purchased 1966

Provenance
Theodore Fink, from 1888 until at least
1918

Exhibitions:
*The Exhibition of the Royal Academy of
Arts*, London, 1887, no.809: 'Priscilla';
*Victorian Artists' Society Catalogue of
Autumn Exhibition, 'Grosvenor' Gallery,
National Gallery of Victoria*, Melbourne,
May 1889, no.57: 'Priscilla – £31.10.0',
illus.; *Centennial International Exhibition
Official Guide to the Picture Galleries and
Catalogue of Fine Arts*, Melbourne, 1888,
Victorian Artists Gallery no.60: 'Priscilla –
Property of Theo. Finke [sic] Esq.',
awarded 3rd Order of Merit

Literature:
Argus, 30 April 1888, p.11; 10 May 1888,
p.8; *Age*, 30 April 1888, p.6; Finemore
1977, p.64, illus.

GEORGE WALTON ▲
Rosalie, 1888
Oil on canvas (laid down on card)
46 x 38 cm
Signed and dated l.r.: Geo. WALTON/1888
Inscribed u.l.: ROSALIE
Craig W. Thomas, Melbourne

Provenance:
Godfrey Hayes, Melbourne, until 1983

Exhibitions:
*Victorian Artists' Society Winter Exhibi-
tion. 'Grosvenor Galleries', National Gallery of Victoria*, Melbourne, May 1889,
no.26: 'Rosalie – £21.0.0', illus.

Literature:
Argus, 4 May 1889, p.12; *Table Talk*, 10
May 1889, p.6

Roberts met Walton while a fellow student
in London and later wrote, 'He was the
best painter of a head when I was at the
Academy schools'.[1] The common roots of
their portraiture are evident in these
examples. In 1884 Walton was in Paris
with John Peter Russell, Mackennal,
Harry Bates and Mouat Loudon. *Priscilla*
was painted when he was living at
Queen's Road Studios, St John's Wood
('where all the R.A.'s live', as Roberts put
it). It was one of a number of portraits
which he brought with him to Australia.
The 'dark eyed beauty named *Rosalie*'
dates from 1888 when he moved into the
new Grosvenor Chambers – purpose-built
studios in Collins Street – along with
Roberts and Abrahams.

[1] Moore 1934, I, p.160.

ARTHUR STREETON
Between the Lights – Princes Bridge, 1888
Oil on canvas
84 x 155 cm
Signed and dated l.r.: ArthuR Streeton –
1888.
Neville Healy, Melbourne

Provenance:
The artist; Commercial Travellers' Association of Victoria, Melbourne, until 1985;
Neville Healy, Melbourne

Exhibitions:
Victorian Artists' Society Catalogue of Spring Exhibition, Melbourne, November 1888, no.44: 'Between the Lights – Princes Bridge – £75.0.0'

Literature:
Argus, 16 November 1888, p.4; *Age*, 16 November 1888; p.8; *Table Talk*, 23 November 1888, p.5; *Illustrated Australian News*, 22 December 1888, p.219, illus.; Galbally 1979, p.219, no.17
Reproduced by courtesy of Mrs Oliver Streeton

'Between the Lights – Princes Bridge', a work which is quite remarkable for the success, however incomplete, with which he has grappled with a singularly difficult subject [the indistinct light of evening]. Omitting the third arch of the bridge, counting from the right, and the sky above it, the picture presents much that will challenge attention and invite praise.
– *The Argus*, 16 November 1888

Princes Bridge, gateway to the city of Melbourne across the Yarra River, was a popular subject for artists. The official opening on 4 October 1888 of this, the third bridge on the site, coincided with Melbourne's centenary celebrations.[1] Designed by J.H. Grainger and built by David Munro, its foundation stone was laid on 7 September 1886 by the Lady Mayoress, Mrs James Cooper Stewart. Two years and £137,000 later, the seven span structure was opened by the Chief Commissioner of Public Works. It was then one of the widest bridges in the world. The Commercial Travellers' Association, who purchased this painting, had opened 'luxuriously furnished' new club rooms in April 1888.[2] Streeton's small oil sketch of the same subject, perhaps included in the 9 by 5 Impression Exhibition the following year, is now in the Australian National Gallery.

[1] For examples by John Mathew and Charles Bennett, showing the second bridge of 1846, see Topliss 1984, p.50.
[2] *Age*, 30 April 1888, p.6.

TOM ROBERTS ▶
Allegro Con Brio, Bourke St. W., [c.1886]
Oil on canvas
51.2 x 76.7 cm
Signed l.r.: Tom Roberts
National Library of Australia
Purchased 1946

Provenance:
The artist; Frederick McCubbin c.1903; Parliamentary Library Committee, Parliament House, Canberra 1920; National Library of Australia 1946

Exhibitions:
Exhibition of Pictures by Fd. McCubbin, Arthur Streeton and Tom Roberts, Gemmell, Tuckett and Co., Melbourne, December 1890, no.3: 'Allegro Con Brio, Bourke St. W. – 30 in x 20 in'; *Victorian Artists' Society Exhibition of Australian Art Past and Present*, National Gallery of Victoria, Melbourne, August 1893, no.153: 'Bourke St., Looking West'; *The Society of Artists Second Spring Exhibition*, Sydney, September 1896, no.41: 'Bourke St, Melbourne, '86 – £31.10.0'; *Exhibition and Sale of Paintings Previous to Leaving Australia*, Society of Artists, Sydney, November 1900, no.51: 'Bourke Street, East, Melbourne, before the trams – 35 guineas'

Literature:
Table Talk, 28 November 1890, p.5; *Argus*, 15 March 1892, p.6; 21 June 1931; 15 September 1931, p.6; Hoff 1951, p.127; Gleeson 1969, pl.14; McCulloch 1969, pp.18, 154; Smith 1971, pp.83, 94; Inson & Ward 1971, p.7; Gleeson 1971, pl.27, pp.92ff.; Finemore 1977, pp.18, 154; Spate 1978, pp.30, 38f., 49, 51; Splatt & Bruce 1981, p.26, pl.13; Downer & Phipps 1985, no.173, p.52; Topliss 1985, no.64

Bourke-street, Melbourne, has suggested an animated subject, abounding in color somewhat after the style of Unterberger's Venetian scenes. The view is taken from the north-side of Bourke-street looking towards Queen-street, thus enabling the artist to focus all the bustle and life that congregates near the Post Office. The coloring is very brilliant, the grouping clever, and the general effect spirited, so that there is no lack of interest in the picture.
– *Table Talk*, 28 November 1890

Allegro Con Brio, Bourke Street.W. was Roberts's first and major urban scene, a celebration of the bustling activity of central Melbourne: a city whose boulevards were compared with those of Paris and whose precocious growth in commerce had by this time earned it titles such as 'The Queen City of the South' and 'The empire-city of Australia'. Roberts painted the section of Bourke Street looking west towards Spencer Street, from a high vantage point beside the Post Office. Just below the main retail district of the city, this block was primarily devoted to the horse trade and horse traffic; the Melbourne *Directory* for 1888 reveals that the majority of businesses were owned by saddlers and harness makers. The buildings – depicted realistically – are identifiable from the Menzies Hotel on the corner of William Street down to Dunn and Collins, booksellers, in Elizabeth Street. P. Philipson and Co. were listed as manufacturing jewellers and opticians; John Danks as gasfitters and brassfounders. A large gathering of people is shown outside the premises of Streetle Stratford and Co.,

a horse and cattle bazaar. According to contemporary accounts:

Bourke Street has other sights. To the west of Elizabeth Street, the space for some distance seems devoted to horses. There are saddlers shops in a row, and then great yards for the sale of horses, carriages and carts. In the morning, horses are being trotted in the street to show their paces.

It is best by daylight also to ascend the hill that leads us to the west end of Bourke Street. At night it is dark, for here no retail shops are found; but tradesmen's places and horse bazaars; grand warehouses... in bluestone upon either hand.[1]

Roberts's accuracy in depicting the buildings would suggest that he was equally precise in his painting of the central section of the thoroughfare with its row of hansom cabs. The first cable tram from North Fitzroy travelled down Bourke Street on 2 October 1886. The painting appears to pre-date this and also to show the street before the wooden blocks were laid – a process which was under way by 1884 but not completed until 1886. The canvas was still in the artist's possession in 1890; for on 29 November his friend Miss Elizabeth Anna Fraser recorded in her diary that he brought it to her house at Heidelberg, set up his easel on the verandah and, with her two sisters also acting as models, added the three figures in the left foreground.[2] *Allegro Con Brio* –'fast with spirit' – formed part of Roberts's title when he first exhibited the work that year. It attests to his interest in Whistler and the musical properties of colour. In Sydney in

1896 the work was exhibited as 'Bourke St, Melbourne, '86'.

Roberts's composition has been compared with the *Boulevard des Capucines* painted by Claude Monet in 1873; however, the format had become comparatively widespread by the early 1880s – when Roberts was in England. Whistler, for example, had employed the high view point and bustling city streetscape in his *St James Street* of 1878. In the Royal Academy exhibition of 1883 (which included work by Roberts) there was a similar painting by Edward Gregory A.R.A. entitled *Piccadilly*. Critics have noted the painting's unprecedented luminosity and attributed this to an 'impressionist' use of coloured shadow, in preference to black or earth-toned shadows but Whistler's use of coloured shadow is a more likely source than 'true' French Impressionism. Roberts's inconsistent placement of shadows points to a certain difficulty in depicting the Australian atmosphere. Unable to envelop the local scene in the atmospheric mist which he had employed in earlier London views, he devised a scale of colours, a subtle gradation of ochres, pinks and mauves, to suggest the spatial recession of buildings on the left. The painting is comparable with Conder's later *Departure of the Orient* in its summary treatment of figures, some arbitrarily cut off at the edges. *Allegro Con Brio, Bourke St. W.* remained unsold when Roberts departed for Europe and he gave or loaned the work to the McCubbins. In 1920 Mrs McCubbin, hearing of Roberts's financial difficulties, sold the picture and sent him the proceeds in England.

[1] *Cassell's Picturesque Australasia*, Melbourne, 1889, and Sutherland 1888, I.
[2] Croll 1935, p.31.

B.W.

TOM ROBERTS ▲
Invitation card, 1888
Printed line drawing
22 x 10 cm
Box Hill City Council

Literature:
Topliss 1984, nos 56-8

Mr Tom Roberts's studio in Grosvenor Chambers, Collins street east, was the *locale* of an interesting exhibition of pictures last friday afternoon, April 20. The studio is a large and well lighted apartment, one side being composed of large glass windows, commanding charming views of the city and Hobson's Bay. The ante-room leading into the studio was beautifully decorated with flowers and pot plants and here afternoon tea was served to the crowd of visitors, in dainty little cups, together with the crispest of crisp biscuits. The exhibition itself was an exceedingly good one all the pictures being meritorious works... Owing to the great interest manifested in the collection by the many visitors, it was somewhat difficult to get a thoroughly good view of them. Taking all things into consideration, the progress of Australian art is decidedly cheering. I hear that the forthcoming exhibition of the Victorian Artists' Society... is expected to be the best display of native art we have yet seen...

GROSVENOR CHAMBERS occupy a frontage of nearly 26 feet to Collins-street east, and extend back for a depth of 130 feet to a lane from Little Flinders-street... A mezzanine below the second floor is devoted exclusively to the accommodation of artists, and consists of a series of studios with ante-rooms attached. The arrangement and lighting of these studios has been made a matter of special study by the architects after long and careful consultation with Messrs T. Roberts, Waite and other artists who have leased them. The lighting is all taken as far as possible from the south. The elevations of the windows is on the principle laid down by Sir Joshua Reynolds: great care has also been taken to avoid all reflected lights by coloring external walls, in the neighborhood of these windows, with dark, absorbent colors. The present artists occupying this floor are Messrs T. Roberts, Waite, Abraham [*sic*] and Walton. The design of the building is in a pure classic style... The architects are Messrs Oakden, Addison and Kemp, and the contractor Mr W. Davidson, J.P., Mayor of Richmond. The total cost will be nearly £6000. The whole of the interior decoration has been carried out by the proprietor, Mr C.S. Paterson, art decorator, under the direction of Mr Monkhouse.

– *Table Talk*, 27 April 1888

FREDERICK McCUBBIN
Melbourne in 1888, [1888]
Oil on canvas (laid down on plywood)
112 x 98.8 cm
National Gallery of Victoria
Presented by Hugh McCubbin 1960

Provenance:
The artist's family; exhibited in *The Paintings of the Late Frederick McCubbin*, The New Gallery, Melbourne, November 1924 as no.3: 'Melbourne in the Eighties – 180 guineas'

Exhibitions:
Victorian Artists' Society Catalogue of Spring Exhibition, Melbourne, November 1888, no.65: 'Melbourne in 1888 – £126', illus.

Literature:
Age, 16 November 1888, p.8; *Argus*, 16 November 1888, p.4; *Table Talk*, 23 November 1888, pp.5f.; *Illustrated Australian News*, 22 December 1888, p.219, illus; Galbally 1981, p.45, pl.5; Downer & Phipps 1985, no.145

The complete painting as originally exhibited, reproduced in *The Illustrated Australian News*, 22 December 1888
Photograph: LaTrobe Collection, State Library of Victoria

FREDERICK McCUBBIN
Melbourne in 1888, [1888]
Oil on canvas
125 x 88.8 cm
Signed and erroneously dated l.r.
Margaret Fink, Sydney
For exhibition in Sydney only

Provenance:
Probably in the artist's family until c.1960, *Exhibition of Australian Marine Painting*, Joseph Brown Gallery, Melbourne, August 1970, no.14 as 'Ship at Victoria Docks'; Christie's Sale no.6, Sydney, October 1977, lot 124; private collection, Sydney

Exhibitions:
Victorian Artists' Society Catalogue of Spring Exhibition, Melbourne, November 1888, no.65: 'Melbourne in 1888 – £126', illus.

Literature:
Age, 16 November 1888, p.8; *Argus*, 16 November 1888, p.4; *Table Talk*, 23 November 1888, pp.5f.; *Illustrated Australian News*, 22 December 1888, p.219, illus.

Turning to the landscapes and sea pieces, we may remark that . . . 'Melbourne in 1888' is not only one of the largest, but one of the best pictures of the kind in the exhibition. Its subject is the by no means 'silent highway' of the Yarra, from a point of view just below the South Wharf, from which a Tasmanian steamer – capitally painted, by the way – is about to be warped off. The atmosphere is murky in places with smoke and steam; the opposite wharf is populous with vessels and the unfinished cathedral is a conspicuous object in the background.
– *The Argus*, 16 November 1888

Melbourne in 1888 was exhibited by McCubbin at the Victorian Artists' Society in November 1888 and reproduced in *The Illustrated Australian News* of 22 December. The painting was subsequently cut in half. The left section remained with the McCubbin family until 1960 when it was presented to the National Gallery of Victoria; the right half, inscribed with the erroneous date 1879, has recently come to light. Both Louis and Hugh McCubbin seem to have restored their father's works to some extent in later years; but it is equally conceivable that McCubbin himself cut the canvas. The original painting was comparatively large and expensive when first exhibited at £126 and this may have been a contributing factor. McCubbin painted many views of Melbourne's docks and the bridges over the Yarra. In 1887, for example, he exhibited *Mel-*

bourne (The Pool), *Smith's Wharf*, and *The City's Toil* with the Australian Artists' Association; and *Coles Wharf, Lower Yarra* and *The Yarra below Princes Bridge* with the Victorian Artists' Society in November 1888. Streeton also exhibited his ambitious picture of the Yarra, *Between the Lights – Princes Bridge*, in this latter exhibition. McCubbin's view reveals the considerable progress made in redeveloping the port of Melbourne between 1882 and 1888. In 1887 only smaller ships could navigate the river; larger vessels had to be unloaded in the bay. The Melbourne Harbour Trust, formed in 1877, had developed the area for shipping by reducing the length of that section of river and by widening areas through reclamation of the West Melbourne swamp. In the left half of the painting the spires of Scots Church, the Independent Church and St Enoch's are visible; and in the right half the unfinished St Paul's Cathedral is depicted. Building work on the Cathedral was halted in 1888 pending final decision on a controversy regarding suitability of the site. A realistic description of the distant city was not McCubbin's prime interest but, rather, depiction of the golden light and haze that suffused the buildings, and the smoke and steam surrounding the activity in the harbour. Not all contemporary reviews of the painting were complimentary; notably that of *The Age*:

> Mr McCubbin is unfortunate both in his subject and in his treatment of it. The Yarra below the Falls-bridge is pretty well exhausted from an artistic point of view, and in the picture under notice, the unlovely components are not grouped in a manner which alone could invest such a scene with a certain poetic charm. To the right is an admirably realistic steamer, stern on, which overbalances the whole composition, the middle distance is a blank, unrelieved even by a boat or some other floating object, and the background is a dreary plane of square blocks of buildings geometrical in form and brick dust in hue.

B.W.

ARTHUR LOUREIRO ▲
Study for 'The Spirit of the New Moon', [1888]
Oil on canvas
56 x 165 cm
Private collection, Melbourne

Provenance:
The artist; until *Catalogue of the whole of the Oil Paintings, Studies, Models, Carved Furniture, &c. of Senhor Loureiro*, Gemmell, Tuckett and Co., Melbourne, 2 August 1907, lot 9: 'The Spirit of the Storm – A quaint conceit, beautifully executed'; Mrs Carrie Templeton, née Taylor, a former pupil; to her niece by descent

Literature:
Table Talk, 19 October 1888, p.4; Clark 1985, p.98

Loureiro was perhaps the first local painter whose work embodies elements of the Symbolist Manifesto that the essential principle of art is 'to clothe the idea in sensuous form' (*Figaro*, 18 September 1886). *Table Talk* stated that this sketch was 'taken from a Portuguese poem' (presumably *The Luisiads* of Camões, VI, 85-91); but the oval finished version was illustrated and catalogued for the Victorian Artists' Society accompanied by verses from Shelley:

> That orbid maiden with white fire laden
> Whom mortals call the moon,
> Glides glimmering o'er my fleece like floor
> By midnight breezes strewn.

It was commissioned by Alderman James Cooper Stewart (whose portrait of 1887 by Loureiro hangs in the Melbourne Town Hall), along with *The Spirit of the Southern Cross*. The pair were not literal illustrations; rather, their loose poetical associations were simply intended to set the keynote of a mood. *The Argus* called them 'thoroughly poetical in conception' (16 November 1888, p.4). *The Illustrated Australian News* described them as 'symbolical . . . graceful and classical, showing that this talented artist has not forgotten his early training' (22 December 1888, p.219).

◀ GIROLAMO PIERI BALLATI NERLI
A Bacchanalian Orgie, 1887
Oil on canvas
55.5 x 91.5 cm
Signed and dated l.r.: G.P. Nerli/Sydney
1887
David R.C. Waterhouse, Sydney

Provenance:
*The Cowlishaw Collection of Early
Australian Colonial Books and Paintings*,
Sotheby's Australia Pty Ltd, 16-17
October 1984, lot 251; David R.C.
Waterhouse, Sydney

Exhibitions:
*The Eighth Exhibition of the Art Society of
New South Wales*, December 1887, no.3:
'A Bacchanalian Orgie – £42.0.0'; *South
Seas Exhibition*, Dunedin, 1889-90
(although not included in the catalogue)

Literature:
Sydney Morning Herald, 8 December
1887, p.7; 18 September 1888, p.5;
Australasian Art Review, 1 June 1899,
p.23; A.H. O'Keeffe, 'Art in Retrospect,
Earlier Dunedin Days – Paint and
Personality in New Zealand', *Art in New
Zealand* XII, 3, March 1940, p. 160;
Entwisle 1984, pp.104f.

The paintings which would arrest the
attention of the spectator by reason of
their pronounced character [include]
'A Bacchanalian Orgie', by Signor
Nerli..., whose talent is very distinct..., one of those dashing, unfinished, bold studies that could only
come from the French or Italian
schools. Bacchantes revelling would
not naturally be a very attractive subject to most people, but Signor Nerli
will no doubt rest content with a recognition of the fact that his dramatic composition and bold free habit of the
brush is recognised in this theme. People are apt here, however, to take too
literally the poetry of the classics, and
its pourtrayal [*sic*] of
   'The lilies and languor of virtue,
   And the roses and rapture of vice'.
...The most characteristic painting in
the exhibition is that of Signor Nerli.
His pictures will stand little chance of
popularity, but there is exceeding
merit in them for all that... Signor
Nerli is entirely unconventional in his
subjects and his artistic habit. He has a
courageous freedom, and an originality that is refreshing... Broad, sympathetic, Signor Nerli certainly is, and his
figure-work deserves high commenda-
tion. It is to be hoped that he will set his
hand to Australian subjects as well.
– *The Sydney Morning Herald*, 8
December 1887

Nerli, an Italian by birth, and with a
thorough European training, was the
first to introduce... the daring independence of Southern néo-Cont-
inentalism (if one may coin the expression for the nonce), in its disregard of
generally accepted trammels and its
frequent substitution of the mere
sketch for finished work, which has
influenced a number of Australian
painters – partly for good, and partly
for ill – but the former on the whole,
more strongly than the latter.
– James Green 'De Libra', *The Australasian Art Review*, 1 June 1899

Sharing a studio with Loureiro in Melbourne, Nerli displayed not only his own
paintings, but also 'sketches and studies'
by several contemporary Italian artists
which he had brought with him from
Europe.[1] Nerli's work was far more
broadly and vigorously painted than that
of most local artists; and showed a fine
colour sense. It was generally well
reviewed by critics in Melbourne and in
Sydney, where he moved in 1886, for
'bold originality' and 'the voluptuous rich-
ness of the Italian school' – despite a lack
of 'finish'. He painted a number of highly
theatrical 'Bacchanalian' scenes.[2]

[1] *Once a Month*, 1 January 1886, p.72.
[2] A sketch for the central portion of this
painting is in the Art Gallery of New
South Wales; another, undated, version is
in the Australian National Gallery.

'A walk from Kew to Heidelberg', in *The Illustrated Australian News*, 1 February 1890 Mitchell Library, State Library of New South Wales

HEIDELBERG SUMMERS

Jane Clark

Landscapes and coast views predominate among the canvases. . . [by] the younger artists more particularly. In fact they may be said to form a little school in themselves; and to have come to an agreement to look at Nature with the same eyes, and to interpret what they see by the same methods.

– *The Argus*, 29 March 1890

The Box Hill camp at Houston's farm broke up towards the end of 1888. Charles Conder arrived from Sydney, where Roberts had met him earlier that year and encouraged him to join the group in Melbourne. He was nicknamed 'K'. 'I get a good deal of fun in Melbourne, much more than I used to in Sydney', he wrote to his cousin, 'I don't let it encroach on my time more than I can help'.[1] This period, which began with the summer of 1888-89 and ended with Conder's departure for France in April 1890, has been called by many writers 'the golden age of Australian painting'.

It was Streeton who discovered the new painting ground which gave the Heidelberg School its name. As he recalled, he had spent a long day painting *en plein air* at Templestowe, following in the footsteps of Buvelot; and returning to Heidelberg railway station, had met a friend from the Gallery School, Miss Janet Davies, with her brother who was part-owner of the nearby 'Mount Eagle' estate. Then and there, apparently, Mr Davies gave Streeton 'artistic possession' of the semi-derelict weatherboard homestead, 'with its 8 or 10 rooms, standing on the summit of the hill, and beautifully surrounded by a little forest of coniferous and other fine trees'.[2] Streeton later wrote:

My first night there I spent alone excepting for the caretaker at the farther end of the house, . . . my boots and coat for pillow. I slept upon the floor, the rooms being bare of furniture. The whole place was creaking and ghostly . . . But tobacco and wine weighed healthily against the darkness and solitude.

He was joined for a short time by Aby Altson and another Gallery student, John Llewelyn Jones. Then Conder and Roberts arrived:

Our beds we made of corn-sacks nailed to two saplings, and supported by upright pieces to raise them from the floor. Our seats were old boxes, our dining table was a box with boards placed across it. Our leg of mutton, potatoes, and so forth were all cooked together in a large pail. Our illumination was tallow candles. Surrounded by the loveliness of new landscape, with heat, drought and flies, and hard pressed for the necessaries of life, we worked hard and were a happy trio.[3]

Conder recorded a glimpse of this convivial domestic scene in one of his small panel 'impressions', probably entitled *Impressionists' Camp*. Indeed titles listed in the famous 9 by 5 Impression Exhibition (see following section in this catalogue) reveal many subjects found in the beautiful ruined Eaglemont garden and the whole 'new landscape' surrounding the camp. Streeton remembered years later:

The brilliant blue mornings with the faint Dandenongs and the round she-oaks all the way down to the Station . . . and Oleander and Japonica and Pinecones scattering on the dewy grass . . . And the thick small cypress trees near the Tennis Court where the balls used to hide, and the Fair Open Hilltop where K. did his 'Evening Star' and the row of Hazel and Pear trees and Pines round the well and the indigestible short cut to Ivanhoe; and the long warm afternoons of coppery light.[4]

Eaglemont had long been a popular beauty spot, with its expansive views eastward across the Yarra valley towards the blue Dandenong Ranges. The village of Heidelberg, first settled in the 1840s, had become a pretty rural backwater easily accessible from the city. The journey by coach took only an hour; or one and a half by the Heidelberg Railway, opened in 1888, which a local dignitary declared was 'the only thing Heidelberg required . . . because nature had supplied everything else'.[5] Conder's friend Miss Fanny Barbour joined a picnic expedition out there in November 1888, with swimming for the boys and sketching for the girls:

I didn't think there was a place about Melbourne so pretty. We bought a big scone & some biscuits in Heidelberg, then we started off up the road; a long dusty road through the green feilds [sic], & hedges – quite English . . . It is jolly going out on little Bohemian excursions like that, when you needn't be particular, put on old things, & scramble about.[6]

Streeton, Roberts and Conder painted at Eaglemont 'luxuriously and successfully for two summers'.

During the week Roberts often worked in his Melbourne studio; and indeed much further afield, for in the spring of 1888 he first visited Corowa in New South Wales and the following year began work in earnest there on *Shearing the Rams*.[7]

Streeton and Conder, who stayed at Eaglemont even through most of the winter, started an informal painting school for young ladies, to keep themselves in funds; McCubbin, having married his long-standing sweetheart in March 1889, came out only at weekends. Walter Withers spent most of the second summer there whilst his homesick English wife visited the 'old country'. Other occasional visitors included Loureiro, Mather, Walton, Tom Humphrey, John Ford Paterson and Percival Ball.[8] The Victorian Artists' Society organized an excursion for sixty members, including many Gallery students, just before Christmas 1889: 'Tennis and rounders formed a great attraction to a number of the guests, the large grounds of the "art camp" at Eaglemont lending themselves admirably to amusements of this kind'. They had a picnic lunch and afternoon tea – to the accompaniment of an orchestra of silver whistles; and finally marched down to the train, lighting their way with dozens of coloured Chinese paper lanterns.[9]

On fine weekends, Streeton recalled, students arrived in great numbers with their various wives and girlfriends. Anna Fraser, whose family lived at Heidelberg at the time, has left an evocative description of these impromptu events – 'in the nature of a pastoral festival' – commencing on Saturday morning and ending late the same night:

> The men brought satchels of painting materials, and helped their women folk with carrying provisions. Leaving the women in charge, the men immediately departed on a sketching jaunt with Roberts and Streeton. They painted, discussed art matters, criticized each other in a healthy manner and, imbued with Roberts's enthusiasm, all worked tirelessly and joyously throughout the long summer day. Late in the afternoon in the shade of the pine trees, the long trestle tables which always stood there for such occasions were set out by the ladies with a feast 'fit for the gods' awaiting the return of their men folk. Then there would be exclamations of admiration at the work achieved during the day and all would settle down to a merry feast accompanied by laughter and badinage, while a marvellously-happy spirit of camaraderie prevailed among the members of the 'big family'. Many a quick sketch was made on the spot with brilliant colour and rich contrasts of light and shade.
>
> At dusk the whole company trooped up to the large studio on the hill, which fore-runners had swept and garnished and also had 'candled' the floor, ready for the evening's enjoyment. Dancing was accompanied by the music of fiddles, mouth organs, jew's harps and any other instrument which could be persuaded to play dance music. Couples wandered off into the garden to 'cool off' while admiring the effect of the moonlight on the old fountain or sampling the filberts on the old nut tree. Finally, a rush was made for the last train leaving Heidelberg by those obliged to return to the City, and arrangements were made for another 'picnic dance' in the near future.[10]

Some of the men would stay overnight in the old house. Louis Lavater, a musician friend from Buonarotti Society student days, remembered finding a tiger snake as a bed companion during one sojourn at Eaglemont; and 'killing it with a walking-stick and nonchalantly turning over and going to sleep again'.[11] Altson later wrote to Roberts from Paris:

> Eaglemont had a great charm to me and it and art seemed inseparables; the most artistic life I ever saw and lived was

there and the pleasantest as well as the most instructive few months I ever spent was when you, K., Smike and Jones and I were out there together; the writing of all your names brings pleasant feelings to me, with which I won't trouble you – perhaps because I should find them difficult to write – and so Goodbye to Aiglemont.[12]

The pictures painted at Eaglemont reveal that the artists had found this new landscape particularly congenial. 'At Heidelberg everything is different', wrote Conder.[13] Their response was often romantic and poetic. Yet to their ambitious large-scale landscape paintings they also brought a degree of objectivity which had existed before only in small *plein air* sketches. Conscious that they were breaking new ground in Australian art they wrote boldly to *The Argus*:

> It is always more or less difficult for the average mind to accept a new beauty or its interpretation... So in judging landscape work in Victoria, the mind is more or less influenced by familiar works. In looking at the works of modern European and American painters, who have in a great measure discarded the studio for their painting ground, and whose aim has been to sacrifice no truth for effect, the spectator may feel a certain want as of finish or arrangement, and here let us leave our mind open, and forget for the moment our own idea of what ought to be in a picture...
>
> In the matter of how much do we see? In a row of cabbages 20 yards from us, how many leaves can we make out? On checking the number how very few! In the clumps of reeds or rushes across the river, how many individuals can we distinguish?[14]

Local writers increasingly criticized the younger *plein air* painters' work as 'impressionist': meaning simply that it was not 'finished' to the polished standard of a canvas by von Guérard, or even one by Buvelot. Their 'independent way of looking at nature' was admired; but, declared James Smith – echoing the famous English critic John Ruskin – 'nature never leaves anything unfinished'.[15]

Nevertheless a visiting American art critic, Sidney Dickinson, coined the name 'Heidelberg School' in a particularly favourable review. 'Mr Streeton's works', he wrote, 'where observed dispassionately, and by comparison, not with other pictures but with the aspects of nature which they describe, are found to be boldly and vigorously painted, broad in effect, and with striking contrasts and robust harmonies of colour'. The 'Heidelberg School' pictures had attracted 'no small amount of attention' in recent exhibitions, he said; 'having shown in marked degree the qualities of original observation and individual treatment... and afford a hopeful augury for the future development of Australian art'.[16] In fact the Eaglemont camp had already disbanded by this time. Roberts was there only briefly during 1891. Streeton, after some months in Sydney, returned in 1891 and 1892; but he usually stayed in Richmond, working in Roberts's Grosvenor Chambers studio and commuting out to paint at Heidelberg on occasions. Mather had built a studio at Healesville. McCubbin's family was growing steadily year by year! Conder and several other Heidelberg School contemporaries had left to try their fortunes in Europe. Many artists still painted around Heidelberg, of course.[17] But as Conder wrote nostalgically from Montmartre:

> I feel more than sorry that [those] days are over, because nothing can exceed the pleasures of that last summer, when

I fancy all of us lost the 'Ego' somewhat of our natures in looking at what was Nature's best art and ideality. Give me one summer again with yourself and Streeton – the same long evenings, songs, dirty plates, and last pink skies. But these things don't happen, do they? And what's gone is over.[18]

[1] Rothenstein 1938, p.29.
[2] Arthur Streeton, 'Eaglemont in the 'Eighties – beginnings of art in Australia', The Argus, 16 October 1934, p.49. Charles Martyn Davies (1856-1937) was one of a syndicate which purchased the 'Mount Eagle' estate in April 1888. It had been developed in 1858 by John Henry Brooke, a member of parliament who became President of the Board of Land and Works and Commissioner of Crown Lands; he landscaped and planted an English-style garden, with a long curving cypress avenue leading from Maltravers Road and along what is now Outlook Drive to the summit of Mount Eagle. Brooke planned to live in a mansion on the hilltop but his fortunes declined and he never built anything more than the house which became the Eaglemont artists' camp; he sold the property to Sir Samuel Wilson, who leased it and departed for England in 1881. In October 1889 Charles Davies married Lucy Walker, a Gallery student and close friend of the Heidelberg painters. His sister, Janet, married David Davies in 1891 (a coincidence of surnames which has caused some confusion in earlier accounts of Eaglemont). Topliss 1984, p.25; and see Patricia Grassick, 'Lucy Walker – the road to Heidelberg', Art and Australia, Autumn 1985, pp.357ff.
[3] Streeton, loc.cit.
[4] Streeton to Roberts, 7 August 1908; Croll 1946, p.93.
[5] Argus, 9 May 1888, p.8.
[6] Fanny Barbour's 'Jottings', 1887-88.
[7] Roberts went to Tasmania for several weeks in 1890. Also that year both he and Streeton did some scene painting for the Bijou Theatre in Bourke Street (Table Talk, 7 February 1890, p.3 and 28 November 1890, p.2); Roberts later denied this!
[8] Streeton, loc.cit.
[9] Table Talk, 26 December 1889, p.11 (the picnic was Sunday 14 December).
[10] Croll 1935, p.30. Anna Fraser and her sister Lottie were the models for Roberts's additions to Allegro Con Brio – Bourke St. W. in 1890. In 1893 Anna married Frederick Williams, a former Gallery student and member of the 'Charterisville' artists' camp, who had moved to Western Australia (Roderick Anderson, Early Western Australian Art from the Robert Holmes à Court Collection, Heytesbury Holdings Ltd, Perth, 1983, p.62.
[11] Argus, 10 August 1929, p.3.
[12] Altson to Tom Roberts, 22 July 1891; Roberts Papers. Mitchell Library, Sydney. MS A 2480, III, 113-14.
[13] Croll 1946, p.126.
[14] Tom Roberts, Chas. Conder, Arthur Streeton, 'Concerning "Impressions" in Painting', The Argus, 3 September 1889, p.7. Although this letter was occasioned by Smith's criticism of the 9 by 5 exhibition, it addressed the whole question of recent public response to the artists' new interpretation of local landscape.
[15] Argus, 11 September 1888, p.33; reviewing the Centennial Exhibition Smith wrote, 'Mr Tom Roberts, Mr F. McCubbin and Mr Arthur Streeton may be grouped together on account of the similarity of their procedure in landscape painting, [and] seem to be falling more and more under the influence of the French impressionists'; although there is absolutely no evidence that any painter of the Heidelberg School was familiar with work by Monet, Renoir, Degas, etc. – the original French Impressionists. The label was used extremely loosely, and increasingly in condemnation, following the example of most contemporary British writers. See the excellent introduction and collection of documents in Flint 1984. In 1886 Smith had praised Mather's An Impression, no.74 at the Victorian Academy of Arts (Argus, 3 April 1886, p.13). A year later, however, he criticized Streeton's Midday at Mentone for being 'not so much a picture as an impression of nature' (Argus, 2 April 1887, p.12).
[16] Australasian Critic, 1 July 1891, p.240. Dickinson was reviewing studio exhibitions of Streeton's and Withers's recent work. For details of his cosmopolitan life history, see Table Talk, 30 August 1889, p.5.
[17] A writer in The Melbourne University Review, October 1891, p.219, said 'We are very glad to know that Heidelberg is becoming more and more popular as a resort for our artists'; citing Streeton, Conder and Richardson as leaders of the 'Australian school'. Withers had moved to 'Charterisville' – within walking distance; see the section on Melbourne in the 1890s in this catalogue. Charles and Lucy Davies, feeling the effects of Melbourne's recession, moved into the 'Mount Eagle' house themselves in about 1894; they had previously lived very nearby, often visited by Roberts and Streeton, in a much grander house called 'Carn'.
[18] To Roberts, 20 August 1890; Croll 1946, p.128.

A few years ago there would have been, perhaps, half-a-dozen pictures in the entire collection which would have owed their origin to the inspiration of the country in which they were painted... Today the visitor is agreeably assured that the sentiment of this new Southern World is beginning to find artistic expression, and that the penumbra of a genuinely Australian School of Art is veritably visible, presaging we know-not-what of excellence in the near future.

– Fred. J. Broomfield, 'Art and Artists in Victoria', *The Centennial Magazine*, I, 1889, reviewing the Victorian Artists' Society exhibition of 1889

The Picturesque Atlas of Australasia ▶
Edited by the Hon. Andrew Garran
Published by the Picturesque Atlas Publishing Co. Ltd, Sydney, 1883-89
LaTrobe Collection, State Library of Victoria

Literature:
Argus, 31 October 1885, p.12; *Australasian*, 2 April 1887; Frederic B. Schell, 'How Books are Illustrated', *Centennial Magazine*, I, 1888, pp.118ff.; *Australasian Art Review*, 1 August 1899, p.26; Moore 1934, I, pp.232f.; John Alexander Ferguson, *Bibliography of Australia*, Angus and Robertson, Sydney, 1963; Astbury 1980, pp.264f.; McCulloch 1984,. pp.867f.; Astbury 1985, in press, pp.67ff.

This was the largest and most lavishly funded of many picture books produced during Australia's centenary decade. (Others include *McKinley's Australian Pictorial Almanac* of 1880, *Cassell's Picturesque Australasia*, 1887-89, and *Victoria and its Metropolis: Past and Present*, 1888.) *The Picturesque Atlas of Australasia* comprised an outline of the discovery, geography and general development of Australia and New Zealand, illustrated with some 800 black-and-white wood engravings: 'representations of the street architecture of Australian towns and cities, specimens of the landscape scenery, flora and fauna of the colonies, typical examples of the aboriginal races, picturesque episodes in the history of the country, &c'.[1] Published in forty-two parts from 1883, it was issued finally as three bound volumes c.1889. The venture was conceived by one Silas Lyon Moffett, an American book canvaser who had already produced *Picturesque Canada* with great success. His art editor, Frederic

Picturesque Atlas
'Rounding up a Straggler on a Cattle-run', c.1887-88, by Frank Prout Mahony, reproduced in *The Picturesque Atlas of Australasia*, vol.2

B. Schell, arrived with two fellow American artists, William Thomas Smedley and W.C. Fitler, plus a team of American engravers led by Horace Baker. Many local artists were attracted to Sydney to work on the project, described by *The Australasian* as 'the most ambitious and the most important piece of artistic work ever yet attempted in the Australian colonies'. There were illustrations by the three Americans, by Louis Buvelot, George and Julian Ashton, W.C. Piguenit, A.H. Fullwood, John Mather, Frank P. Mahony, Tom Roberts, Madame Roth and others. William Macleod, who did most of the portraits, became chairman of directors of

the Atlas Publishing Company; and afterwards manager of the Sydney *Bulletin*. The Americans excelled in the genre of wet city street scenes. Mahony later produced a large-scale oil version of his illustration entitled *Rounding up a Straggler*, which was purchased by the Art Gallery of New South Wales. Their drawings, made in a variety of media, were transferred onto wood blocks for engraving by a mod-

◀ ALBERT HENRY FULLWOOD
Sturt Street, Ballarat, [c.1887]
Watercolour and pencil on card
40 x 56.5 cm
Signed l.l.: A. Hy. FULLWOOD
Ciy of Ballarat Fine Art Gallery
Gift of 3BA and the Ballarat *Courier* 1978

Exhibitions:
A collection of black-and-white work for *The Picturesque Atlas* at J.R. Lawson's, June 1895; *Catalogue of Original Drawings of the Picturesque Atlas of Australasia*, James R. Lawson, Sydney, 21 September 1897, lot 2: 'Sturt Street, Ballarat' (auction sale)

Literature:
Daily Telegraph, 4 June 1895; Anne Gray, *A. Henry Fullwood, War Paintings*, Australian War Memorial, Canberra, 1983, pp.11f.; Rich 1984, no.55

This was one of Fullwood's many contributions to *The Picturesque Atlas of Australasia*, vol.2. Having arrived in Sydney in 1883, he shared a studio with Frank Mahony and joined Julian Ashton, Conder and others for *plein air* painting excursions. He worked as a lithographic draughtsman and designer and drew illustrations for the *Australian Town and Country Journal*. Employment as staff artist for the Atlas Publishing Company took him south to the Victorian gold mining towns and as far afield as the north of Queensland. As Frederic Schell explained in his article 'How Books are Illustrated', drawings for reproduction by wood engraving could be made in pencil, watercolour, lamp black and Chinese white or even oils.

'Saturday Night in George Street', 1886, by William Thomas Smedley, reproduced in *The Picturesque Atlas of Australasia*, vol.1

ern photographic process, described in detail by Schell in an article for *The Centennial Magazine*. 'For subtle effect and delicacy of expression', he declared, 'it is universally conceded that the Americans have, within the last decade, surpassed all others . . . And to prove that the results of this progress have been felt in Australia, I have only to point to the fact that a colony educated under these influences has been during three years engaged in producing an illustrated work fully comparable to any publication of the kind in Europe or America'. Unfortunately, this great production was a financial fiasco – shareholders lost 2/6 in the pound. It was, however, an artistic success, which did much to interest Australians in their own continent as a source of enormously varied subject matter for art.

[1] *Argus*, 31 October 1885, p.12: reviewing a Melbourne exhibition of drawings for the work in progress.

CHARLES CONDER
Departure of the Orient – Circular Quay,
1888
Oil on canvas
45.1 x 50.1 cm
Signed and dated l.l.: CHAS CONDER/
SYDNEY/1888
Art Gallery of New South Wales
Purchased 1888

Provenance:
The artist

Exhibitions:
*Annual Exhibition of the Art Society of
New South Wales*, Sydney, September
1888, no.140: 'Departure of the Orient –
Circular Quay – £21.0.0'; *Official
Catalogue of Exhibits World's Columbian
Exposition*, Chicago 1893, p.163, no.57:
'Departure of the "Orient"'; *Exhibition of
Australian Art in London*, Grafton
Galleries, London, April 1898, no.311:
'Departure of the "Orient"– Lent by
Trustees of Sydney Gallery'

Literature:
Sydney Morning Herald, 18 September
1888, p.5; *Catalogue of the National Art
Gallery of New South Wales*, 4th edn.,
Sydney, 1888, no.146 (and later edns);
Table Talk, 5 April 1889, p.6; *Tatler*, 5 June
1898, p.24; *The British Australasian*, 1898;
Moore 1934, I, p.73; Hoff 1960, no.10;
Gleeson 1969, pl.18; McCulloch 1969,
pl.14; Inson & Ward 1971, p.8; Gleeson
1971, pl.46; Hoff 1972, no.C20, p.23;
Hughes 1977, p.70; Sandra McGrath &
Robert Walker, *Sydney Harbour Paintings
from 1794*, Jacaranda Press, Milton, 1979,
pp.46f.; Splatt & Bruce 1981, pl.22;
Astbury 1985, in press, fig.92

> Mr. Conder has studied the impression-
> ist school... 'The Departure of the
> Orient, Circular Quay' is one of the
> most character-marked pictures in the
> exhibition this year – misty and dim in
> tone, showing the scene on a drizzling
> morning, with groups of figures mov-
> ing rapidly away, and the effect losing
> itself in the dull grey and mirk of a
> lowering sky. The contrast between
> the tone of this picture and that of
> other by Mr. Conder... is very distinct
> and bold.
> – *The Sydney Morning Herald*, 18 Sep-
> tember 1888

Conder's essay in harbourside life was
done soon after Roberts had returned to
Melbourne. Largely painted on the spot,
from a hotel balcony overlooking the
scene, it shows the ferry berths at Circular
Quay in Sydney Cove.[1] However, Conder
was less interested by topography than
the life around him and the atmosphere of
the wet winter's day. The opposite shore is
completely shrouded in mist. Large ships
and small boats provide notes of sharp
tonal contrast against a flat grey sea; and
accents of red on their hulls echo those on
hats, umbrella and flagpoles which lead
the eye up the picture plane and into
depth. The complex composition is based
on the bold diagonals of the wharf but
cleverly disguised by a seemingly haphazard arrangement of little figures and dancing reflections upon the slippery
pavement.

Conder's theme of rainy weather
derives originally from Japanese art, via
Whistler and other European contemporaries; he probably knew Whistler's Thames etchings of the 1850s and watery
Venice Set, published in 1880. Foreground
figures cut off by the frame show an
awareness of developments by such artists as Degas, inspired by the effects of
modern photography. The high bird's-eye
viewpoint, made familiar by Whistler and
the French Impressionists, had been used
by Roberts in *Allegro Con Brio: Bourke
St.W.* and for a number of urban street-
scapes in *The Picturesque Atlas of Australasia*. Nevertheless, Conder's *Departure of
the Orient* is informed by a subtle wit that
is all his own. As the steamer prepares to
cast off, a small crowd disperses – doubtless nostalgically mindful of 'Home' across
the sea. On the right a young lady raises
her umbrella and hitches up her skirt,
whilst an umbrella... less porter employs
his tray of oranges as makeshift shelter. In
the far left a pair of mamas with a match-
ing pair of little daughters nod and bob in
conversation. The painting was acquired
by the Art Gallery of New South Wales in
September 1888 – one of its first Australian purchases described as 'impressionist'; and the proceeds enabled Conder to
move to Melbourne the following month.

[1] Tate Gallery Archives, London, MS
7910.16 (Amandeus J. Fisher, Sydney).
Circular Quay took its name from the
semi-circular sea wall and quay
constructed 1837-44, the last great work
of convict labour in New South Wales; it
was gradually straightened during the
latter part of the 19th century as new
docks were built for the steam ferries.

TOM ROBERTS
An Autumn Morning, Milson's Point, Sydney, 1888
Oil on canvas
45.7 x 76 cm
Signed and dated l.l.: Tom Roberts/
Sydney. 88
Art Gallery of New South Wales
Purchased 1983

Provenance:
Mr R.W. Knightly Goddard, London; Miss
S.B. Cornock D'oyley Goddard, London;
private collection, New York; Sotheby's,
Melbourne, March 1983, lot 54

Exhibitions:
*Victorian Artists' Society Catalogue of
Autumn Exhibition, 'Grosvenor Gallery',
National Gallery of Victoria*, Melbourne,
May 1888, no.87: 'An Autumn Morning,
Milson's Point, Sydney – £50.0.0'

Literature:
Table Talk, 27 April 1888, p.2; *Argus*, 30
April 1888, p.11; *Age*, 30 April 1888, p.6;
Pearce 1983, no.16; Topliss 1985, no.103

'An Autumn Morning, Milson's Point,
Sydney', is a new departure on the part
of the artist, and has a dash of originality about it. It portrays the smoke and
mist rising from the city in the early
morning, flushed with a rosy glow by
the newly risen sun, which sheds its
strong white light upon the pier and
vessels in the foreground, while the
surface of the harbour gives back a
reflection of the blue sky overhead.
–The Argus, 30 April 1888

Roberts visited Sydney early in 1888,
apparently on some business connected
with his work for *The Picturesque Atlas of
Australasia*. He met Conder through
Madame Constance Roth, who had
recently arrived from England, and who
maintained a fashionable *salon* for fellow
artists and writers. Evidently they quickly
became friends for Roberts stayed with
Conder's aunt and uncle for the remainder
of his time in Sydney. In March at Milson's
Point he made a small oil sketch on
wooden panel, inscribed 'North Shore
24.3.88' (now in a private collection). The
finished version, *An Autumn Morning,
Milson's Point, Sydney*, is much larger, and
painted on canvas; however it retains the
effect of pink-brown polluted waterside
atmosphere which Roberts had obtained
initially by means of the background colour of his preliminary sketch on wood.

Indeed *The Age* reviewer commented on
the 'colouring of the buildings and ferry
boats on the right, and the middle distance . . . set off by the somewhat murky
background, reminding the spectator that
this is a city consuming fossil coal and not
charcoal'.

Although Milson's Point, now the northern end of the Sydney Harbour Bridge,
had been settled as early as 1806, any
connection with the city by road involved
very lengthy detours. From 1860, vessels
of the North Shore Steam Ferry Company
crossed the harbour from Circular Quay
to Milson's Point. Each ferry, as depicted
by Roberts, could take in tow a pair of
large vehicular punts.[1] Rapid expansion of
this punt-ferry service contributed to the
development of North Sydney's residen-
tial suburbs; less fashionable than those on
the city side of the harbour, perhaps, but
very beautiful – especially further eastward of busy Milson's Point. Roberts himself lived at Mosman in the early 1890s.

[1] P.R. Stephenson, *The History and
Description of Sydney Harbour*, Rigby,
Adelaide, 1966. In 1889 the North Shore
Steam Ferry Company became Sydney
Ferries Ltd.

CHARLES CONDER ▶
Coogee Bay, 1888
Oil on board
26.6 x 40.7 cm
Signed, dated and inscribed: CHARLES
CONDER COOGEE EASTER 88
National Gallery of Victoria
Purchased with assistance of a special
grant from the Government of Victoria
1979

Provenance:
Possibly taken by Conder to London in
1890; Joseph Gee, London; John Young of
Macquarie Galleries, Sydney (purchased
in London 1921); John McDonnell,
Sydney; on loan to Sir George Paton,
University of Melbourne 1951-61; Jack
Manton, Melbourne 1961-79

Exhibitions:
*Victorian Artists' Society Catalogue of
Spring Exhibition*, Melbourne, November
1888, no.25: 'Coogee Bay – £10.0.0'

Literature:
Argus, 16 November 1888, p.4; Hoff 1960,
n.6; McCulloch 1969, pl.12; Gleeson 1971,
pl.45; Hoff 1972, no.C21, p.21; Radford
1975, no.3; Spate 1978, p.52; McCaughey
1979, p.98; Splatt & Bruce 1981, pl.24

TOM ROBERTS ▶
Holiday sketch at Coogee, 1888
Oil on canvas
40.3 x 55.9 cm
Signed, dated and inscribed l.l.: Holiday
sketch at Coogee Tom Roberts- /April 88
Art Gallery of New South Wales
Purchased 1954

Provenance:
H. Walter Barnett, Sydney, photographer
and a friend of Roberts, c.1890; *Early
Work of Arthur Streeton, Tom Roberts and
others*, Anthony Hordern and Sons Ltd,
Sydney, December 1925, no.16: 'Coogee
Bay – 135 guineas'; Sir Reginald Marcus
Clarke K.B.E.; his estate sale, James R.
Lawson, Sydney, 16 June 1954

Literature:
Sydney News, 2 December 1925, p.164;
Croll 1935, p.22; Croll 1946, p.10; Daniel
Thomas 1969, p.470; Gleeson 1969, p.60;
McCulloch 1969, p.27; Radford 1975,
no.30; Spate 1978, p.52, pl.12; Burn 1980,
pp.92, 240; *Fifteen Decades of Australian
Painting*, Art Gallery of New South Wales,
1981, no.6; Pearce 1983, no.15; Topliss
1985, no.104

To the eastward of the village of
Randwick and on the shore, is Coogee
Bay. The whole beach is reserved for
the public from point to point, and on
both rocky headlands there are liberal
spaces in frequent use as picnic
grounds. The beach is a popular prom-
enade and a favourite bathing place,
the tramway running down to its edge
bringing on holidays multitudes of the
city folk to enjoy the freshness of the
pure salt water and Pacific breezes.
– *The Picturesque Atlas of Australasia*,
1883-89

Conder and Roberts spent Easter 1888
painting at Coogee, working side by side
and using much the same format; however, their results reveal striking differences in artistic temperament. Roberts's
Holiday sketch is more strictly naturalistic.
It records the sun's glare on bright blue sea
and bleached white sand, golden sandstone, dry grass and spindly seaside vegetation. The brilliant colour and bold
handling express his excitement with the
intensity of Sydney's light. Conder's version is characteristically decorative. He
focuses on the pretty silhouettes of foreground figures; deliberately bends his tall
tree to echo the curve of the bay; blurs
superfluous details in a softer sunlight and
smoother paint surface. Remembering his
and McCubbin's first encounter with
Streeton on the beach at Mentone,
Roberts wrote back to 'the Prof' in Melbourne, that he had discovered another
'genius'.[1] Roberts's influence on the younger painter was to be profound: six
months later Conder joined the group of
artist friends in Melbourne.

[1] MacDonald 1916, p.58.

CHARLES CONDER ▶
Bronte Beach, 1888
Oil on cardboard
22.7 x 33 cm
Signed and dated l.l.: Chas Conder-
Bronte Beach/1888
Australian National Gallery
Purchased from Gallery admission
charges 1982

JULIAN ASHTON ▶
The Corner of the Paddock,1888
Watercolour, gouache and pencil on
cardboard
40.5 x 59 cm
Signed and dated l.r.: J.R. ASHTON/JUNE
1888
National Gallery of Victoria
Purchased with assistance of a special
grant from the Government of Victoria
1979

Provenance:
Original owner unknown; Leonard Joel,
Melbourne 1960; Jack Manton, Mel-
bourne

Exhibitions:
*Annual Exhibition of the Art Society of
New South Wales*, Sydney, September
1888, no.43: 'The Corner of the Paddock –
£26.5.0'

Literature:
Sydney Morning Herald, 18 September
1888, p.5; Moore 1934, I, p.95; Radford
1975, no. 2; Gleeson 1969, pl.11;
McCaughey 1979, pl. 10, p.36
Reproduced by permission Julian Ashton
Art School

Painted at Richmond, on the lower
reaches of the Hawkesbury River, *The
Corner of the Paddock* embodies Ashton's
'aim for Australian art' that painters must
work only from first hand experience:
familiar scenes, landscape 'which charms
the eye', 'the lovely blue of the distant
hills', 'the lovely colour on the cheek of a
child'.[1] Its suggestion of a story and the
little milkmaid's rather stiffy held pose are
legacies of the artist's successful career as
a newspaper and magazine illustrator; the
fluent draughtsmanship and free use of
gouache are typical of his early watercolour style. However, the rich yellow pastureland, purple-blue distance and the
feeling of crisp winter sunlight establish
his work as a vital link between earlier
plein airism of Buvelot (a close friend during his five years in Melbourne) and later
developments of the Heidelberg School.

[1] Julian Ashton, 'An Aim for Australian
Art', *The Centennial Magazine*, 1888,
pp.30f.

CHARLES CONDER
Spring-time, 1888
Oil on canvas
44.1 x 59 cm
Signed and dated twice – l.r.: Charles
CONDER AUG.1888;
and – l.l.: CHARLES CONDER AUG.88
National Gallery of Victoria
Felton Bequest 1941

Provenance:
J.A. Springhall, Melbourne, who according to Mr Skewes was presented with it by a close friend who may have got it from the artist; to his son-in-law C.T. Skewes

Exhibitions:
Annual Exhibition of the Art Society of New South Wales, Sydney, September 1888, no.137: 'Spring-time – 12 guineas'

Literature:
Sydney Morning Herald, 19 September 1888, p.12; Hoff 1960, no.15; Hoff 1972, C37, pl.12

The overgrown orchard at Griffith's farm provided Conder with subjects for several paintings.[1] '"Spring-time" is a delicate idyll, flushed with soft sweet colour, and clear in the crisp spring air', said *The Sydney Morning Herald*. No doubt the blossoms reminded Conder of England. As his Sydney friend, the artist D.H. Souter, wrote:

> We had always been unable to decide whether the Hawkesbury looked best in the spring attire of pink and green or in the more sombre robes of early autumn . . . The farm yards are ever interesting, littered with implements of quaint design that have seen their day of service, and are now rusting honourably near the field of their former triumphs.[2]

Another friend from Richmond days recalled that 'Conder was not a hard worker; he spent most of his time chasing girls round the Haystacks'.[3] *Spring-time* shows the second of three Griffith daughters, Abigail Celeste; the baby was her niece, Linda, and the other two were children of her elder brother. Members of the family regularly sat for visiting artists: their father owned the Royal Hotel at Richmond.

[1] See *Sydney Morning Herald*, 18 September 1888, p.12. These include *Tea Time* (Art Gallery of South Australia) and *An Early Taste for Literature* (City of Ballarat Fine Art Gallery); see Hoff 1972 for others. Fullwood's large *Early Spring, Near Richmond, N.S.W.*, a goosegirl amidst blossom trees, painted at the same time, was exhibited at the same Art Society exhibition of 1888 as no.112; now in a private collection in Great Britain.
[2] D.H. Souter, 'From a painter's point of view', *The Australian Magazine*, 30 March 1899, p.37.
[3] Letter from Mann to Louis McCubbin. LaTrobe Collection, State Library of Victoria. Hoff Conder papers MS 9678.

CHARLES CONDER
The Farm, Richmond New South Wales,
1888
Oil on canvas
45.6 x 51.3 cm
Signed l.l.: Charles Conder 1888
National Gallery of Victoria
Purchased with assistance of a special
grant from the Government of Victoria
1979

Provenance:
Julian Ashton – purchased October 1888
when Conder left for Melbourne; Anthony
Hordern's Art Gallery, Sydney 1948; Lady
Tooth, Queensland; Jack Manton,
Melbourne 1975-79

Literature:
Moore 1934, I, p.95; Croll 1946, p.46; Hoff
1960, no.14; Hoff 1972, no.C 36, pl.11;
McCaughey 1979, pl.42

Thomas Griffith's old farm, on the Richmond side of the Hawkesbury River, was a favourite *plein air* painting ground for Sydney artists such as Julian Ashton, Alfred Daplyn, A.H. Fullwood and Frank Mahony. As Ashton later recalled:

It was in the early part of August 1888 that I persuaded Conder to come away with me and see the old farms at Richmond under their spring bloom. We stayed at a little old time Hotel about a mile and a half from Richmond on the way to Kurrajong. The scene of this painting was an old ruined orchard close by the Hotel looking towards the high hill known as 'The Terrace'... For 4 or 5 weeks,... Conder with his painting materials formed the last figure in a small procession, which included a little girl and a calf, to the spot at which he worked. The calf which had so inconspicuous a place in his painting was a source of great irritation to Conder... When he left Sydney at the end of 1888 for Melbourne, I

purchased this painting from him and have had it ever since.[1]

Ashton had painted *The Corner of the Paddock* earlier that year and Conder's work shows some similarities in subject matter and... the sharp graphic treatment of foreground details. However, Conder combined observation with the highly decorative element so characteristic of his style in these Australian years. Fragile blossoms springing from dark gnarled tree trunks were a favourite theme in Japanese woodcuts; also of Whistler, van Gogh, John Peter Russell, and many contemporaries who came more or less under the sway of Japanese art in the later 19th century.

[1] 1 August 1920; letter formerly attached to the back of the painting. LaTrobe Collection, State Library of Victoria. Hoff Conder papers MS 9678.

CHARLES CONDER ▶
Cove on the Hawkesbury, [c. 1888]
Oil on cardboard
37 x 22 cm
Signed: l.r.: CONDER
National Gallery of Victoria
Bequeathed by Mrs Mary Helen Keep
1944

Provenance:
Mrs Ernest E. Keep (née Mary Helen Gibson, sister of Conder's friend and biographer, Frank Gibson), whose family may have obtained the painting directly from the artist

Literature:
Hoff 1960, no. 21; McCulloch 1969, pl.19; Smith 1971, p. 95, pl. 78; Hoff 1972, no. C17

GIROLAMO PIERI BALLATI NERLI ▲
Street scene on a rainy night, [c.1890]
Oil on pulpboard
31 x 23.2 cm
Signed l.l.: G.P. Nerli
National Gallery of Victoria
Purchased 1951

Literature:
Astbury 1985, in press, fig.95

Nerli's work was admired by fellow artists for its gusto and spontaneity. As one Sydney critic explained, he 'espoused the system of painting generally called, though perhaps not very happily or relevantly, "Impressionism" (for surely "Sketchism", or some such word would be a more accurately descriptive term)'.[1] Streeton called Nerli 'brilliant' and Conder owned one of his sketches. However, this street scene must have been painted after Nerli had seen Conder's *Departure of the Orient* acquired by the Art Gallery of New South Wales in 1888; and indeed, later than November that year when electric street lighting was first installed in Sydney.[2] He would certainly have known the black-and-white illustrations of wet city streets in publications such as *The Picturesque Atlas of Australasia*, 1883-89 or *Victoria and its Metropolis: Past and Present*, 1888.[3] In 1890 Nerli exhibited a large canvas entitled *Winter in Sydney*, a 'clever' view of the *Sydney Morning Herald*'s Hunter Street offices with figures in the foreground.[4] His smaller *Street scene on a rainy night* may well have been a preparatory study for that oil painting.

[1] James Green 'De Libra', *Australasian Art Review*, 1 August 1899, p.22.
[2] Arc-lights of the type shown by Nerli were first introduced at Tamworth (*Sydney Morning Herald*, 9 November 1888). According to research by Bettie Currie, they were soon operating in districts closer to the city – at Penrith and Mossvale by 1889; at Redfern by 1892; in Sydney itself from 1904. (Girolamo P. Nerli, Fine Arts Honours thesis, University of Melbourne, 1976, p.27.)
[3] For example W.T. Smedley's 'Saturday Night in George Street' in *The Picturesque Atlas*, vol.1, and a rainy night scene of 'The Queen's Jubilee in Melbourne 1887', *Victoria and its Metropolis*, vol. 1.
[4] *Art Society of New South Wales Catalogue of Spring Exhibition*, Sydney, September 1890, no. 116: 'Winter in Sydney – £105.0.0'. Described in *The Sydney Morning Herald*, 6 September 1890, p.5; *The Illustrated Sydney News*, 27 September 1890, p.19. In 1893 he exhibited *A Wet Winter Day* at the Otago Art Society in New Zealand (perhaps the same painting).

CHARLES CONDER ▲
A Holiday at Mentone, 1888
Oil on canvas
46.2 x 60.8 cm
Signed and dated l.r.: CHAS. CONDER-
1888
Art Gallery of South Australia
Government grant with the assistance of
Bond Corporation Holdings Ltd through
the Art Gallery of South Australia
Foundation, to mark the Gallery's
centenary 1981
For exhibition in Melbourne and Adelaide
only

Provenance:
Dr Douglas Stewart, Melbourne; until his
Art Sale of a Fine Private Collection...,
Gemmell, Tuckett and Co., Melbourne, 30
April 1920, lot 28; J.R. Lawson, Sydney –
to Mr and Mrs M.S. Atwill, Sydney; Sir
John and Lady Atwill

Exhibitions:
*Victorian Artists' Society Catalogue of
Spring Exhibition*, Melbourne, November
1888, no.8: 'A Holiday at Mentone
£21.0.0'

Literature:
Argus, 16 November 1888, p.4; *Table Talk*,
23 November 1888, p.6; Hoff 1960, no.30;
Daniel Thomas 1963, pp.40f.; Gleeson
1969, pl.19; McCulloch 1969, pl. 63;
Gleeson 1971, pl.50, pp.94, 101; Hoff
1972, no.C45, pl.13; Hughes 1977, p.72;
Horton & Thomas 1981, pp.63f.

Painted at Mentone, about fifteen miles
down the bay from Melbourne, this was
the first Victorian scene publicly exhibited
by Conder. Its luminous atmosphere
relates more closely, perhaps, to his paintings of Bronte Beach in Sydney than to
Roberts's Mentone view of 1887. Only the
seascape itself was executed on the spot.
Conder added the figures later, as crucial
elements in a boldly calculated formal
structure.[1] The wooden footbridge leading across to the Mentone baths (half visible on the right hand side) provides a
strong geometrical framework. Its vertical supporting piers are echoed by the
upright gentleman in front and the dark
silhouettes behind; whilst the prostrate figure, lying parallel with the rails of the
bridge, the horizon and shadow, is an
example of Conder's delight in pattern-
making pushed almost to absurdity. As in
his *Departure of the Orient*, touches of red
guide the eye: from parasol to bonnet to
newspaper and again on the frieze of
smaller figures set in relief against the
aerial depth of blue sky.

Beach scenes were a favourite subject
of the French Impressionists and many
contemporary painters. Conder may have
been familiar with the composition of
Degas's *Bains de Mer; Petite fille peignée
par sa bonne*, no.50 in the Third Impressionist Exhibition, Paris, 1877: immediate
parallels are the high horizon line, the
patterning of dark figures, umbrella and
clothing against pale sand and the overall
mood of quiet sociable activity at the seaside.[2] Although *The Bridge* by Philip
Wilson Steer is an evening scene, it shares

many features in common with Conder's
treatment of the theme: 'snapshot' effect,
figures in silhouette against white railings,
a range of blues, pink and cream, with
black used as a positive colour.[3] Conder,
like Steer, would certainly have known
Whistler's famous bridge compositions –
the etching of Old Putney Bridge and oil
paintings of Battersea Bridge – indebted in
their turn to Japanese woodcut prints by
Hiroshige and Hokusai of a narrow
wooden bridge set high in the image.
Roberts had used this same motif in *Winter Morning after Rain, the old bridge,
Gardiner's Creek*, c.1885, which was still
in his studio when Conder joined the
group in Melbourne.[4] *A Holiday at Mentone* ranks among Conder's most striking
achievements. The composition is held
together by sunlight: bright in the clear
blue sky and reflected upwards from sand
and sea. The brushwork is careful and
delicate, but never 'finikin' – to borrow a
useful adjective from Tom Roberts. The
strands of seaweed are almost calligraphi-
cally treated. And Conder's ever-ready
wit is epitomized by his placement of the
open Japanese umbrella: blown unob-
served by the sea breeze from its rightful
place beside its owner's feet – for all the
world like a Japanese printer's seal gone
astray from beneath its line of characters.

[1] Inspection of the paint surface clearly
reveals the figures added over the
background. A delightful 'impression' of
the same young woman reading on the
beach is now in a private collection. Hoff
1972, no.C25; properly entitled *The Sun
and I*, no.49 in the 9 by 5 Impression
Exhibition and no.47 in *The George Page
Cooper Collection*, Leonard Joel,
November 1967.
[2] Martin Davies, *French School, Early
19th century, Impressionists, Post-
Impressionists etc.*, The National Gallery,
London, 1970, no. 3247.
[3] Laughton 1977, no.34, pl.19; probably
painted 1887, exhibited at Grosvenor
Gallery's summer exhibition 1888,
no.105.
[4] Hoff 1972, pp.21, 30; Topliss 1985, no.
53.

ARTHUR STREETON ▲
Early Summer – Gorse in bloom, 1888
Oil on canvas
56.2 x 100.6 cm
Signed and dated l.l.: Arthur Streeton 1888
Art Gallery of South Australia
Art Gallery of South Australia Foundation 1982
For exhibition in Melbourne and Adelaide only

Provenance:
James William Hines; John H. Connell, Melbourne; Leonard Joel, Melbourne, 25 September 1953, lot 169; John and Sunday Reed, Melbourne

Exhibitions:
Victorian Artists' Society Catalogue of Spring Exhibition, Melbourne, November 1888, no.38: 'Early Summer – Gorse in bloom £40', illus.; *Catalogue of the Diamond Jubilee Loan Exhibition in the National Gallery of Victoria, in commemoration of the 60th Year of the Reign of her Majesty Queen Victoria*, Melbourne, June 1897, no.44: 'Early Summer, Gorse in Bloom – Lent by James William Hines, Esq.'

Literature:
Age, 16 November 1888, p.8; *Argus*, 16 November 1888, p.4; *Table Talk*, 23 November 1888, pp.5f.; Streeton 1919, pl.IV; Streeton 1935, no.38; John Reed, 'Streeton Memorial Exhibition – the Decay of an Artist', *Angry Penguins*, December 1944; John Reed, *Australian Landscape Painting*, Melbourne, 1965, p.5; Radford 1974, no.38; Galbally 1979, no.18; Richard Haese, *Nolan, the city and the plain*, National Gallery of Victoria, Melbourne, 1983, pp.12f.
Reproduced by courtesy of Mrs Oliver Streeton

In 1888 Streeton was still an apprentice lithographer, only spending weekends painting at the Box Hill camp. Neverthe-less, reviewing the first Victorian Artists' Society exhibition in that year, *Table Talk* extolled 'the wonderful aerial effect' in his pictures; 'while as an example of impressionist work, there is nothing better in the exhibition than his "Early Summer, Gorse in Bloom"'. James Smith of *The Argus*, however, equated 'impressionism' with laziness and 'slapdash brushwork'. Although he admired a 'clever vagueness' in *Early Summer – Gorse in bloom*, 'everything being dextrously indicated and nothing clearly defined except the post and rails', he refused to consider it as a finished painting. It was a sketch, 'an impression merely', he wrote, 'an exceedingly graphic memorandum of form and colour'. Of course it was precisely this bold construction and the brilliant colour under blazing Australian sun which appealed so strongly to the Reeds and their artist friends at 'Heide' in the 1940s. 'For sheer delicacy and feeling for its subject, it would hold its own in any country', John Reed declared. Streeton was not interested in painting narrative subjects such as those explored by Roberts and McCubbin; the figures in this painting tell no obvious story. Indeed close inspection reveals numerous *pentimenti* and changes of mind about their relative positions – essentially as structural components of the landscape.

CHARLES CONDER ▲
The Fatal Colors, 1888
Oil on board
35.5 x 20.3 cm
Signed l.l.: CHAS CONDER/1888
Inscribed l.r.: THE FATAL COLORS
Private collection, Melbourne

Provenance:
Lawrence Abrahams (Louis Abrahams's younger brother) probably from the artist; until *The Magnificent Collection of Australian Pictures – the late Lawrence Abrahams*, Decoration Co., Melbourne, 20 June 1919, lot 36 [50 guineas]; George Page Cooper, Melbourne (not in his sale at Leonard Joel, June 1967); Mrs G.M. Chartres; Leonard Joel, Melbourne, November 1980; Lauraine Diggins, Melbourne; private collection, Melbourne

Literature:
Gibson 1914, p.93; Hoff 1960, no. 26, p.38; Hoff 1972, no. C23, fig. 6

ARTHUR STREETON ▲
Yarra valley at Heidelberg, 1888
Oil on canvas
40.8 x 76.2 cm
Signed and dated l.l.: A. Streeton/1888
National Gallery of Victoria
On loan from the estate of Sunday Reed

Provenance:
Original owner unknown; the first painting bought jointly by John and Sunday Reed, 1930s

Exhibitions:
Possibly *Victorian Artists' Society Catalogue of Spring Exhibition*, Melbourne, November 1888, no.46: 'Evening with Bathers – £25.0.0'[1]

Literature:
Richard Haese, *Nolan, the city and the plain*, National Gallery of Victoria, Melbourne, 1983, pp.11f.
Reproduced by courtesy of Mrs Oliver Streeton

Heidelberg was a popular picnicking spot and painting ground for years before the semi-permanent artists' camp at Eaglemont. In 1865, for example, one amateur versifier's 'Australian Rambling Rhyme' had described the dusk and rising moon:

> With sad sheoaks, and here and there a gum,
> For variations to the river's hum![2]

In November 1887 Conder's friend, Miss Fanny Barbour, explained in her diary that the 'the tour out there' took only an hour on the Heidelberg coach, followed by a walk to the river. 'The Yarra is quite clear up here', she wrote, 'The banks are thickly wooded . . . The grass is very long and green. We loafed about in the afternoon. Ern [her cousin] went for a swim'. Streeton's informal style matches the intimacy of his subject matter: an idyll of everyday life, suffused with warm twilight.

[1] Described briefly in *The Age*, 16 November 1888, p.8 and *The Argus*, 16 November 1888, p.4. A number of Streeton's bathing scenes from the late 1880s are listed in Streeton 1935 and Galbally 1979.
[2] See Topliss 1984, pp.23ff.

ARTHUR STREETON ▲
Golden Summer, Eaglemont, 1889
Oil on canvas
81.3 x 152.6 cm
Signed, dated and inscribed l.l.: Pastoral/
Arthur Streeton/1889
Inscribed l.r.: Eaglemont
William J. Hughes, Perth

Provenance:
Taken to London by Conder in April 1890;
purchased on the opening day of the Old
Salon, Paris, 1892, by Mr Charles Mitchell
of Armstrong, Whitworth and Co.,
Newcastle-on-Tyne, an artist (died 1903);
re-acquired by Streeton from Mitchell's
widow in 1919 for £60; cleaned and
slightly retouched by Streeton for
exhibition in Melbourne and Sydney
1920-24; and on loan at the Art Gallery of
New South Wales; purchased by a
Victorian private collector from *Arthur
Streeton's Exhibition of Paintings*, Fine Art
Society, Melbourne, March-April 1924,
no.4: 'Golden Summer – 1,000 guineas';
William J. Hughes, Perth, since May
1985

Exhibitions:
*Victorian Artists' Society Catalogue of
Winter Exhibition at 'Grosvenor Gallery',
National Gallery of Victoria*, Melbourne,
May 1889, no.15: 'Golden Summer,
Eaglemont – £100', illus.; *The Exhibition
of the Royal Academy of Arts*, London
1891, no.84: 'Golden Summer, Australia';
*Catalogue illustré de peinture et sculpture
Salon de 1892*, Paris 1892, no.1560:
'Golden Summer' (hung on the line and

awarded *Mention honorable*); *Exhibition
of Australian Art in London*, Grafton
Galleries, London, April 1898, no.87:
'Golden Summer – lent by C.W. Mitchell,
Esq.'

Literature:
Table Talk, 26 April 1889, p.5; 10 May
1889, p.6; 26 July 1889, p.8; *Argus*, 4 May
1889, p.12; 15 May 1889, p.9; 30
November 1892, p.7; 29 June 1895, p.4; 16
October 1934, p.49; *Centennial Magazine*,
I, 1889, p.884; *Melbourne University
Review*, October 1891, p.219; *Magazine of
Art*, May 1898, illus.; Lionel Lindsay,
'Arthur Streeton's Place in Australian Art',
Art in Australia 2, 1917; *The Home*,
September 1920; *Art in Australia*, Special
Numbers 1919 and 1931; Moore 1934, I,
p.72; Streeton 1935, no.43, p.33; Lindsay
1938, p.15; Croll 1946, pp.5, 34, 36, 115f.,
126, pl.1; McCulloch 1969, p.196, pl.219;
Smith 1971, p.119; Galbally 1979, no.33,
pl.7A; Topliss 1984, p.27
Reproduced by courtesy of Mrs Oliver
Streeton

This 'large summer landscape... is an
excellent illustration of the scenery
around Heidelberg; a long undulating
plain, which, lying in all the glory of a
warm sunny afternoon, appears as a
stretch of golden meadow land, while in
the distance the purple shadows are fast
creeping over the hills, and lurking in little
patches among the hollows of the
ground', reported the critic for *Table Talk*.
'Mr Arthur Streeton, in *Golden Summer,
Eaglemont*, abundantly testifies to his per-

fect sense of colour'. Contemporary critics
were quickly aware of Streeton's great
strengths in painting Australian colour
and capturing the quality of light: 'He
paints summer effects as if he loved the
country'.[1] For this work he began by making a brilliant oil sketch on the spot in full
sunlight, overlooking the Yarra basin and
the blue ranges to the east, and north.[2]
'Oh, the long, hot day. Oh, the gift of
appreciation', he wrote to Roberts. 'I sit on
our hill of gold, on the north side; the wind
seems sunburnt and fiery as it runs
through my beard. Yes, rather, see, look
here: north-east the very long divide is
beautiful, warm blue, far, far away, all
dreaming and remote. Now to the east a
little . . . Yes, I sit here in the upper circle
surrounded by copper and gold, and smile
joy under my fly net as all the light, glory
and quivering brightness passes slowly
and freely before my eyes'.[3] The finished
canvas, however, was essentially a poetical response to his total experience of the
landscape at Eaglemont. As he wrote later
to Roberts, 'Fancy if you could grasp all
you feel and condense your thoughts into
a scheme which would embrace sweet
sound, great colour, and all the slow soft
movement'.[4] The high key of his original
'impression' is mellowed to what he called
the 'coppery light' of a long afternoon; the
full moon has risen, surrounded by a halo
of mare's-tail clouds. The tall running figure of the sketch is now standing still,
further distant, and replaced in the foreground by a little boy, a magpie and delicate, closely focused details of foliage. The

◄ARTHUR STREETON
Near Heidelberg, 1890
Oil on canvas
53.5 x 43 cm
Signed and dated l.l.: A. Streeton. 90
National Gallery of Victoria
Felton Bequest 1943

Provenance:
Possibly in the sale of *Australian pictures collected by the late Louis Abrahams*, Decoration Co., Melbourne, 15 August 1919, lot 16: 'Near Heidelberg' [31 guineas]; Mrs Jerome Tuomy, East St Kilda, until 1943

Literature:
Inson & Ward 1971, p.7; Gleeson 1971, pl. 56; Galbally 1979, no. 34, pl. 1
Reproduced by courtesy of Mrs Oliver Streeton

'Nothing happier than this... Oh, that I could roll some up – as a present. Oh, I'll try'. Thus wrote Streeton to Roberts from Eaglemont; and most nostalgically, in another letter, 'Well, we can't have last summer again till, well...'[1] Eaglemont became something of an informal art school when Streeton and Conder were living there and supplementing their income giving lessons to young women. At weekends, as their friend Anna Fraser remembered, they were joined by Roberts, McCubbin and other painters, as well as students and numerous casual visitors.[2] Streeton recalled 'How we made sketches of the girls... The lovely pure muslin, and gold sweet grass-seeds'.[3] The artists also learned a great deal from one another, working together and painting the same views. All of them painted from this hillside.[4] Streeton learned, from Conder in particular, the decorative deployment of landscape features: the slender silhouetted gum tree motif in *Near Heidelberg*, for example, also appears in Conder's 9 by 5 impression, *Dandenong from Heidelberg*. The 'square brush' method of paint application is a legacy of Roberts's training in England. The brilliant blue-and-gold palette was perhaps Streeton's particular contribution: continuing as a hallmark of his interpretation of Australian landscape for the remainder of his long career.

[1] Streeton to Roberts, from Eaglemont, c.1890; Croll 1946, p.6.
[2] Moore 1934, I, p.72; Croll 1935, p.30.
[3] Croll 1946, p.6.
[4] See Topliss 1984, pp.26f.

sheep are no longer breaking away up the hillside, but moving quietly homeward to the slow rhythm of day's end. Turning once again to Streeton's own recollection of Eaglemont, 'Its suggestion is a large harmony, musical...'[5] One critic called *Golden Summer* 'an Australian idyll'; in which the artist 'had set himself to idealize even the most commonplace scenery'.[6] When the painting was hung at the Salon in Paris, John Longstaff reported 'that it created quite a sensation and stood out in oneness and quality all through everything else on the walls'.[7] By 1920 Lionel Lindsay considered that amongst 'the swagger company' of Streeton's latter-day canvases *Golden Summer* looked 'as if it belonged to another age – an age of romance and of youth's reverence and delight. It was like a poem set singly in a book of deliberate but brilliant prose'. To Lindsay, it was the cornerstone of the 'Australian' vision of the Heidelberg art-

ists.[8] Although man's hand is marked indelibly upon the landscape in farm buildings and fences, there is a poignant mood of transience – passing time and passing youth – inspired perhaps by Streeton's reading with Conder of romantic 17th century poetry by Robert Herrick.

For information concerning provenance, I am most grateful to John Jones of the Australian National Gallery.

[1] *Table Talk*, 26 April 1889, p.5; 10 May 1889, p.6.
[2] See following section on the 9 x 5 Impression Exhibition in this catalogue.
[3] Undated letter, probably from the summer of 1888-89; Croll 1946, p.6.
[4] 1890; ibid., p.14.
[5] ibid.
[6] *Table Talk*, 10 May 1889, p.6; 26 July 1889, p.8.
[7] *Argus*, 29 June 1895, p.4.
[8] *The Home*, September 1920; and Lindsay 1938.

ARTHUR STREETON
Spring, 1890
Oil on canvas
80.6 x 152.8 cm
Signed and dated l.r.: Arthur Streeton
1890
Inscribed l.l.: Heidelberg Spring of 1889
National Gallery of Victoria
Presented by Mrs Margery Pierce 1978

Provenance:
On the market c.1910 (Moore 1934, p.72);
Sir Walter Baldwin Spencer (on loan to the
Art Gallery of New South Wales 1916-17;
the painting was not catalogued for
Baldwin Spencer's sale in 1918); Alfred
Nicholas, 1930s; to his daughter, Mrs
Margery Pierce

Exhibitions:
*Victorian Artists' Society Catalogue of
Winter Exhibition*, Melbourne, March
1890, no.84: 'Spring – £70', illus.; *Art
Society of New South Wales Spring
Exhibition*, Sydney, September 1890,
no.191: 'Spring Pastoral – £100'; *Pictures
of Fd. McCubbin, Arthur Streeton and
Tom Roberts*, Gemmell, Tuckett & Co.,
Melbourne, December 1890, no.4: 'Spring
Pastoral, Heidelberg – 60 x 32 ins';
Streeton's Art Union at Buxton's Art
Gallery, Melbourne, 1891, illustrated on
the ticket; Art Gallery of New South Wales
1916-17

Literature:
Table Talk, 7 March 1890, p.6; 3 April
1890, p.7; 19 September 1890, p.7; 28
November 1890, p.5; *Argus*, 29 March
1890, p.11; 15 May 1891, p.6; *Melbourne
University Review*, March 1890, p.27:
probably the painting described as a view
of the Yarra at Heidelberg; *Sydney Morning Herald*, 6 September 1890, p.5; *Australasian Builder & Contractors' News*, 13
September 1890, p.198; *Illustrated Sydney
News*, 27 September 1890, p.19; 'Sir W.
Baldwin Spencer's Collection of Australian Pictures', *Architecture*, February
1917, pp.56f., illus. as 'Springtime, Heidelberg'; Moore 1934, I, pp.72f.; Streeton
1935, p.114, no.49 as 'Spring Pastoral'
Reproduced by courtesy of Mrs Oliver
Streeton

His latest work is an effective study of
spring or early summer, before the
grass has lost its greenness and while
the wild flowers are still in blossom.
The foreground is filled with an extent
of grassy land, and forms a tender contrast to the waterpool in the left of the
picture, where some children are bathing under the shade of a group of trees.
In all Mr Streeton's work, his effort is to
impart the quality of 'air' throughout
the landscape, a feat he has never so
successfully achieved as in this picture.
– *Table Talk*, 7 March 1890

Spring, or 'Spring Pastoral' as Streeton
later renamed it, was painted at Heidelberg and exhibited in 1890 along with *Still
glides the stream*. . . 'The landscape is one
of the most attractive in the exhibition',
said *The Argus*. 'The delicate tone of the
picture is remarkable, while the freshness
and originality of method is beyond question', reported *Table Talk* (3 April). Nevertheless, as usual, Streeton's neglect of
'finish' was remarked upon; and when the
painting was shown in Sydney the same
critic reported that 'some of his efforts
savour too much of impressionism' (19
September). Interestingly, a writer for *The
Melbourne University Review* was somewhat concerned by 'one discordant feature': the nearest figure on the river bank,
'which, though very finely painted. . . has
about it a painfully pronounced suggestion of the absence of clothes'!

ARTHUR STREETON
Still glides the stream, and shall for ever glide, 1890
Oil on canvas
82 x 153 cm
Signed and dated l.l.: Arthur Streeton-1890 -/Heidelberg
Art Gallery of New South Wales
Purchased 1890

Provenance:
The artist

Exhibitions:
Originally called 'An Australian Gloaming'; *Victorian Artists' Society Catalogue of Winter Exhibition*, Melbourne, March 1890, no.47: '"Still glides the stream, and shall for ever glide" – £70.0.0', illus.; *Streeton's Sydney Sunshine Exhibition*, Melbourne, December 1896, no.36: 'Still Glides the Stream Lent by the Art Gallery of New South Wales'; *Exhibition of Australian Art in London*, Grafton Galleries, London, April 1898, no.284: 'Still Glides the Stream, Lent by Trustees of Sydney Gallery'

Literature:
Argus, 29 March 1890, p.11; *Table Talk*, 3 April 1890, p.7; 18 April 1890, p.12; *Illustrated Sydney News*, 1 August 1891, p.6; *The Year's Art*, London, 1891, illus.; *Daily Telegraph*, 5 May 1898, p.6; *The Australian Magazine*, 17 August 1899, p.346, illus.; *The Australasian Art Review*, 1 December 1899, p.24; Lionel Lindsay, *Art in Australia*, 1917 and 'Streeton's Loan Exhibition', *Art in Australia*, February 1932, p.8; Moore 1934, I, pp.76, 90, 234; Streeton 1935, no.50; Ashton 1941, pp.100ff.; Olsen 1963, pp.161ff.; McCulloch 1969, pp.49f., 174; Smith 1971, pp.79f.; Hughes 1977, p.63; Smith 1979, p.95; Galbally 1979, no.35; pl.7B; Terry Smith 1982, pp.29ff.; Pearce 1983, no.19
Reproduced by courtesy of Mrs Oliver Streeton

I see what was, and is, and will abide;
Still glides the Stream, and shall
forever glide;
The Form remains, the Function
never dies;
While we, the brave, the mighty and
the wise,
We Men, who in our morn of youth
defied
The elements, must vanish; – be it so!
Enough, if something from our hands
have power
To live, and act, and serve the future
hour;
And if, as toward the silent tomb we
go,
Through love, through hope, and
faith's transcendent dower,
We feel that we are greater than we
know.
– William Wordsworth, 1820

The stream is the Yarra as it meanders through the flats near Heidelberg, which are half in light and half in shadow; with the uplands beyond catching the last rays of the declining sun, and the full moon rising from behind the ranges, which detach their misty blue silhouettes from the still warm sky.
– *The Argus*, 29 March 1890

. . . perhaps the finest he has ever painted – the entrancing 'Still Glides the Stream and Shall for Ever Glide', now in the National Art Gallery of New South Wales. Taken from a little rise at Heidelberg, the near half of the canvas, with its winding stream and wading cattle, is seen in shadow; while the further slopes yet warm themselves in the declining sun's last golden beams, to which an exquisite contrast is afforded by the silver moon just rising above the faint blue far-off hills that bound the purples of the mid-distance. The scene is suffused not only with an exquisitely artistic light, but with a strong poetic feeling, which is emphasised with subtle touch by the birds in the foreground flying home to roost.
– *The Australasian Art Review*, 1 December 1899

Still glides the stream, and shall for ever glide is the same size as *Golden Summer, Eaglemont* and *Spring*; and organized spatially and tonally in a similar way. The River Yarra flows down from the distant blue Dandenong Ranges, winding through settled pasture land; although visually its course takes the eye back into the painting from the narrow foreground strip, broadly brushed and dotted with palette-knife details of vegetation. Magpies hover in the gentle breeze. Cattle meander towards the river for their evening drink. Doncaster Tower catches the last glint of sunlight on the horizon. Time itself is moving visibly. Streeton originally called this painting 'An Australian Gloaming';[1] however, just before publication of the Victorian Artists' Society exhibition catalogue, he gave it a long poetical title taken from the 'After-Thought' to William Wordsworth's sonnet of 1820 on the River Duddon.[2] McCubbin had already called a small painting *Still glides the stream* in the previous year.[3] Both artists, like Wordsworth, recognized that Nature – 'what was, and is, and will abide' – persists long beyond the lives of individual men. Rarely, however, a man may create something lasting – a poem, a masterpiece of art, an act of faith:

> . . . if something of our hand have power
> To live, to act, and serve the future hour.

Thus by quoting Wordsworth in association with his painting, Streeton was not merely fashionably mouthing English Romantic poetry in a foreign land. As Terry Smith points out, he was proud that a sight such as the Yarra valley could provoke poetic transports just as deeply felt and as significant as those aroused in Wordsworth himself by other landscapes of acknowledged beauty.[4]

'Ah I feel more than I can ever write about this', Streeton said to Roberts of their years at Eaglemont; and he wrote later of his ambitions in painting Australian landscape to 'translate some of the great hidden poetry that I know is here'.[5] Although *Still glides the stream*... is inscribed 'Heidelberg' he intended the work less as a record of specific locality than as a generalized statement about a *type* of place. (Indeed there is an amusing story of his response to a Sydney trustee who refused to approve purchase of the painting because he considered that the foreground grasses looked typical of New South Wales rather than Victoria. Streeton politely concurred, adjusted the colour range, added some flowers; and the objection was withdrawn.[6]) Compositionally the slender eucalypts are reminiscent of trees painted by Corot, whose work in reproduction Streeton claimed to have first introduced to Melbourne artists.[7] As the *Table Talk* critic wrote, a 'wonderful effect of distance and atmospheric space is the principal feature' of the painting. 'Even now, as a colorist, he is without an equal', the review continued. 'This young artist is making such rapid strides in his profession, that, without exaggeration, it may be said that he is regarded as the coming Australian landscape painter' (3

April 1890, p.7). Purchase of *Still glides the stream*... by the Art Gallery of New South Wales meant at once the climax and the end of Streeton's Heidelberg camping days: for with £70 in hand he decided to move north to Sydney.

---

[1] McCulloch 1969, p.49.
[2] Terry Smith 1982, pp.34ff: a very interesting discussion of various different levels at which the painting may be interpreted.
[3] *9 by 5 Impression Exhibition*, Melbourne, 1889, no.177. Many of the Heidelberg painters read widely. Roberts mentions Shelley, Browning, Kipling and William Morris, amongst other poets and writers. Streeton admired Boccaccio, Herrick, Addison, Reynolds, Blake, Wordsworth, Byron, Shelley, Keats, Swinburne, Browning, Joachim Miller, Thomas Hardy, Thackeray, Dickens and Victor Hugo. Croll 1935, pp.184, 193-5; 1946, pp.9, 29, 40-2; Smith 1975, p.253. He took titles for other paintings from Shelley, Walt Whitman and, locally, Adam Lindsay Gordon.
[4] Terry Smith, op.cit., p.41.
[5] Croll 1946, pp.16, 40.
[6] Ashton 1941, p.100.
[7] *Argus*, 16 October 1934, p.49.

TOM HUMPHREY ▲
Summer walk, [late 1880s]
Oil on canvas
45.5 x 61 cm
Signed l.l.: Tom Humphrey
National Gallery of Victoria
In memory of Ann Wilkinson, Gallery Society (1967-78); donated by her friends 1979

Humphrey probably visited Eaglemont from time to time during the summer of 1889, for McCubbin and John Mather were among his regular painting companions. The high tonality and free brushwork of *Summer walk* show how much he had learned from the *plein air* practices of the leading Heidelberg School painters; in the 1890 Victorian Artists' Society exhibition his landscapes were admired as 'characteristic of the country and marked by harmonious colour' (*Table Talk*, 3 April 1890, p.8). Humphrey also painted at Olinda around this time and later at Templestowe and 'Charterisville'.

CHARLES CONDER ▲
The Yarra, Heidelberg, 1890
Oil on canvas
49.9 x 90.2 cm
Signed, dated and inscribed l.r.: CHAS.
CONDER/HEIDELBERG 1890
J.O. Fairfax, Sydney

Provenance:
The artist's sister Alice; to her son, C.J.W.
Lillie; Sotheby's, London, 15 December
1965, lot 54

Exhibitions:
*Victorian Artists' Society Catalogue of
Winter Exhibition*, March 1890, no.42:
'The Yarra, Heidelberg – £26', illus.

Literature:
Table Talk, 7 March 1890, p.6; 3 April
1890, p.7; *Argus*, 29 March 1890, p.11;
Age, 29 March 1890, p.15; Gibson 1914,
pp.28f., 94; Hoff 1970, p.35; Hoff 1972,
no.C78, pl.17

Conder spent much of his last Australian summer painting at Eaglemont, 'most of his subjects being chosen from that locality'.[1] *The Yarra, Heidelberg* is among his clearest observations of that landscape – simple and objective – with its muddy river flats, dead wood and tangled reeds. Here is a private corner of nature shared by willy-wagtails in the foreground and cattle on the cleared hills beyond; sheltered from rising clouds as twilight approaches. Conder rarely worked on such a large scale. Probably he was encouraged by the success of Streeton's pictures of boys bathing, especially *Spring*, painted at much the same spot only a few months before. Roberts seems to have been the first of the group to try the theme: with his seaside *The Sunny South* in 1887.

At Conder's farewell dinner several speakers mentioned influences on his work from Streeton. And Conder agreed: 'I feel a good deal of truth about this, but if they'd then said Roberts they might have been nearer the mark'.[2] The mutual experience of the painting camps – 'early companionships and the way we had to try out things – how we were led and misled, and did the best in our innocence', Roberts recalled[3] – was of course central to the artistic development of all three. Conder took this painting with him when he sailed for home and gave it to his sister in England. He never forgot the Yarra valley at Heidelberg. 'Give me one summer

again with yourself and Streeton', he wrote to Roberts from his studio in Montmartre, '... the same long evenings, songs, dirty plates, and last pink skies. But these things don't happen, do they? And what's gone is over'.[4]

[1] *Table Talk*, 7 March 1890, p.6.
[2] Conder to Roberts, 2 May 1890; Croll 1946, p.127.
[3] Roberts to McCubbin, 23 October 1906. LaTrobe Collection, State Library of Victoria. MS 8188.
[4] Croll, op.cit., p.128.

CHARLES CONDER ▶
Rickett's Point, 1890
Oil on canvas
31 x 77 cm
Signed l.r.: CHAS. CONDER/1890
National Gallery of Victoria
Purchased 1951

Provenance:
Theodore Fink (from the artist); to his son, Thorold Fink, 1942; Mrs Alexander de Bretteville (formerly Mrs Thorold Fink)

Exhibitions:
Victorian Artists' Society Catalogue of Winter Exhibition, Melbourne, March 1890, no.8: 'Rickett's Point – 15 guineas', illus.

Literature:
Table Talk, 7 March 1890, p.6; 3 April 1890, p.7; Rothenstein 1938, p.286; Hoff 1960, no.41, pl.20, p.14; Gleeson 1971, pl.47; Hoff 1972, no.C73, pl.19, p.47

Contemporary critics considered *Rickett's Point* 'noticeable for clever summer colouring' and 'full of varied colour and clever effects'; but they felt it was too slight for public exhibition as a 'finished' picture – simply a stretch of bayside beach midway between Sandringham and Mordialloc. The painting is much less formally structured than *A Holiday at Mentone*, but its apparent spontaneity is carefully balanced by Conder's decorative instinct. The long narrow canvas is divided horizontally – half sea, half sky – by a boldly brilliant stripe of blue horizon; and diagonally by the foreground waterline and the treetops dissolved in a shimmer of light. It is a vignette of happy idleness from the artist's last Australian summer. On 17 April 1890, the Victorian Artists' Society gave Conder and George Walton a grand farewell dinner at Legal's French restaurant in Spring Street; about ten days later Conder departed for Europe.

TOM ROBERTS ▲
Moonlight, [c.1889-90]
Oil on canvas (mounted on hardboard)
24.5 x 59.5 cm
Signed l.l.: Tom Roberts
Sir Andrew and Lady Grimwade, Melbourne
For exhibition in Melbourne only

Provenance:
Original owner unknown; Leonard Joel, Melbourne, 17 June 1965, lot 288

Literature:
Topliss 1984, no.46; Topliss 1985, no.83

This twilight view probably dates from the time when Streeton was working on *Still glides the stream. . .*; and Roberts himself painted a little 9 by 5 landscape panel of the same Yarra valley vista looking eastward to the Dandenong ranges from Heidelberg. The white tower in the distance is Doncaster Tower, a popular scenic lookout and local landmark for thirty-five years. Situated on Clay's Hill in Doncaster Road, the steel and oregon structure 285 feet high was erected in 1879 by Mr A.O. Hummell, an engineer, gentleman farmer, hotel builder and entrepreneur, who was eager to promote the area as a 'beauty spot'. Visitors paid sixpence to climb to the top. In October 1889 the first electric tram route in the Southern Hemisphere was opened from Box Hill station to the Doncaster Tower (2¼ miles in 15 minutes for 9 pence; or 1/6 return by train plus tram from Princes Bridge)[1]. Contemporary advertising declared: 'To Doncaster Tower by Electric Tram is one of the most pleasant, novel and withal cheapest of outings. Magnificent view from the Tower'.

[1] *Doncaster Templestowe & Warrandyte since 1837, a short history*, compiled by the Doncaster-Templestowe Historical Society, [c.1970]. I am grateful to Mr Jack McLean of the Box Hill Historical Society for information about the lookout tower. The painting has also been called 'Moonrise at Box Hill' but the orientation of the view and the short distance between Doncaster and Box Hill make this impossible.

CHARLES CONDER ▶
Yarding sheep, 1890
Oil on canvas
35.5 x 56 cm
Signed and dated l.r.: CHAS CONDER/
MELBOURNE. 1890
National Gallery of Victoria
Bequeathed by Mrs Mary Helen Keep
1944

Provenance:
Mrs Ernest E. Keep, née Mary Helen
Gibson, whose family may have acquired
the picture from the artist

Literature:
Hoff 1960, no.37; Gleeson 1969, pl.20A;
McCulloch 1969, pl. 64A; Inson & Ward
1971, p.33; Hoff 1972, no.C79, pl.18

Shortly after his arrival in Australia, Conder had about two years experience of bush life whilst working as an apprentice at various trigonometrical survey camps with the New South Wales Lands Department. However, he never aspired to such large-scale national outback subjects as Tom Roberts's *Shearing the Rams* – completed in the same year as *Yarding sheep*. Dust-laden air and shimmering heat haze, which Conder must have known well at first hand, justify its lack of definition. Conder had experimented with the theme of searing Australian heat in *The Hot Wind* of 1889, an allegorical female figure representing 'insatiable summer', which was not greatly appreciated by the critics and was caricatured by *Melbourne Punch* in a cartoon entitled 'Boiling the Billy'.[1] *Yarding sheep* is a realistic evocation of action and atmosphere. There is no narrative as suggested, for example, in Buvelot's dusty road with homeward bound flock of sheep; it has none of the drama of Roberts's *The Break Away*, painted in 1891. (Conder wrote sympathetically to Roberts of the tremendous 'difficulties of sheep in motion [which] need a deuce of a lot of study and memory'.)[2] The closest parallel is perhaps Streeton's *Impression for 'Golden Summer'*. Both are small-scale notations of a fleeting moment: men and working dogs in action, sheep moving across a hot dry land, intense light, brilliant colour, rapid brushwork. Conder may have taken *Yarding sheep* home to England with him in April 1890 for it later belonged to the sister of his biographer, Frank Gibson.

[1] *Melbourne Punch*, 16 May 1889, p.306; present whereabouts of the painting unknown.
[2] From Paris, 22 May 1891; Croll 1946, p.136.

THE 9 BY 5 IMPRESSION EXHIBITION, 1889

Jane Clark

Such an exhibition of impressionist memoranda as will be opened today at Buxton's Art Gallery, by Messrs. Roberts, Conder, Streeton, and others fails to justify itself. It has no adequate 'raison d'être'. It is as if a dramatist should give a performance on the stage of such scraps of dialogue, hints of character, ideas for incidents, and suggestions of situations as had occurred to him while pondering over the construction of a play, or as if a musician should invite people to listen to crude and disconnected scraps of composition, containing the vaguely indicated theme for a cantata, a symphony, or an opera; or as if a sculptor should ask us to inspect certain masses of marble from which he has just blocked out the amorphous outlines of various pieces of statuary. None of these is to be regarded as a work of art. Neither is a painter's 'impression'. It is simply a record in colour of some fugitive effect which he sees, or professes to see, in nature. . . The modern impressionist asks you to see pictures in splashes of colour, in slap-dash brushwork, and in sleight-of-hand methods of execution leading to the proposition of pictorial conundrums, which would baffle solution if there were no label or catalogue. In an exhibition of paintings you naturally look for pictures, instead of which the impressionist presents you with a varied assortment of palettes.

– James Smith, *The Argus*, 17 August 1889

The 'nine by five' exhibition of artists' impressions just now being held at Buxton's Art Gallery by Mr. Arthur Streeton, Mr. Charles Conder, Mr. Tom Roberts, and Mr. Frederick McCubbin, is an attractive display of clever little sketches. The mysterious words 'nine by five'. . . merely refer to the size of the 'impressions', which are nearly all 9 inches long and 5 inches broad. To lovers of the beautiful – and beauty is, after all, as Browning says, 'about the best thing God invents' – the arrangements of the exhibition must strongly appeal. Scarves and draperies of soft clinging silk, of the reds that Millais has made popular, and the greens, beloved of the aesthetic, hang from picture-frames and overstands and carved cabinets. The great blue and green vases that stand in various parts of the gallery were filled on the opening day with japonica and roses, violets and jonquils, and the air was sweet with the perfume of daphne. The motto of the impressionists might be ' Nature versus Artificiality ', as the main idea of the impressionist movement is a revolt against conventionality. . .

– 'Viva' (Miss Edith Castilla) in *The Daily Telegraph*, 24 August 1889

The 9 by 5 Impression Exhibition opened to the public on Saturday morning, 17 August 1889, in the upstairs gallery of Mr James Buxton's art supplies establishment in Swanston Street, opposite the Melbourne Town Hall. Probably the most famous exhibition in Australian art history, Streeton wrote later that it marked a turning point – 'the first definitive upward move' – in Australian painting.[1] It was calculated to provoke the local critics and certainly did so; to assert the artists' independence and group identity; and to interest the buying public. In fact almost all the exhibits were sold within two weeks.

The venture was instigated by Tom Roberts – renowned for his skills in public relations. *Table Talk* had announced the first plans almost a month in advance:

The three principals in the movement are Mr Tom Roberts,

Mr Charles Conder and Mr Arthur Streeton. These three artists are generally considered to be the leaders of impressionism here, while Mr Frederick McCubbin may possibly be added as a fourth.

At that stage Roberts intended to hold the exhibition in his own studio and 'most of the members of the Victorian Artists' Society' were to contribute a total of some 130 works. Many local artists had 'caught the infection from the above mentioned Impressionist quartette, and are hard at work painting all sorts of attractive little subjects'.[2] In the event, the four leaders were joined only by Charles Douglas Richardson, Roger Falls and Herbert Daly. Roberts contributed sixty-two items, Conder forty-six, Streeton forty, Richardson twenty-five, including six sculpted 'impressions'. McCubbin produced five, Falls three and Daly, at almost the last moment, added no. 40a. (As Gallery School students Falls and Daly certainly knew McCubbin; and had probably joined weekend excursions to Eaglemont. Both had social connections which would have been helpful in attracting influential patrons.)[3]

Marketing was clearly an important consideration. Sixpence for admission included a 'dainty little catalogue', designed by Conder and printed on handmade paper. The pictures themselves were small – most were painted on cedar cigar-box lids – and affordable, the majority being priced between one and three guineas and the most expensive at nine.[4] Most critics thoroughly enjoyed the press preview on the afternoon of Friday 16 August. The following morning Lady Robinson (wife of the Administrator of the Government of Victoria in the absence of Sir Henry and Lady Loch), was invited as guest of honour; and the general public arrived. Lists of purchasers printed by *Table Talk* include many prominent figures in Melbourne's social and intellectual circles, as well as personal friends of the artists (23 and 30 August 1889). The exhibition was open daily from 10 a.m. to 5.30 p.m. and on Friday evenings from seven until ten, with tea every afternoon at four o'clock and 'musical selections' each Wednesday. The very title of the exhibition was 'provocative of inquiry and speculation', wrote Captain Gurnet for *The Age*. Sheer novelty was a major attraction. So too was a degree of intellectual snobbery. As *Table Talk* observed, 'so much has been said and written about impressionism in art'; and Miss Castilla of *The Daily Telegraph* remarked, in a slightly superior tone, that it was 'an educated taste'. A 'Lady Representative' from *The Evening Standard* advised her readers:

These daring young Impressionists, who are making an effort to educate amateur art-lovers by presenting, for the first time in Australia, a series of their 'impressions', aim at conveying in their pictures a broad effect of tone and colour without the eye being attracted by detail. Some of the 'impressions' were caught and painted in a quarter of an hour . . . Persons interested in art should not fail to visit it. If they have no other satisfaction it will be a gain to have ocular demonstration of what an artist's 'impression' means.[5]

The story of the original French Impressionist exhibition of 1874 is now very well known: thirty participants made history by mounting the first large-scale independent collection of *avant-garde* art intended as a direct challenge to the Paris Salon and academic officialdom.[6] In Melbourne, however, artists, critics and public alike had no real knowledge of that movement. Information about European art invariably reached Australia via England and English critical opinion; and

by 1889 'impressionism' was used by writers as a label for almost any slightly controversial departure from the academic norm.[7] Claude Monet himself declared: 'I am still and I always intend to be an impressionist . . . but I see only very rarely the men and women who are my colleagues. The little clique has become a great club which opens its doors to the first come dauber'.[8] The nine by five inch panels of the Melbourne exhibition were in no way comparable with large French Impressionist canvases such as Monet's *Impression, Sunrise* which gave the movement its name. Fresh colours, casual compositions and free brushstrokes are the only common factors. Nevertheless the term 'impression' had long been used in Europe for exactly such small-scale, quickly worked studies of the transient moods of nature: intended as notations for future reference in painting full-scale compositions.

The local audience simply equated 'impression' with 'oil sketch', and the artists themselves called the works 'impressions and sketches' in their letter to *The Argus* replying to James Smith's criticisms. The *9 by 5 Impression Exhibition* catalogue addressed the public as follows:

'When you draw, form is the most important thing; but in painting the first thing to look for is the general impression of colour'. – GEROME

TO THE PUBLIC

An Effect is only momentary: so an impressionist tries to find his place. Two half-hours are never alike, and he who tries to paint a sunset on two successive evenings, must be more or less painting from memory. So, in these works, it has been the object of the artists to render faithfully, and thus obtain first records of effects widely differing, and often of very fleeting character.[10]

Conservative critics and some academic painters considered that oil sketches were part of an artist's preparatory 'raw material' – not appropriate for public exhibition. Increasingly, however, they were viewed as works of art in their own right. Corot's 'impressions' or 'effects', for example, were eagerly sought by European collectors who admired their freshness and spontaneity. Whilst Melbourne reviewers described the 9 by 5s as 'skeleton pictures' or 'artistic jottings . . . many of which are excellent studies in the rough', only James Smith objected on principle to their public display; although *Melbourne Punch* felt that perhaps picture buyers 'should be supposed to know nothing of the machinery that produces the effects that please them – behind the scenes'.[11]

In England, throughout the 1880s, James McNeill Whistler painted and exhibited small panel sketches – which he called 'curious little games' – as independent finished works. He also considered himself superior to his contemporaries across the Channel and actively tried to make the word 'Impressionism' synonymous with his own painting style. Tom Roberts almost certainly saw Whistler's much publicized exhibition of these panels, entitled 'Notes'–'Harmonies'–'Nocturnes', in London in May 1884. It was described as 'the principal artistic event of the year', held at Dowdeswell's Gallery in Bond Street, which Whistler had arranged himself as 'a pretty decorative *ensemble*'.[12] Whistler's notorious entrepreneurial 'stage-managing' was undoubtedly an inspiration to Roberts, as were the little paintings themselves. Many of them survive: exquisite, yet broadly painted, atmospheric, evoking the intangible; subtle and consciously aesthetic – with musical titles such as *Harmony in Rose* or *Arrangement in Black*. *Table Talk* observed quite correctly that 'Messrs. Tom Roberts, Conder and Streeton are not at all free from the charge of Whistlerism' (23 August 1880, p.4). And Miss Castilla admired their 'harmonies in grey and yellow, arrangements in orange, blue and white, and symphonies in rose, black and grey, after the manner of Mr James Whistler, the first of the English Impressionists'.[13]

The décor of the 9 by 5 exhibition was eminently fashionable. As reported in *The Daily Telegraph*, 'The first impression upon entering [was a pun intended?] is that one has strolled into the sanctum of some art-loving esthete'. The room was coloured by a 'flood of light' from a stained-glass window at one end. One wall was lined with dark red cloth. Mr Cullis Hill, a leading local decorator, had supplied – free of charge – the 'art' furniture, 'art pottery' in the form of agate-ware vases and 'handsome Bretby jardinieres', Japanese umbrellas, screens and 'whistler draperies' of 'soft Liberty silk of many delicate colours [which] were drawn, knotted and looped' amongst the exhibits.[14] This 'Aesthetic' style of interior decoration – pioneered by Whistler, among others, in England – reached its peak of popularity in Melbourne during the 1880s. Indeed many local artists decorated their studios with exactly the same Aesthetic paraphernalia. Roberts used blue muslin draperies, oriental rugs and leopard skins, a harpsichord and large Japanese vases filled with flowers or feathery grasses. Roger Falls's 'artistic nook' had red walls, Indian draperies, a Japanese screen, cabinet and vases and 'some very fine Australian rugs thrown negligently here and there'. Conder furnished with 'soft draperies of Madras muslins, liberty silks, and other lightly falling fabrics', along with 'fans and other odds and ends of curious little articles' and numerous sketches by artist friends.[15] Mr Buxton's gallery was thus fitted out for the occasion to resemble as closely as possible a comfortable, fashionably Aesthetic, upper middle class domestic interior – in which the 9 by 5 impressions became indispensable decorative accessories.[16]

Almost every reviewer emphasized that the exhibition was something new for Australia. In fact George Rossi Ashton had organized an independent group show in October 1888, including Roberts, Streeton, McCubbin, John Mather, Phil May and George Walton: 'making a sale of Australian artists' work in a private studio, which is a distinct innovation on whatever has gone before'.[17] There was no local precedent, however, for the Whistlerian co-ordinated décor, the unity of scale and the comparative unity of treatment in the 9 by 5 exhibition. *The Evening Standard* went so far as to declare the display as a whole 'far more finished than those held in London and Paris'! Even the frames were carefully designed 'in keeping with the paintings' and in harmony with the total ensemble. Wide and flat, cut from lengths of pine obtained cheaply at a local timber yard, they were inspired by Whistler's own 'anti-academic' picture frames. *Table Talk*'s critic saw Roberts, Conder and Richardson splashing gold, silver and bronze enamel paint onto dozens of neat, unpolished rectangles during the week before opening day. (Whistler had likewise used 'frames in three shades of metal colour' at Dowdeswell's Gallery in 1884.)[18] One journalist described how in some cases 'an idea suggestive of the "motive" of the picture is carried out on the woodwork of the frame'.[19]

Although the majority are now untraced, contemporary descriptions and titles in the catalogue show that the 9 by 5s were as mixed in style, subject matter and mood as the multifarious – and often conflicting – influences which exercised the seven young artists' fertile imaginations. The 9 by 5 were a culmination of at least four years of experimentation by members of the Heidelberg School. (One should remember that Roberts, who was working on his great *Shearing the Rams* at exactly this time, had shown a sentimental narrative entitled *Jealousy* at the most recent Victorian Artists' Society exhibition in May 1889.) Many were certainly, as they claimed, self sufficient 'first records of effects widely differing, and often of very fleeting character'. The best surviving examples are sensitive renderings of a particular moment in time, often changing effects of atmosphere or weather with the emphasis on delicate colour values – some light, others dark in tonality. The recognizably local subjects had immediate popular appeal. Others, by Roberts and Richardson, were European scenes. There were several figure subjects – like a number of Whistler's 'Notes' and 'Arrangements'. Streeton's no. 31, *Impression for 'Golden Summer'* was, however, a preliminary study for his recently exhibited major canvas *Golden Summer, Eaglemont*. Richardson's *Gold, Green and White* – a naked girl reclining on the beach and attended by a flock of seagulls – was evidently a sketch for *A Nereid*, which he showed at the Victorian Artists' Society exhibition of 1892.[20] His moulded wax and terracotta impressions, admired by most critics and interpreted as *maquettes* for 'bronze and marble statuary', were clearly not transcripts of nature. Richardson also contributed quasi-allegorical subjects: no. 65, *Entanglement*, for instance, showed 'a young lady attired in a pair of very small butterfly wings, caught in a flowery maze'. Numerous simple subjects were endowed with poetic or anecdotal significance by their titles. In many of Conder's there is a touch of wit, epigrammatic in its brevity. Streeton's no. 122, *Back in Five Minutes* depicted a temporarily unattended bird's nest full of eggs (its label actually read 'Gone for lunch – Back in 5 minutes').

Some journalists enjoyed flexing their own literary muscles at the artists' expense: '"Bananas and Japonica" is a realistic bit of still life', said *Melbourne Punch*. 'The bananas especially have an extremely natural look. They seem to be whispering to each other, "Wait till we get on the pavements, and won't we lay the mighty low"'. But this sort of commentary apparently had little effect on popular response – or on sales. Nor did the remarks of a well-known temperance advocate and social reformer 'that if his little boy of five could not do better than that he would hang him' (a reactionary opinion of a sort still to be heard at almost any art exhibition which breaks new ground). The artists simply pasted up amusing or derogatory printed reviews outside the door – thereby attracting passing pedestrians who might not otherwise have entered the gallery.[21]

James Smith of *The Argus*, as a National Gallery trustee and Melbourne's most respected critic, was the only writer whose comments the artists took seriously; for his passionate attacks struck at the underlying ideas which had motivated their exhibition. In his opinion 'impressionism' could never be considered as 'true art' fit for public display. Much of these Impressionists' subject matter was commonplace, he felt – and therefore inartistic. Above all, he condemned the absence of 'exquisite finish and perfection'; the exhibition was, he said, thus 'destitute of all sense of the beautiful' and 'whatever influence it was likely to exercise could scarcely be otherwise than misleading and pernicious'. Smith's philosophy was based on that of John Ruskin, that 'nothing can be perfectly beautiful unless complete'. Ruskin, of course, had been Whistler's arch-opponent. And Smith's condemnation of the 9 by 5s echoes *The Argus* critique (presumably his own) four years previously, of Whistler's *A Note in Blue and Green*, then on show in Melbourne along with paintings by Whistler's Australian-born 'disciple', Mortimer Menpes.[23] Most of the 9 by 5 impressions, he said, were a pain to the eye. One resembled 'a hydrocephalous doll'; 'others suggest that a paint-pot has been accidentally upset over a panel nine inches by five' (the famous Ruskin *versus* Whistler libel case had originated with Ruskin's remark that Whistler had thrown a pot of paint in the public's eye).[24]

Roberts, Conder and Streeton wrote jointly to *The Argus* a letter entitled 'Concerning "Impressions" in Painting' (3 September 1889, p.7) which may be accepted as a manifesto of their artistic aims at that time. They proclaimed their freedom of choice in both subject and technique. They defended their right to paint as 'very seriouse [sic] well considered efforts' those 'effects and moods and thoughts of nature' which had impressed them strongly, and which they wished 'in turn to impress upon the lovers of their art'. And they continued:

> Let us then try to state our case of the principles upon which we have worked, and as well as we can put them in writing. They are these:– That we will not be led by any forms of composition of light and shade; that any effect of nature which moves us strongly by its beauty, whether strong or vague in its drawing, defined or undefinite in its light, rare or ordinary in colour, is worthy of our best efforts and the love of those who love our art. Through and over all this we say we will do our best to put only the truth down, and only as much as we feel sure of seeing. . .

Undoubtedly their attitudes changed over the years. Streeton was always impatient of theory: he commented to Roberts on John Peter Russell's letters about French art, 'He seems to love the open air very much and, therefore, must be a fine chap . . . But he does seem to me to bother too much about the ways and means – really there's not time enough to do that. I should think it would take a man off his inspiration or idea'.[25] Roberts, in particular, constantly adapted his style to suit the circumstances of each new commission or chosen project. But they were all well aware that 'in the formation of taste in this new country where art is so young and so tentative, every public expression of opinion and every show of works must have a more or less strong influence in the making of that taste'.

Roberts and his colleagues deliberately cultivated their fashionably bohemian image – as innovators but not dangerous radicals. Together with many Australian contemporaries, they exhibited small oil sketches (and large-scale paintings in a comparable freely painted style which critics continued to label 'impressionist') for years to come. As their tripartite letter of September 1889 concluded:

> In doing so, we believe that it is better to give our own idea than to get a merely superficial effect, which is apt to be a repetition of what others have done before us, and may shelter us in a safe mediocrity, which, while it will not attract condemnation, could never help towards the development of what we believe will be a great school of painting in Australia.

[1] Croll 1935, p.15.

[2] *Table Talk*, 28 June 1889, p.3; 2 August 1889, p.7. Edward Alexander Vidler (1863-1942), art critic for this popular weekly newspaper 1889-1902, was clearly in sympathy with the Heidelberg School artists. His week by week account of preparations for the 9 by 5 exhibition aroused a sense of excited anticipation. His regular column, 'Art and Artists', documented their work, studios and painting excursions. The prominence given by *Table Talk* to art and related issues also reflected the interests of its cosmopolitan editor, Maurice Brodsky.

[3] Other prospective exhibitors presumably pulled out because of increasingly adverse comments by critics about 'impressionist tendencies' in local painting. As *Table Talk* observed, 'some sections of the Melbourne Press have treated impressionism with a good deal of rather unnecessary abuse'. Roberts's neighbours in Grosvenor Chambers, for example – the Misses Sutherland, Southern and Price – had 'caught the "impression" fever, and show a great variety of charming little sketches, which however are not intended for exhibition'. Now, a fortnight before the opening, some Melbourne artists were 'looking coldly at the movement, and holding aloof', reported *Table Talk*; 'but it is none the less certain that the much abused Impressionists will have public favour with them. This is pretty well instanced by sketches being already sold in the studios' (2 August 1889, p.7).

[4] The Heidelberg School painters obtained cigar-box panels from Louis Abrahams, whose family owned a cigar import and packaging business; and from Aby Altson's brother, B.H. Altson, tobacconist of Elizabeth Street. Not all the 9 by 5 impressions were painted on cigar-box lids, however. See individual entries which follow for examples of different supports – cardboard or canvas – and varying dimensions.

[5] *Age*, 17 August 1889, p.15; *Daily Telegraph*, 17 August 1889, p.7 (see also 24 August 1889, p.10); *Evening Standard*, 17 August 1889, p.1 – the 'Lady Representative' was Miss Conor O'Brien, a young New Zealand journalist.

[6] See Rewald 1973; Paul Tucker, 'The first impressionist exhibition and Monet's *Impression, Sunrise*: a tale of timing, commerce and patriotism', *Art History* 7, no. 41, December 1984, pp.465ff. It opened under the title of *Société anonyme des artistes, peintres, sculpteurs, graveurs, etc.* on 15 April 1874 in former studios of the notorious Parisian photographer Nadar; the décor was red – red wallpaper and hangings, red attendant's uniform – to match Nadar's red hair and walrus moustache. The leaders were Monet, Degas, Pissarro, Renoir and Sisley. Over 200 works were seen by about 4,000 visitors; including some rather unsympathetic critics, one of whom coined the originally derisive label 'Impressionist'.

[7] English interpretations of Impressionism are fully documented and discussed by Flint 1984. Although both Roberts and Richardson had considerable opportunity to see French Impressionist paintings, in London if not in Paris, there is no evidence that they did so. The Australian artists would have read numerous articles on Impressionism in English and American magazines but these were not often illustrated.

[8] 1880; quoted by Rewald, op. cit., p.447.

[9] See Boime 1971, especially pp. 170ff. (Many English and European painters used cigar-box panels for their oil sketches from time to time.)

[10] The quotation from Jean-Léon Gérôme was a legacy of Roberts's very brief sojourn in that master's atelier at the Académie Julian in Paris in 1884. Roberts is said to have first learned something of Impressionism from Loreano Barrau, one of the Spanish art students encountered during the walking tour with John Peter Russell in 1883, who had been a pupil of Gérôme. The quotation is somewhat ironical and

clear evidence of a very superficial knowledge of French art; for Gérôme was a leading academic genre painter who called Impressionism 'the dishonour of France' and a sign of 'great moral depravity'.

[11] *Melbourne Punch*, 22 August 1889, p.116.

[12] For descriptions of this exhibition and Whistler's gallery décor see *The Artist and Journal of Home Culture*, 1 June 1884, p.164; *The Portfolio*, 1884, p.144; Walter Dowdeswell, 'Whistler', *The Art Journal*, April 1887, pp.97ff. (also printed in *The Magazine of Art*). For titles and Whistler's address to the public, 'Proposition No. 2', see the catalogue *'Notes' – 'Harmonies' – 'Nocturnes'* (an original copy is held by the State Library of Victoria). For examples still extant, see McLaren Young et al 1980.

[13] *Daily Telegraph*, 24 August 1889, p.10.

[14] *Table Talk*, 16 August 1889, p.6; 23 August, 1889, p.4; described in less detail in other newspapers.

[15] Roberts's studio is described in *The Illustrated Sydney News*, 1 August 1891, p.6 and elsewhere; for Falls's, see *Table Talk*, 7 February 1890, p.5 and Conder's in *Table Talk*, 5 April 1889, p.6.

[16] Galbally 1980, pp.130ff. discusses the exhibition in the context of the modish Aesthetic style of interior decoration. For an excellent account of Aestheticism in Melbourne, see Lane 1984. The Aesthetic movement had originated in England in the 1860s, seeking to bring 'taste' and beauty to all spheres of design from architecture to dress. Initially it had a firm philosophical and literary base; and a considerable influence on painting and sculpture. By 1880, however, when it reached the Melbourne general public at the International Exhibition, it was thoroughly commercial and somewhat superficially faddish: largely 'sunflower adoration and too-too-ism' (*Once a Month*, 15 October 1884, p.299). It drew heavily for inspiration upon Japanese design but increasingly embraced a rag-bag of styles from Jacobean to Adam revival. The movement and its 'high priest', Oscar Wilde, were much satirized in the years around 1880 by caricaturists such as George du Maurier and in the musical comedies of Gilbert and Sullivan (for example the 'greenery-yallery Grosvenor Gallery'). Cullis Hill opened his importing and manufacturing New English Art Furniture Warehouse at 62 and 64 Elizabeth Street, Melbourne, on 18 July 1881. Liberty's of London had agents throughout the civilized world by the 1880s, advertising fine Indian silk as 'invaluable for artistic draping'; Bretby 'Art Pottery' was listed in their catalogues by at least 1890. Liberty's also sold a very wide range of *japonaiserie* from fans, lacquer ware and screens to 'Tokio Tooth Powder'. *Liberty's 1875 – 1975 an exhibition to mark the firm's centenary*, Victoria and Albert Museum, London, 1975, pp.10,17.

[17] *Table Talk*, 5 October 1888, p.4.

[18] *The Portfolio*, 1884, p.144.

[19] *Table Talk*, 16 August 1889, p.6 and 23 August 1889, p.4; *Daily Telegraph* and *Evening Standard*, locs cit. See also Moore 1934, I, p.74 and Croll 1935, p.25. Although artists such as Rossetti had used painted frames with poetic inscriptions earlier in the century, Whistler's were especially famous. See T.R. Way, *Memories of James McNeill Whistler, the artist,* John Lane The Bodley Head, London and New York, 1912, p.54. Many *avant-garde* European painters had particular ideas about the framing of their work; see, for example, a letter from Pissarro, also commenting on Whistler. John Rewald (ed.), *Camille Pissarro, Letters to his son Lucien*, Kegan Paul, Trench, Trubner and Co., London, 1943, pp.22f. Unusual frames were also a feature of the New English Art Club, 'every artist having some special device of his own' (*Westminster Times*, 9 April 1887). All paintings exhibited at the Royal Academy still had to be framed in gold; black or 'dark natural wood' were allowed at the Salon.

[20] No.69, *Gold, Green and White* was described in *Melbourne Punch* and *The Evening Standard*: one of a 'series of "impressions" (chiefly ideal) for decorative panels'. *A Nereid* is illustrated as no. 152 in the Victorian Artists' Society catalogue of May 1892.

[21] Moore 1934, I, p.75. Both, Whistler in February 1883, and the French Impressionists exhibiting in London, April-July 1883, had collected and publicised adverse criticisms to attract further interest. See Burns A. Stubbs, *James McNeill Whistler, a biographical outline illustrated from the collection of the Freer Gallery of Art*, Smithsonian, Washington, 1950, p.22; Cooper 1954, p.23.

[22] *Argus*, 4 September 1889, reprinted in full by Smith 1975, pp.208ff.

[23] *Argus*, 26 October 1885, p.7. Whistler's painting (probably quite a large canvas, now unfortunately untraceable) was included in an exhibition sent to Sydney and Melbourne by the Anglo-Australian Society of Artists: 'The place of honour in it has been assigned to "A Note in Blue and Green", but the note is written in some cryptic character, which is unintelligible to the uninitiated. There are some dabs of green paint which highly imaginative persons are requested to regard as waves of the sea; and there are some eccentric smears of blue and grey, which you are invited to accept as representations of cloud-form . . . The Whistler cult has found a reverential devotee in Mr. Menpes, who appears to have made a special study of deformed, ricketty and hydrocephalous children . . . It is with no inconsiderable sense of relief that we turn from these fantastic productions to the fine workmanship, the homely feeling, the nice sense of colour, and the loyal truth to nature manifested by Mr Walter Langley . . .' (Langley was a founder of the *plein air* Newlyn School).

[24] Whistler sued Ruskin and won, in 1878, damages of a farthing but was bankrupted by his own costs. Richardson later recalled long discussions with Roberts and McCubbin on the 'Ruskin and Whistler libel case'. Richardson 1918, p.7.

[25] c.1896; Croll 1946, p.63. For Russell's letters to Roberts, see Galbally 1977.

Catalogue.

			Guineas
1	Fog, Thames Embankment	*Tom Roberts*	1
2	After the Play ...	... *Chas. Conder*	1½
3	Grey and Purple ...	*Arthur Streeton*	1
4	Collins St. 11 a.m.	... *Chas. Conder*	1½
5	At Sandridge ...	... *Tom Roberts*	1
6	Winter's Evening ...	... ,,	1½
7	The Wave	... ,,	*(Lent)*
8	The Milky Way ...	... ,,	3
9	Fisherman's Bend ...	*Arthur Streeton*	1½
10	Looking over to Williamstown	*R. E. Falls*	2
11	The National Gallery	*Arthur Streeton*	1½
12	Yellow and Grey ...	... ,,	1
13	Andante	... *Tom Roberts*	*(Lent)*
14	Going Home ...	... ,,	2
15	By the Treasury ...	... ,,	2
16	Cometh not	... ,,	5
17	Quiet Study ...	... ,,	2
18	Black & Red & White ...	,,	5
19	She-oak and Sun-light ...	,,	2
20	Perplexed	... ,,	7

The 9 by 5 Impression Exhibition, 1889
Catalogue – with cover and advertisement designed by Charles Conder
Printed by Fergusson and Mitchell, Art Printers, Fancy Stationers, Collins Street, Melbourne
Wood engraving on handmade paper, twenty pages
17.7 x 10.6 cm
Private collection, Victoria

Provenance:
Charles Douglas Richardson; estate of Stephanie Taylor, a pupil of Richardson, 1973; Richard Berry, Melbourne 1974; private collection

Literature:
Smith 1971, pp.95ff.; Peers 1985, no.55

Conder's design for the *9 by 5* catalogue cover was intended both as a witty statement about the title of the exhibition and, more seriously, as an allegory of the artists' aim to flout convention. The figures '9' and '5' are set against wooden discs cut along and across the grain respectively: just as the length of a cedar cigar-box panel is normally cut with the grain and the width against it. A rather bad-tempered looking young woman represents 'Art bound by convention' (her bindings are thus labelled); her torch smoulders on the point of extinction. Various emblems of transience symbolize the 'fleeting character' of the Impressionists' subject matter: the sun shines forth from the lower left hand corner; petals fall from a branch of blossom; the dragonfly – according to natural history folklore – lives only for a day. This is an early example of Conder's lifelong love of allegory and symbol; and his innate decorative emphasis – with an element of *art nouveau* stylization. As *Table Talk*'s critic remarked, the catalogue was 'quite an elegant little souvenir'.[1]

[1] 23 August 1889, p.4. Conder also designed an allegorical catalogue cover for the *Victorian Artists' Society Winter Exhibition*, March 1890.

TOM ROBERTS ▶
Thames scene, [c.1884]
Oil on wood panel
12.7 x 22.9 cm
Verso: label written by a previous owner,
November 1955, repeating information
from Clive Stephen that the painting was
said to have been included in the 9 by 5
Impression Exhibition of 1889
Private collection, Melbourne
For exhibition in Melbourne only

Provenance:
The artist's studio; Mrs Fanny Burchill (his
sister-in-law); Dr Clive Stephen (sculptor)
until 1955; private collection, Melbourne

Exhibitions:
9 by 5 Impression Exhibition, Melbourne,
August 1889, possibly no.1: 'Fog, Thames
Embankment – 1 guinea'

Literature:
Age, 17 August 1889, p.15; Spate 1978,
pp.24,27,30, pl.3; Topliss 1985, no.41, p.6

Roberts brought home a number of his
Whistlerian oil sketches on panel when he
returned from London in 1885. This one
was painted from the Thames Embankment looking across to the mist-shrouded
Houses of Parliament.

CHARLES CONDER ▶
*A winter Sunday at Heidelberg with Tom
Roberts and Arthur Streeton*, 1889
Oil on board (in original signed frame)
13.9 x 24 cm
Signed l.r.: Charles Conder
Inscribed l.c.: Sunday, July 27. 1889.
Heidelberg
Australian National Gallery
Gift of Mr and Mrs Fred Williams and
family 1979

Provenance:
Mr Cholmondeley, London; Arthur
Chomley 1961; J.R. Lawson, Sydney, 27
November 1963, lot 32 (unsold); Mr and
Mrs Rudy Komon 1966; Mr and Mrs Fred
Williams

Exhibitions:
9 by 5 Impression Exhibition, Melbourne,
August 1889, probably no.47: 'Impressionists' Camp – 1 guinea' (bought by Mr
A'Beckett)

Literature:
Table Talk, 30 August 1889, p.6; Hoff
1964, p.34; Hoff 1972, no.C54; Splatt &
Bruce 1981, pl.35; Daniel Thomas 1982,
p.220; Topliss 1984, no.49

The unframed picture hanging on the wall
appears to be Streeton's *Impression for
'Golden Summer'*.

◀ CHARLES CONDER
Sketch Portrait, [c.1889]
Oil on panel
15.3 x 10.5 cm
Signed 1.1.: Charles Conder
Inscribed l.r.: SKETCH PORTRAIT
National Gallery of Victoria
Purchased 1970

Provenance:
Theodore Fink, Melbourne – probably
from the artist in 1889; bequeathed to his
daughter, Mrs W.M. Timmins; to Rodney
G. Timmins, by descent; Christie's,
Melbourne, 16 September 1970, lot 89

Exhibitions:
9 by 5 Impression Exhibition, Melbourne,
August 1889, either no.43 or no.107:
'Sketch Portrait – 1 guinea'

Literature:
Gibson 1914, p.93; Rothenstein 1938,
p.286; Hoff 1960, no.31, pl.16; Hoff 1972,
no.C48, p.32, fig.9

ARTHUR STREETON ▲
Impression for 'Golden Summer', [c. 1888]
Oil on canvas (on board)
29.6 x 58.7 cm
Signed l.l.: A. Streeton
Ledger Collection
Benalla Art Gallery

Provenance:
Given by Streeton to John Llewelyn
Jones, a fellow artist at Eaglemont, in
1888; sold to Harold Desbrowe Annear
(architect) before 1935; L.H. Ledger,
Benalla

Exhibitions:
9 by 5 Impression Exhibition, Melbourne,
August 1889, no.31: 'Impression for
"Golden Summer" (*kindly lent by J.L.
Jones, Esq.*)'

Literature:
Streeton 1935, no.40; Splatt & Bruce 1981,
pl.30; Topliss 1984, no.63
Reproduced by courtesy of Mrs Oliver
Streeton

Several of the 9 by 5 impressions were
related to full-scale paintings. Streeton
had exhibited *Golden Summer, Eaglemont* with the Victorian Artists' Society in
May 1889.

ARTHUR STREETON ▼
A Road to the Ranges, [c. 1889]
Also known as 'Impression – roadway'
Oil on cardboard
14.3 x 24 cm
National Gallery of Victoria
Purchased 1955

Provenance:
Original owner unknown; R.T. Miller,
Carnegie c.1955; purchased from
Decoration Co., Melbourne, June 1955

Exhibitions:
Perhaps *9 by 5 Impression Exhibition*,
Melbourne, August 1889, no. 38: 'A Road
to the Ranges – 3 guineas'

Literature:
Streeton 1935, no.69; Galbally 1979,
no.28; Splatt & Bruce 1981, pl.33; Downer
& Phipps 1985, no.189
Reproduced by courtesy of Mrs Oliver
Streeton

This impression is now tentatively identified as *A Road to the Ranges*: much
admired by *The Evening Standard* in 1889
as a sunny landscape, the road dotted with
travellers 'on the wallaby' and 'the ranges
showing up darkly blue in the distance'.

CHARLES CONDER ▲
All on a Summer's Day, 1888
Oil on wood panel
40.6 x 28.8 cm
Signed and dated l.l.: CHARLES
CONDER/APRIL-1888-
Inscribed l.r.: ALL.ON.A.SUMMER'S.DAY.
M.J.M. Carter Collection, Adelaide

Provenance:
Dr Douglas Stewart 1889; probably until
his *Art Sale of a Fine Private Collection . . .*,
Gemmell, Tuckett and Co., Melbourne, 30
April 1920 (? as part of lot 91); P.L. Pickles,
Sydney, November 1980; Lauraine
Diggins; M.J.M. Carter, Adelaide

Exhibitions:
9 by 5 Impression Exhibition, Melbourne,
August 1889, no.54: 'All on a Summer's
Day – 1½ guineas'

Literature:
Table Talk, 30 August 1889, p.6; Gibson
1914, p.93; Hoff 1964, pp.31, 35; Hoff
1970, no.C24

HERBERT JAMES DALY
'Barfold', 1888
Watercolour and bodycolour on paper
33 x 42.3 cm
Signed and dated l.l.: Herbert
Daly/EASTER 1888
Private collection, Melbourne
For exhibition in Melbourne only

Daly's single contribution to the 9 by 5
exhibition has not been traced. This
bird's-eye view of his wife's family
homestead, 'Barfold', on the Campaspe
River, near Kyneton in Victoria is a rare
example of his early painting style.

CHARLES CONDER ▲
A Dream of Handel's Largo, [c. 1889]
Oil on cedar panel (cigar-box lid)
26.6 x 16.1 cm
M.J.M. Carter Collection, Adelaide

Provenance:
The Daley family (label verso, now destroyed); Sir Keith Murdoch; until *A Collection of Antiques, the property of Sir Keith and Lady Murdoch*, Decoration Co., Melbourne, 20 August 1947, lot 200; J.M. Edwards; until Leonard Joel, Melbourne, 20 June 1969, lot 55, illus.; M.J.M. Carter, Adelaide

Exhibitions:
9 by 5 Impression Exhibition, Melbourne, August 1889, no.117: 'A Dream of Handel's Largo – 3 guineas'

Literature:
Gibson 1914, p.94; Rothenstein 1938, p.36; Hoff 1960, no.36; Hoff 1972, no.C52

CHARLES CONDER ▲
The Happy Days of Wooing, [c.1889]
Oil on card, in original painted pine frame decorated with pink blossom
23.6 x 11.6 cm
Signed l.l.: CHARLES CONDER
William J. Hughes, Perth

Provenance:
Mr and Mrs J.W. Traill; Lauraine Diggins, May 1984, no. 19; William J. Hughes, Perth

Exhibitions:
9 by 5 Impression Exhibition, Melbourne, August 1889, no.120: 'The Happy Days of Wooing – 1 guinea'

Literature:
Gibson 1914, p.94; Radford 1974, no.3, as 'Lovers' Walk'; Topliss 1984, no.62

CHARLES CONDER ▲
How We Lost Poor Flossie, [1889]
Oil on panel
25 x 9.2 cm
Signed l.l.: CONDER
Art Gallery of South Australia
Purchased through the Elder Bequest
1941
For exhibition in Melbourne and Adelaide
only

Provenance:
Given to McCubbin by the artist in 1889;
sent for sale at Christie's, London, before
1918; John Young of Macquarie Galleries,
Sydney, who brought it back to Australia

Exhibitions:
9 by 5 Impression Exhibition, Melbourne,
August 1889, no.111; 'How We Lost Poor
Flossie – 2 guineas'

Literature:
*Bulletin of the Art Gallery of South
Australia*, III, 1, 1941; Hoff 1960, no.33;
McCulloch 1969, pl.62; Gleeson 1971,
pl.52, p.101; Hoff 1972, no. C51, pl.15,
p.38; Astbury 1980, p.265; Horton &
Thomas 1981, pp.61, 64; Astbury 1985, in
press, p.72

Flossie was Fred McCubbin's dog, who
vanished whilst out walking one rainy
day. According to McCubbin's daughter,
Conder's original wide frame for this
impression was painted with a series of
vignettes to illustrate preceding episodes
in the sorry tale.[1] The soft mauve tonality
is distinctly Whistlerian and the bold vertical format is *japoniste*. Conder was clearly
inspired by the atmospheric wet city
street scenes of many European and
American contemporaries.

[1] Such *'remarques'* or marginal sketches
were an established stylistic trait in late
19th century French art, brought to
perfection, perhaps, by Felix Buhot
(1847-98) in his *japoniste* etchings – very
often of wet street scenes; Buhot gave
them the delightful name *marges
symphoniques* or 'symphonic margins'.

TOM ROBERTS ▲
Evening Train to Hawthorn, [c.1889]
Oil on cedar panel
14 x 22.6 cm
Private collection, Sydney

Provenance:
Miss Sylvia Bertha Purves (the artist's
niece), then known as 'Evening, Princes
Bridge'; William Ellenden, Sydney, May
1976, lot 118, as 'Spencer St. Station'; Chris
Deutscher, Melbourne 1977; Mr and Mrs
Rob Andrew, Melbourne; private col-
lection, Sydney

Exhibitions:
9 by 5 Impression Exhibition, Melbourne,
August 1889, no. 77: 'Evening Train to
Hawthorn – 1 guinea'

Literature:
Topliss 1985, no. 127

Painted from the Yarra bank facing across
the old Princes Bridge railway station;
Scots Church and the Independent
Church spires can be seen in the centre
(on the Collins Street hill). Quite a number
of the 9 by 5s treated railway subjects and
'bits of tram life'.

ARTHUR STREETON ▲
The Long Road, 1889
Oil on cedar panel (cigar-box lid)
25 x 11 cm
Signed and dated l.r.: Streeton, 89
Verso: paper cigar-box label
Shepparton Art Gallery
Purchased 1958
Also known as 'The Old Road'

Provenance:
Unknown, probably Theodore Fink,
Melbourne – died 1942

Exhibitions:
Probably *9 by 5 Impression Exhibition*,
Melbourne, August 1889, no.124: 'The
Long Road – 1 guinea' (bought by
Theodore Fink – *Table Talk*, 23 August
1889, p.4)

Literature:
Streeton 1935, no.76; Radford 1973,
no.43; Perry 1980, no.47; Splatt & Bruce
1981, pl.36
Reproduced by courtesy of Mrs Oliver
Streeton

TOM ROBERTS ▲
Harper's Weekly, [c. 1889]
Oil on cedar panel (cigar-box lid)
23.8 x 14.2 cm
Inscribed verso: 'Bought from Tom
Roberts/NINE by FIVE Impression
Exhibition/Aug. 1889/J.W. Springthorpe';
and printed stamp 500/"Claro Colorado"
National Gallery of Victoria
Purchased 1958
Previously called 'Quiet Study'

Provenance:
Dr John William Springthorpe, Mel-
bourne 1889; until *The Springthorpe
Collection of Australian Pictures*, Leonard
Joel, Melbourne, 24 May 1934, lot 61: 'Girl
Reading (a 9 x 5)'; Mrs Simpson (the artist's
sister-in-law); her daughter Miss 'Nellie'
Eleanor Lil Simpson; R.J. Allsop, Eltham

Exhibitions:
9 by 5 Impression Exhibition, Melbourne,
August 1889, no.139: 'Harper's Weekly – 3
guineas'

Literature:
Daily Telegraph, 17 August 1889, p.7;
Table Talk, 23 August 1889, p.4; Hughes
1977, p.56; Spate 1978, pl.15; Splatt &
Bruce 1981, pl.32; Downer & Phipps 1985,
no.175; Topliss 1985, no.140, but see also
no. 138

Under the title of 'Harper's Weekly', Mr
Roberts has drawn a young girl reading that paper. The pose of the young
student is very natural, and the subdued colouring remarkably effective.
– *The Daily Telegraph*, 17 August 1889

This impression is very closely comparable Whistler's little panel, *Arrangement
in Black – Reading*, which Roberts probably saw in the 'Notes' – 'Harmonies' –
'Nocturnes' exhibition at Dowdeswell's
Gallery, London, in 1884 (no.26). For
many years it has been identified as *Quiet
Study*, catalogue no.17 in the 9 by 5 exhibition; however, it is much more likely to
be no.139 which was purchased by Dr
Springthorpe. *Harper's Weekly, A Journal
of Civilization* was widely read in Melbourne at the time. (McCubbin's scrapbook contains numerous cuttings.)
Advertisements declared it to be 'The
Leading American Illustrated Weekly. In
the best sense of the term it is an American
educator. It fills a large place in the minds
of the coming men and women'.

TOM ROBERTS ▲
Perplexed, [c.1889]
Oil on cedar panel
26.6 x 16.9 cm
Private collection, Melbourne

Provenance:
Dick Roberts, the artist's brother; Mrs
Fanny Burchill, his widow; private
collection, Melbourne

Exhibitions:
9 by 5 Impression Exhibition, Melbourne,
August 1889, probably no.20: 'Perplexed
– 7 guineas'

CHARLES DOUGLAS RICHARDSON ▲
Wind, 1889
Wax on cedar panel
16.3 x 11.2 cm
Signed with initials and dated l.r.: CDR/
1889
Inscribed c.l.: WIND
Australian National Gallery
Rudy Komon Fund 1981

Provenance:
Bertram Joseph Bryning, painter,
Melbourne; to his son Frank Bryning,
Brisbane in the 1940s; Phillip Bacon
Galleries, Brisbane 1980-81

Exhibitions:
9 by 5 Impression Exhibition, Melbourne,
August 1889, no.119: 'Wind *(Wax)* – 3
guineas'

Literature:
Age, 17 August 1889, p.15; *Argus*, 17
August 1889, p.10; *Table Talk*, 23 August
1889, p.4; Sturgeon 1978, pp.75f.; Radford
1980, p.36; Daniel Thomas 1982, p.220;
Peers 1985, no.32

Mr Richardson's sketches in wax are
noticeably good, and are the one
exhibit which has had the good fortune to meet with general approval.
– *Table Talk*, 23 August 1889

Literature:
*A Memorial Exhibition of Paintings of the
late Tom Roberts*, Fine Art Society,
Melbourne, June 1932, no.55, as 'Portrait,
Miss Walker', with a note that it had been
included in the 9 by 5 Exhibition of 1889;
Croll 1935, p.138; Spate 1978, p.68 as 'Girl
in a hammock'; Topliss 1985, no.145 as
'Portrait, Miss Walker'

The subject of this impression is said to
have been Miss Lucy Walker, a former
Gallery School student and close friend of
the Heidelberg artists. Her pose is very
similar to that of the dark-haired girl holding a fan in Roberts's *Jealousy*, painted the
same year and first exhibited as *'One, not
easily Jealous, but, being wrought, per-
plex'd in the extreme'*.[1] The oriental bro-
cade which forms the background was
one of the exotic appurtenances in
Roberts's studio.

[1] From Shakespeare's *Othello*, IV, iii.
Another example of Roberts's rather
wittily cryptic titles in the 9 by 5
exhibition was no. 171, *La Favorita*,
taken from the cigar brand name
stamped on the back of that panel (Topliss
1985, no.141). *Jealousy* is now in the Art
Gallery of New South Wales; according to
Table Talk, 10 May 1889, p.3, 'the model
for the dark woman in Tom Roberts's
"Jealousy" was Miss Bevan, the actress'.

TOM ROBERTS ▲
*Her Majesty's Mail, O'Meara's Skipton
Road*, [c.1889]
Oil on cedar panel
13.2 x 16.8 cm
Inscribed on label verso: 'Given by Tom
Roberts the artist to Fanny Bristow after
singing at the Exhibition of small paintings
on August 17th 1889'
The Robert Holmes à Court Collection

Provenance:
Fanny Bristow; by descent to her grand-
son, F.H. Lemann, Bowral, New South
Wales; Thirty Victoria Street, Sydney
1980; private collection, Sydney; Robert
Holmes à Court, Perth 1985

Exhibitions:
9 by 5 Impression Exhibition, Melbourne,
August 1889, no.102: 'Her Majesty's Mail,
O'Meara's Skipton Road – 2 guineas'

Literature:
Topliss 1985, no.120

O'Meara's Hotel, on the south side of Skipton Road, was a regular stop for Cobb &
Co. coaches carrying the Royal Mail; in
the paddock opposite, two upright posts
and a cross bar form a gibbet used in
stringing up cattle for slaughter. This
'impression' was chosen by Miss Fanny
Bristow as her payment for singing at the
exhibition on the opening day (and again
on Thursday, 29 August).

ARTHUR STREETON ▲
Princess' & Burke & Wills', 1889
Oil on panel
20.3 x 15.4 cm
Signed and dated l.r.: STREETON. 89
Elders IXL Collection
Purchased 1969

Provenance:
Lawrence Abrahams until *The Magnificent Collection of Australian Pictures, late Lawrence Abrahams*, Decoration Co., Melbourne, 20 June 1919, lot 30 [5 guineas]; Mr H.L. Johnson, Kew; Leonard Joel, Melbourne, 7 March 1969, lot 47; Clune Galleries, Sydney

Exhibitions:
9 by 5 Impression Exhibition, Melbourne, August 1889, no.144: 'Princess' & Burke & Wills' – 3 guineas'

Literature:
Streeton 1935, no.86; Galbally 1979, no.29, pl.6B; Radford 1984, no.35
Reproduced by courtesy of Mrs Oliver Streeton

The Burke and Wills memorial statue of 1865, by Charles Summers, was moved from its original position at the intersection of Collins and Russell Streets when tramlines were laid in 1886. It stood opposite the Princess Theatre in Spring Street until 1980, when moved to its present site in the City Square.

TOM ROBERTS ▲
Impression, 1888
Oil on cedar panel (apparently prepared for use in a *plein air* 'painting kit')
11 x 18.5 cm
Signed with monogram and dated l.l.: TR 88 [incised]
National Gallery of Victoria
Purchased 1955

Provenance:
Original owner unknown; J.H. Minogue, East Malvern (an artist) until 1955; purchased from Decoration Co., Melbourne, June 1955

◄ CHARLES CONDER
An Impressionist, [c.1889]
Oil on panel (cigar-box lid)
Panel 28.5 x 23.4 cm; image: 28 x 14.7 cm
Signed and inscribed u.r.: SKETCh OF MR TOM ROBERTS/C/-hAR/-LES/ CONDE/R
Inscribed verso: 'about 1889'
Private collection, Melbourne

Provenance:
John H. Connell, Melbourne; bequeathed to Caleb Roberts, 1953; by descent in the artist's family until 1985;
private collection, Melbourne

Exhibitions:
9 by 5 Impression Exhibition, Melbourne, August 1889, probably no.179: 'An Impressionist – 1 guinea'

Literature:
Hoff 1960, no.32, pl.17; Hoff 1972, no.C47; *Joseph Brown Gallery*, September 1981, no.40; Splatt & Bruce 1981, p.4; Topliss 1984, no.3, as 'An Impressionist'

Exhibitions:
Probably included in the 9 by 5 Impression Exhibition, Melbourne 1889, although it is difficult to find a precise title for it in the catalogue

Literature:
Spate 1964, p.263; Spate 1978, pp.66, 85, pl.16; Splatt & Bruce 1981, p.53, pl.31; Topliss 1985, no.124

CHARLES CONDER ▲
Herrick's Blossoms, [c.1889]
Oil on cardboard
13.1 x 24 cm
Signed l.i.: CHARLES CONDER
Label verso: '*Blossoms* was painted after reading *Herrick's Blossoms*. Noted to that effect by the artist on the back of the picture: A.S. McMichael'
Australian National Gallery
Purchased 1969

Provenance:
A.S. McMichael, Melbourne; W.G. Buckle; Leonard Joel, Melbourne, 7 March 1969, lot 46, illus.

Exhibitions:
9 by 5 Impression Exhibition, Melbourne, August 1889, no.141: 'Herrick's Blossoms – 3 guineas'

Literature:
Gibson 1914, p.94; Rothenstein 1938, p.36; Hoff 1960, no.28; Hoff 1972, no.C38, pl.9; Splatt & Bruce 1981, pl.46; Daniel Thomas 1982, p.219

To Blossoms
Fair pledges of a fruitful tree,
Why do ye fall so fast?
Your date is not so past;
But you may yet stay here a while,
To blush and gently smile;
And go at last.

What, were ye born to be
An hour or half's delight;
And so bid good-night?
'Twas pity Nature brought ye forth,
Merely to show your worth,
And lose you quite.

– Robert Herrick (1591-1674)

CHARLES CONDER ▲
Dandenong from Heidelberg, [c.1889]
Oil on cardboard, in original painted pine frame
11.5 x 23.5 cm
Signed l.r.: CHARLIE CONDER
M.J.M. Carter Collection, Adelaide

Provenance:
Miss Fanny Barbour 1889; to her niece Mrs L.D. Bayer, Berwick; Leonard Joel, Melbourne, 20 June 1969, no.21, illus.; Mr and Mrs Rob Andrew, Melbourne until 1984; M.J.M. Carter, Adelaide

Exhibitions:
9 by 5 Impression Exhibition, Melbourne, August 1889, no.148: 'Dandenong from Heidelberg – 1 guinea'. As this was Fanny Barbour's only recorded purchase at the 9 by 5 exhibition (*Table Talk*, 30 August 1889, p.6), the catalogue ascription of no.148 to Tom Roberts was presumably a misprint; research has revealed other errors – probably due to hasty printing!

Literature:
Table Talk, 30 August 1889, p.6; Hoff 1972, no.C59; Topliss 1984, no.59; Alison Carroll, *East and West: the meeting of Asian and European cultures*, Art Gallery of South Australia, 1985, no.213

ARTHUR STREETON ▲
Mentone Beach, [c.1889]
Oil on card
13.2 x 21.8 cm
Signed with initials l.r.: A.S.
Private collection, Victoria

Provenance:
Original owner unknown; by descent in
the present owner's family

Exhibitions:
9 by 5 Impression Exhibition, Melbourne,
August 1889, perhaps no.131: 'Sunny
Sandringham – 2 guineas'

Literature:
Radford 1974, no.39
Reproduced by courtesy of Mrs Oliver
Streeton

TOM ROBERTS ▼
Across the Dandenongs, [1889]
Oil on cedar panel (cigar-box lid)
13.6 x 23 cm
Signed l.l.: Tom Roberts
Dated l.r.: June 30 1889
Verso: Cigar label fragment and 'Favorita'
stamp
National Gallery of Victoria
Purchased 1962

Provenance:
Original owner unknown; B. W. Harting
until August 1962

Exhibitions:
9 by 5 Impression Exhibition, Melbourne,
August 1889, no. 97: 'Across the
Dandenongs – 3 guineas' or no. 167:
'Across to the Dandenongs – 2 guineas';
Table Talk recorded a Mr Harty, as buyer
of 'Across the Dandenong [*sic*]'

Literature:
Table Talk, 30 August 1889, p.6; Topliss
1985, no. 129

This Heidelberg vista was also depicted in
Roberts's *Moonlight* and Streeton's *Still
glides the stream*. . . of 1890.

TOM ROBERTS ▲
Woman at the piano, [c. 1889]
Oil on cedar panel
26 x 13.1 cm
M.J.M. Carter Collection, Adelaide

Provenance:
Original owner unknown; private
collection, Melbourne; Chris Deutscher,
Melbourne; M.J.M. Carter, Adelaide

Exhibitions:
Probably in the 9 by 5 Impression
Exhibition, Melbourne, August, 1889

Literature:
Topliss 1985, – Disc 10 No.93a

Several of the 9 by 5 catalogue titles
reflect Roberts's interest in music. No.13,
Andante, purchased by Miss Sutherland,
was one example; no.147, *Lieder ohne
Worte* (songs without words) another. 'I
think there is such affinity between the
sister arts', he told *Melbourne Punch*, 'that
I am disposed to believe that what impre-
sses itself deeply upon the practitioner of
one will not be without corresponding
influence on the worker in the other' (6
May 1889, p.300).

ARTHUR STREETON ▶
The National Game, [c.1889]
Oil on cardboard
11.8 x 22.9 cm
Signed with initials l.r.: A.S. [incised]
Art Gallery of New South Wales
Purchased 1963

Provenance:
J.W. Maund, Sydney; Coleman Page Pty
Ltd, Sydney (auction sale including estate
of the late Mrs G.C. Maund), 7 June 1963,
lot 235

Exhibitions:
Probably *9 by 5 Impression Exhibition*,
Melbourne, August 1889, no.150: 'The
National Game – 1 guinea'

Literature:
Streeton 1935, no.87; Olsen 1963, p.164;
Inson & Ward 1971, p.105; Galbally 1979,
no.27, pl.6A; Leonie Sandercock, *Up
Where Cazaly? The Great Australian
Game*, Granada, London, Sydney etc.,
1981, reproduced on jacket; Downer &
Phipps 1985, no.190, p.53
Reproduced by courtesy of Mrs Oliver
Streeton

Australian rules – 'colonial football' –
amazed at least one visitor to Melbourne
in the 1880s:

> What I saw of it struck me as the fastest
> game I have ever seen. Hands are
> used, legs, heads, everything, in break-
> ing down all the rules of other football
> systems, with the one object of speed.
> Science must therefore to a great
> extent suffer. Every man seems to play
> his best individually. The combination
> is nothing compared with the combi-
> nation in any other football I have
> seen; although, no doubt, it exists. The
> science of the Victorian game of foot-
> ball may be too quick for a stranger to
> grasp at first sight, or an artist to depict
> with justice.[1]

Streeton remembered painting this impression at East Richmond or Burnley in
1889. Perhaps it was a practice session, or
an amateur match, for none of the major
teams wore these colours at that date and
long trousers had already been abandoned by most players.

[1] Harry Furniss, *Australian Sketches
Made on Tour*, Ward Lock and Co.,
London, New York and Melbourne 1888,
pp.74f.

FREDERICK McCUBBIN ▲
Petit déjeuner – sketch for *After Breakfast*,
[c.1889]
Oil on cedar panel (cigar-box lid)
11 x 22.3 cm
National Gallery of Victoria
Purchased 1956

Provenance:
Hugh McCubbin, the artist's son

Literature:
Hoff 1955

McCubbin's larger, oil on canvas version
of this subject was exhibited at the Victorian Artists' Society in March 1890 (no.87)
and well received by the critics as 'a pleasant little *genre* picture'; it is now in a private collection.

ROGER EYKYN FALLS ▼
Port Phillip Heads (from Point Lonsdale),
1888
Oil on canvas
30.7 x 102 cm
Signed and dated l.l.: R.E. Falls 1888
Geelong Art Gallery
Presented by H.G. Oliver 1935

Provenance:
Harry Glen Oliver, Lara, secretary and
engineer to the Corio Shire Council

Literature:
Geelong Advertiser, 14 December 1934,
p.6; *Geelong Art Gallery Annual Report of
Trustees*, 1934

> Mr Falls' sketches have such a finished
> appearance that they are something
> more than 'Impressions'.
> – *Table Talk*, 23 August 1889

> Mr Falls' landscapes are distinguished
> by their tender atmospheric effect, and
> the delicacy of his tones in 'sea and sky'
> subjects.
> – *Table Talk*, 7 February 1890

NATURALISM AND NATIONALISM

Jane Clark

During the 1890s the Heidelberg School painters worked on a grander scale than ever before. They were older, with more confidence in their own powers; each aware of his own particular artistic strengths. By 1895 *The Argus* considered:

> There can be no doubt that an Australian School of painting is in process of birth. A certain indefinable something runs through the works of Messrs McCubbin and Streeton, Roberts... and others, which makes them as of the same class of inspiration.[1]

According to Streeton, it was Tom Roberts who first urged fellow artists to leave 'the suburban bush and paint the national life of Australia'.[2] In part they were responding to calls by writers such as Sidney Dickinson, who declared that 'it should be the ambition of our young artists to present on canvas the earnestness, vigour, pathos and heroism of the life around them'.[3] In particular, the aggressively nationalistic Sydney *Bulletin* – with its slogan 'Australia for Australians' – called upon the painter to meet 'the artistic needs of his public' and to depict the 'real Australia' of the outer pastoral regions.[4] Roberts once rode 170 miles through northern New South Wales on his mare, Black Bess, from 'Yugilbar' on the Clarence River to 'Newstead' station near Armidale. He spent at least three seasons in the Riverina at 'Brocklesby' station. Streeton wrote to him in about 1892:

> I'm not a bit tired of Australia... I want to stay here, but not in Melb. If I can raise this coin I intend to go straight inland (away from all polite society), and stay there 2 or 3 years and create some things entirely new, and try and translate some of the great hidden poetry that I know is here, but have not seen or felt.[5]

Outback and pioneering subjects, they believed, distinguished Australian life from that of any other nation.

Earlier colonial artists had, of course, painted Australian 'types' such as stockmen and goldfields workers: Conrad Martens, S.T. Gill, William Strutt, for example. James Alfred Turner's pictures were popularly considered 'typical of Australian bush-life [for] Mr Turner has travelled all over the colonies and is thoroughly conversant with station life'.[6] Nevertheless, his illustrative canvases, usually fairly small in scale, were scarcely different from the anecdotal 'pictures of character' and 'bush types' produced by contemporary photographers or by black-and-white newspaper artists. Indeed the Heidelberg painters' own experience of these two popular media was a most important factor in conditioning their ideas and building up their visual vocabulary.[7]

One influential English writer said that in 'a country full of fine effects and unhackneyed compositions, the Australians should require no other stimulus to produce really artistic work of an original sort'.[8] But only an academically trained painter, such as Roberts, could handle a complex composition of figures in action on the ambitious scale of *Shearing the Rams*. The younger generation, trained overseas or at the Gallery School, was at last capable of creating a strong figurative tradition in Australian art. (Streeton, who had little formal instruction, often said that he envied McCubbin's skill as a figure painter.) Several of them were planning, as 'a new departure... considered to be the crucial test', to send paintings for exhibition at the Royal Academy in London.[9] Their subject matter was not new but it was given a new significance by their ambitious treatment. They endowed images of Australian life or pioneering history with overtones of heroic grandeur and nobility.

Mainstream European art was both an inspiration and a yardstick by which Australians could measure their own achievements. The theme of men at work, for example, had been advocated by leading French artists as early as the 1860s. 'Look at these young fellows', Thomas Couture had written, 'so well built,... their heads generally fine, burned by the sun; see the rich amber colour... Who are these men? These are new subjects'.[10] Roberts's first essays in national working life were *Wood Splitters* and *End to a Career – an old Scrub Cutter*, 1888 (present whereabouts unknown). The theme of 'strong masculine labour' reached heroic proportions in his great shearing subjects and *The Break Away* of 1891. Streeton's *Fire's On*, 1891, records a team of toiling 'big brown men' pitted against the harsh Australian land and climate. Thus when John Peter Russell, writing from Paris, described *Shearing the Rams* as naturalistic art' and 'rational impressionism', he was grouping Roberts with a whole generation of European painters. The 'Naturalist' successors of Jean François Millet and Gustave Courbet asserted that art should treat local and contemporary life 'in all forms and on all levels, and that its sole aim is to reproduce nature by bringing it to its maximum strength and intensity'.[11] As Roberts wrote in defence of his own work, 'by making art the perfect expression of one time and one place, it becomes art for all time and of all places'.[12]

Naturalism was an attitude towards subject matter and the role of art, rather than a single style or a 'school' – with all the strictures and limitations that term implies. By about 1890, however, what Russell called 'rational Impressionism' was indeed a hallmark of most naturalist work, not only in France, but throughout Europe, in England, America and Australia. Artists combined some impressionist elements – bright colours, freer brushwork and atmospheric distance – with basically academic methods of careful underlying composition and accurate drawing in the figures and foreground details. Its most celebrated exponent was Jules Bastien-Lepage, who became something of an international *plein airist* hero when he died young in 1884.[13]

Many naturalist painters chose to record characteristic 'types' engaged in activities which, due to the 19th century's rapid social and industrial progress, would soon be history. In Australia two thirds of the population lived in cities and towns by 1891. City and country had acquired new importance as categories of thought and imagery in both art and literature: the booming cosmopolitan metropolis *versus* the unspoilt 'Great Australian Bush'. Roberts and McCubbin certainly saw themselves as chroniclers of passing ways of life. In Sydney Roberts told the Society of Artists:

> They had the beauties of all the Pacific slopes to paint – right away to the north where they were fishing for bêche-de-mer, away to the far west where gold was being mined for, and down to the southern coast, where pursuits were more agricultural – all this they had to paint. They were now living in one of the most interesting epochs of time in these colonies. They were getting the last touch of the old colonial days. Men who came to paint here in 20 years' time would know nothing of it. Artists of the present time had the chance to paint it, and this they were trying to do. It was a life different from any other country in the world.[14]

Although McCubbin remained in the 'suburban bush' – tied by family and teaching duties – he embarked on a series of major paintings in celebration of Australia's pioneer settlers: 'that union of landscape and bush episode which he has somewhat made his own'.[15] And he followed most faithfully the methods of Bastien-Lepage, working some of his largest canvases entirely out-of-doors.

For Streeton, the Australian landscape and light were themselves heroic. Just after the Melbourne Gallery had purchased his *Purple noon's transparent might* in 1896, he told Roberts:

> I must work more and produce bigger, more serious things... I picture in my head the Murray and all the wonder and glory at its source up toward Kosciusko..., and the great gold plains, and all the beautiful inland Australia, and I love the thought of walking into all this and trying to expand and express it in my way. I fancy large canvases all glowing and moving in the happy light...[16]

And Roberts spoke in a similar vein, of his yearning to 'ride all day and camp at intervals and boil the quart and sleep at night and lay by the banks of a new big river and back... to the home station and to think if one could express it all, make others feel what beauty there is in it. Australia hasn't been fairly touched yet'.[17]

---

[1] *Argus*, 24 August 1895, Editorial, p.6.

[2] Croll 1935, p.16.

[3] Sidney Dickinson, 'What should Australian artists paint?', *The Australasian Critic*, 1 October 1890, p.22. Calls for specifically Australian subject matter had come particularly thick and fast since the Centennial Exhibition of 1888: for example, James Smith in *The Argus*, 11 September 1888, p.33; Julian Ashton, 'Art in Australia and its possibilities', *Table Talk*, 27 January 1888, p.3, and 'An Aim for Australian Art', *The Centennial Magazine*, I, 1889, pp.31f.; Fred. J. Broomfield, 'Art and Artists in Victoria', *The Centennial Magazine*, I, 1889, pp.882ff.; the Heidelberg School's friend and patron Henry Laurie, Professor of Moral Philosophy at Melbourne University, in a speech to the Victorian Artists' Society, *Table Talk*, 7 June 1889, p.5, and *The Centennial Magazine*, II, 1889, p.37; and many more.

[4] See Astbury 1980 and 1985 ,in press . Frederick Broomfield later became a sub-editor of *The Bulletin*.

[5] Croll 1946, p.40.

[6] *Table Talk*, 4 December 1885, p.2. He sent paintings entitled *On the Wallaby Track*, *Ringing Timber* and *Bailed Up* to the Colonial and Indian Exhibition in London; all subjects treated later – and very differently – by the Heidelberg School.

[7] Leading illustrative photographers in the 1870s and 1880s were J.W. Lindt and Nicholas Caire. See Daniel Thomas 1976 and Astbury 1985; also Lindt's *A Few Notes on Modern Photography*, Melbourne, 1888.

[8] R.A.M. Stevenson, 'Art in Australia', *The Magazine of Art*, 1886, p.399: reviewing the Colonial and Indian Exhibition at which Roberts and other Melbourne artists were represented; illustrated with a 'pioneer' figure subject by George Rossi Ashton.

[9] *Table Talk*, 30 August 1889, p.5. The writer named Roberts, Streeton, Richardson, Walton and John Ford Paterson; and continued, 'Once admitted within those walls – which all British artists consider sacred – Australian art will receive the impetus of which it so sorely stands in need at the present time'.

[10] Thomas Couture, *Conversations on Art Methods*, tr. S.E. Stewart, G.P. Putnam's Sons, 1879, first printed privately in France in the 1860s; reprinted in Nochlin 1966, p.7. Couture himself was famous for vast *machins salonniers*; he was Folingsby's former master (also Manet's and Puvis de Chavannes's).

[11] Russell to Roberts, c.June 1890; printed in Galbally 1977, p.94. The term 'Naturalism' was first used in France to distinguish a younger generation from the older 'Realist' painters, by [Jules Antoine] Castagnary in his *Salon de 1863*, reprinted in *Salons (1857-1870)*, Paris, 1892; Nochlin, op.cit., pp.63ff. See also Weisberg 1980. By the later 1880s naturalism was current throughout Europe and America.

[12] *Argus*, 4 July 1890, p.10.

[13] Bastien-Lepage was much admired by Russell (Galbally 1977, p.21); and by McCubbin (cf. reproductions in his scrapbook and letter to Roberts, 1 June 1892. LaTrobe Collection, State Library of Victoria. MS 8910 1205/3(c) and Croll 1935, p.173). Followers admired by members of the Heidelberg School include the English George Clausen, Henry La Thangue, Stanhope Alexander Forbes, Thomas Cooper Gotch and other Newlyn painters, the Irish John Lavery, the 'Glasgow Boys', the Portuguese Souza Pinto, and Americans Thomas Alexander Harrison and William Morris Hunt. Their popular style of 'impressionism made palatable' is now often termed *juste milieu* or 'middle-of-the-road' by art historians. See Boime 1971; House & Stevens (eds) 1980.

[14] *Sydney Morning Herald*, 21 October 1895, p.3.

[15] *Australasian Art Review*, 1 December 1899, p.25.

[16] Croll 1946, pp.63f.

[17] Roberts to S.W. Pring, from Newbold, Copmanhurst, 16 January 1897. Mitchell Library, Sydney. MS 1367/2 no.18.

FREDERICK McCUBBIN
Down on his Luck, 1889
Oil on canvas
114.5 x 152.8 cm
Signed and dated l.r.: F. McCubbin/1889
Art Gallery of Western Australia
Purchased 1896

Provenance:
William Fergusson, from the artist, until
January 1896

Exhibitions:
*Victorian Artists' Society Winter
Exhibition, 'Grosvenor Gallery', National
Gallery of Victoria*, Melbourne May 1889,
no.25: 'Down in his Luck – £100.0.0', illus.;
*Exhibition of Works of Victorian Artists
and a Loan Collection of Pictures*,
Exhibition Buildings, Melbourne 1890,
no.135: 'Down on His Luck – Lent by W.
Fergusson, Esq.'; *Victorian Artists' Society
Exhibition of Australian Art Past and
Present*, Melbourne, August 1893, no.36:
'Down on his Luck (1889) – Lent by
Fergusson, Esq.'

Literature:
Table Talk, 26 April 1889, p.5; 10 May
1889, p.6; *Argus*, 4 May 1889, p.2; 25
October 1894, p.6; *Centennial Magazine*,
I, July 1889, p.882 , illus.; *Age*, 20
December 1890, p.10; 12 August 1893,
p.15; *Australasian Critic*, January 1891,
p.95; *The Studio*, 1897, p.152; MacDonald
1916, pp.58ff., pl.i; Moore 1934, I, p.71;
Lindsay 1938, p.46; Hoff 1955, no.8; *The
Western Australian Art Gallery Monthly
Feature*, 4, 7, July 1966; McCulloch 1969,
pp.22ff.; David Thomas 1969, p.72; Inson
& Ward 1971, p.79; Smith 1971, p.86;
Hughes 1977, p.67; Smith 1979, p.125,
pl.44; Astbury 1980, pp.263, 266; Galbally
1981, pp.70, 79ff., pl.14; Astbury 1985, in
press, pp.88ff., pl.13

Mr. McCubbin in his present picture,
'Down on his Luck' has left all his
former work far behind, and raises
expectation in no ordinary degree as
to what he will yet accomplish. The
scene represents a forest glade, with
the evening shadows gradually steal-
ing over the trees, and causing them,
as they recede into the forest, to be
enshrouded in a faint grey mist. In the
foregound is a human figure seated on
the ground, after the style of a bushman, and yet conveying the idea that
he has once been far different. The
face tells of hardships, keen and blight-
ing in their influence, but there is a
nonchalant and slightly cynical
expression, which proclaims the
absence of all self-pity . . . McCubbin's
picture is thoroughly Australian in
spirit . . .
– *Table Talk*, 26 April 1889

McCubbin's large picture of an unsuccessful gold digger sadly brooding over his fate was very well received by contemporary viewers. It was sold within an hour of opening at the Victorian Artists' Society exhibition in April 1889; and reproduced photographically by Fergusson and Mitchell in 1894. 'His swag is lying on the ground, and he is ruefully reflecting upon the unsatisfactory nature of his position and prospects', wrote *The Argus*. The landscape itself, with its subdued light, grey-green foliage and warmer touches of brown, seems to share the mood of its solitary human occupant. The subject derives ultimately from illustrations by such artists as S.T. Gill in the 1850s. In those gold rush days, however, the unlucky miner was usually presented as a humorous rather than a sympathetic figure. Gill's anecdotal watercolour, *Bad Results*, 1852, is one early version of the theme.[1] By the late 1880s, when Melbourne's gold-based prosperity reached its peak, the same character could be viewed with romantic nostalgia. Gill's image, for example, was adapted in 1888 for an illustration in *Victoria and Its Metropolis* entitled 'The gold-digger: down on his luck'; and accompanying text described 'the early diggings...full of tales of the silent solitary stranger' whose golden dreams dwindled down to the mere hope of finding enough to keep the spark of life within him.[2] A photograph by Nicholas Caire bears a remarkable resemblance to McCubbin's painting.

Down on his Luck was painted in the Box Hill bush, which McCubbin preferred to the more open landscape of Eaglemont where Streeton and Conder were camping that year. He has left a description of the problems of *plein air* painting on such a large scale (following the methods of Bastien-Lepage): setting up the canvas securely, meeting with the changing weather and carrying home a large wet oil painting – especially if it turned windy. Nevertheless, the posed figure (Louis Abrahams was the model) is rendered with a sharpness of detail which suggests additional studies made in the studio under clearer, artificial light.

[1] Astbury 1980, p.226; an excellent article to which this discussion is much indebted.
[2] Alexander Sutherland, *Victoria and Its Metropolis: Past and Present*, Melbourne, 1888, I, pp.346; II, p.708.

TOM ROBERTS
Sketch portrait – Alexander Anderson (Snr), 1889
Oil on canvas
25.4 x 20.3 cm
Signed and dated u.l.: Tom Roberts/Sep. 24th 1889
Castlemaine Art Gallery and Historical Museum
Purchased with assistance of Caltex – Victorian Government Art Fund and Public Appeal 1979

Provenance:
The artist; Charles Anderson (the subject's son); Misses I.M. and W.M. Anderson (his daughters); Miss F.M. Anderson (his granddaughter)

Literature:
Terry Smith 1980, pp.116, 244; Topliss 1985, no.154

Alexander Augustus Anderson was one of the proprietors of 'Brocklesby' station at Corowa, in the south central Riverina district of New South Wales, where Roberts painted *Shearing the Rams* and *The Break Away*; and 'with much courtesy and kindness [he] arranged all matters to suit, as far as possible, the artist's convenience' (*The Argus*, 26 June 1890). Roberts is said to have met him aboard the 'Lusitania' in 1885. The two men became close friends; and Roberts's brother, Dick, married Anderson's only daughter.

TOM ROBERTS
'First Sketch for Shearing...', [c.1888]
Gouache and pencil on buff paper
22.3 x 30 cm
Signed and inscribed l.l.: 'First sketch for/ Shearing/[? To my] friend C.S. Paterson-/ 1890./Tom Roberts-/Brock[lesb]y'
National Gallery of Victoria
Purchased 1974

Provenance:
Charles Stewart Paterson (friend, patron, decorative artist and builder of Grosvenor Chambers), from the artist, 1890; Mr and Mrs T.L. White, from a local auction, date unknown

Literature:
Astbury 1978, pp.68f.; Terry Smith 1980, p.101; Jaffé 1982, p.32; Topliss 1985, no.149a; Astbury 1985, in press, pp.107, 111, fig.147

The inscribed date 1890 refers to the time of Roberts's gift of the sketch to Paterson. It was presumably done in 1888 before Roberts had finally resolved the composition of *Shearing the Rams*. It is a straightforward record, one glimpse of the animated shearing line: one of his seventy or eighty preparatory studies of 'the light, the atmosphere, the sheep, the men and the work'.

TOM ROBERTS
Shearing the Rams, 1890
Oil on canvas (lined on to board)
121.9 x 182.6 cm
Signed and dated l.l.:
TOM ROBERTS/1890
National Gallery of Victoria
Felton Bequest 1932

Provenance:
Edward Trenchard, of Edward Trenchard and Co., Queen Street, Melbourne, 1890; C.W. Trenchard, until 1932

Exhibitions:
Special viewing at Roberts's studio, Grosvenor Chambers, Melbourne, May 1890; Gemmell, Tuckett and Co., (auctioneers), Melbourne,1890; *Exhibition of Works of Victorian Artists and a Loan Collection of Pictures*, Exhibition Building, Melbourne, December 1890, no.19: 'Shearing the Rams – lent by Edw. Trenchard and Co.'; *Catalogue of the Diamond Jubilee Loan Exhibition in the National Gallery of Victoria, in commemoration of the 60th Year of the Reign of her Majesty Queen Victoria*, Melbourne, June 1897, no. 126: 'Shearing the Rams – lent by Edward Trenchard Esq.'; displayed in Robertson and Moffat's window, Melbourne, August 1900 (they had published reproductions); *Victorian Gold Jubilee Exhibition Art Catalogue*, Bendigo 1901, no.126: 'Shearing the Rams – £350.0.0'

Literature:
Corowa Free Press, 29 November 1889; *Age*, 30 May 1890, p.7; 20 December 1890, p.10; *Argus*, 31 May 1890, p.4; 24 June 1890, p.6; 26 June 1890, p.9; 28 June 1890, pp.8,10; 4 July 1890, p.10; 9 July 1890, p.5; 30 March 1920, p.8; *Table Talk*, 27 September 1889, p.4; 11 October 1889, p.4; 16 May 1890, p.8; 30 May 1890, p.7; 18 July 1890, p.10; 13 September 1900, p.11; *Illustrated Sydney News*, 2 August 1890, p.13; 1 August 1891, p.6; *Australasian Critic*, January 1891, p.95; Moore 1934, I, p.129; Croll 1935, pp.32ff.; Croll 1946, p.128; Hoff 1951, p.129; Spate 1964, p.262; Gleeson 1969, p.62; McCulloch 1969, pp.52, 54, 154; pl.22; Inson & Ward 1971, p.82; Smith 1971, pp.88, 90, 120; Gleeson 1971, pl.34; Finemore 1977, p.26; Hughes 1977, pp.57f.; Astbury 1978, p.68; Spate 1978, pp.19, 69, 85ff.; pl.23; Burn 1980, p.94; Lendon 1980, pp.73ff.; Terry Smith 1980, pp.99ff.; Splatt & Bruce 1981, p.67; Jaffé 1982, pp.30ff.; Topliss 1985, no.149, pp.8,11,14,17ff.; Astbury 1985, in press, pp.6ff., 107ff., pl.17

There is at present on view at Mr Tom Roberts's studio, Grosvenor-Chambers, Collins street, the most important work of a distinctively Australian character which has been completed up to the present time.
– *The Age*, 30 May 1890.

It seems to me that one of the best words spoken to an artist is, 'Paint what you love and love what you paint', and on that I have worked; and so it came that being in the bush and feeling the delight and fascination of the great pastoral life and work I have tried to express it . . . So, lying on piled up wool-bales, and hearing and seeing the troops come pattering into their pens, the quick running of the wool-carriers, the screwing of the presses, the subdued hum of hard, fast working, and the rhythmic click of the shears, the whole lit warm with the reflection of Australian sunlight, it seemed that I had there the best expression of my subject, a subject noble enough and worthy enough if I could express the meaning and spirit – of strong masculine labour, the patience of the animals whose year's growth is being stripped from them for man's use, and the great human interest of the whole scene.
– Tom Roberts to the editor, *The Argus*, 4 July 1890

The image of the hard-working, hard-living shearer had a strong romantic appeal and a special place in Australian folklore. Wool was Australia's staple industry (the national economy 'rode on the sheep's back' until the depression of the 1890s); with the woolshed as the 'one centre . . . through which the accumulated growth and wealth of the year is carried'.[1] The subject had therefore been treated pictorially by earlier colonial painters, photographers; and, most frequently, by popular illustrators for newspapers, magazines and descriptive books such as *The Picturesque Atlas of Australasia*, 1883-89 or *Cassell's Picturesque Australasia*, 1888.[2] What made *Shearing the Rams* absolutely exceptional in 1890 was its grand scale: Roberts's conscious heroization of pastoral labour. He worked solidly on the painting for a total of eight months – two shearing seasons over two years – and almost certainly intended to send it to London for exhibition at the Royal Academy, as a subject 'with a decided leaning towards nationality'.[3]

Melbourne critics admired his bold palette and light tonality, capturing the characteristic light and atmosphere; the 'subdued brilliance that is not once broken in the whole of the work' (*Table Talk*, 30 May 1890, p.7). 'Through the open door at the far end of the shed is seen a glimpse of sunlit bush, and the artist has been most successful in catching the idea of intense heat so often associated with bush scenes' (*The Age*, 30 May 1890, p.7). As Roberts wrote himself, explaining his aims in the painting, 'By making art the perfect expression of one time and one place, it becomes art for all time and of all places' (*The Argus*, 4 July 1980, p.10).

Although he derived the general composition from local sources, he was equally indebted to wider European academic and realist traditions. Identifiable sources range from Italian High Renaissance art (for the boy on the left) to French Realism (possibly Courbet's *The Stonebreakers*, of 1849) and Ford Madox Brown's famous social documentary, *Work*, painted in 1863. He probably saw Robert William MacBeth's *Sheep-shearing* exhibited in London in 1883: a large-scale academic rendering of 'strong masculine labour', closely comparable with *Shearing the Rams*.[4] True to his own academic training, Roberts commenced by making sketches on the spot, at 'Brocklesby' station near Corowa, in the late spring of 1888: 'studies of the light, the atmosphere, the shed, the sheep, the men and the work. Between seventy and eighty sketches were made in this way, and when all were done it was too late to begin seriously on the big picture. The artist returned to town, worked at portrait painting through the autumn and the winter of that year and in the next spring went out again'.[5] For this second season he set up his canvas inside the shearing shed. He paid £12 to 'the most characteristic and picturesque of the shearers: to pose as required for a good many days'. (Their average weekly wage for shearing was £3). As a result, remarked *Table Talk*, 'There is no hesitation about the modelling, each figure is firmly and spiritedly drawn, and of itself worth separate study'.[6] The 'champion of the shed', in the foreground, was one Jim Coffey; shown shearing the 'long blow', the length of the animal's side. 'Down the board – to use the expressive vernacular of the country' – his fellows are variously posed removing neck, belly and shoulder wool, in a rhythmic description of the repetitious motions which make up the shearing process.[7] Rams – as opposed to ewes or wethers – were still hand shorn after the introduction of machine shearing (in 1888) because hand-held shears allowed greater control.[8] (Interestingly, however, when the painting was eventually acquired to hang in the office of Edward Trenchard

and Co., leading stock and station agents, *The Illustrated Sydney News* pointed out that it was 'very valuable not only as a work of art, but also as representative of a style of shearing which in pastoral history will soon be a thing of the past'.) The bearded pipe-smoker squatting down on the right was a neighbouring 'cockatoo' farmer, Frank Barnes. The 'merry-faced tar boy', ready to staunch any accidental wounds, was in fact ten-year-old Susie Bourne, daughter of a local stockman, who received additional sixpences from Roberts for 'keeping the dust kicked up to create a hazy atmosphere'.[9] Roberts's easy and natural manner evidently appealed to the local population. He not only sketched the shearers. He also transcribed their fruity vernacular in his note books:

Scene Shearing Shed.

One Shearer to another.

'I goes to the Cove & Sez J. do you want Shearers. Yes sez he & he puts me on. So I spots my stand, waltses into the canary cage, catches my bird, gives him two blows, from his sneezer to his breezer. When the Cove sez. Sez he, that shearing wont do my man. So I ship my b – y tongs across the dancing board, straddles my crock, & takes to the water like a b – y rat'.[10]

In his painting, however, Roberts gave no hint of the problems of labour relations which were beginning to beset the Australian wool industry at just this time.[11]

'He worked all through the shearing, packed his canvas then, and returned to town, stretched it again in his studio, and began the long work of finishing.'[12] Roberts's method of working – from sketch 'impressions' and detailed drawings, to the full-scale canvas on location, and completion in the studio – was standard 19th century 'Naturalist' painting procedure. Visual facts, carefully collected over a long period of time, are precisely arranged to express his chosen theme of 'strong masculine labour'. His serious academic treatment elevates essentially popular subject matter to the status of 'High Art'. Indeed Roberts's great achievement in *Shearing the Rams* is his balance between the particular and the typical, the individual and the universal. 'He was well pleased and almost satisfied', reported *The Argus*, 'when framed at length in heavy gold, and backed by dark maroon hangings, its truthful beauty was all displayed on the studio wall'.[13]

Shearing the Rams provoked more press comment than any other contemporary Australian picture, and lively speculation as to its fate.[14] Even in an unfinished state *The Corowa Free Press* considered it a 'masterpiece of artistic skill which would be worthy in a national gallery'. However, James Smith, as *Argus* art critic and one of the Melbourne Gallery trustees, considered that the picture was too naturalistic and therefore did not embody those 'universal' qualities necessary to great art (28 June 1890, p.10); he did not recommend its acquisition for the National Gallery of Victoria. Roberts, in an eloquent reply, defended his right to paint such subject matter and explained the new significance he had given it in the context of Australian art. *The Age* critic wrote, more prophetically than Smith, 'The work as a whole will appeal not only to the small minority who know something of art methods, but to the immense majority who like a painting that tells its own story' (30 May 1890, p.7). And *Table Talk* declared, 'Shearing the Rams is a work that will live and a work by which Mr. Roberts' name will always be remembered' (30 May 1890, p.7).

'Sheep Shearing', c.1888, by George Rossi
Ashton, reproduced in *The Picturesque Atlas of
Australasia*, vol.3
LaTrobe Collection, State Library of Victoria

[1] *Argus*, 4 July 1890, p.10.
[2] Photographic and illustrative
precedents are reproduced and fully
discussed by Astbury 1978 and 1985; and
Terry Smith 1980.
[3] *Table Talk*, 30 August 1889, p.5. It was
not ready in time for the 1890 Royal
Academy exhibition and was sold before
1891.
[4] David Jaffé kindly drew my attention to
this painting, reproduced in Henry
Blackburn's *Grosvenor Notes* for 1883,
no. 74; and described in W.E. Henley, *A
Century of Artists, a Memorial of the Loan
Collection of Painting and Sculpture,
International Exhibition Glasgow 1888*,
James MacLehose and Sons, Glasgow,
1889, p.107. Helen Topliss has recently
suggested that Roberts was also inspired
by the novel *Far from the Madding
Crowd* by Thomas Hardy (a native of
Dorset, like Roberts himself); chapter 22
contains an atmospheric and compelling
description of 'The Great Barn and the
Sheep-Shearers'. Interestingly, the great
medieval barn described by Hardy could
very well be the setting of MacBeth's
shearing scene. See especially Spate
1978, pp.88.ff.; Jaffé 1982 and Topliss
1985, p.113.
[5] *Argus*, 24 June 1890, p.6.
[6] *Table Talk*, 30 May 1890, p.7.
[7] Jaffé, op.cit. p.31.

[8] ibid.; and see Kelly 1981.
[9] Interview with Susan Davis, née
Bourne, in *The Age*, 12 October 1979.
Other local personalities were identified
in *The Corowa Free Press*, 29 November
1889.
[10] LaTrobe Collection, State Library of
Victoria. MS 8061 Box 641/4 (c). Undated
notes; possibly c.1895 and therefore from
'Newstead' rather than 'Brocklesby'
Station. 'Tongs' was the shearers' word
for hand shears, as opposed to the new
shearing machines; the 'Cove' was the
station-manager or proprietor.
[11] Terry Smith, op.cit.; Kelly, op.cit. For
one amusing contemporary city dweller's
view see *Table Talk*, 26 September 1890,
p.3. Members of the Amalgamated
Shearers' Union, founded 1886, called
themselves 'brother Knights of the Blade'.
See also Patsy Adam-Smith, *The
Shearers*, Nelson, Melbourne, 1982.
[12] *Argus*, 24 June 1890, p.6.
[13] ibid.
[14] Conder evidently heard a rumour that
it has been sold well before completion,
for he wrote to congratulate Roberts on 7
February 1890 (Roberts correspondence
vol. II, Mitchell Library). It was not
finished in time for the Victorian Artists'
Society autumn exhibition in March. A
number of writers hoped it would be
purchased for the National Gallery of
Victoria; or meet 'the better fate of being
known throughout the colony as an
engraving' (*Table Talk*, 30 May 1890, p.7).
Its eventual sale was announced in July
1890. In 1900 it was apparently sent to
England for reproduction by
photogravure; offered for sale in Bendigo
1901; and finally purchased by the
Gallery in 1932 from the family of the
original owner.

FREDERICK McCUBBIN ▶
A Bush Burial, 1890
Oil on canvas
122.5 x 224.5 cm
Signed and dated l.r.: F. McCubbin/1890
Geelong Art Gallery
Purchased by subscription 1900

Provenance:
J. Falkingham, Melbourne 1890-1900

Exhibitions:
*Victorian Artists' Society Catalogue of
Winter Exhibition*, Melbourne, March
1890, no.57: 'A Bush Burial – £220.0.0',
illus.; *Exhibition of Works of Victorian Art-
ists and a Loan Collection of Pictures*,
Exhibition Building, Melbourne, Decem-
ber 1890, no.203: 'The Last of the Pioneers
– Lent by the Artist'; *Exhibition of Pictures
by Fd. McCubbin, Arthur Streeton and
Tom Roberts*, Gemmell, Tuckett and Co.,
Melbourne, December 1890, no.19: 'The
Last of a Pioneer – F. McCubbin'; *Victorian
Artists' Society Exhibition of Australian
Art Past and Present*, National Gallery,
Melbourne, August 1893, no.74: 'The
Bush Burial, 1890 – Lent by J.
Falkingham, Esq.'; *Catalogue of the Dia-
mond Jubilee loan exhibition in the
National Gallery of Victoria in commemo-
ration of the 60th Year of the Reign of her
Majesty Queen Victoria*, Melbourne, June
1897, no.24: 'A Bush Burial – Lent by J.
Falkingham, Esq.'; Messrs Naylor, Forbes
and Co., auctioneers, painting sale for
J. Falkingham, Esq. June 1899 (passed in);
published as a chromolithograph by
Troedel and Co. (date unknown).

Literature:
Table Talk, 14 March 1890, p.5; 3 April
1890, p.7; 28 November 1890, p.5; *Age*, 29
March 1890, p.15; 12 August 1893, p.15; 9
June 1899, p.16; *Argus*, 5 April 1890, p.6;
24 April 1890, p.11; *Melbourne University
Review*, May 1890, p.82; *Australasian
Critic*, January 1891, p.95; *Australasian
Art Review*, 1 July 1899, p.11; 1 December
1899, p.24; MacDonald 1916, pl.II;
Colquhoun [1919]; Hoff 1951, p.127; Hoff
1955, no.9; David Thomas 1969, pp.70f.;
Gleeson 1969, p.56; McCulloch 1969, p.22,
pl.24B; Gleeson 1971, pl.19; Smith 1971,
p.86; Hughes 1977, p.67; Robin da Costa,
Blackburn A Picturesque History, Pioneer
Design Studio, Lilydale 1978, frontispiece;
Astbury 1978a, pp.52ff.; Smith 1979,
p.125; Astbury 1981, pp.31ff.; Astbury
1985, in press, pp.136ff., pl.23

The remains of the deceased, doubtless the wife of the grey headed old man reading the service, are already lowered into the trench recently excavated, and the group is completed by the stalwart son or son-in-law, his weeping wife and child, and a dog. the accessories are vernal rather than autumnal, suggesting life hereafter and better things to come. The work is one which will do much to enhance Mr McCubbin's reputation.
– *The Age*, 29 March 1890

Nowhere could a subject be found more affecting in its pathos, more picturesque in its setting, and more truly characteristic of national experience and environment. The picture strikes the first dominant note that has been heard in purely Australian art and should stimulate others to investigate also the life of this continent.
– Sidney Dickinson, letter to *The Argus*, 24 April 1890

In *A Bush Burial* of 1890, McCubbin has taken a favourite subject of English Victorian period narrative painting – the graveside or funeral scene – and set it in local Australian landscape. It was a theme already established in colonial art and literature. The 'Bush Funeral', a colour lithograph in S.T. Gill's *Australian sketchbook*, 1865, is a rather clumsy early example. In 1873 a writer for *The Australasian Sketcher* commented that 'the first generation of settlers is passing away, leaving but a meagre history of their personal doings and feelings to those who succeed them'.[1] By the 1880s, a nostalgic reverence for pioneering history was widespread among the predominantly urban community. Indeed for a time McCubbin altered the title of his *A Bush Burial* to 'The Last of the Pioneers'. The painting bears compositional similarities to William Strutt's drawings of *The Burial of Burke*, well known in the late 80s through reproductions for the popular press: in the grouping of the figures over the open grave, the implements and freshly dug soil in the foreground.[2] McCubbin nevertheless chose to depict anonymous domestic characters rather than any specific national hero. He embraced the ideals of simple dignity, piety and lasting family ties. *A Bush Burial* was immediately acclaimed by critics and public alike. Newspaper reviewers reconstructed the 'story' to their own satisfaction: failing to agree about who exactly was being buried but unanimous in their praise for the picture's 'pathos' and its nationalistic theme. It was reproduced as a colour lithograph by Troedel and Co.

A Bush Burial manages to hold in subtle balance a lyrical mood, the 'touching and tender sentiment' and McCubbin's artistic aim of realistic observation. In fact it was painted on the suburban fringes of Melbourne in the Blackburn area, with McCubbin digging a grave in his own back garden (lot 52 Wolseley Crescent). His models for the elder bearded 'pioneer' were a Mr John Dunne and David Houston on whose farm at Box Hill McCubbin and Roberts had their first *plein air* painting camp[3]; the other figures were Mrs McCubbin and various friends and relatives. 'They stand out as types of character', said *Table Talk*, 'The sentiment of the picture is so poetic and yet so perfectly true to nature that the artist has gained his ends without recourse to any tricky methods of idealization. The work is sincerely full of genuine feeling and thoroughly national'.

[1] *Australasian Sketcher* I, 17 May 1873, p.39; quoted by David Thomas 1969, p.72.
[2] Astbury 1981, pp.32ff. Strutt's painted version of *The Burial of Burke* (now in the State Library of Victoria) was not executed until 1911, in London; and clearly indicates a reciprocal influence from McCubbin's burial composition of 1890.
[3] John Dunne certainly modelled for the features of 'the grey headed old man'; information from his grand-daughter.

TOM ROBERTS
The Break Away, [1891]
Oil on canvas
137.2 x 168.1 cm
Signed l.l.: Tom Roberts
Art Gallery of South Australia
Purchased 1899, Elder Bequest Fund
For exhibition in Melbourne and Adelaide
only

Provenance:
The artist

Exhibitions:
Roberts's Studio, Grosvenor Chambers,
Melbourne, July 1891; Gemmell, Tuckett
& Co., auctioneers, Melbourne, July 1891;
*Victorian Artists' Society Exhibition of
Paintings, Sculpture & Drawings
Illustrated Catalogue*, Melbourne, May
1892, no.195: 'The Break Away – 300
guineas', illus.; *Art Society of New South
Wales Catalogue of Spring Exhibition*,
Sydney, September 1893, no.176: 'A
Breakaway – £265.0.0', illus.; *Exhibition
of Australian Art in London*, Grafton
Galleries, London, April 1898, no.40: 'A
Break Away'; *South Australian Society of
Arts, The Second Federal Exhibition*,
Adelaide, November 1899, no.51: 'A
Breakaway – £220'

Literature:
Argus, 17 July 1891, p.5; *Table Talk*, 13
February 1891, p.12; 17 July 1891, p.17;
27 May 1892, p.7; *Sydney Morning Herald*,
1 September 1893, p.6; 2 September 1893,
p.6; *The Year's Art*, London, 1895, p.222;
Daily Telegraph, 5 May 1898, p.6; 12 May
1898, p.6; 21 May 1898; *Magazine of Art*,
1898, pp. 378, 383, illus.; *Tatler*, 4 June
1898, p.24; *Bookfellow*, 29 April 1899,
p.31; *Australasian Art Review*, 1 December 1899, p.25; Moore 1934, I, p.129; *Herald*, 1 August 1935; Croll 1935, pp. 33, 35
ff., 120, 173f.;Lindsay 1938, p.40; *The Australian Artist*, I, 3, 1948, p.33; Hoff 1951,
pp.129f.; McCulloch 1969, pp.58, 158;
Smith 1971, pp.90f.; Gleeson 1971, pl.37;
Finemore 1977, pp. 25ff.; Hughes 1977,
p.57; Astbury 1978, p.73; Spate 1978,
pp.86, 90f., 97, pl.24; Astbury, 1980b,
pp.2ff.; Horton & Thomas 1981, pp.48, 64;
Splatt & Bruce 1981, p.76; Topliss 1985,
no.170; Astbury 1985, in press, pp.113ff.,
pl.18

Mr Tom Roberts' New Picture
A new picture by the painter of Shearing the Rams is always worth going to
see, and it is no disappointment to the
visitor to Mr Tom Roberts' studio in
Collins-street to view the new painting,
A Break Away! The subject is an excellent one for a great work. A bit of arid
country, with ragged gum trees and
stunted box positively frizzling in the
heat of a January day; an ultramarine
sky, with the tall column of a dust
whirlwind on the horizon; a red, dusty
track down which the vanguard of a
mob of sheep rush to the water pool
just visible on the right corner of the
foreground. A horseman vainly strives
to check the mad death rush of the
sheep; another is just emerging from
the dust cloud that conceals the main
body of the sheep. An Australian incident – tragic, realistic, picturesque.
– *Table Talk*, 17 July 1891

Roberts returned to Corowa for some months early in 1891 'to depict on canvas scenes of Australian life'. In March he was visited there by a newspaper reporter, who subsequently wrote a long article for *The Argus* entitled 'A "Bush" Studio; and the picture in it'.[1] The 'studio' was the 'Brocklesby' woolshed, Roberts's setting for *Shearing the Rams*. The picture was *The Break Away*. 'A still holding pool in Riverina has been selected by the artist', wrote the visitor, 'and in Riverina, as a rule, only sheep are now depastured'. The theme of a breakaway by drought-stricken cattle, maddened at their first scent of water, had been treated frequently by illustrators documenting Australian pastoral history.[2] However, as this reporter recognized, such stampedes were now very rare indeed; it is most unlikely that Roberts ever witnessed one, although he spent 'six weeks on the roads' with drovers collecting visual material for the subject.[3] The practice of driving stock over long distances had almost disappeared by the 1880s. Widespread use of wire fencing, vast extension of the railway network and the increased size of selections were rapidly transforming the pastoral industry of the district. *The Break Away* was thus Roberts's somewhat nostalgic contribution to a larger contemporary process of apotheosis of the Australian bushman by an urban-based society.[4] His protagonists are anonymous; but their drama is portrayed on a heroic scale:

'Mustering Sheep', 1888, by William Hatherell, in *Cassell's Picturesque Australasia*, vol.2 LaTrobe Collection, State Library of Victoria

One feels that one has arrived on the scene just a moment too late to witness the first grand rush...The crashing gallop...of the swearing, dust-covered horseman, as he strains every nerve to bear his share in preventing what he fears will result in severe loss, completes the *life* of the picture.[5]

Roberts made oil sketches in the open air: one of the old-fashioned chock-and-log fence, for example, 'with effects so strongly marked as to suggest fierce overhead sunlight – a dazzling glare'.[6] His visitor admired the brightness, the 'strong reds, blues, and yellows' of the full-scale canvas in progress. The high key of the finished painting, the broad brushwork of the landscape and the distinctive purple-mauve and blue shadows are all results of his initial outdoor studies. The foreground horseman, however, stands out against the dust with somewhat unnatural clarity: an inevitable consequence of completing the work inside the 'bush studio.' The *Table Talk* critic considered this lack of unity between foreground and background a serious fault (17 July 1891, p.16). One pencil drawing shows how carefully Roberts composed the picture from its earliest stages, with the powerful diagonal thrust of the panicking mob countered by the action of horse and rider. It was an '*apparently* haphazard arrangement'; with, consequently, 'marvellous seeming reality' such as he admired in certain 19th

century French paintings.[7] 'Looking at the large canvas, one feels the story', said *Table Talk*. According to Roberts's stated aim, *The Break Away* captured one concept, one scene and one mood; indeed as he told A. G. Stephens, writer for *The Bookfellow*, he prized it 'as the work in which his art has so far most nearly realized his idea'.[8]

[1] Reprinted by Croll 1946, pp. 35ff.
[2] Astbury 1980b discusses and reproduces various precedents from the illustrated press.
[3] Lionel Lindsay, *Catalogue of the Jubilee Exhibition of Australian Art*, 1951, p.14.
[4] Astbury, op. cit., cites a number of parallels from contemporary literature. For Roberts's view of art as historical record, see Topliss 1985, p.18.
[5] Croll 1946, p.37.
[6] ibid.; related studies are catalogued by Topliss 1985, nos 170a – b, 171 and Sketchbook III, p.242.
[7] *Argus*, 31 October 1891, p.4. In this article discussing the collection of the Art Gallery of New South Wales, Roberts singled out Etienne Dinet's *Snake Charmer* for its unconventional composition and intense sunlight effects: 'we come back to this Eastern piece, as from a dull common room to a brilliant open air, with a sense of freshness and healthfulness'.
[8] Interview reprinted by Croll, op.cit., pp.56ff.

ARTHUR STREETON
Fire's On, 1891
Oil on canvas
183.8 x 122.5 cm
Signed and dated l.l.: Arthur Streeton.
1891.
Art Gallery of New South Wales
Purchased 1893

Provenance:
The artist

Exhibitions:
Victorian Artists' Society Exhibition of Paintings, Sculpture & Drawings Illustrated Catalogue, Melbourne, May 1892, no.140: 'Fire's On – 150 guineas', illus.; *Art Society of New South Wales Catalogue Spring Exhibition*, Sydney, August 1893, no.239: '"Fire's On" (Lapstone Tunnel) – £157.10.0'; *Streeton's Sydney Sunshine Exhibition*, Melbourne, December 1896, no.37: 'Fire's On – Lent by the Trustees, Sydney Art Gallery'; *Exhibition of Australian Art in London*, Grafton Galleries, London, April 1898, no.94: 'Fire's On – lent by Trustees of Sydney Gallery'

Literature:
Age, 27 May 1892, p.6; *Illustrated Australian News*, 1 July 1892, p.7; *Sydney Morning Herald*, 1 September 1893, p.6; *Table Talk*, 8 September 1893, p.10; *The Year's Art*, London, 1895, p.222; *Daily Telegraph*, 5 May 1898, p.6; 12 May 1898, p.6; *Australasian Art Review*, 1 December 1899, p.25; Souter 1905, p.225; Streeton 1919, pl.X; Lionel Lindsay, 'Streeton's Loan Exhibition', *Art in Australia*, February 1932, p.8; Moore 1934, I, p.96; Croll 1935, pp.185ff., 195; Streeton 1935, no.114; Ashton 1941, pp.102f.; Croll 1946, pp.19ff.; Hoff 1951, p.131; McCulloch 1969, p.176; Gleeson 1969, pl.22; Smith 1971, pp.91ff.; Gleeson 1971, pl. 62; Hughes 1977, pp.54, 61ff., 80; Galbally 1979, no.44; pl.17; Burn 1980, p.89; *Fifteen Decades of Australian Painting*, Art Gallery of New South Wales, 1981, no.7; Splatt & Bruce 1981, p.75; Hugh Speirs, *Landscape Art and the Blue Mountains*, Alternative Publishing Co-operative Ltd, Chippendale, 1981, pp.60f.; Martin Terry, 'Conrad Martens and the Zig Zag', *Art and Australia* 21, 4, Winter 1984, pp.503ff.
Reproduced by courtesy of Mrs Oliver Streeton

Bulldog, there is a great chance up here; if possible...I'll put in all the next long Bright Gold Summer...
– Streeton to Roberts, from Glenbrook, New South Wales, 5 October 1891

I'm in the Blue Mountains...The sun is beautiful in the morning...I follow the railway line for 3/4 of a mile through a canyon or gully where big brown men are toiling all the hot day excavating and making a tunnel, which will cost thousands (about 1/2 mile long), but will save (apparently) wearing out a great number of engines on the first Zig Zag. I've past the west mouth and now am arrived at my subject, the other mouth, which gapes like a great dragon's mouth at the perfect flood of hot sunlight... Right below me the men work, some with shovels, others drilling for a blast. I work on the W.Color drying too quickly and the ganger cries 'Fire', 'Fire's on'; all the men drop their tools and scatter and I nimbly skip off my perch and hide behind a big safe rock. A deep hush is everywhere – then, 'Holy Smoke!'... All at work once more – more drills; the rock is a perfect blazing glory of white, orange, cream and blue streaks here and there where the blast has worked its force... I'll soon begin a big canvas (oilcolor) of this. I think it looks stunning. 'Tis like painting in the 'Burning Fiery Furnace'; so beautiful and bright and yet so difficult to attain.
– To McCubbin, October 1891

This morning, hot, windy, and warm, as I travel down the line, and the mirage sizzling and jiggering over the railway track. I arrive at my cutting, 'the fatal cutting', and inwardly rejoice at the prosperous warmth all glowing before me...; is it worth painting? Why, of course, damn it all! that is providing I'm capable of translating my impression to the canvas – all is serene as I work and peg away...12 o'clock...and now I hear 'Fire, fire's on', from the gang close by...BOOM! and then rumbling of rock, the navvy under the rock with me, and watching, says, 'Man killed'... More shots and crashing rock, and we peep over; he lies all hidden bar his legs. All the shots are now gone except one, and all wait, not daring to go near; then men, nippers, and a woman hurry down, the woman with a bottle and rags;...and they raise the rock and lift him on to the stretcher, fold his arms over his chest, and slowly six of them carry him past me...
– To Roberts, 17 December 1891

A striking picture is that of Mr. Arthur Streeton's Fire's On – not merely on account of the light and force which characterise it, but because of its new world associations and the spirit of innovation it breathes... Such a subject as the blasting of a tunnel will strike many people as unpicturesque and inartistic, but it is only because they will not realise that in reflecting the contemporaneous life and activity of a new continent and a new race Australian art will most surely find its keynote... Australian art has all its traditions to make, and this is a conviction that we feel to be expressed in Mr. Streeton's picture.
– *The Age*, 27 May 1892

Streeton spent almost three months at Glenbrook in the Blue Mountains late in 1891, exploring the landscape of inland New South Wales. In a series of sketches and more finished watercolours he recorded the blasting of Lapstone railway tunnel through the mountainside: culminating in his largest oil painting to date.[1] *Fire's On* balances bravura technique with strong emotion: inspired as much by the landscape itself as by dramatic events witnessed. (Two workers died and another was seriously injured whilst Streeton was there: 'at seven bob a day – the hardest work in the country for the money I'll bet', he wrote.) The drama of the dead man being carried from the tunnel mouth is subordinated to towering cliffs and giant boulders; the brilliant ochres of the gashed sandstone and mol-

ten blue of the sky; the very sensation of intense summer heat. A critic for *The Age* noted this 'ant-like activity' of Streeton's human subjects, confronted by 'the inert, stubborn resistance' of nature itself. Here was a new type of 'heroic' landscape painting, intended by Streeton and recognized by reviewers as distinctively national.[2] As Julian Ashton told the president of the Sydney Gallery trustees, 'Well, first of all it does not rely for its success upon any one of the usual sentimental transcripts of nature . . . ; and one is struck by the simplicity of the means used, each brush-stroke saying unfalteringly what it has to say with very few colours, telling the story of the everyday life and toil of men in this vast continent'.

[1] A highly finished watercolour version, *Cutting the Tunnel, Lapstone*, 1892, is now in the Art Gallery of New South Wales. The engineering of this railway line, with its 'Great Zig Zag' into the Blue Mountains, was considered 'one of the greatest wonders of the colony – perhaps it may be said – of the world'. Josiah Hughes, *Australia Revisited in 1890, and excursions in Egypt, Tasmania and New Zealand*, London, 1891, pp.222ff. Conrad Martens had painted a 'Turneresque' watercolour of *The Zig Zag*, c.1873 – that is, before the cutting of Lapstone Tunnel (Australian National Gallery, Canberra). See also Speirs 1981.

[2] See especially *The Age*, 27 May 1892, p.6; as that critic pointed out, it was unusual subject matter for a major painting. Streeton would have seen one English precedent, *A Railway Cutting* by Edwin Buckman, reproduced in *The Magazine of Art*, 1879, p.120. (I am most grateful to David Jaffé for this reference). Buckman was also praised for showing 'modern every-day pursuits in their real picturesqueness . . . the felicitous subject of a railway cutting with the navvies at work . . . ' (p.118). Buckman's painting, however, was simply a view of men at work: of 19th century progress through human labour. Although Streeton, too, admired the toiling 'big brown men'; his response to the subject was very different.

ARTHUR STREETON ▲
Sketch – Blue Mountains, 1891
Watercolour on paper
32.5 x 23 cm (sight)
Signed l.r.: A. Streeton
Inscribed l.l.: Blue/Mountains/91
Private collection, Adelaide

Provenance:
J. Shirlaw (?); W.G. Speirs; private collection, Adelaide

Exhibitions:
Victorian Artists' Society Exhibition of Paintings, Sculpture & Drawings Illustrated Catalogue, Melbourne, May 1892, probably no.234: 'Sketch – Blue Mountains, watercolour – 3 guineas' or no.238: 'Cutting a Tunnel (sketch), Blue Mountains, watercolour – 3 guineas'; *Society of Artists, South Australia*, Adelaide, date unknown: as 'Blasting on Blue Mountains – n.f.s.'

Literature:
Argus, 30 May 1891, p.7
Reproduced by courtesy of Mrs Oliver Streeton

What a boom of thunder shakes the rock and me. It echoes through the hills and dies away 'mid the crashing of tons of rock; some lumps fly hundreds of feet sometimes and fall and fly everywhere among the trees; and then a thick cloud laden with fumes of the blasting powder.
– Streeton to McCubbin, October 1891

I've been pegging in at my work between the 'blasts', and have not been here a fortnight, but have done

two watercolour gems, besides a number of sketches – and I can do very little more to 'em, strikes me . . . The men are very interested in the tunnel one; I get on fine with some of them; big chaps they are, and swear very little.
– To Roberts, October 1891

Streeton has captured the very moment of an explosion in this watercolour: one of his many sketches of work on the railway tunnel at Glenbrook. 'There is a cutting through the vast hill of bright sandstone', he wrote to McCubbin; 'the walls of rock run high up and are crowned by gums bronze green'. It appears to have been painted early one morning, unlike the finished oil on canvas where the scene is bleached by a blazing midday sun.

FREDERICK McCUBBIN
The North Wind, 1891
Oil on canvas (lined on to plywood)
91 x 152.7 cm
Signed and dated l.l.: F. McCubbin/1891
National Gallery of Victoria
Felton Bequest 1941

Provenance:
Sedon Galleries, Melbourne, September
1941

Literature:
Hoff 1955, no.10; McCulloch 1969, pl.27B;
David Thomas 1969, p.72; Inson & Ward
1971, p.26; Galbally 1981, p.87, pl.17;
Astbury 1981, pp.35ff.; Astbury 1985, in
press, pp.139ff., pl.24

They toiled and they fought through
the shame of it –
Through wilderness, flood and
drought . . .
– Henry Lawson, *How the land was
won*, 1899

Hardship in the face of nature was a fact of
life for the small selector in 'Droughtland'
Australia. As Francis Adams wrote in *The
Australians: a Social Sketch*, 1893, 'the
average selector finds it possible nowa-
days to gain little more than a mere living
by the exercise of unremitting and monotonous toil'. Hot winds, 'which invariably
come from the north', were feared from
the earliest days of colonial exploration.
They 'traverse an arid and burning desert
in the interior, before reaching the settlement', wrote E. Lloyd in 1846; 'hot as out
of a furnace', said William Howitt.[1]
McCubbin himself wrote of 'the awful Hot
Winds that blew in summer – and the
fearful dust storms'.[2] Memories of 'Black
Thursday' were etched indelibly on the
Australian imagination: on 6 February
1851 some fifty miles of country near
Mount Macedon had been devastated by
bushfires fanned by the 'fierce north
wind'. (William Strutt's famous painting of
this event, well known to McCubbin, was
exhibited several times in Melbourne during the 1880s and 1890s). The great

drought of summer 1888 was also fresh in
popular memory when McCubbin painted
The North Wind. By the 1890s economic
recession was casting a shadow of gloom
over Melbourne. City dwellers recognized
(in contemporary literature and the press)
a dual image of rural settler as 'heroic
pioneer' and, increasingly, as 'wretched
small-holder, eking out a miserable existence'. Here McCubbin focuses on one family, isolated, pitted against the elements.
The man struggles on foot. His wife sits in
the cart with their meagre possessions
and shields their small baby from the
swirling red dust. Have they been driven
from their property by drought? Or is this
perhaps a more optimistic image of stoic
perseverance? McCubbin leaves these
questions open.[3]

[1] E. Lloyd, *A Visit to the Antipodes with
Some Reminiscences of a Sojourn in
Australia, by a Squatter*, London, 1846,
pp.142f.; William Howitt, *Land, Labour,
and Gold*, London, 1855, vol. I, p.203;
quoted by Astbury 1981, pp.37, 52.
[2] Galbally (ed.) 1979, p.73.
[3] Astbury discusses these alternatives,
citing precedents in colonial art and
literature for different interpretations of
the 'plight of the selector', pp.35f.

TOM ROBERTS ▲
Sketch – shearing shed, Newstead, [c.1894]
Oil on wood panel
23.5 x 35.6 cm
Signed and inscribed l.c.: Tom Roberts to DSA (with ideogram of a 'Bulldog')
Private collection, Sydney

Provenance:
Duncan Anderson; Alick Anderson (his son); R.W. Anderson; private collection, New South Wales

Exhibitions:
Exhibition and Sale of Paintings Previous to Leaving Australia, Society of Artists, Sydney, November 1900, no.3: 3 guineas

Literature:
Topliss 1985, no.217

> The springtime it brings on the shearing,
> And then you will see them in droves,
> To the west-country stations all steering,
> A seeking a job off the coves.
>
> With a ragged old swag on my shoulder,
> And a billy quart-pot in my hand,
> And I'll tell you we'll 'stonish the new-chum
> To see how we travel the land.
> – Shearers' song

Roberts painted at 'Newstead' station, New South Wales, during the shearing season of 1894. By curious coincidence, the owner's name was Duncan Anderson; but no relationship with the Andersons of 'Brocklesby' has been established. In a letter to *The Argus* (4 July 1890) Roberts had described just such a scene: 'the coming of Spring, the gradual massing of the sheep towards that one centre, the woolshed'. Now, four years later, he produced *Shearing at Newstead*, which he regarded as his great sequel to *Shearing the Rams*. *Shearing at Newstead* was exhibited at the Art Society in 1894 and acclaimed as 'the great picture of the year . . . strongly painted, full of research'. It was purchased by the Art Gallery of New South Wales for £275, under 'its second and more poetic title' – *The Golden Fleece*.[1]

---

[1] *Sydney Morning Herald*, 28 September 1894, p.3. For a discussion of this major work, see Topliss 1985, no.216.

FREDERICK McCUBBIN ▶
Bush Idyll, 1893
Oil on canvas
119.5 x 221.5 cm
Signed and dated l.r.: F. McCubbin 1893
David R.C. Waterhouse, Sydney

Provenance:
Louis Abrahams after 1899 – said to have paid £35; until *Australian Pictures Collected by the late Louis Abrahams*, Decoration Co., Melbourne, 15 August 1919, lot 18: 'A Bush Idyll' (£262.10.0); purchased by Hugh D. McIntosh; probably taken to London in the 1920s; private collections, England, until 1984; David R.C. Waterhouse, Sydney

Exhibitions:
In McCubbin's studio at Blackburn, called by a visiting reporter 'Bush Pastoral', February 1894; Art Union exhibition to raise funds for the new Victorian Artists' Society building, June 1894, as 'Bush Idyll' (no catalogue located); *South Australian Society of Arts Federal Exhibition*, Adelaide, November 1898, no.98: 'A Bush Idyll – £94.0.0'; McCubbin's studio at the National Gallery of Victoria, November 1899

Literature:
Age, 10 February 1894, p.15; 12 June 1894, p.6; 16 August 1919, p.14; *Argus*, 8 June 1894, p.6; 23 November 1899, p.3; MacDonald 1916, pp.32, 59, 96; *Herald*, 12, 16 and 21 August 1919

> Mr. McCubbin shows us one of those woods with whose soft greys and greens he has made us familiar. The foreground is in shadow, but in the background a pool of water, beside which cattle are grazing, reflects a blue sky, and the trees bordering the pool are gilded by the approaching sunset. In the soft shadowy atmosphere of the foreground Mr. McCubbin has placed the figures of his 'Idyll', a boy seated on the grass in rough working clothes, his felt hat drawn over his eyes playing on a tin whistle, and a girl of about the same age stretched beside him, listening with an expression which would lead you to believe that the humble instrument must be as tuneful as any shepherd's pipe of old. Her face, which is not pretty in the everyday sense of the word, is beautiful with emotion which spiritualises it for the moment. There may be some incongruities in the details of the picture, the dress of the girl as compared with that of her companion for instance, but the harmony of the composition as a whole, the sentiment conveyed, and the decorative qualities of the painting make this work perhaps the most pleasing and important that Mr. McCubbin has yet executed.
> – *The Age*, 10 February 1894

McCubbin's relationship with the Australian bush was quieter and more intimate than Streeton's or Roberts's. As *The Age* reporter observed, he 'reveals a delicacy and a tender grace in the Australian landscape . . . He avoids what he himself admits to be the repellent side of our bush scenery – such as, for instance, the noontide glare of a midsummer sun seen over endless tracts of monotonous gum forest'. Specific areas of bushland suggested artistic motifs to him, as he explained to the same reporter: 'Nature under our Australian sky seems to me like a shy, reserved person, ready to repel you; but you have only to wait and watch her varying moods, and you will find all the beauty you can desire'.[1] *Bush Idyll* was painted at Blackburn, described at the time as 'a sort of Australian Barbizon'. *The Argus* critic saw in the work 'something of the feeling that Millet gets in his pictures of French rural character'. The influence of Bastien-Lepage is particularly apparent in the enveloping soft grey light and the foreground foliage; and in such details as the youthful swain's 'rough working clothes' and rustic boots – a distinctive characteristic of countless country children painted by Lepage and his Naturalist followers.[2] McCubbin's love of children is certainly well documented: he had six of his own. In 1893, the year in which he painted *Bush Idyll*, he also exhibited *Found*, continuing the theme of children lost in the bush but now ending happily ever after. During the 1890s he seems to have felt increasingly that children saw things with greater clarity and intensity than most adults. The bush was no longer threatening but, rather, a source of mystery and enchantment. Contemporary poets, too, began to present it as an arcadian setting where classical nymphs or sprites might find a home[3]. *Bush Idyll*, however, remains firmly rooted in reality: it was probably

largely executed on the spot in the outer suburbs of Melbourne and, as reviewers noted, the young pair are by no means 'idealized'.[4] Instead of classical pan-pipes, the boy plays a common tin whistle – as McCubbin often did himself! And his attentive companion is evidently dressed in her Sunday-best attire. *Bush Idyll* was very popular, for many years hanging in the artist's studio at the National Gallery. As one English reviewer observed, 'In everything Mr. McCubbin paints there is that spirit of truth: which wins the sympathy of the heart. He tells us everyday stories, and we feel they are true. With an innate love for bush subjects, and with the scent of the eucalyptus in his being, he can depict, with sympathetic feeling, scenes which appeal to Australian hearts'.[5]

I am extremely grateful to Mary Eagle of the Australian National Gallery for first identifying this recently re-discovered painting as *Bush Idyll* and for indispensable assistance with research. John Jones has also been most generous with assistance.

[1] *Age*, 10 February 1894, p.15.

[2] *Pas mêche*, 1882 (National Gallery of Scotland) is probably the best known example by Bastien-Lepage; see Astbury 1985, in press, p.110. McCubbin had recently read, and recommended to Roberts, André Theuriet's biography *Jules Bastien-Lepage and his Art*, 1892. He had an engraved reproduction of Lepage's famous *Joan of Arc listening to the Voices* in his scrap-book; also a photograph of George Clausen's *Girl at the gate* – wearing rustic boots.

[3] See Galbally 1981, pp.107ff. and Astbury 1985, pp.173ff. for visual parallels in McCubbin's later work; and *Table Talk*, 10 May 1895, p.7, for the prevalence of 'Idylls' in contemporary exhibitions.

[4] A small oil on cardboard version of the boy's figure in bush landscape (Savage Club, Melbourne) was more probably painted after the major work than as a preliminary sketch. It is signed l.r. and inscribed u.r. 'Melbourne/SAVAGE Club/ Smoke Concert/Oct. 20th/1900'; it was apparently used as a programme cover design. John Jones of the Australian National Gallery kindly drew my attention to this work. The girl was Miss Mary Jane Lobb (b.1881) of Blackburn; information from her son.

[5] *The Studio*, 1897, p.69.

TOM ROBERTS ▶

Bailed Up, 1895/1927
Oil on canvas
134.5 x 182.8 cm
Signed (in 1928) l.l.: Tom Roberts/95 = /27
Art Gallery of New South Wales
Purchased 1933

Provenance:
The artist; until his *Exhibition of Oil Paintings*, Macquarie Galleries, Sydney, June/July 1928, no.18: 'Bailed Up – 500 guineas', bought by J.W. Maund and placed anonymously on loan to the Art Gallery of New South Wales until 1933

Exhibitions:
Society of Artists, First Exhibition, Sydney, September 1895, no.29: 'Bailed Up – £275', illus.; *Victorian Artists' Society Annual Exhibition Catalogue of Paintings, Studies, Sketches &c.*, Melbourne, October 1896, no.41: 'Bailed Up – £275'; *Exhibition and Sale of Paintings Previous to Leaving Australia*, Society of Artists, Sydney, November 1900, no.20: 'Bailed Up – 70 guineas'; *Victorian Gold Jubilee Exhibition*, Bendigo 1901, no.52: 'Bailed Up'

Literature:
Daily Telegraph, 27 September 1895, p.6; *Sydney Morning Herald*, 27 September 1895, p.6; 14 November 1900, p.5; 2 March 1928, p.13; 28 June 1928, p.8; 14 July 1928, p.11; 10 November 1947, p.7; *Argus*, 23 October 1896, p.6; *Table Talk*, 23 October 1896, p.16; *Age*, 24 October 1896, p.11; Moore 1934, I, p.128; Croll 1935, pp.38, 129, 176f.; Lindsay 1938, p.41; Hoff 1951, p.130; Spate 1964, p.263; McCulloch 1969, pp.64, 88, 158; Gleeson 1969, pl.16; Daniel Thomas 1969, p.473; Smith 1971, p.90; Hughes 1977, p.57; Spate 1978, pp.73, 92ff., pl.26; Smith 1979, pp.125, 167, 242; Burn 1980, p.89; Splatt & Bruce 1981, pp.76f; Topliss 1985, no.234, pp.19f., 139; Astbury 1985, in press, pp.125ff., pl.21

Mr Tom Roberts, the chairman of the Society of Artists sets a good example by sending characteristically Australian subjects... Mr Roberts's chief work is 'Bailed Up' (No.29), a clever picture, the title of which tells the whole story. The artist shows a mountain road at the base of a hill rising steeply behind, dazzlingly near the spectator under the fierce light of a brilliant day. Dwarfed by the heights above are the figures of mounted bush-rangers rifling a Cobb's coach which has been brought to a standstill. The glossy dark-brown horse in the foreground is beautifully drawn and painted, but the drawing of the grey is weak, and the figures generally are not entirely convincing. The best view of this clever composition is got by standing very far back.
– *The Sydney Morning Herald*, 27 September 1895

Bailed Up by Mr Tom Roberts, is an ambitious composition full of achievements and failures. The steep rise against which the coach has been arrested with its parched sunlit grass and gum trunks is painted with the vigor and charm of color familiar to us in Mr Roberts's landscapes. But the length and slimness normal in the gum tree are abnormal in the legs of the bushrangers, and though the outline and movement of the horses have been accurately observed, the living lustrous quality of their skin is not given;... As a narration of an episode in the history of the bush, there is an amusing lack of any dramatic element. The whole affair is conducted à l'aimable. The grey leader alone appears startled. One man as a matter of form points his revolver at the impassible coachman, while another member of the long-legged fraternity chats at the coach door to a lady passenger...
– *The Age*, 24 October 1896

In *Bailed Up*, begun 1893, Roberts's romantic historicizing attitude to his 'national' subject matter was unequivocal. *Table Talk* reported that the painting showed an incident from the novel *Robbery Under Arms*.[1] A writer in *The Sydney Morning Herald* stated that 'on the occasion of a dinner at Newstead, Mr Roberts expressed a wish that he might obtain some data which would enable him to paint a picture... typifying the early days of New South Wales in the bush-ranging era. The Messrs Anderson [owners of 'Newstead' station] entered into the spirit of the project enthusiastically.: Cobb and Co's coach, with the old leather braces, was commandeered as was the driver, Robert Bates, well known in those

days...'[2] Mr Bates himself reluctantly admitted having been 'stuck up' some thirty years before, in the 1860s, and described his memories of that event. Roberts then followed Bastien-Lepage's recommended procedure for history painting, reconstructing the incident as accurately as possible in an appropriate setting.[3] (Not long before Roberts had written admiringly of those contemporary European artists who 'insist that any subject painted must be done true to the conditions under which it is supposed to have existed'.)[4] Essentially, however, his progression from numerous sketches to the full-scale canvas was traditional academic method: as in the painting of all his grand 'machines'.[5] A local official recalled, 'The scene of the sham hold-up was at a place known as Wall's Hill... At that time it was a rough and lonely bit of road well suited for the setting of the picture'. Roberts painted only the landscape background there, on the old Armidale to Inverell road five kilometres from 'Newstead' and three from 'Paradise' station (where he was staying as guest of Mr Russell Hughes). He chose a bend in the road bordered by steep hills, grasstrees and heavy timber; and constructed a high wooden platform, his 'Perch', on which to work. The canvas was transferred to Inverell for addition of 'the principal factors in the incident' – the coach and driver; 'Station hands and others were run in as bushrangers, passengers, etc., and the scene was complete'.[6] Alick Anderson remembered that the finishing touches were added at Newstead, 'and some of the horses were ours, and some of the bushrangers our men'.[7] (In fact Roberts retouched the landscape to some extent in 1927.)

Now that highway robbery had become a part of 'colonial history', the public relished dashing tales such as 'Reminiscences of the Bushranging Days', published over several weeks during 1890 in *The Illustrated Sydney News*. A number of artists had already treated the theme. The prolific illustrative painter, J.A. Turner, had sent his own *Bailed Up* to the Colonial and Indian Exhibition of 1886. William Strutt had already returned to London by 1887, when he painted his very large historical *Bushrangers, Victoria, Australia 1852*; and wrote, 'I brought the costumes over from Australia and they are the very ones worn by the Colonists at that time'.[8] Frank Mahony's swashbuckling 'As in the Days of Old', 1892, was much admired as 'a spirited delineation of a stirring bushranging episode,... full of life and motion [and] galloping horses'.[9] By contrast, when Roberts's *Bailed Up*

was first exhibited, most reviewers were either 'thoroughly unconvinced' or somewhat puzzled by its comparative lack of drama. They wanted to feel 'the thrill of excitement that such a scene should engender'.[10] In fact the old coach driver, Bates, relating his own experience for Roberts, had emphasized 'the quiet way the whole thing was done'.[11] Roberts's avoidance of histrionics was deliberate. (Interestingly, the mood of Strutt's *Bushrangers*, which Roberts probably never saw, is similar.) The strange, slow quiet of this 'stick up', and the frieze-like arrangement of its main motif in such shallow pictorial space, lend *Bailed Up* a timeless, almost classical authority.[12]

[1] 23 October 1896, p.16.
[2] Quoted by Moore 1934, I, p.128.
[3] Spate 1978, p.73. Bastien-Lepage's method was quoted by R. Muther, *The History of Modern Painting*, London, 1896, III, p.14.
[4] *Argus*, 31 October 1891, p.4.
[5] He filled almost a whole sketchbook with drawings. For numerous related pencil and oil studies, see Topliss 1985, nos 234a-h. Roberts probably worked on the subject from December 1893 to mid-1895.
[6] Moore, op.cit., p.128.
[7] 'Some recollections of Tom Roberts by Mr Alick Anderson, of Garrawilla, N.S.W.', quoted by Croll 1935, p.168.
[8] Curnow 1980, p.42. Strutt's *Bushrangers* was exhibited at the Royal Academy in 1887.
[9] *Argus*, 23 October 1986, p.6; now in the Art Gallery of New South Wales.
[10] ibid.
[11] Moore, op.cit., p.128.
[12] A number of art historians have commented on Roberts's admiration for Pierre Puvis de Chavannes (1824-98) in relation to *Bailed Up*. Puvis became something of an idol of *avant-garde* European painters at the end of the 19th century because of the decorative and calm abstract qualities of his art. See Spate 1978, p.95.

ARTHUR STREETON ►

The purple noon's transparent might, 1896

Oil on canvas

121.8 x 122 cm

Signed and dated l.l.: ARTHUR STREETON/1896

National Gallery of Victoria

Purchased 1896

Provenance:

The artist

Exhibitions:

Society of Artists Second Spring Exhibition, Sydney, September 1896, no.23: 'Hawkesbury Landscape – £210.0.0', illus.; *Streeton's Sydney Sunshine Exhibition,* Melbourne, December 1896, no.5: 'The purple noon's transparent light [*sic*]'; *Exhibition of Australian Art in London,* Grafton Galleries, London, April 1898, no.62: "Purple Noon's transparent light [*sic*]" – Hawkesbury River, N.S.W. – lent by Trustees of Melbourne Gallery'

Literature:

Sydney Morning Herald, 5 September 1896, p.7; *Table Talk,* 4 December 1896, p.7; 11 December 1896, pp.1,7; *Age,* 11 December 1896, p.7; *Daily Telegraph,* 7 September 1896; 12 September 1896; 5 May 1898, p.6; *Magazine of Art,* 1898, pp.379, illus. 383; *Studio,* May 1898, illus.; MacDonald 1916, p.89; Streeton 1919, pl.XIII; Moore 1934, I, p.96; Streeton 1935, no.172; Croll 1946, pp.61f.; Hoff 1951, p.131; Cox 1970, p.425; Gleeson 1969, pl.24; McCulloch 1969, pp.64, 66,176; Smith 1971, pp.91f.; Gleeson 1971, pl.66; Hughes 1977, p.63; Galbally 1979, no.80, p.29, illus.13; Splatt & Bruce 1981, pl.56

Reproduced by courtesy of Mrs Oliver Streeton

The sun is warm, the sky is clear,
The waves are dancing fast and bright;
Blue isles and snowy mountains wear
The purple noon's transparent might
– Percy Bysshe Shelley (1792-1822)

. . . a beautiful foreground of translucent blue water stretching out to the shallows and shelving rocks of the higher reaches of the river, and miles of green fields hemmed in at last by the haze-enveloped hills. There is a feast of colour in this fine work.
– *The Sydney Morning Herald,* 5 September 1896

Streeton had written to Roberts of his intention 'to go straight inland (away from all polite society), . . . create some things entirely new, and try and translate some of the great hidden poetry that I know is here.'[1] His painting trip to the upper reaches of the Hawkesbury River in 1896 was made with that ambition in mind. This vast panoramic view, looking across to the Blue Mountains, was painted from a natural rise known as 'The Terrace' between Richmond Bridge and Windsor; according to the artist, 'in two days and during a shade temperature of 108 degrees'. At first he called it simply 'Hawkesbury Landscape'; but when he brought it to Melbourne for his one-man-exhibition in December that year he changed the title to 'The purple noon's transparent light [*sic*]' – a quotation from Shelley's romantic poetry.[2] Later Streeton recalled that he had worked on the canvas in a state of 'artistic intoxication with thoughts of Shelley in my mind'.[3] 'My work may perish but I must work so as to go on, on', he wrote (almost incoherently) to Roberts, 'a man wants all the bother of drawing & drying and blending & so on, all just in his hand . . . & then put forth his mind and out with all he has till he's exhausted, then rest and sleep and on again and on'.[4] Contemporary critics recognized this fervour in the painting itself: 'The gaiety of the color and the facility of the execution impress the spectator immediately. Nature has been rendered with passion rather than the long patience of genius, and with a sensuous charm that, like all strong emotions, communicates itself readily'.[5] Streeton's bravura rendering of light, heat and distance in this Hawkesbury series revealed 'his great qualities as a landscape painter'. One of the smaller canvases in the series (probably *Hawkesbury River*) was 'an exquisite transcript of silvery light', said *The Age.* The heroic *Purple noon* . . . was 'remarkable for its fine and beautiful color, the "inner radiance" of the pale, hot sky and haze enveloped mountains'. Lindsay

Bernard Hall, as director of the Melbourne Gallery, wrote to his trustees:

With regard to the exhibition being held in town by Mr Arthur Streeton, I have to advise you of its general excellence, & to recommend *you most strongly* to purchase something important for the Gallery from him before he leaves Australia for Europe. Just such a picture exists in No.5 – *'The purple noon's transparent light'* – on the Hawkesbury River. As it would come under the classification of 'the best work by the best men', I strongly advise the Trustees not to miss the opportunity of acquiring it, and of adding to the Australian section what is *most characteristically* Australian in the way of pictorial presentment.[6]

Largely due to the support of John Mather as a trustee, who agreed to the asking price of £150 whilst one of the others tried to beat the artist down to 125 guineas, this most popular work became the first by Streeton acquired for the National Gallery of Victoria.

[1] Croll 1946, p.40.

[2] In the catalogue for *Streeton's Sydney Sunshine Exhibition* of 1896, line 4 of Shelley's *Stanzas written in Dejection – December 1818, near Naples,* was misquoted 'The purple noon's transparent light'. This was repeated in catalogues of 1898, 1918 and 1923. However, in the *Loan Exhibition of the Works of Arthur Streeton* at the Art Gallery of New South Wales, November 1931-January 1932, the quotation was corrected to read 'The Purple Noon's Transparent Might' (no.49). As first published, the poem read '. . . transparent light' (Mary Shelley (ed.), *Posthumous Poems,* 1824, and also in 2nd edn , 1839). All editions from 1847, however, follow Shelley's fair copy, probably of 1820: Pierpoint Morgan Library M.A. 406; indeed, 'light' is the rhyme-word for the line following, which Mary's 1824 version of the poem omitted. Streeton's own edition, which read 'might', was E. Moxon and Son, London, 1877. According to the artist's son the change was made by Streeton himself; and as it was maintained in later literature within his lifetime, we have waived our 'first exhibited title rule' and continue to call the painting *'The purple noon's transparent might'.* I am most grateful for information from Peter Naish, Department of English, Monash University.

[3] Handwritten note, quoted by Galbally 1979, p.34. Streeton often took volumes of poetry with him on his solitary painting

expeditions; as did Roberts, Streeton identified his own response to the landscape with the romantic mood of Shelley's verse. In addition it is very likely that the particular words, 'The purple noon's transparent might', associated itself in his mind with the hazy distance and the purple-blue shadows cast by vegetation under the zenithal sun. Professor Bernard Smith observes that 'Streeton's sensitive perception of colour values is here remarkably well sustained throughout the whole canvas. There are few paintings as large as this one which are so consistently based upon the careful painterly assessment of retinal impressions . . . [V]isual perception and painting technique are wonderfully balanced'.

[4] Probably 1896. Tom Roberts correspondence, Mitchell Library, Sydney, MS A2480, vol.I.

[5] *Age*, 11 December 1896, p.7.

[6] 7 December 1896, to the Chairman of trustees, quoted by Cox 1970, p.425.

FREDERICK McCUBBIN
The Pioneer, 1904
Oil on canvas (triptych)
223.5 x 86 cm; 224.7 x 122.5 cm;
223.5 x 85.7 cm
Signed and dated in each panel l.l.:
F. McCubbin/1904
National Gallery of Victoria
Felton Bequest 1906

Provenance:
The artist

Exhibitions:
Mr Fred McCubbin's Exhibition of Australian Paintings, Athenaeum Upper Hall, Melbourne, April 22, 1904, no.6: 'The Pioneer – £525.0.0' (with a poem written by the artist William Blamire Young); *Victorian Artists' Society Winter Exhibition, Illustrated Catalogue*, Melbourne 1905, no.43: 'The Pioneer – £367.10.0', illus. in original frame

Literature:

Age, 22 April 1904, p.8; 16 August 1905, editorial, p.6; 27 March 1906, p.4; 30 March 1906; *Argus*, 22 April 1904, p.7; *Herald*, 13 July 1905; Moore 1906, illus.; *Australia Today*, 1 December 1909, p.77, illus. in original frame; Colquhoun [1919], illus.; MacDonald 1916, pl.XVII, pp.65ff.; Moore 1934, I, p.126; Hoff 1951, p.128; Hoff 1955, no.20; Hoff 1956, p.304; McCulloch 1969, pp.80ff.; Gleeson 1969, pp.56f.; David Thomas 1969, p.73; Smith 1971, p.88; Gleeson 1971, pl.21; Hughes 1977, p.68; Smith 1979, p.125; Galbally 1981,pl.19,pp.95ff.; Astbury 1981, pp.45ff.; Downer & Phipps 1985, no.147; Astbury 1985, in press, pp.150ff., pl.26

The big picture is to my mind my best effort in Art.
– McCubbin to Roberts, 14 June 1904

The large canvas is divided into three panels to enable the painter to give pictorial insight to three episodes in the life history of those strong spirits who opened up this Continent... In the first panel the forest twilight is deepening under the fires of sunset. The young, free selector has pushed into the depths of the bush. Having unharnessed his pair of horses from the covered cart which has carried all his belongings this far, he is lighting the fire to boil the billy for the evening meal... In the foreground the centre of interest is the sweet face of the selector's young wife... She is thinking of the home she has left far away, of the many human ties broken, that part of this gigantic forest may be cleared for human habitation... But this note of gloom is not sounded too deeply. The face of the young woman shows that she is strong enough to be chastened by the quiet half hour of personal sadness. The onlooker is sure that she will soon be setting about her duties with the blithe wifely spirit of the pioneer woman. The forest color in this panel is very lovely indeed. The fallen gum leaves and bark weave their mysterious tangle of browns and purples under foot, while the fern, dimly lit from the twilight sky through the leafage over head, shimmer a quiet sylvan green... In the next panel we see that the great wonder of the bush has been achieved [by] the strong arm of the man... His cottage nestles in the clearing. In the foreground he sits smoking the pipe of peace on the trunk of the last giant to crash before the axe that lies beside him. With the fallen leaves and bark are now mingled the chips that mark his slow dogged struggle with exuberant Nature... The young wife stands in front of him, a child in her arms. The figure has the same lithe elegance as before, but the despondency of the twilight hour has gone. The new life and the child have paramount claim on her energies...
The last panel is the triumphal stanza of the whole color poem. A country youth, with reverent fingers, clears away the undergrowth from the rough wooden cross marking the last resting place of the gallant couple. In the distance the spires and bridges of a glorious young city and the stooks of a rich harvest field tell of the joys that another generation is reaping from the toil of the once lusty pioneers now

gone to dust... This picture of Mr. McCubbin's is to be hailed as an irrefutable demonstration that Australia can produce a strong and beautiful national art of her own.
– The Age, 16 August 1905

The Pioneer represents the culmination of McCubbin's paintings on the theme of pioneering Australian settlement. By choosing a triptych format, traditional in religious art, he deliberately raised his theme to a level of reverence: 'telling its own legend of the useful toil, the homely joys and destiny obscure of the pioneer...'[1] There are many echoes from his earlier paintings. The pensive young wife in the first panel, for example, is reminiscent of the lonely swagman in Down on his luck, 1889. The second section portrays a family group, as does McCubbin's On the Wallaby Track of 1894 (Art Gallery of New South Wales). The final scene recalls The Bush Burial. However, The Pioneer – painted three years after Federation – is more self-consciously nationalistic; proud of 'the prosperity of the fine city seen in the background'.[2] Its mood of quiet optimism is unqualified. The Age called it 'a poem of democracy'.[3] McCubbin began work on The Pioneer in 1903. He was then living with his family at Mount Macedon, in the house which he called 'Fontainebleau' after the famous village near Paris where Corot and his followers had painted en plein air. As The Argus critic remarked, 'Mr. McCubbin has attempted to do for Macedon and Woodend something of what the Frenchman did for the forests of Fontainebleau'.[4] For probably the last time in a large-scale work, he followed Bastien-Lepage's recommended procedure in order to paint the entire picture in the open air. Rather than building a scaffold to reach the top of the painting, he lowered the canvases into a deep trench – the remains of which can still be seen in the garden at Macedon. This was a daunting task. As he wrote to Roberts in September 1903, 'I am pegging on at The Pioneer and I feel like the poor devils I am painting in the picture... Sometimes up and sometimes down'.[5] McCubbin first exhibited The Pioneer in 'one of the most notable "one man shows" to have been held in Melbourne' (The Age, 22 April 1904, p.8). He showed it once again the following year, at the Victorian Artists' Society, when critics noted that the distant city had been retouched 'in the manner of Turner'.[6] 'It will certainly be a cause of humiliation to Victoria if the trustees of the National Gallery do not secure this beautiful poetical landscape and deeply sympathetic historical picture', declared The Age editorial. In fact the acquisition

was fraught with disputes amongst the trustees and considerable disillusion for poor McCubbin himself. Fortunately, John Mather was re-elected a trustee in 1906; and finally The Pioneer became one of the first Australian paintings purchased for the National Gallery of Victoria by the Felton Bequest – although at £175 less than the artist's original asking price.

[1] Argus, 22 April 1904, p.7.
[2] ibid. For the contemporary context of nationalistic fervour see Galbally 1981, p.95 and especially Astbury 1981, pp.47f.; also J.B. Hirst, 'The Pioneer Legend', Historical Studies, 18, 71, October 1978.
[3] 16 August 1905, p.6.
[4] Argus, loc.cit.
[5] McCubbin to Roberts (in London), 3 September 1903. Roberts correspondence, vol. II, Mitchell Library, Sydney. MS A2480.
[6] Astbury points out that McCubbin's longstanding admiration for Turner had been rekindled by The Studio special issue on that artist's work, 1903-4. Astbury, op.cit., p.47.

SYDNEY HARBOUR

Jane Clark

Hymn to Sydney

City of laughing loveliness! Sun-girdled Queen!
Crowned with imperial morning, bejewelled with joy,
Raimented soft like a bride, in virginal sheen,
Veiled in luminous mist, blushing maidenly-coy
In shyly opening dawntide of youthful-sweet beauty:–
Earth and Air, and the Heavens, and wondering Ocean salute thee!

– G.W.L. Marshall-Hall, 1897, dedicated to Arthur Streeton

We call at island stations for passengers, look up long arms of harbour and some projecting
capes, at each place dropping or taking in passengers. These projecting capes, with their
far-reaching creeks, are sprinkled with good stone buildings, and beautiful villas peep out
from amongst the dense growth surrounding them. The rugged, broken nature of the friable
sandstone rocks, covered with acacias and eucalyptus, make up picture after picture as we
steam in and out among them.

– Josiah Hughes, *Australia Revisited in 1890. . .* , London, 1891

Streeton left Melbourne for Sydney in May 1890, with 'one or two commissions awaiting him', as he told *Table Talk*'s reporter.[1] Having sold his *Still glides the stream. . .* so recently to the Art Gallery of New South Wales, he was warmly welcomed by the trustees. Julian Ashton described him as 'a slim, debonair young man of about twenty-four years of age, with a little gold pointed beard and fair complexion. When he wasn't painting he was quoting Keats and Shelley'.[2] E.L. Montefiore, the other artist trustee, accompanied him to the Gallery. He visited Fullwood, Frank Mahony, Nerli and other local painters; and various places, such as Coogee Bay, where he knew Roberts and Conder had worked two years earlier.

There was much less sense of an artistic community in Sydney than in 'the sister state'; as D.H. Souter explained, 'Sydney had no accumulation of excellence. . . Julian Ashton was still considered a visitor from Melbourne'.[3] Many of the *Picturesque Atlas* artists had left by 1890. W.C. Piguenit was certainly recognized as a master of Australian landscape; but was said to be isolated by 'his modesty and retiring nature. . . and absolutely refuses to take pupils'.[4] Indeed before long Streeton was writing to Roberts, 'At present I don't think there are very many *great* painters in Sydney – between you and me'; and later, 'Things are very slow here, and I don't do any work and don't feel inclined to commence anything else. And the Victorian people, I think, are a bit quicker to feel Art'.[5]

Sydney nevertheless offered two great attractions for painters. For one thing, Ashton had carried a resolution 'that not less than five hundred pounds be spent annually on the purchase of Australian works of art'. As Sidney Dickinson remarked, the Art Gallery of New South Wales was 'known to Victorian artists as almost the only influential patron that they have'![6] Secondly, there was the natural beauty of Sydney Harbour with its mild climate and brilliant sunshine. 'From Milson's Point to Middle Head was unbroken bushland, with the exception of two or three old settlers' homes', Julian Ashton wrote.[7] His son, Howard Ashton, declared that 'Sydney is a poem itself' and that the harbour landscape inspired pictures almost without study.[8] *Table Talk* soon reported that Streeton, having intended to stay four weeks in Sydney, had been there four months. In spite of poor sales at the Art Society's exhibition (he had to ask his father to pay for the frames), he decided to remain. Roberts joined him the following year.

Living was cheap, for Sydney was affected later than Melbourne by the impending depression. Sydney's economy was founded more securely on pastoral wealth – rather than massive foreign investment in 'mushroom' banks and dubious financial institutions; in 1891 there were sixty million sheep in New South Wales compared with Victoria's six million. And McCubbin wrote to Roberts, 'I think you must get more of the sun than me and it makes you chirpy'.[9] There was, however, a chronic housing shortage (notwithstanding more than twice the number of boarding houses than in Melbourne).[10] By October 1891 Streeton and Roberts were living at Curlew Camp on Little Sirius Cove with a postal address of Saunders' Boat House, Mosman's Bay.

Unlike the Box Hill and Eaglemont camps, Curlew Camp was not inhabited exclusively by artists. It was a semi-permanent institution during the 1890s, tenanted by a great variety of characters who could not or would not make a 'respectable' living. (Both Roberts and Streeton also took city studios when they could afford the rent.) Reuben Brasch, known as 'the father of the camp', pitched a tent there with his three brothers. Other neighbours included Sidney Barberfield, the interstate footballer William Galloway, and champion runner R. White; F.S. Delmer, a linguist friend of Streeton and Roberts, who later taught at the Universities of Königsberg and Berlin; as well as artists Fullwood, Daplyn, William Lister Lister and Nelson Illingworth. There was a man to do the cooking and a youth to attend to the odd jobs, the campers 'living like fighting-cocks on £1 a week'.[11] Professor Marshall-Hall, on one of his periodic visits from Melbourne, 'enjoyed the skies and the harbour; and was suppered by a tribe of congenial Bohemians' nearby at Cremorne.[12] Artists' reminiscences of the period abound. Streeton and Roberts were evidently greeted by one local who said, 'We are glad to see you chaps. But what are you poor devils going to do?' Harry Weston, an architect and cartoonist, remembered 'a strange sense of unreality about the art life of those days. It was after the land boom had burst; and on the rare occasions you received a cheque, you rushed to the Bank, feeling certain it would be stopped'.[13] And William Moore relates:

At the lunch hour the painters used to commiserate in the Growlers' Corner – one of the corners near the door in the lounge of the Café Français, George Street. Another haunt was the Empire Hotel, Hunter Street. Here Roberts used to line up the squad to see if they were physically fit. If an artist could drain a half-pint without a gasp he was fit, if not he had to try another.[14]

The impact of the former Heidelberg artists was considerable – even though both Streeton and Roberts often travelled far away from Sydney to work on their various great New South Wales outback subjects. (Streeton also spent much of 1892 in Melbourne, still corresponding regularly with Roberts.) Fullwood admired their painting for 'the dash and vigour of the workmanship, the evident open air feeling which permeated the whole'.[15] *The Bulletin* called Streeton 'the Australian high priest of the school [of the] "impressionist" craze' (6 October 1894). 'Ashton, Fullwood and myself were painting in low tones', wrote Lister Lister, 'but, after seeing Streeton's work, we began to observe that the colour and atmosphere of the landscape were brighter than we had previously realized'.[16] Critics recognized the extent to which Streeton's and Roberts's paintings strengthened the local exhibitions; later along with other Victorian entries sent up from Melbourne by McCubbin, Mather, Longstaff, Davies, Fox, Tucker, Loureiro and others. Streeton, Fullwood, Mahony, Julian Ashton, Sydney Long and J.S. Watkins were described by *The Daily Telegraph* as the radicals of the Sydney studios'.[17]

Howard Ashton's work was soon described as 'Streetonesque'. Sydney Long was also said to be much influenced by the Melbourne 'vogue of Impressionism'.[18] As always, however, artistic influences worked in two directions. Although Streeton wrote scathingly that he had not 'the faintest interest' in Long and considered his ideas 'very objectionable & very inartistic',[19] both Streeton and Roberts responded to the strong decorative trend in Sydney painting of the 1890s. Long's incipient Symbolism and *art nouveau* style received official recognition in 1897 when *The Spirit of the Plains* was praised by the critics; and his *Pan*, inspired by poetry of Elizabeth Barrett Browning, was acquired by the Art Gallery of New South Wales in 1898.[20]

Just as in Melbourne a decade before, Roberts soon moved easily in local high society – 'on the dining list of most people who had over a couple of thousand a year'; and took a prominent role in art politics. He became, with Julian Ashton, one of Sydney's most sought-after portrait painters. Indeed portraiture was, in terms of output, his most constant preoccupation during these years. Even Sir Henry Parkes, K.C.M.G., G.C.M.G., wrote in 1894:

My dear Mr Roberts,
Sitting to you means a frightful interruption to the full course of life and this personal freedom the most precious thing that life holds for an old man. However, I am prepared to suffer martyrdom for the cause of art and Tom Roberts . . .[21]

He and Streeton opened a teaching studio in Pitt Street:

There is a Mrs Tom Roberts now, and she aids her husband in making his studio a pleasant meeting place on Thursday afternoons. He has two rooms in Vickery-chambers, quite a haunt of artists now, where Hall Thorpe, of the 'Sydney Mail', Sid Long, and others have their studios. The larger room is artistically got up in terra-cotta, with many jars and art objects around, brightened with flowers and draperies. There are usually one or two poets to be found here, A.B. ('Banjo') Paterson and H. Morant, alias 'The Breaker'.[22]

According to Souter, 'Tom brought an air of Piccadilly into Studioland. In the evenings he wore a dress cape and an opera hat, which were astounding in those days'. He was the first artist to sign his name in the visitors book at Government House. He also introduced 'stage management in art shows', wrote Sydney Long, 'and so he started a movement which gave the society's exhibitions a certain social attraction'.[23] In August 1895 Roberts, Streeton, Fullwood and others led a breakaway group from the Art Society of New South Wales and formed the Society of Artists of New South Wales. Membership was confined to professional artists and a few selected 'friendly laymen who helped by their sympathies and guineas'. Roberts was elected the first president.[24]

Early in 1898, Julian Ashton led a joint committee made up of members of the two Sydney art societies to select a vast exhibition of Australian work for the Grafton Galleries in London. Organized by the Art Gallery of New South Wales and sponsored by a generously wealthy Sydney citizen, Miss Eadith Walker, the exhibition received a rather mixed press from English critics. It was probably far too large. It was appallingly badly hung.[25] Streeton had already left for London, sailing via Cairo, towards the end of 1897. Roberts remained in Sydney a further three years; for harbourside life was still generally cheerful. Now, as Miss Florence Blair of *The Argus* reported most fulsomely to her Melbourne readers:

Possessors of artistic temperament, that delight in sensuous beauty which induces a longing to express itself in a way most congenial to the possessor, are a numerous band in Sydney. And they are very earnest and enthusiastic, and don't put on any swaggering airs, but are sociable and form a little kindgom of their own, a Bohemia of the true sort, which includes much meeting in studios reeking of paint and very dusty, much pipe-smoking, much drinking of tea (probably whisky, when ladies have been politely bowed out), many harbour excursions, meals at cafes, Tivoli parties, and much real hard work, which results in London exhibitions and Gallery purchases.[26]

[1] *Table Talk*, 16 May 1890, p.8.
[2] Ashton 1941, p.102. Ashton was then the most prominent figure in the Sydney 'art scene'.
[3] Souter 1905, p.224. David Henry Souter (1862-1935) was best known as an illustrator; he joined *The Bulletin* in 1892.
[4] James Green 'De Libra', 'The Fine Arts in Australasia, their progress, position and prospects', *The Australasian Art Review*, 1 June 1899, p.26. William Charles Piguenit (1836-1914) was born in Hobart, exhibited in Sydney from 1875 and settled there in 1880; he resigned from the Art Society because of his profound antipathy for the influence of 'impressionism' in the 1890s.
[5] Croll 1946, pp.10f. Mackennal, also visiting Sydney in 1890, wrote to the Heidelberg artists' friend and patron Theodore Fink: 'In fact, I like the place very much, but I could not earn my drink here, no money for luxuries, vile sculpture, it would make a leopard vomit'. Fink papers, Education Department, University of Melbourne.
[6] Sidney Dickinson, 'The National Galleries of Victoria and New South Wales', *The Australasian Critic*, 1 March 1891, p.142.
[7] Ashton, op.cit., p.33. Arriving from Melbourne in 1883 he was particularly taken with the winding streets and picturesque buildings of the older city. Robert Louis Stevenson was likewise charmed in 1893 by 'its little bits of Paris and London. And there is certainly something very Continental in the way that Bohemia spreads itself about among different cafes, and takes up new fads . . . The Continental atmosphere is marked in Sydney'; quoted by Florence Blair, 'In Sydney Studios', *The Argus*, 28 May 1898, p.4.
[8] Howard Ashton, 'The Lure of Sydney', *Art in Australia* I, 1916, unpaginated.
[9] 1 June 1892. LaTrobe Collection, State Library of Victoria. MS 8910 1205/3(c); printed in Croll 1935, pp.172f.
[10] Davison 1978, p.193.
[11] Moore 1934, I, p.246. Other accounts have Streeton living on 12/6 per week; and even Roberts and Streeton jointly on 8/- during 1893. For example, Galbally 1979, p.25; Croll 1935, p.66; see also Les G. Thorne, *A History of North Shore Sydney, from 1788 to Today*, rev. edn, Angus and Robertson, Sydney, 1979, p.27. Little Sirius Cove is a small arm of Mosman's Bay (formerly known as Greater Sirius Cove); named after the ship which in 1789 brought supplies from Capetown and thereby saved the struggling young colony of Sydney from starvation. Ashton and Livingston Hopkins ('Hop' of *The Bulletin*) established a similar camp at Balmoral for about two years in the 1890s.
[12] *The Bookfellow*, 25 March 1899, p.13.
[13] Quoted by Moore 1934, I, p.166.
[14] ibid., pp.245f.
[15] Quoted by Souter, op.cit., p.225.
[16] Quoted by Moore in 'An Artistic Trio – Streeton, Roberts and Conder', *The Sydney Morning Herald*, 28 November 1931, p.9. Lister Lister (1859-1943) was unkindly dismissed by Streeton in a letter of 1890 with a bracketed aside, 'poor work'. Moore also quotes Hans Heysen: 'It was by a bright painting by Streeton, shown at the South Australian Society of Arts, that the movement for open-air was awakened in a small coterie of artists in Adelaide. The sunny nature of the picture touched the imagination and opened our eyes to the fact that our Australian sunshine was radically different from that of the European pictures in the Gallery'. Some allowance should be made for the chauvinistic myth-making of the 1930s when writers such as Moore and Lionel Lindsay tended to present Streeton as the hero of Australian art. However, comparable claims were certainly made at the time: for example by a critic in *The Daily Telegraph*, 5 September 1896, p.3, 'It must be conceded that a few of our local men are in a fair way to losing individuality in their attempt to imitate Mr Streeton's methods, even down to his mannerisms. That the influence is a good one few will be inclined to question, but when it appears as a faithful reproduction of a particular form of cloud effect and the like one begins to wish that the "trail" were not quite so marked'.
[17] 'It is in the breaking of new ground in methods of treatment that they claim the title of Progressionists'. *The Daily Telegraph*, 27 June 1895.
[18] *The Bulletin* writers, in particular, disapproved of 'impressionism' and the growing 'pretentions' of artists in Sydney. Long's *By Tranquil Waters*, repeatedly described as 'impressionist' and certainly influenced by the Heidelberg School, was purchased by the Art Gallery of New South Wales in 1894. Mendelssohn 1979, no.10; see also James Green 'De Libra', *The Australasian Art Review*, 1 August 1899, pp.25ff.
[19] Streeton to S.W. Pring, from Palings Buildings, Sydney, c.1895. Mitchell Library, Sydney. MS 1367/1.
[20] *The Spirit of the Plains*, 1897, is now in the Queensland Art Gallery. Mendelsshon 1979, nos 49 and 60.
[21] 16 May 1894. Mitchell Library MS A2480, vol.III, p.124. For Roberts's portraits of Parkes, see Topliss 1985, nos 193 and 228. Streeton wrote inviting Parkes to visit his and Roberts's shared studio, 99n Pitt Street, Sydney (11 January 1893). Mitchell Library MS A 908, vol.38, p.216.
[22] *Argus*, 28 May 1898, p.4. Roberts had married Miss Lillie Williamson, a former Gallery student, in Melbourne on 30 April 1896; he then left Mosman to live in Balmain. By about 1899 Curlew Camp was largely abandoned by artists. John Hall Thorpe (1874-1947) was described in 1895 as 'one new comet and the only one [that] has appeared on the horizon' (*The Daily Telegraph*, 27 September 1895, p.6).
[23] Souter, quoted by Moore 1934, I, p.246 and Croll 1935, pp.40f.; and Long quoted ibid., p.168. Long also bought a top hat to wear to Vice-Regal functions; although later it was said his real purpose was 'to make himself look taller against a tall slim young lady' (that is, the artist Thea Proctor). Mendelssohn, op.cit., p.30. See also George A. Taylor, '*Those Were the Days*', *Being Reminiscences of Australian Artists and Writers*, Tyrell's, Sydney, 1918, for Roberts's involvement in the Dawn and Dusk Club and the Supper Club.
[24] See *The Sydney Morning Herald*, 21 October 1895, p.3; James Green 'De Libra', op.cit., pp.22f.; Moore 1934, I, pp.168f. The first council consisted of Roberts, Streeton, Fullwood, Mahony, Long, Souter and Watkins. Julian Ashton became president in 1897 and Sydney Long in 1898.
[25] The selection committee comprised Ashton, Roberts, Long, Mahony, Lister Lister and Piguenit. The layout of the exhibition was described in *The Daily Telegraph*, 5 May 1898, p.6. See also James Green 'De Libra', op.cit., pp.27ff.; and a number of contemporary reviews reprinted in *The Daily Telegraph*, 12 and 21 May 1898, and Smith 1975, pp.215ff.
[26] 28 May 1898, p.4.

ARTHUR STREETON ▶
Sunny South – Coogee Bay, 1890
Oil on canvas
29 x 59 cm
Signed, dated and inscribed l.l.:
Coogee/Steeton [*sic*] 1890
Inscribed l.r.: Sunny South
Private collection, Melbourne

Provenance:
Lawrence Abrahams, purchased from the
artist 1890; Mrs Alice Phipps, his daughter

Exhibitions:
*Art Society of New South Wales Spring
Exhibition*, Sydney, September 1890,
no.187: 'Sunny South – 15 guineas'; probably *Exhibition of Pictures by Fd. McCubbin, Arthur Streeton and Tom Roberts*,
Gemmell, Tuckett & Co., Melbourne, 5
December 1890, no.16: 'Coogee Bay – 24
x 12 ins'

Literature:
Sydney Morning Herald, 6 September
1890, p.5; *Table Talk*, 28 November 1890,
p.5; *Australasian Builder & Contractors'
News*, 29 November 1890, p.401; Hoff
1967, pp.386ff.; Galbally 1979, no.37 (as
'Coogee Beach')
Reproduced by courtesy of Mrs Oliver
Streeton

'What a lovely little place. Sand, bananas,
empty bottles & color & pretty children.
Shall do some good work there I think',
Streeton wrote to Roberts after he first
saw Coogee Bay in 1890.[1] It was his first
plein air painting spot in Sydney; and he
returned again and again during his
repeated visits to New South Wales
between 1890 and 1896 and many years
later.[2] Streeton certainly knew both
Roberts's and Conder's paintings of Coogee from Easter 1888; and seems to have
stood in almost the same spot to paint
Sunny South. Even his choice of title harks
back deliberately to happy times with 'K'
and 'Bulldog' – 'the days that are no more'
at Heidelberg and Mentone. Streeton evidently brought the picture home to Melbourne for inclusion in an exhibition and
sale held jointly with Roberts and McCubbin in December. It was purchased by
Lawrence Abrahams (Louis Abraham's
younger brother), who refused to part
with it even when Streeton himself hoped
to buy it back many years later.[3]

[1] Streeton to Roberts, September 1890.
Mitchell Library, Sydney, MS A2480.
Roberts correspondence, vol.I.
[2] For example, see Galbally 1979, nos 38,
39, 78.
[3] Information kindly suppplied by the
present owner. It was also withdrawn
before sale from *The Magnificent
Collection of Australian Pictures – late
Lawrence Abrahams*, Decoration Co., 20
June 1919, lot 25.

TOM ROBERTS ▶
Aboriginal Head (Charlie Turner), 1892
Oil on canvas (mounted on pulpboard)
39.4 x 29.8 cm
Signed and dated l.l: Tom Roberts/1892
Inscribed verso: Arneham/Wolnall Tribe/
Port Darwin
Art Gallery of New South Wales
Purchased 1892

Provenance:
The artist

Exhibitions:
*Art Society of New South Wales, Catalogue
of Spring Exhibition*, Sydney, September
1892, no.78: 'Aboriginal Head (Charlie
Turner) – £21.0.0'.; *Official Catalogue of
Exhibits World's Columbian Exposition*,
Chicago 1893, p.163, no.60: 'Aboriginal
Head'; *Exhibition of Australian Art in
London*, Grafton Galleries, London, April
1898, no.41: 'Aboriginal Head – lent by
Trustees of Sydney Gallery'

Literature:
Sydney Morning Herald, 2 September
1892, p.2; *Australasian Art Review*, 1
August 1899, p.23; Croll 1935, pp.208ff.;
McCulloch 1969, pp.60, 158; Daniel
Thomas 1969, p.470; Spate 1978, pl.105;
Geoffrey Dutton, *White on Black: The
Australian Aboriginal Portrayed in Art*,
Melbourne, 1974, p.59; Topliss 1985,
no.183, pp.19f.; Helen Topliss, 'Tom
Roberts's Aboriginal Portraits: An aspect
of his Outback Vision', paper delivered at
'Australia and the European Imagination'
Conference, Canberra, May 1981; to be
published in T. & I. Donaldson (eds), *Seeing
the First Australians*, Allen and Unwin

'An Aboriginal Head' is painted with so
much strength and fidelity, that its
value will grow year by year with the
gradual disappearance from our midst
of the original possessors of the soil.
Thus it has a permanent, if melancholy
interest, which justifies its inclusion in
our national collection.
– *The Sydney Morning Herald*, 2 September 1892

Charlie Turner was presumably one of the
Port Darwin Aboriginals whom Roberts
met at Cooktown in August 1892. He had
travelled northwards on the ship *Jessie*,
working as a seaman for his passage, one
of his aims being to make studies of various native peoples. He was consciously
painting for history: 'an interesting record
of a passing race'.[1] A number of artists had
already depicted Australian Aboriginal
characters (as something more than anonymous black figures in bush landscape) –
Robert Dowling, Julian Ashton, Arthur
Loureiro, for example. Roberts's *Aboriginal Head (Charlie Turner)* is, however, a
particularly sympathetic portrait.

[1] Roberts quoted in a press cutting,
c.1920-21, in his scrapbook (Mitchell
Library PX*D 310).

TOM ROBERTS ▲
Smike Streeton age 24, 1891
Oil on canvas
45.7 x 35.7 cm
Signed and dated l.l.: Tom Roberts 91
Scratched in paint u.r.: Smike/Streeton/
age 24
Art Gallery of New South Wales
Purchased 1945

Provenance:
The artist; Mrs Roberts (née Jean Boyes)
1931; Miss Helen W. Boyes; purchased
from her estate January 1945

Literature:
McCulloch 1969, p.61; Daniel Thomas
1969, pp.469, 477; Spate 1978, p.117;
Smith 1979, pl.37; Topliss 1984, no.5;
Topliss 1985, no.173; Nancy Underhill,
'The profile in nineteenth century
portraiture and Tom Roberts' *Smike
Streeton age 24*: a friendship portrait',
Australian Journal of Art IV, 1985, pp.64ff.

Roberts always kept this portrait: clearly
prized as a memento of his artistic heyday
with Streeton. It was probably painted
when the two were camping at Little
Sirius Cove.

TOM ROBERTS ▲
Lily Stirling, [c.1892]
Oil on canvas
85.5 x 63.5 cm
National Gallery of Victoria
Purchased with assistance of a special
grant from the Government of Victoria
and the Chase Manhattan Bank 1981

Provenance:
Dr Stirling, Melbourne; to the sitter (later
Mrs Fenner); purchased by her cousin and
close friend, Miss Edna Tatchell,
Melbourne; given to her nephew, Rev. Ian
H. St Clair, Melbourne; Christies, Sydney,
September 1970, lot 52, illus.; Jack
Manton, Melbourne

Exhibitions:
Probably *Victorian Artists' Society
Exhibition of Australian Art Past and
Present*, Melbourne, August 1893, no.103:
'A portrait – lent by Dr Stirling'

Literature:
McCaughey 1979, p.42, pl.13; Marion
Fletcher, *Costume in Australia 1788-1901*,
Oxford University Press, Melbourne,
1984, p.188, pl.159

Eight-year-old Lily (Lilian) Stirling was one
of Roberts's most engaging sitters; possibly painted on a visit to Sydney, for
Roberts was there during most of 1892.
Her father was a Collins Street doctor and
a friend of the artist. Here she is fashionably dressed for an outing. (The American
magazine *Harper's Bazaar* had illustrated
a very similar little girl's *ensemble* in
1890.) Her hat is just like mama's – except
for the ribbons tied under her chin. Her
white overcoat is trimmed with fur; and at
the back a large bow, looking rather like a
bustle, gives her an amusingly modish silhouette. She is presented as a diminutive
'Symphony in White' – like Whistler's
famous portraits of the *Little White Girl*,
which Roberts knew well from reproductions.

Tom Roberts is noted for his portraits, and especially for his studies of women. He has an instinct of accuracy which makes good likenesses, and an instinct of art which makes charming likenesses. The distinction may come from a turn of the chin, or the softening of bright eyes and cheeks under a gossamer veil... or a cunning bit of colour in the hat...
– *The Bookfellow,* 29 April 1899

Mrs Eileen Tooker (née Aird) had married in Ireland and emigrated to settle at Rockhampton, Queensland, with John Tooker and his brother. Evidently she was not happy there; and before long she left the property and her husband. She may have sat for Roberts during his trip north to Queensland and the Torres Strait Islands in 1892. Her veil creates an aura of mystery, distancing her from the viewer despite her proximity to the picture plane; it softens both her profile and the contrasts of light and dark in her pale complexion and shadowed eyes. Roberts's experience with photography had taught him to analyze his sitters and position them to their best advantage. Hanging at the Art Gallery of New South Wales, *Eileen* must have made an excellent advertisement of Roberts's skills as a portrait painter. He was frequently praised by contemporary reviewers for the charm and delicacy of his female portraits. (He kept a photograph of this example in his own scrapbook.)

TOM ROBERTS ▲
Eileen, 1892
Oil on canvas
49 x 36 cm
Signed and dated l.l.: Tom Roberts 92
Inscribed u.r.: EILEEN
Art Gallery of New South Wales
Purchased 1892

Provenance:
The artist

Exhibitions:
Art Society of New South Wales Catalogue of Spring Exhibition, Sydney, September 1892, no.54: 'Eileen – £52.10.0'; World's Columbian Exposition, Chicago 1893, exhibited at the New South Wales Government Building, Australia House, and therefore not included in the *Official Catalogue*

Literature:
Sydney Morning Herald, 2 September 1892, p.21; *The Year's Art*, London, 1893, p.206, illus.; *Australasian Art Review*, 1 August 1899, p.23; McCulloch 1969, pp.60, 67, 158; Daniel Thomas 1969, pp.470f.; Hughes 1977, p.61; Spate 1978, p.117; Topliss 1985, no.187, p.21

MADAME CONSTANCE ROTH, née H. ▶
Constance Jones
Apples, 1890
Oil on cedar panel
24.8 x 91 cm
Signed and dated l.l.: H.C. Roth/1890
Art Gallery of New South Wales
Purchased 1890

Provenance:
The artist

Exhibitions:
Art Society of New South Wales Catalogue of Spring Exhibition, Sydney, September 1890, no.189: 'Apples – £12.12.0'; *First Australian Exhibition of Women's Work*, Exhibition Building, Melbourne, October – November 1907, p.201: 'Apples'

Literature:
Illustrated Sydney News, 30 August 1890, p.5; *Australasian Builder & Contractors' News*, 13 September 1890, p.198; *Table Talk*, 19 September 1890, p.7; 10 October 1890, p.6; Galbally 1979, pp.22f., illus.7

Madame Roth had been working, teaching and exhibiting in both Sydney and Melbourne for about five years when her *Apples* was acquired by the Art Gallery of New South Wales. After training in London, she became manager of a decorative firm in Glasgow where 'she found an outlet for that graceful talent of adorning panel, wall and mantel'.[1] In her exotic Sydney studio she conducted a *salon* for artists, actors and musicians (Roberts first met Conder there): 'The walls are in a shade of Indian red, with the doors and woodwork, olive green and painted by the lady herself'.[2] The fashion for elongated panel paintings had originated in England and Europe along with the cult of *japonaiserie*. Streeton produced a very similar panel of *Bananas*, no.148 in this same Art Society exhibition of 1890 (now in the University of Queensland collection); and he adopted the same format for many of his Sydney Harbour views.

[1] *Illustrated Sydney News*, 14 November 1890, p.20.
[2] *Table Talk*, 11 July 1890, p.5.

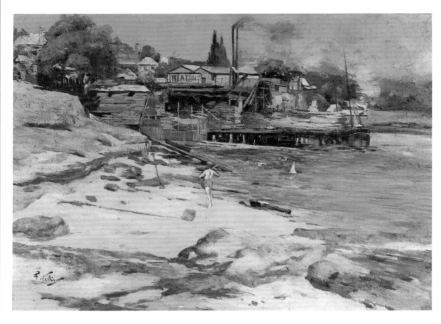

GIROLAMO PIERI BALLATI NERLI ▲
Beach and timber mill – Berry's Bay, Sydney, [1890s]
Oil on canvas
53.5 x 74 cm
Signed l.l.: G.P. Nerli
City of Ballarat Fine Art Gallery
Purchased 1966

Literature:
Sandra McGrath & Robert Walker, *Sydney Harbour Paintings from 1794*, Jacaranda Press, Milton, 1979, pp.32f.

Nerli was in Sydney for about three years from 1886 to 1889; and again in 1890, 1892 and 1899. This is one of his few known paintings of the harbour; interestingly prosaic in choice of subject matter. Berry's Bay and adjoining Lavender Bay were semi-industrial even at this comparatively early date. Weaton's was one of several waterside timber mills in the area, along with boatbuilders and related manufacturers. Here piles of raw timber are stacked on the jetty, ready for loading onto an island schooner. Black smoke belches from tall chimneys and hangs like a pall in the middle distance. The broad brushwork of the rocks in the foreground is closely comparable with Streeton's

painting style in a number of Sydney beach scenes from the mid-1890s.[1] The theme of boys bathing was, of course, a favourite of the Heidelberg painters.

[1] For example, *Sirius Cove*, 1892 (New England Regional Art Museum); *Manly Beach*, 1895 (Bendigo Art Gallery); *Holiday at Coogee*, 1895 (Elders IXL); and others in the present exhibition.

ARTHUR STREETON ▲
Musgrave Street Wharf, 1893
Oil on canvas
38 x 25.5 cm
Signed and dated l.r.: Streeton/93
Dr D.R. Sheumack, Sydney

Provenance:
Samuel Henry Ervin, Sydney (collection sold by John Brackenreg, Artarmon Galleries, September 1958); Dr D.R. Sheumack, Sydney

Literature:
Galbally 1979, no.52, pl.13; Dysart 1982, no. 96; Pearce 1983, no. 22
Reproduced by courtesy of Mrs Oliver Streeton

Old Musgrave Street Wharf was on the eastern side of Curraghbeena Point, opposite Cremorne. The intensity of colour in this painting reflects Streeton's delight in his surroundings. Fully half of the canvas is occupied by water, quietly dancing in the late afternoon light; and delicately balanced by the bushy shoreline, little dinghies and rose-coloured smoke from the ferry in the upper section.

◀ARTHUR STREETON
Sirius Cove, [c.1894]
Oil on cedar panel
68.8 x 16.8 cm
Signed l.l.: A.S.
Australian National Gallery
Purchased 1973

Provenance:
Oliver Streeton; Clune Galleries, Sydney 1973

Literature:
Galbally 1979, no.42, pl.15B; Daniel Thomas 1982, p.220
Reproduced by courtesy of Mrs Oliver Streeton

> The ocean is a big wonder, Bulldog. What a great miracle . . . The slow, immense movement of this expanse moves one very strongly. You're made to clutch the rocks, and be delighted, a dreadful heaving and soft eternity.
> – Streeton to Roberts, Sydney, c.1890

This vertical 'slice' of *Sirius Cove* is one of Streeton's most radical Sydney Harbour views. It is reminiscent of several '9 by 5 impressions', painted by both Streeton and Conder, with *japoniste* vertical format and subdued Whistlerian tonality. Yet this panel is at once more realistic and more abstract. Streeton describes the passing life of Little Sirius Cove – a tiny rowing boat and a distant steamer – just as though glimpsed from his own tent at Curlew Camp; whilst the foreground rocks, confidently brushed in with only few broad strokes, are as subtle as landscape forms in a Chinese scroll painting or Japanese woodblock 'pillar' print. His playfully ambiguous perspective is, again, somewhat oriental in spirit. Although Streeton painted very many views around Sirius Cove in later years, perhaps no other was such a timeless masterpiece of understatement.

ARTHUR STREETON ▲
The Long Wave, Coogee, 1895
Oil on wood panel
9.2 x 54.5 cm
Signed and dated l.l.: A. Streeton – 95
National Gallery of Victoria
Purchased 1959

Provenance:
Carl Pinschoff, Melbourne; to his daughter
Mrs W. Moore Finlay, New South Wales

Literature:
Streeton 1935, no.151 (wrongly dated);
Hoff 1967, p.389; Galbally 1979, no.78,
p.27, pl.8; Splatt & Bruce 1981, p.74, pl.49
Reproduced by courtesy of Mrs Oliver
Streeton

> Coogee is a very jolly place, on warm
> days the place (which is like a nest) is
> filled with smiles and sweet humanity.
> – Streeton to Withers, 1890s

Coogee Bay was one of Streeton's
favourite painting grounds in Sydney. The
eccentric narrow format of this panel
makes for a daring composition: capturing perfectly the long rolling surf as it
breaks on the shoreline, the bluff headlands and gold-coloured sandstone cliffs.
(One of the panels in the 9 by 5 exhibition
of 1889 had also shown 'a blue sea breaking on a long line of sand'.[1] Streeton's
Sydney beach scenes are vigorously
painted; filled with youth and gaiety. This
one was purchased by Herr Carl Pinschoff, Austro-Hungarian Consul in Melbourne, a long-standing patron and friend
of the Heidelberg School artists.

[1] *Herald*, 16 August 1889, p.2.; (and
Whistler had painted similar head-on
breaking waves: *Grey and Silver:The
Angry Sea*, for example, included in his
Dowdeswell Gallery exhibition in 1884).

ARTHUR STREETON ▼
Circular Quay, 1893
Oil on wooden panel
14 x 63.5 cm
Signed and dated l.l: Streeton/93.
Inscribed verso: Sketch Circular Quay
Arthur Streeton
National Gallery of Victoria
Purchased with the assistance of a special
grant from the Government of Victoria
1979

Provenance:
Original owner unknown; W.Oswald Burt,
Melbourne, until 1969; Jack Manton,
Melbourne

Literature:
Galbally 1979, no.57; McCaughey 1979,
p.84, pl.34; Splatt & Bruce 1981, pl.51
Reproduced by courtesy of Mrs Oliver
Streeton

> Yesterday I commenced on a nice little
> bit of Circular Quay. Bright coloured
> stone and greening-blue water – must
> be like Venice – and little steamers
> speeding through the blue tide with
> their bows well up – superb, Prof – oh
> and to be on a boat in the harbour . . .
> wonderful.
> – Streeton to McCubbin, 1890s

One of several views of Circular Quay by
Streeton, the panoramic composition of
this example is reminiscent of harbour
scenes painted by Roberts, McCubbin and
others in the 1880s.[1] Its format, however,is
decidedly decorative: perhaps influenced
by works such as Madame Constance
Roth's *Apples*. Long narrow wooden panels, with an excellent surface for painting,
were readily available from drapers (the
discarded 'cores' from bolts of woollen
cloth); cheapness presumably added to
their popularity in the depression years of
the 90s. *Circular Quay*'s bright colour

scheme is characteristic of Streeton's Sydney period. The novelist Joseph Conrad,
visiting Australia a few years earlier, had
observed that the comings and goings of
ships were a constant and colourful feature in the lives of Sydney residents; and
that Circular Quay was 'no walled prison
of a dock, but the integral part of one of
the finest, most beautiful, vast and safe
bays the sun ever shone upon'.[2]

[1] Streeton's larger canvas of *Circular
Quay*, c.1893 is now in the Australian
National Gallery; and a sketch for the
same work is in a private collection.
Streeton exhibited a 'Sketch from
Circular Quay' at the Victorian Artists'
Society in 1893. See Galbally 1979, nos
51, 53, 58.
[2] Autobiography quoted by Sandra
McGrath & Robert Walker, *Sydney
Harbour Paintings from 1794*, Jacaranda
Press, Milton, 1979, p.46.

ARTHUR STREETON ▲
The Railway Station, 1893
Oil on canvas
40.8 x 61 cm
Signed and dated l.r.: Arthur Streeton/
1893 –
Art Gallery of New South Wales
Presented by Lady Denison 1942

Provenance:
Leonard Dodds, Sydney, 1893-1922 (on loan to the Art Gallery of New South Wales, May 1920-January 1922); Sir Hugh R. Denison (on loan to the Art Gallery of New South Wales, January 1924–May 1926); Lady Denison (his widow), until February 1942

Exhibitions:
Art Society of New South Wales Catalogue of Spring Exhibition, Sydney, September 1893, no.162: 'The Railway Station – Property of Leonard Dodds'; *Streeton's Sydney Sunshine Exhibition*, Melbourne, December 1896, no.11: 'Redfern Station'

Literature:
Sydney Morning Herald, 1 September 1893, p.6; Moore 1934, II, p.27; Streeton 1935, no.110; Olsen 1963, p.163; McCulloch 1969, p.71; Gleeson 1969, pl.23; Inson & Ward, 1971, p.13; Smith 1971, pp. 83f.; Gleeson 1971, pl.63; Hughes 1977, p.63; Galbally 1979, no.50, pl. 18; Splatt & Bruce 1981, p.74; Pearce 1983, no.21
Reproduced by courtesy of Mrs Oliver Streeton

Streeton was clearly impressed by his friend Conder's rainy cityscape, the *Departure of the Orient* of 1888, when he saw it hanging in the Art Gallery of New South Wales. He would also have seen wet street scenes by Nerli exhibited in Sydney. His own *Railway Station* is a wonderfully subtle study of half-light on a wet winter's day. The pavement reflects a saturated sky. Trees, buildings and hurrying figures are united in a grey, drizzle-soaked atmosphere, thickened by puffs of steam. Streeton is here 'the painter of modern life'; interpreting the urban scene in a spirit akin to the famous *Gare Saint-Lazare* series by Claude Monet – although his painting style is altogether different. Trains and railways had become an important theme of modern European literature and Naturalist painting, especially since Turner's great *Rain, Steam, Speed* of

1844. As Emile Zola declared in France: 'Our artists must find the poetry of railway stations as our fathers found the poetry of forests and rivers'.[1]

It is recorded that Streeton worked on *The Railway Station* for only three hours: thus realizing the Heidelberg School's concept of 'impressionism' as capturing 'first records of effects... often of very fleeting character' and 'the *general impression* of colour'.[2] Old Redfern Station was the terminus for Sydney trains until the present Central Station opened in 1906. With a largely floating population – and innumerable boarding houses in the 1890s – it was a rather grim area, as described by the poet Henry Lawson:

> For where the nearest suburb and the
> city proper meet
> My window-sill is level with the faces of
> the street;
> Drifting past, drifting past,
> To the beat of the weary feet –
> While I sorrow for the owners of those
> faces in the street.
> And cause have I to sorrow, in a land
> so young and fair,
> To see upon those faces stamped the
> marks of Want and Care...[3]

Streeton's interest in the subject was, however, more painterly than narrative. His subdued colour scheme, his 'oriental' exploitation of empty space punctuated here and there by brighter touches and the dark notes of figures, are extraordinarily reminiscent of Whistler's wintry *Grey and Gold – Chelsea Snow*. In particular, the isolated black silhouette in the foreground echoes Whistler's painting, which Streeton might well have seen reproduced in the *Goupil Album* of 1892.[4] Whistler himself had chosen this composition to illustrate his aesthetic theory on the irrelevance of narrative subject matter in art:

> My picture of a 'Harmony in Grey and Gold' is an illustration of my meaning... I care nothing for the past, present or future of the black figure, placed there because the black was wanted at that spot. All that I know is that my combination of grey and gold is the basis of the picture... [You should] know that the picture should have its own merit, and not depend upon dramatic, or legendary, or local interest.
>
> As music is the poetry of sound, so is painting the poetry of sight, and the subject matter has nothing to do with harmony of sound or of colour.[5]

The Railway Station is Streeton's outstanding essay in Whistlerian 'arrangement' and tonal impressionism. Interestingly, when the painting was exhibited, *The Sydney Morning Herald* considered it 'clever' but 'rather mannered in style'. And William Moore wrote later of the change in taste since 1893: 'When Mr Leonard Dodds gave £12 for Streeton's impression of the old Redfern railway station he was paying a fair price at the time.... Impressionism was new then, and Mr Dodds' friends told him frankly he was "balmy" to pay such a price. But time works its changes'.[6]

[1] April 1877. Monet exhibited several views of the *Gare Saint – Lazare* in the third Impressionists Exhibition, Paris, 1877. See Daniel Wildenstein, *Claude Monet, Biographie et catalogue raisonné*, La Bibliothèque des Arts, Lausanne and Paris, 1974, nos 438-40. Zola's own 'railways novel', *La Bête humaine*, was published in 1890. Streeton probably knew J.M.W. Turner's *Rain, Steam, Speed*, in the London National Gallery, from reproductions. Quite a number of the 9 by 5 impressions were of train and tramway subjects.
[2] *9 by 5 Impression Exhibition*, 'To the Public'.
[3] Henry Lawson, 'Faces in the Street', *The Bulletin*, 28 July 1888, p.17; quoted in part by Davison 1978, p.193.

[4] *Nocturne: Grey and Gold – Chelsea Snow*, 1876 (Fogg Art Museum, Harvard University, Cambridge, Mass.), was re-exhibited in both Paris and London in 1892, reviewed extensively and reproduced that year in the *Goupil Album*, pl.16. See McLaren Young et al. 1980, no.174.
[5] Whistler, 'The Red Rag', *The World*, 22 May 1878. Conder had painted a small wintry street scene entitled *The Gray and Gold* in 1888 for the Sydney artist D.H. Souter; and a number of the 9 by 5 impressions had Whistlerian titles.
[6] Moore 1934, II, p.27 (Dodds eventually sold it for 360 guineas).

JULIAN ASHTON ▲
A Sydney Wharf, 1895
(also known as 'A hot wind, Sydney Harbour')
Oil on wood panel
13 x 34.2 cm
Signed and dated l.r.: J.R. ASHTON/'95
Inscribed verso, in ink: 'A Sydney Wharf'
National Gallery of Victoria
Purchased 1948

Literature:
Dysart 1981, no.45
Reproduced by permission Julian Ashton Art School

Ashton's *plein air* painting style changed dramatically under the influence of Sydney sunshine and, undoubtedly, of Streeton's elongated harbour views. Here one of the small jetties around Mosman Bay is set against a purple headland and sparkling, aquamarine sea. The paint is briskly applied, with neat square brushstrokes; and so thinly in places that the unprimed wood panel shows through. As a very popular teacher and founder member of the Society of Artists, Ashton was one of Sydney's leading artistic personalities. This may well have been one of the 'panels of local scenery' which he exhibited for sale in June 1895.[1]

[1] An exhibition of 'plein air studies' organized as a commercial venture by 'half a dozen of the most progressive artists', to be sold by J.R. Lawson, auctioneer; reported in *The Sydney Morning Herald* and *Daily Telegraph*, 27 June 1895.

TOM ROBERTS ▶
Mosman's Bay, 1894
Oil on canvas
63.5 x 106.2 cm
Signed and dated l.l.: Tom Roberts 94
New England Regional Art Museum, Armidale, New South Wales
Presented by Howard Hinton 1933

Provenance:
Original owner unknown; Howard Hinton, Sydney; presented to the Armidale Teachers' College in January 1933

Literature:
A Memorial Volume to Howard Hinton, Patron of Art, Sydney 1951, no.22, illus.; Spate 1978, p.70; Sandra McGrath & Robert Walker, *Sydney Harbour Paintings from 1794*, Jacaranda Press, Milton, 1979, p.41; *Focus on the Hinton Collection*, Armidale, 1980, p.29; Splatt & Bruce 1981, p.77; Pearce 1983, p.41, pl.23; Topliss 1985, no.222

...Mosman, which has lately come to the front as a beauty spot, also a fashionable suburb. It undoubtedly has a charm of its own. Near enough to the city to have a twopenny fare, it has an air of remoteness as if its tiny, secluded bay were leagues from the madding crowd... Consequently Mosman is much patronized by youthful enthusiasts, who gaze at the scene with thrown-back head, through half-closed eyes, and interrupt your most interesting remarks with an abrupt, 'There. That's a lovely bit. Look at those purple shadows'. The shadows look quite black to you, but you don't like to say so, fearing to be taken for an utter Philistine. And at every exhibition, 'The Harbour from Mosman's'. 'View from Mosman', 'Mosman's Bay by Moonlight'... decorate the walls by the square yard.
– Florence Blair, 'In Sydney Studios', *The Argus*, 28 May 1898

Nature here has dealt most kindly,
In a smiling dreamy way
And hath shower'd adornments richly,
All around fair Mosman's Bay.

Here, the silv'ry waters dancing,
O'er the golden pebbled shore;
And sea-gulls, with pride are skimming
Keeping time with crests that soar –

Here the native creepers clinging,
Seek the sun's resplendent rays,
And, the foliage 'round is sparkling,
With translucent dazzling sprays.

Mosman's Bay – thy many sisters,
Near by thee, are wondrous rare,
Do their old rocks echo whispers?
Yes! the winds reflected dare

Tell, through Neptune's Nymphs, the story,
Of the Bays, fair to behold;
Grouped away, in Southern glory,
Nestling, in their harbour's fold . . .

Rest ye bays, in loving beauty,
Let your waters, calmly sweep,
O'er the rocks, whose lasting duty,
Is eternal trust to keep.

Thou great part of Nature's fulness;
When we gaze, on thy pure face,
Comes the thought, of God's great goodness;
Fashioned to express His grace.
– Joan Torrance, *Mosman's Bay, Sydney Harbour*, 1890s

Mosman's Bay, a beautiful retired cove on the northern shore of Sydney Harbour, was first settled in 1831 by Archibald Mosman and his whaling establishment. (One of his storehouses was used as a roller skating rink in the 1880s and still stands today.) Within ten years, however, Mosman had sold out; the estate was soon advertised as 'extremely valuable and eligible suburban property' (1843-44). Two large residences from that period can be seen in the background of Roberts's painting. By the mid – 1890s vessels of Sydney Ferries Ltd plied regularly between Circular Quay and Mosman's Bay. In 1894 Roberts himself was still living at the Mosman camp. The artists there were 'a numerous band . . . they are very earnest and enthusiastic and don't put on any swaggering airs, but are sociable and form a little kingdom of their own, a Bohemia of the true sort, which includes much meeting in studios . . . many harbour excursions, meals at cafes, Tivoli parties, and much real hard work'.[1] This is a view from Saunders Boat House, Roberts's first postal address in Sydney, where daytrippers could hire dinghies for their harbour excursions. Roberts painted fewer landscapes in Sydney than he had in Melbourne. His colour scheme in *Mosman's Bay* is more decorative than realistic: owing something, perhaps, to Streeton's harbour paintings which were consistently more decorative in intent than Roberts's. The young couple in the foreground – he in a straw boater, she with scarlet parasol – and the gaily dressed spectators on the quay seem to hark back to Conder's pretty figures-in-landscape of the 1880s.

[1] Florence Blair, 'In Sydney Studios', *The Argus*, 28 May 1898, p.4.

ARTHUR STREETON ▲
Cremorne Pastoral, 1895
Oil on canvas
91.5 x 137.2 cm
Signed and dated l.l.: Arthur Streeton/
Sydney. 1895.
Art Gallery of New South Wales
Purchased 1895

Provenance:
The artist

Exhibitions:
Society of Artists First Exhibition, Sydney,
September 1895, no.24: 'Cremorne Pasto-
ral – £157.0.0'; *Streeton's Sydney Sunshine
Exhibition*, Melbourne, December 1896,
no.39: 'Cremorne Pastoral – lent by the
Trustees, Sydney Art Gallery'

Literature:
Daily Telegraph, 27 September 1895, p.6;
Sydney Morning Herald, 27 September
1895, p.2; R.F.I., 'Impressionism in Art',
The Australian Magazine, 17 August
1899, p.347; *New South Wales Art Gallery
Pictures*, Art in Australia, Sydney, 1931,
p.18; Moore 1934, I, p.96; Streeton 1935,
no.148; Galbally 1979, no.67, p.122;
Pearce 1983, no.25
Reproduced by courtesy of Mrs Oliver
Streeton

Mr Streeton's chief landscape is a view
from Cremorne, the foreground of
sunburnt grass and tangled foliage
occupying the greater portion of the
canvas, and the shores of Rose Bay,
with the varied buildings of the city
seen in the distance. It is a sunny picture, though not as brilliant as some
that Mr Streeton had flashed upon us in
years past. What is more important,
however, is that it is a picture combin-
ing tenderness and strength and
breadth of treatment in the most con-
spicious degree.
– *The Daily Telegraph*, 27 September
1895

One of the most beautiful areas within
easy reach of the Mosman camp was Cremorne – named after the famous Cremorne Gardens in London by the
promoters of a commercial pleasure garden there during the 1850s. In 1893, when
a significant coal discovery was announced there, public opposition to its exploitation was vociferous and the venture was
abandoned; Cremorne Point was left to its
virgin magnificence, overlooking the
sparkling sea. Streeton's *Cremorne Pastoral* of 1895, a celebration of this natural
beauty, was described by *The Daily Telegraph* as 'perhaps the best landscape ever

painted in New South Wales'. At the close
of the inaugural Society of Artists exhibition that year, Roberts claimed that the
keynote of the paintings on show was
sunny optimism. He said the old 'note of
melancholy, which was supposed to be
characteristic of the Australian bush',
dwelt upon by earlier colonial writers
Marcus Clark and Adam Lindsay Gordon,
was no longer to be seen in contemporary
art.[1] Streeton revelled in Sydney's
warmth and bright sunlight. As Howard
Ashton admiringly wrote, 'from his work
around Heidelberg, [he] came up to the
harbour and blossomed forth in gold and
blue'.[2] To the end of his life Streeton used a
palette on which he had painted the
device of a shining sun; and he even
marked his linen with the same emblem.

[1] *Sydney Morning Herald*, 21 October
1895, p.3.
[2] Howard Ashton, 'The Lure of Sydney',
Art in Australia 1, 1916.

HOWARD ASHTON ▲
Through Sunny Meadows, [1898]
Oil on canvas
71.1 x 142.3 cm
Signed l.l.: Howard Ashton
Art Gallery of New South Wales
Purchased 1898

Provenance:
The artist

Exhibitions:
Society of Artists Spring Exhibition, Sydney, September 1898, no.57: 'Through Sunny Meadows – £52.10.0', illus. in original frame inscribed with title

Literature:
Daily Telegraph, 27 August 1898, illus.; *Sydney Morning Herald* 27 August 1898, p.7; R.F.I., 'Impressionism in Art', *The Australian Magazine*, 17 August 1899, p.347, illus.; Pearce 1983, no.31
Reproduced by permission Julian Ashton Art School

Mr F. Howard Ashton's 'Through Sunny Meadows', thoroughly Australian in its character, has value for the effect of brilliant sunlight suffused throughout, and there is feeling for colour in the harmonious gradations of tone from sky to water and to purple hill in the background. All this, and the clump of trees in the middle distance, is very good . . . The general style may be described as strongly 'Streetonesque'.
– *The Sydney Morning Herald*, 27 August 1898

'Sydney is a poem itself', wrote Howard Ashton, who had grown up there and trained as a painter at his father's Academy Julien. He loved the 'graceful distances, and . . . cobalt blue stretches of harbour water'.[1] *Through Sunny Meadows* was probably painted in the Cremorne area: *The Daily Telegraph* described it as a 'landscape of the Cremorne type' and certainly it is indebted to Streeton's *Cremorne Pastoral*, purchased three years before by the Art Gallery of New South Wales. Ashton readily acknowledged the impact of Streeton's work on the younger Sydney artists – including himself.

[1] Howard Ashton, 'The Lure of Sydney', *Art in Australia* 1, 1916.

TOM ROBERTS ▲
Landscape, Cremorne, 1894
Oil on canvas mounted on wood panel
18.5 x 42.3 cm
Signed and dated l.l.: Tom Roberts/94.
National Gallery of Victoria
Purchased 1946

Literature:
Topliss 1985, no.221

With its narrow horizontal format and thick fluid pigments this briskly worked painting shows the influence of Streeton's Sydney Harbour views. Roberts also 'blossomed forth in gold and and blue' when he painted at Cremorne. Later he used the same setting, peopled with dancing figures, for an etching entitled *Ring O'Roses*.[1]

[1] An oil version of uncertain date is in the Australian National Gallery. Topliss 1985, nos 690 and 766.

ARTHUR STREETON ▲
Portrait of a young girl, [c.1894]
Oil on panel
40.7 x 25.5 cm
Private collection, Adelaide

Provenance:
Original owner unknown; John Young of
Macquarie Galleries, Sydney; his widow
Mrs E.C. Young; Thirty Victoria Street,
Sydney; private collection, Adelaide

Literature:
Galbally 1979, no.59
Reproduced by courtesy of Mrs Oliver
Streeton

During the 1890s, in both Sydney and
Melbourne, Streeton found himself painting a number of portraits to help make
ends meet; (he even portrayed a pair of
large red setters on one occasion). 'And I
enjoy figure painting so much now', he
wrote to Roberts, 'and am improving a bit,
I think'.[1]

[1] 1 April 1892. Croll 1935, p.190.

ARTHUR STREETON ▲
Hawkesbury River, 1896
Also known as 'Grey Day on the
Hawkesbury'[1]
Oil on canvas
61 x 81.5 cm
Signed and dated l.r.: A. Streeton. 96 –
National Gallery of Victoria
Purchased with the assistance of a special
grant from the Government of Victoria
1979

Provenance:
Dr J.W. Springthorpe, 1896; until *The
Springthorpe Collection of Australian
Pictures*, Leonard Joel, Melbourne, 24
May 1934, lot 55; Charles Ruwolt, 1934;
until *The Charles Ruwolt Collection of
Australian Paintings*, Leonard Joel,
Melbourne, November 1966, lot 17; Jack
Manton, Melbourne

Exhibitions:
Streeton's Sydney Sunshine Exhibition,
Melbourne, December 1896, probably
no.14: 'Hawkesbury River' [£50];
*Catalogue of the Diamond Jubilee Loan
Exhibition in the National Gallery of
Victoria in commemoration of the 60th
Year of the Reign of her Majesty Queen
Victoria*, Melbourne, June 1897, no.112:
'A Grey Day on the River – Lent by Dr J.W.
Springthorpe'

Literature:
Table Talk, 11 December 1896, p.1; Moore
1934, I, p.96; Streeton 1935, no.169; Croll
1946, p.62; Gleeson, 1971, pl.65;
Finemore 1977, p.20; Galbally 1979,
no.82, p.34, pl.25; McCaughey 1979, p.88,

pl.36; Splatt & Bruce 1981, pl.54
Reproduced by courtesy of Mrs Oliver
Streeton

Although painted about the same time as
The purple noon's transparent might this
view reveals the Hawkesbury landscape
in a different mood. The brushwork is
quieter; the colours softer and more
voluptuous. In his Hawkesbury River
series of 1896 Streeton's fascination with
the changing face of nature shares something of Monet's attitude towards differing
effects of light on grain-stacks, waterlilies,
the façade of Rouen Cathedral and so on,
during the 1890s. Streeton studied the
river in early morning light, under the
blazing sun; and, here, in the shimmering
haze of a cloudy summer day. As he had
explained, along with Roberts and Conder, in 1889: 'An effect is only momentary,
so an impressionist tries to find his place.
Two half hours are never alike . . .'

[1] The painting has been known as 'Grey
Day on the Hawkesbury' since the *Loan
Exhibition of the Works of Arthur
Streeton*, Art Gallery of New South Wales,
1931-32; however Streeton himself called
it 'Hawkesbury River' in 1935.

economy. During the 1890s, as Roberts became Sydney's most sought-after society painter, his portraits of friends and acquaintances were most often intimate, rapidly worked studies such as this one. Not long before Roberts left Sydney in 1901, Miss McDonald visited his studio once again to tell him she was to be married. He asked her to select one of his paintings as a wedding present: and she chose a watercolour landscape – which remained in her elder daughter's possession until 1978 when it was left to Roberts's Tasmanian widow.

[1] See John H. Pearn, *A Worthy Tradition – The Biography of Sydney Fancourt McDonald*, University of Queensland, 1985; Julie K. Brown and Margaret Maynard, *Fine Art Exhibitions in Brisbane 1884-1916,* University of Queensland, 1980. Further information kindly supplied by Dr Pearn; the sitter's daughter, Mrs Celia Taylor, and niece, Mrs Helen Vellacott.
[2] Isobel's mother, Amelia, was a younger sister of Mrs Herbert Daly, née Kitty Mitchell. When in Melbourne, Isobel usually stayed with the Edward Mitchells.

TOM ROBERTS ▲
Profile portrait of a young girl in a straw hat, 1895
Oil on canvas
46.5 x 41.8 cm
Signed and dated l.l.: Tom Roberts/Dec 5/95
National Gallery of Victoria
Purchased 1957

Provenance:
Original owner unknown; sold by James R. Lawson, Sydney c.1928; Mr John Young of Macquarie Galleries, Sydney 1950s; Mrs B.E. Mendell (from her father), Sydney, until August 1957

Exhibitions:
Possibly *Society of Artists of New South Wales Autumn Exhibition*, Sydney, March 1896, no.38: 'Head Study – £12.12.0'

Literature:
McCulloch 1969,pl.38B; Topliss 1985, no.243

The subject of this portrait has recently been identified as Miss Isobel Agnes McDonald (1871-1926). Born in Victoria, she moved with her family to Queensland in early childhood; but was educated in Melbourne. Her uncle by marriage, Herbert Daly, was one of the almost-forgotten contributors to the 9 by 5 Impression Exhibition with Roberts, Streeton and Conder in 1889.[1] Isobel McDonald attended the Gallery School in 1888-89 and in 1895, becoming a favourite pupil of McCubbin. She is also said to have taken painting lessons from Roberts; and certainly joined some of the weekend artistic expeditions to Heidelberg. Although she returned to Queensland in 1894, she seems to have visited Melbourne and Sydney quite regularly. Roberts painted this sketch portrait on 5 December 1895, when his studio address was Commercial Chambers, Bathurst Street, Sydney. He used a favourite combination of pinks and greens (as in his *Smike Streeton* of 1891): very thinly painted, the facial features and details of dress described with utmost

ARTHUR STREETON ▲
'Oblivion' (suggested by Tennyson's Lotus-Eaters), [c.1892-95]
Oil on canvas
56.2 x 100.5 cm
Signed and dated l.l.: Arthur Streeton
Private collection

Provenance:
The artist, who took it to England in 1898; Mr Jules Fuerst, until after 1935; Norman G. Clark c.1937; his son, Norman K. Clark, until 1985; private collection

Exhibitions:
Society of Artists First Exhibition, Sydney, September 1895, no.26: '"Oblivion" (suggested by Tennyson's Lotus-Eaters [*sic*]) – £157.10.0', illus.; *Streeton's Sydney Sunshine Exhibition*, Melbourne, December 1896, no.1: 'Oblivion' – offered as the major prize in 'Streeton's Art Union of Pictures to be drawn in December' (later announced as 'drawn in February'; no record traced of outcome)

Literature:
Daily Telegraph, 27 September 1895, p.2; *Sydney Morning Herald*, 27 September 1895, p.2; *Table Talk*, 4 December 1896, p.7; *Australasian Art Review*, 1 August 1899 p.23; Streeton 1935, no.120; Galbally 1979, no.72
Reproduced by courtesy of Mrs Oliver Streeton

THE LOTOS-EATERS
'COURAGE!' he said, and pointed toward the land,
'This mounting wave will roll us shoreward soon'.
In the afternoon they came unto a land
In which it seemed always afternoon.
All round the coast the languid air did swoon . . .

THERE is sweet music here that softer falls
Than petals from blown roses on the grass,
Or night-dews on still waters between walls
Of shadowy granite, in a gleaming pass;
Music that gentlier on the spirit lies,
Than tir'd eyelids upon tir'd eyes;
Music that brings sweet sleep down from the blissful skies.

How sweet it were, hearing the downward stream,
With half-shut eyes ever to seem
Falling asleep in a half-dream! . . .
To hear each other's whispered speech;
Eating the Lotos day by day,
To watch the crisping ripples on the beach,
And tender curving lines of creamy spray;
To lend our hearts and spirits wholly
To the influence of mild-minded melancholy;
To muse and brood and live again in memory,
With those old faces of our infancy . . .
– Alfred, Lord Tennyson (1809-92)

. . . in point of fact, a girl lying in the sunshine on a marble slab, with loose draperies but half concealing her charms, whilst the blue sea breaks on the shore beyond . . . The drapery and the barely suggested landscape are done to perfection, and the gradual transition from the snow-white robes to the delicate flesh tints of the bust, and the crimson tenderly suffusing the cheeks, and finally concentrating itself in the lips, is one of the most poetic schemes of color that we have seen for a very long time.
– *The Daily Telegraph*, 27 September 1895

Towards the end of his career, Streeton wrote to a previous owner of *Oblivion*: 'I was living with the late Tom Roberts in our tents at Sirius Cove at [the] time your picture was painted. We posed a model in our Studio for the students of our class to study from: & I did my picture while they made their studies'.[1] During the mid-1890s in Sydney he painted a number of ambitious allegorical subjects, often loosely inspired by poetry. In 1893, for example, he exhibited *'Twilight (allegorical)'* and *'Cupid'*, which was catalogued with a long quotation from William Blake. At the Society of Artists in 1895, together with *Oblivion*, he showed *'Herrick's Blossoms'*: another particularly exotic reclining female figure.[2] One enthusiastic reviewer called *Oblivion* 'the very marvel of soul and skill; . . . perhaps the most

charmingly subtle effect to which Mr Streeton's genius has yet given expression'.[3]

[1] 23 November 1937. 'I think that after taking it to England in 1898 I cut it down to its present size, & sold it to a Mr Jules Fuerst' (18 November 1937). Mr Norman K. Clark kindly showed me these letters addressed to his father.
[2] Although several of these paintings are described by contemporary reviewers, most are at present unlocated. One panel entitled *Pastoral* is now in the Art Gallery of New South Wales (Art Society 1894, no.372). In 1935 Streeton wrote that he had painted *Oblivion* in 1892; however, as he spent a large part of that year in Melbourne, rather than sharing a Sydney studio with Roberts, he may well have been mistaken in this recollection: a dating of 1894-95 is more probable. Arthur Loureiro and Charles Douglas Richardson were probably the first local artists to exhibit poetical/allegorical maidens – in the late 1880s in Melbourne.
[3] *Daily Telegraph*, 27 September 1895, p.6.

TOM ROBERTS ▲
Adagio, [1899]
Oil on academy board
25.6 x 51 cm
Art Gallery of New South Wales
Purchased 1947

Provenance:
Original owner unknown; James R. Lawson, Sydney, April 1947; Mrs Clarice Thomas until November 1947

Exhibitions:
The Society of Artists Spring Exhibition, Sydney, August 1899, no.69: 'Adagio – £21.0.0' (the original label is still on the back of the panel); *Exhibition and Sale of Paintings Previous to Leaving Australia*, Society of Artists, Sydney, November 1900, no.5: 'Girl with Violin – 5 guineas'

Literature:
Spate 1964, pp.260, 262; Daniel Thomas 1969, p.478; Spate 1978, pp.73, 97, 99ff., 103, 117, pl.28; Topliss 1985, no.212

To allude, to suggest – therein lies the dream.
– Stéphane Mallarmé (1842-98)

At the Society of Artists exhibition of 1899, wrote the Sydney critic James Green, Tom Roberts surpassed himself 'in the realms of Imagination, of which . . . he had but previously crossed the threshold'.[1] Green was referring to *A Circe* (now known only from photographs), *Study for Jepthah's Daughter* (purchased by the Art Gallery of New South Wales) and *Adagio*. On one level these 'imaginative' paintings represented an extension of Roberts's increasing preoccupation in the 1890s with female portraiture.[2] Musical titles were by no means a new idea. (*Adagio*

translates literally as 'slowly'.)[3] With *Adagio*, however, he came closer than at any other time to elements of the Symbolist aesthetic then current in European painting: evoking feelings and ideas inexpressible by any art which limits itself to visual reality.[4] The painting is not a descriptive statement but, rather, a starting point for speculation. As the Australian Symbolist poet, Christopher Brennan, wrote:

The I of my verses is not necessarily ME
A poem is the expression of a mood
A mood need not be a confession of faith
. . . nor yet a record of real events
All the sincerity required in art is that you should have thoroughly felt your mood.[5]

The landscape setting of *Adagio* is indeterminate, glowing with unnatural crimson and sulphur lights. The mysterious violinist in profile is placed close to the picture surface, yet remains psychologically distant; her thoughts are private and indefinable.[6] Like the European Symbolists, Roberts was intrigued by relationships between musical and pictorial expression. And he had many highly articulate musical friends. Professor Marshall Hall, for example, may well have introduced him to the work of Wagner – musical hero of the Symbolists (and much admired by Brennan). *Adagio* expresses on a modest scale Wagner's theory of the 'total work of art': in which sight, sound and emotion are equally balanced and indivisibly fused. In fact Roberts's response to the decorative and Symbolist tendencies influencing Australian art was comparatively belated. Melbourne artists, such as Loureiro,

Richardson and Conder, had produced imaginative allegories in the late 1880s. Streeton, too, turned increasingly to poetry and romantic unreality for inspiration. Sydney Long's *Pan* – a fantasy of dancing nymphs and fauns – was acquired by the Art Gallery of New South Wales in 1898. Perhaps Roberts's artistic ambitions were too various for single-minded concentration in any one area: in 1898 he painted the outback *Mountain Muster* and in 1901 he began work on his vast documentary *Opening of the First Federal Parliament*. In April 1899, the year in which he exhibited *Adagio*, an interviewer in Sydney explained: 'And Tom Roberts teaches and paints portraits, and paints portraits and teaches...; and hopes for a chance to get on canvas some and other characteristic scenes and incidents of Australia... "Do I still attempt the ideal? Yes, I could show you some pictures, suggestions, sketches..." And Tom Roberts is off with the gleam of the Ideal in his eye'.[7]

[1] *Australasian Art Review*, September 1899, p.8.
[2] Helen Topliss has recently suggested that *Adagio* was painted some years earlier than 1899: making comparisons with his portrait of *Lena Brasch*, c.1893 and '*Plink-a-Plong*', 1893, a girl playing a banjo. In fact his 'exotic' female subjects span the 1890s: for example, *A Modern Andromeda* and *Odalisque* in 1896, *A Circe* and *Jepthah's Daughter*, 1899, *Rose of Persia*, 1900. It would seem that exact dating remains inconclusive.
[3] Roberts had given musical titles to paintings many years before: for example, in the 9 by 5 Impression Exhibition of 1889. Miss Jessie L. Evans had produced a painting called *Adagio* at the Melbourne Gallery School in 1890: no.15 – exhibited with the poetic subtitle 'Soft and slow, Ever a gentle underflow'. Howard Ashton included an *Adagio* in the Grafton Galleries exhibition of 1898 (present whereabouts unknown).
[4] Virginia Spate 1978 discusses the Symbolist context of *Adagio*: especially pp.101,142, notes 63 and 64. See also Philippe Jullian, *Dreamers of Decadence, Symbolist painters of the 1890s*, Pall Mall, London, 1971 and Edward Lucie-smith, *Symbolist Art*, Thames and Hudson, London 1972.
[5] c.August 1896; quoted by Axel Clarke, *Christopher Brennan: A Critical Biography*, Melbourne University Press, Melbourne, 1980, p.88. Brennan returned to Sydney from Berlin in 1894; he was probably introduced to the artists at Curlew Camp by the linguist F.S. Delmer who lived there for some time and was a close friend of Roberts and Streeton; he

almost certainly met Marshall Hall there in summer 1898-99 and later wrote that he admired the art of the Heidelberg painters.
[6] Comparable paintings of mysterious female subjects, close-up, were painted by a number of European Symbolists in the 1890s. Roberts certainly would have seen reproductions in journals such as *The Studio*. In addition, he still corresponded with friends from his years at the Royal Academy, such as Grieffenhagen and Anning Bell (the latter sent photos of his recent paintings), whose work was increasingly abstract and decorative.
[7] *The Bookfellow*, 29 April 1899, p.33.

ALFRED JAMES DAPLYN ▶
The Australian Artist's Dream of Europe,
[1898]
Oil on canvas
77.5 x 55.6 cm
Signed l.r.: A.J. Daplyn
Frank McDonald, Thirty Victoria Street, Sydney

Exhibitions:
Art Society of New South Wales Illustrated Catalogue of the Nineteenth Annual Exhibition, Sydney, September 1898, no.46: 'The Australian Artist's Dream of Europe – £63.0.0', illus.; *South Australian Society of Arts Federal Exhibition*, Adelaide, November 1898, no.11A: 'The Australian Artist's Dream of Europe – £52.10.0'

Literature:
Daily Telegraph, 8 September 1898, p.3; *Sydney Morning Herald*, 10 September 1898, p.4

> For all time we must look to Europe as the world's art centre – the great university whereto all artists gravitate, and where for many years yet they must graduate before receiving the world's hallmark of approbation.
> – D.H. Souter, Sydney[1]

Australian artists had always dreamed of making their name (and fortune) in Europe. 'They mastered the grammar of their art in the Melbourne schools, came to Paris to learn, and finally to London to sell', said the English *Magazine of Art* in 1895.[2] Of course some of the travellers eventually returned to Australia. During the depressed 1890s, however, as antipodean artists found it more and more difficult to earn a living, the wider opportunities offered by London and Paris must have seemed increasingly attractive.

'I love Australia... and shall be beastly sorry to go away', wrote Streeton. 'I don't grumble a bit but it's unfortunate. This country is full of wealth, but somehow can't afford artists yet. Why, dammit, bricklayers, scene shifters, office boys, all get their work recognized and are able to go on – and if I were recognized more I could PAINT MORE. Perhaps I'd have the same trouble in Europe, but I must risk it...'[3] Streeton had never studied overseas, unlike Daplyn; or indeed Roberts, to whom he said, 'I think if I were away in Europe, Florence, or somewhere, I would work much harder... I've been reading Reynolds' lectures, and really it makes me quite ambitious to get on in a way'.[4] In 1897 the patriotic celebrations in honour of Queen Victoria's Diamond Jubilee highlighted Australia's great distance from the centre of Empire. Streeton left for Europe later that year, writing to Roberts from London: 'I feel convinced that my work hereafter will contain a larger idea and quality than before, after seeing Constable, Turner, Titian, Watts, and all the masters. I wish you and the Prof. could have a trip here; I think it's necessary for one's work'.[5] Daplyn had worked in England, France, Italy and America before emigrating to Australia. As first 'art instructor' at the Art Society of New South Wales, and Honorary Secretary from 1898, he knew only too well the problems faced by local painters. *The Australian Artist's Dream of Europe* was doubtless more than somewhat autobiographical; indeed the slumbering figure appears to be a self-portrait. Earlier in 1898 he had sent work to London for inclusion in the Grafton Galleries exhibition of Australian art. R.A.M. Stevenson, who knew Daplyn from their student days together in Paris many years before, praised his paintings as 'quiet, unaffected, and without any swagger of brushwork' (*The Pall Mall Gazette*, 4 April 1898). According to *The Times*, the exhibition as a whole showed that Australian art was much influenced by those 'English and Australian teachers who had first learned what the Paris ateliers had to teach them... Mr Daplyn and some other teachers are instances of this'.[6] In this rather extraordinary picture, of that same year, the artist is visited in his studio by a bevy of figures from famous masterpieces of Titian, Raphael, Michelangelo and their peers. 'Mr Daplyn has succeeded completely in the imaginative portion of his theme', said *The Sydney Morning Herald*, 'the romantic suggestion of "unsubstantial pageant" in the airy places and Madonnas of the vision'. *The Australian Artist's Dream of Europe* was intended not only as a vision of expatriate experience, but

ARTHUR STREETON
Standing female figure, 1895
Oil on cedar panel
58.1 x 39 cm
Signed and dated l.r.: A. STREETON/1895
The Joseph Brown Collection, Melbourne
For exhibition in Melbourne only

Provenance:
Original owner unknown; Gordon
Galleries, 1970; Christie's, Sydney,
October 1971, lot 327; Joseph Brown,
Melbourne

Literature:
Daniel Thomas 1980, no.47
Reproduced by courtesy of Mrs Oliver
Streeton

According to a previous owner, Streeton
painted this decorative panel for a
wardrobe belonging to Dame Nellie
Melba. It may represent the predatory
goddess Circe, archetypal *femme fatale*,
who ensnared innocent lovers with her
beauty and then magically transformed
them into swine. Mackennal's standing
bronze statue of *Circe* had been acclaimed
at the Royal Academy in 1894. Roberts
exhibited an allegorical painting entitled
A Circe, in 1899.

also as a concrete demonstration of
Daplyn's own cosmopolitan credentials as
a professional painter and teacher in Sydney.

[1] *Art and Architecture* V, 1908, p.6; on the
occasion of his friend Fred Leist's
departure for Europe.
[2] Jope-Slade 1895, p.389.
[3] Croll 1946, p.64.
[4] Croll 1935, p.193.
[5] Croll 1946, p.67.
[6] *The Times*, 4 April 1898, p.15; both
articles were quoted in *The Argus*, 11
May 1898, p.7 and reprinted in full by
Smith 1975, pp.211ff.

The Victorian Artists' Society, East Melbourne
The new building, designed by Mr. R. Speight, jun. in the Queen Anne style, has been successfully completed . . . The interior is spacious and most commodiously planned. A large hall on the ground floor, in which the statuary has been arranged, opens on to a library, a club room, the secretary's room and cloak rooms. In the centre of this room is a wide, bluestone staircase, from which two smaller flights branch off to the right and left, leading to the picture galleries, north and south, in which the lighting arrangements have been admirably provided for . . . A magnificent collection of ferns and pot plants has been artistically disposed about the hall and staircase.

The Age, 27 May 1892
Photographs: LaTrobe Collection, State Library of Victoria

MELBOURNE'S ANSWER IN THE 90s – 'CHARTERISVILLE'

Bridget Whitelaw

This is Melbourne, Marvellous Melbourne; what an empty boast of pride,
While its poverty is swelling like a mighty ocean tide
– G.H. Willoughby, *Marvellous Melbourne and Other Poems*, 1898

It is a pleasure to turn to the works of those who, in all the fret and fume of the last eight years, have tried to look into the deep quiet face of Nature; lingering where the winding, almost silent river bathes the feathery wattle branches; sometime on a hillside watching the sun setting while the far-off hills go distant and more distant in the grey dusk until the moon rises in the quiet east; finding beauty in odd corners of some country shanty, or by some lagoon which palely reflects the banks all bathed in a great shimmer of trembling, brilliant sunlight. . . We can see, too, the development of the men, how the tendency of the painting is certainly towards light and air, and, with an atmosphere familiarly Australian, whether it is the tender grey of the diffused daylight, or the dazzling sunshine; there are one or two deep notes that touch the tragedy of human life, yet the general tone is joyous.
– Tom Roberts, *The Argus*, 30 September 1893

The predominance, in Melbourne in the 90s, of such poetic landscapes as Roberts praised, cannot be attributed solely to the effect of the depression and consequent idealization of rural life. Trends in contemporary European art brought back to Melbourne by artists such as Fox, Tucker, Withers and Longstaff had considerable impact on the circle of artists remaining there in the 1890s, especially in extending the practice of *plein air* painting, already well established in the late 1880s. For those artists staying in or returning to Melbourne, life seemed bleak. Many of their friends had departed: Conder for Europe, Roberts and Streeton to Sydney. Indeed McCubbin wrote to Roberts at Mosman's Bay in 1892: 'Tucker is to arrive in the *Arcadia*, and Withers and family are off as soon as they can get to London; he says Melbourne is played out for the next seven years, and, by gum, it looks like it'.[1]

These artists had a strong desire for international experience and recognition; and, while many of them chose to study in Paris, they still looked to London for professional and social recognition. In fact, Longstaff, Tucker, MacKennal, Streeton and Conder all settled in London. Several of them sent paintings from Australia for exhibition in Paris at the Salon or London at the Royal Academy; and some exhibited with the more radical New English Art Club. Only a small proportion of these expatriates remained permanently overseas, however; the majority returned to Melbourne after interludes abroad –

albeit with the desire for some continuing exposure in Europe. As Fox wrote to McCubbin, 'I am quite certain the only way is to exhibit alongside the best of the work here, and that one man shows and colonial or Australian exhibitions in London are of very little good'.[2]

The difficulty of making ends meet forced most artists to take teaching positions or accept the constraints of portrait commissions: indeed for Longstaff and Fox such work provided much of their income. The need to satisfy the taste of the patron led to an increase in conventional portraiture by the late 90s: '. . . the true artist is one who works for the love of his profession and ignores such considerations as the profitable sale of his pictures. In practice, however, it is found that he is like other men in having a stomach to fill and a back to cover, and that, while he may work with all sincerity and earnestness, he is compelled by necessity to touch the taste of his public'.[3] Yet critics noted that 'Mr Tucker and Mr Fox work by the light of their French ideals and for this reason are more interesting to the artist than the art lover'.[4]

The reluctance of the Melbourne Gallery to purchase works by these Australian artists was a source of further frustration. The more adventurous buying policy of the Gallery in Sydney, advised by Julian Ashton, prompted the comparison:

While the National Gallery of Victoria remains practically stationary and contents itself with present possessions, that of New South Wales shows some marked advance with every year . . . Not only is this so, but it is known to Victorian artists as almost the only influential patron that they have, and is gradually bringing together a collection which will one day be of priceless historical value, as showing the early achievements of that Australian school whose vigorous existence may fairly be anticipated.[5]

When the first of these artists' paintings were acquired for Melbourne in 1894, they included David Davies's *Moonrise* , Frederick McCubbin's *Feeding Time*, Tom Humphrey's *Under a Summer Sun* and Walter Withers's *A Bright Winter's Morning*. At the direction of Bernard Hall, however, *Feeding Time* and *A Bright Winter's Morning* were returned to the artists and exchanged respectively for *A Winter Evening* and *Tranquil Winter*. Such lack of conviction did not pass the notice of a critic in October 1895 who commented on 'the very gradual recognition of power in the Australian artist' and condemned the trustees as 'unguided and composed of a body of members possessing the little knowledge which is as dangerous in art as in science'.[6] Teaching provided local artists with sufficient income to survive the lean years:

> It is well known that for the last two or three years the painting of pictures has been the most precarious of professions, and that in consequence of this Melbourne has lost several of her most talented artists; while others, unable to break up their homes and go elsewhere, have been obliged to devote all their time to teaching, an occupation that in such cases is well termed drudgery . . . Pictures are a luxury everyone can dispense with, if need be, but he who makes them, and who feels himself impelled to do so by a demand that springs from his own higher nature . . .[7]

The euphoria associated with the camp at Eaglemont may have dissipated but, for the circle of artists remaining, 'Charterisville' provided a focus for continuing the more progressive developments of *plein air* painting in Melbourne. Part of the old stone mansion 'Charterisville', built about 1840 by David Charteris McArthur, had been sub-let from 1890 to Walter Withers; and the cottages in the grounds occupied by artists who included Tom Humphrey, Hal Waugh and Leon 'Sonny' Pole. The house, cottages and gardens provided both an exquisite setting and ample accommodation for an artists' colony, which survived in various forms throughout the decade:

> Not far from Eaglemont, but lower down near the Yarra, stood a fine old stone mansion with a large barn and stables. It was in a wild romantic garden, a profusion of lilac, white and purple, and roses of many kinds, spreading out in entangled masses. A dilapidated summer-house, a broken fountain, and an odd pedestal here and there suggested the glory of other days. Below the terrace in front of the house there was a straggling vineyard, tall willows flanking the landing place on the bank of the river.[8]

In 1894 the tenancy was formally taken over by Phillips Fox and Tudor St George Tucker, providing studios and a location for the summer school they were to conduct as an extension of their Melbourne Art School, which they opened in June 1893 in the Cromwell Buildings in Bourke Street. According to the prospectus, it was 'founded for the purpose of providing a thorough art education on similar lines to the best Parisian Schools'.[9] The course included drawing from the cast and painting and drawing from life. This life class attracted many students from the Gallery School and by January 1895 a critic praised Fox and Tucker's success:

To establish a school of art in Melbourne such as these young men had in their minds, meant slow work. They were brought into direct collision with the Victorian National Gallery, which thanks to its solid Government subsidy, is enabled to throw its doors open to pupils for a mere trifle in the way of fees . . . Their exhibition of pupils' work last year, though not important, amply proved the thorough training to which the students were subjected. The exhibition now open makes it evident that the Melbourne School of Art is the only academic school here, with the same facilities for study as are provided in the leading studios in Europe, barring of course, the access to the famous picture galleries of the old world. The masters are fortunate in their pupils, who have entered on their studies with enthusiasm, and better still, with earnestness and determination.[10]

The constant availability of a live model and the stress on colour rather than a rigorous course of drawing prior to entry (as was the case at the Gallery School) contributed to its popularity with students: able 'to paint occasionally while [they were] . . . learning to draw, the Masters believing that the absorbing fascination of colour is in itself an aid to good careful drawing'.[11]

The introduction of *plein air* instruction at 'Charterisville' for students selected from the Melbourne School was an innovative step. The summer school was held there at weekends from 1894, but by 1897 had developed into a two month camp each autumn, 'whose cottages and outbuildings are like so many swallows' nests for the Melbourne artists, which they leave, and to which they return, to take their artistic flight with a more or less assured stroke'. It must have proved an 'idyllic' form of instruction – as Violet Teague, one of the students, recalled:

> The garden which sloped down to the Yarra was as beautiful and neglected as it could be. There was a wonderful variety of subjects. We chose our own, and setting up our easels we started to work. Mr. Fox would come round and looking over a canvas would wriggle a brush in the sky, pull it all together and fuse the warring elements. If the light was good we worked all day and did about four oil sketches which in the evening were put in a room, which we named 'Burlington House', where Mr. Fox judged them. Any one which he particularly favoured was put on the wall of the dining-room, which we called 'The Chantrey Bequest' . . . You would need to live in a community like that to fully appreciate Mr. Fox's kindness and his humility as regards his own work, combined with a burning enthusiasm to get even with nature in her most subtle harmonies and rapid changes. He had a very strong influence on his school and made it pre-eminently a colour school.[12]

This out-door schooling enabled Fox and Tucker to share with students their knowledge of the practices of the *plein air* colonies of France and England. Student recollections focus on progressive techniques such as a limited palette, liberal use of white and a direct and rapid method of painting: 'plenty of panels and paint were always on hand . . . we were encouraged to take another panel when Nature's mood changed'.[13] A critic of the school's annual exhibition in 1898 noted that 'the landscape generally is true to the tenets of the plein-air school. There is poetry, vagueness, airiness and space in even the least of the sketches which are also characterized by a fresh moist look'.[14]

Of all the artists returning to Melbourne from Europe in the 90s, Fox and Tucker appear to have had most impact on the local scene both through their teaching and the exhibition of work. 'The return of Mr Fox and Mr Tucker has had a great influence on the work [at the Victorian Artists' Society exhibition]', said *The Sun*, 'for both these artists exhibited many clever studies of the plein-air school, a certain section of their Melbourne brethren immediately took the hint and indirectly profited by the training of the Australians'.[15]

More problematic, however, is the extent of their influence on established artists such as McCubbin who stayed in Melbourne throughout the 90s. McCubbin's biographer, James MacDonald, noted:

> He had not been long in Brighton when Fox and Tucker who had been studying in Paris returned in a manner somewhat like the return of Roberts, for they brought back new ideas which much impressed McCubbin and caused him to break away largely from the usual style of work he was up till then doing... McCubbin had anticipated the refraction of colour theory brought back triumphantly from Paris by Fox and Tucker... [McCubbin] himself says that the desire to test the limits of high key which these new notions permitted brought his work dangerously near being anaemic in colour...[16]

MacDonald's desire to see McCubbin as an innovator has clouded the truth for although some of his works of the late 90s, such as *Autumn Memories*, show evidence of a new, freer technique and are painted in a warmer key, the majority still reflect an interest in the silvery grey tonal landscapes of Bastien-Lepage. In 1891 McCubbin wrote, 'I have a small photo of a landscape by Lepage, a hillside it is so lovely. The hill is so that you might walk over it'.[17] Moreover his letters to his wife from Europe in 1907 contain only fleeting reference to the French Impressionists but dwell on the art of the Newlyn School, George Clausen and Turner.

The degree of influence of French Impressionism on Fox and Tucker and its consequent effect on Melbourne's more progressive artists is complicated by the critics' imprecise application of the term 'impressionist' to their works. The semantic confusion over the use of the term which existed in the 1880s continued:

> For the younger generation of the time it boiled down to whether you did or did not accept Impressionism which many loved to talk about, but few understood. We had not learned to distinguish between the impressionism of Whistler and Velasquez which meant seeing a scene broadly as a whole and enveloping it in air and light and the impressionism or (luminism) of Monet and Renoir which further meant analyzing the colour in shadows and ruling out all neutral tints. In England at all events 'impressionism' meant Whistler.[18]

Most Melbourne critics in the 1890s used the term 'impressionist' as a synonym for unfinished:

> All this is clearly traceable to the spread of 'impressionism' ...An artist has to be an expert, both in depicting form and handling colour, before he can become a successful impressionist. The men – here in Melbourne – who really know and understand the subject have drifted into either carelessness or heedlessness, judging by their exhibits, and those who rush to copy these returned students from European centres, change celerity of execution into slapdash effects, in which colour is splashed about by the pound.[19]

Impressionism was equated with sketchiness: 'When, say, Mr Emanuel Fox hits off an illustration of "mistiness after rain", his admirers exclaim, "How clever!" Undoubtedly it is clever, but would not Mr Fox be a much greater artist if he painted something enduring, and not set a bad example to a score of youthful aspirants who are really only enthusiastic over what is easy, and who are tumbling over each others heels in their haste to secure the coveted short cut'.[20] However, Russell wrote to Roberts from Paris in 1890, 'Understood here it [impressionism] consists not of hasty sketches but in finished work in which the purity of colour and intention is kept'.[21]

Of all the artists painting in Melbourne in the 1890s, Fox had the greatest understanding of Impressionist principles. This was often counteracted in his work by other influences; for example, the muted colours and narrative element of his *Convalescent* reflect the *plein airism* of Newlyn and St Ives where the painting was completed. Similarly, *Art Students*, criticized by the Melbourne press for its 'tendency towards impressionism', was more accurately compared with aspects of British art when it was exhibited in the Grafton Galleries exhibition of 1898. However, Fox's knowledge of Impressionist techniques is more clearly evident in the broken brushstrokes of his 90s landscapes – for example, *Moonrise, Heidelberg*, on which the press commented adversely: 'His brushstroke is a little too apparent in the technique'.[22] Davies's *Moonrise* of 1894 was also criticized, for 'a tendency toward mannerism in thick laying on of colour almost in relief on the canvas'[23]; yet he was rarely associated with French Impressionism. MacDonald noted that Tucker 'preached the gospel of broken colour with Monet as its prophet'[24] and critics recognized his influence on local *plein air* painting and the introduction of French techniques, with the laudatory qualification: 'Mr Tucker however, is not an "impressionist" although his pictures have the above-mentioned characteristics. In the first place he is too good a draughtsman, and in the second, he takes pains to work up a study to as near a reproduction of nature as he believes to be correct'.[25]

The debate over 'impressionist' influence tended to obscure the variety of overseas influences these artists experienced. Fox, Tucker, Withers and Longstaff chose to study in Paris rather than at the Royal Academy or Slade School in London where artists such as Roberts and Russell had enrolled in the previous decade. However, by the 1890s, Paris was no longer the centre of *avant-garde* French art; it was, rather a haven for academic artists and the *juste-milieu* or 'middle-of-the-road' followers of Impressionism. Contact with 'original' 1870s French Impressionism appears to have been peripheral rather then direct for these Australians who joined the many foreign art students, especially Americans, then studying in Paris. Interestingly, Conder wrote in 1890 that 'the American students here tell me that Tucker is the strongest man from Australia in Paris, and Fox is also thought a great deal of'.[26]

The ethos of European landscape painting brought back by these artists was in accord with that of the 90s in Melbourne, when the bush came to be depicted as a place of mystery and romance. Views of early morning mists and moonrises replaced the bright light of midday favoured in the 1880s; and twilight scenes, already popular in the late 80s, became remarkably preponderant. In 1899, James Green wrote of the previous decade of art in Melbourne: 'It is this poetic distillation of Australian nature apart from mere literal transcription or excellence of technique that our painters are now learning so specifically to excel'.[27] The number of such landscapes included in the Victorian Artists' Society winter exhibition of 1895 prompted one critic to exclaim:

> Three-fourths of the exhibits are landscapes, studies and sketches, which are intended, should opportunity arise, to be developed into more important work. This explains the presence of so many 'grey days', 'misty mornings', 'summer evenings', and so forth. Probably they will all emerge into idylls later on, with some central idea to give them force. At present, the combined amount of greyness and mistiness requires some heroism to face. One grey day, or perhaps two, or three at the outside is sufficient for anyone, even of the most despondent temperament, but when 'grey days' and 'misty mornings' can be measured out by the square yard, surely there is some excuse for adopting the same view as Mark Twain's Blue Jay, and object that it is becoming 'monotonous'. There are few 'hot days' thank heaven! Perhaps, some time – before the millennium – 'grey days' and 'misty mornings' may, too, be no more.[28]

The preference for such landscapes by these Melbourne artists became associated with the spirit of nationalism and the emergence of an Australian school of painting. James Green wrote, 'the landscape of a country is the distilled aroma of her being and when truthfully translated upon canvas remains her esoteric own and essentially none other's'.[29]

Although critics, such as the artist Sydney Long, wrote somewhat scathingly of Melbourne's art in the 90s as being overly dependent on European models, most disagreed with his view that:

> The work of the Victorian artists has always been pitched in a greyer key than those of N.S.W. But it is not the grey of Australia; it rather shows the influence of the 'French Grey' School. Although they are more workmanlike in their methods, due to a large proportion of them being trained abroad, I should say that their work was more unAustralian than any of the other States. Unfortunately, too, they show a strong tendency to stick to the old hackneyed subjects of the European studios.[30]

The exhibition of Australian art in London at the Grafton Galleries in 1898 included many such works: Fox's *My Cousin* and *Art Students*, Davies's *Moonrise*, McCubbin's *A Winter Evening*, Withers's *Tranquil Winter*, and landscapes by Sutherland, Tucker and Humphrey. While frequent comment was made on the influence of French and English *plein air* painting, the majority of reviews praised the development and distinctiveness of Australian art. 'The pictures represent very faithfully the country of their origin and they stamp the individuality of the artists...', reported *The Tatler*, 'In the future more than at present the art of Australia will be seen to be a thing of its own and a very worthy one into the bargain. Even now the Australian artist is distinctive and creditably so'.[31]

[1] Quoted in Croll 1935, p.55.

[2] LaTrobe Collection, State Library of Victoria. McCubbin papers MS8525 987/2. Letter from Fox to McCubbin, 16 May 1903.

[3] Dickinson 1890, pp.21f.

[4] *Sun*, 25 August 1893, p.7.

[5] Sidney Dickinson, *The Australasian Critic*, 1 March 1891.

[6] *Age*, 29 October 1895.

[7] *Age*, 25 October 1894, p.6.

[8] Moore 1934, I, p.77.

[9] State Library of Victoria. A.A.A. file on E.P. Fox.

[10] *Table Talk*, 11 January 1895, p.9.

[11] *Sun*, 3 February 1893, p.13.

[12] Violet Teague, quoted by Moore 1934, I, pp.78f. 'Burlington House' was a reference to the Royal Academy and 'The Chantrey Bequest' to the Tate Gallery in London.

[13] Mrs Felix Meyer, quoted by Zubans in Ph.D. thesis, p.114.

[14] *Table Talk*, 7 January 1898, p.5.

[15] *Sun*, 21 April 1893, p.5.

[16] LaTrobe Collection, State Library of Victoria. Lothian papers, Box 31; cf. Astbury 1979, p.80.

[17] McCubbin to Roberts, 26 March 1891. Roberts correspondence vol.II, Mitchell Library, Sydney.

[18] Frank Rutter, *Art in My Time*, 1933, pp.57-8, quoted in Flint 1984, p.57.

[19] *Table Talk*, 10 May 1895, p.7.

[20] ibid.

[21] Reprinted by Galbally 1977, p.95.

[22] *Age*, 10 May 1895, p.6.

[23] *Age*, 25 October 1894. See Lothian papers, Box 31; quoted in Astbury 1979, p.80.

[24] Lothian papers, loc. cit., quoted in Astbury.

[25] *Table Talk*, 5 July 1895, p.7.

[26] *Table Talk*, 1 August 1890, p.15.

[27] *Australasian Art Review*, 1 September 1899, p.2.

[28] *Table Talk*, 10 May 1895, p.7.

[29] *Australasian Art Review*, 1 September 1899, p.2.

[30] Smith 1975, p.260.

[31] *Tatler*, 18 June 1898, p.19.

EMANUEL PHILLIPS FOX ▶
Convalescent, 1890
Oil on canvas
95 x 77 cm
Signed and dated l.r.: E.P. FOX, 90. St. Ives
The Robert Holmes à Court Collection

Provenance:
Original owner unknown; private collection, Melbourne (purchased in St Kilda 1950); Leonard Joel Melbourne, November 1979, lot 95 as 'Two Sisters'; The Robert Holmes à Court Collection, Perth

Exhibitions:
Catalogue illustré de peinture et sculpture, Salon de 1891, Paris 1891, no 646: '*Convalescente*', illus. p.158; at the Austral Salon, Melbourne, December 1892, no.11 – 75 guineas; Art Union exhibition to raise funds for the new Victorian Artists' Society building, June 1894; at the Athenaeum Hall, Melbourne, February 1916

Literature:
Argus, 6 December 1892, p.7; *Table Talk*, 9 December 1892, p.4; *Sun*, 9 December 1892, p.14; *Age*, 12 June 1894, p.6; Terry Ingram, *Financial Review*, 22 November 1979; Zubans 1980, pp.135, 142ff.

> Mr Fox seems... anxious to communicate the visual impression which he himself has received from his subject, and this is exemplified in *The Convalescent*... he appears to have been most struck by the effect of firelight on the pallid face of the invalid and on the white draperies of her bed.
> – *The Argus*, 6 December 1892

The painting which attracts most notice is undoubtedly the one entitled Convalescent, exhibited at the Salon of 1891. It was painted at St Ives, and is an admirable example of the teaching of the Cornish school, [in] that it is the probable and unexpected incident which an artist should choose for illustration. A girl of about fourteen years of age, clad in white reclines in a wicker arm chair, placed so close against the mantel piece that the golden light of the fire shines upon her frock, though the grate itself is unseen. A younger child, standing behind the chair, is arranging the pillow on which the invalid's head is resting. There are no deep shadows, and the fire-light plays in patches over the white dress like molten gold. The wan, patient face of the convalescent tells its own story of wearying suffering, and the attitude of the other child is expressive of affectionate solicitude. The contrast of flesh tints between health and sickness is masterly, and the drawing is vigorous yet soft in outline. The chief defect in the realism of the picture is that of the hands of the girl, which, correct enough in drawing, are too plump and firm in comparison with the worn face.
> – *Table Talk*, 9 December 1892

Convalescent was painted at St Ives, Cornwall, in 1890, soon after Fox's arrival from Paris where he had studied for three years. As one of the paintings Fox included in his one man exhibition in Melbourne it attracted considerable attention on his return to Australia in 1892. It highlights the English influences which the artist had absorbed during his overseas studies and modifies the traditional view that his contribution to the Melbourne art scene in the 1890s was predominantly French Impressionist.[1] Muted colours and a narrative element in the work contrast with brightly coloured paintings which he had produced earlier in France. Although hung in the Salon of 1891 and well reviewed by the Melbourne press in 1892, *Convalescent* evidently did not appeal to local patrons for it remained unsold at the artist's death.

[1] A typical example of contemporary Cornish work is Thomas Gotch's *Mental Arithmetic*, painted at Newlyn in 1883 and presented to the National Gallery of Victoria by the artist's cousin J.S. Gotch in 1884. T.C. Gotch had visited Australia in 1883 and later befriended Rupert Bunny in Europe.

TUDOR ST GEORGE TUCKER ▲
Young girl in a garden, [c. 1896]
Oil on canvas on board
52 x 44.5 cm
Signed in monogram l.r.: T.S.G.T.
The Robert Holmes à Court Collection

Provenance:
Private collection, New Zealand; Thirty Victoria Street, Sydney; The Robert Holmes à Court Collection, Perth

[His paintings] belong to the modern French school, whose principal tenets are an insistence on atmospheric effect, a preference for neutral colour and an absence of detail. Nature is regarded from afar off, when outline becomes indistinguishable and merges into colour . . . Mr Tucker, however is not an 'impressionist' although his pictures have the above-mentioned characteristics. In the first place he is too good a draughtsman, and in the second he takes pains to work up a study to as near a reproduction of nature as he believes to be correct.
– *Table Talk*, 5 July 1895

This wistful study of a young girl clasping a spray of eucalyptus was probably painted in the garden at 'Charterisville' where Tucker worked from 1894. Tucker's prime interest was the sensitive modelling of the girl's face and the effects of sunlight on her golden hair; the distant landscape is only hazily sketched in. His liberal use of white in the dress and hat, broadly and rapidly applied, is suggestive of the 'impressionist' technique, brought back from France, which he and Fox taught their students at the 'Charterisville' summer school: combined in his finished works with more conservative elements of style.

EMANUEL PHILLIPS FOX ▶
Portrait of my Cousin, [c.1893]
Oil on canvas
205.5 x 91.5 cm
Signed l.r.: E. Phillips Fox
National Gallery of Victoria
Felton Bequest 1925

Provenance:
The artist's family until *Catalogue of Pictures by the late E. Phillips Fox*, auction sale by the Fine Arts Society in conjunction with Leonard Joel, Melbourne, 12-13 May 1925, lot 27

Exhibitions:
Catalogue illustré de peinture et sculpture, Salon de 1894, Paris 1894, no.759: 'Portrait de ma cousine' (gold medal); *The Exhibition of the Royal Academy of Arts*, London, 1895, no.16; *Exhibition of Australian Art in London*, Grafton Galleries, London, April 1898, no.56: 'Portrait of My Cousin'; *Catalogue of the Victorian Artists' Society Exhibition*, National Gallery of Victoria, Melbourne, [July] 1898, no.48: 'Portrait of My Cousin'; *The Commonwealth Exhibition of Australian Art*, Sydney, 1901, no.87: 'Portrait of My Cousin'

Literature:
Table Talk, 12 July 1895, p.2; 8 November 1895, p.2; *Standard*, 4 April 1898; *Daily Telegraph* (London), 7 April 1898; *Daily Telegraph* (Sydney), 5 and 12 May, 1898, p.6; *Daily News* (London), 9 April 1898; *Magazine of Art*, May 1898, illus.; *Sketch*, June 1898, illus.; Fox 1969, p.19; Zubans 1970, pp.61f.; Zubans 1980, p.144

The pose of the standing figure – reflected vaguely in the long mirror in a shadowed space to the right – is of admirable and complete refinement. The broad-faced, placid, far from inanimate model, stands her lips parted a little, and with glove in hand, in Empire dress; short-waisted, therefore, with arms bare to the elbow. The painter has been entirely worthy of his theme, and has produced a canvas so elegant and distinguished that there is no modern Gallery in which it might not appropriately hang.
– *The Standard*, 4 April 1898

This tender portrait of Lottie Phillips, the artist's cousin, was completed soon after his return to Australia. According to family tradition, Fox was romantically attached to Lottie at the time but the romance did not continue;[1] and the painting itself was finished with European exhibitions in mind. It won a gold medal at the Paris Salon of 1894 and was widely acclaimed in London when exhibited at the Royal Academy in 1895 and the Grafton exhibition of 1898. Fox later commented to McCubbin on the great importance of such official recognition.[2] The influence of Whistler, suggested in the sitter's pose, her reflection in the mirror, the placement of the patterned carpet and fur rug, was noted by many contemporary reviewers. *The Daily News*, for example, said, 'We have a suggestion of Mr Whistler's style of his breadth of his chiaroscuro if his subtlety has not quite been reached'. Fox almost certainly saw the Whistler exhibition held at the Goupil Gallery in London in 1892 and his interest would have been fostered by his association with the artists at St Ives (Whistler painted there in 1883-84) and his American former teacher, Thomas Alexander Harrison, who knew Whistler. *Portrait of my Cousin* has similarities with Whistler's *Symphony in White no.2: The Little White Girl* or *Harmony in Pink and Grey: Portrait of Lady Meux*, both included in the Goupil Gallery exhibition.[3] The work also reveals a high degree of finish and formality, attributable both to Fox's desire to have the portrait accepted in academic circles and to his working methods. (According to his niece, he completed a charcoal sketch directly onto the canvas and then a number of small oil studies before painting the final version.) At this time, in Melbourne in the 90s, Fox received numerous commissions for portraits which comprised many of the works he exhibited at the Victorian Artists' Society. With Roberts in Sydney, John Longstaff was his only major rival as a portraitist. Such commissions and his earnings from the Melbourne School of Art formed the basis of his income during this Australian decade.

[1] Fox 1969, p.19.
[2] LaTrobe Collection, State Library of Victoria. MS 8525 987/2. McCubbin papers: letter from Fox to McCubbin, 16 May 1903.
[3] McLaren Young et al. 1980, nos 52 and 229; also no.38, the famous *Symphony in White no.1: The White Girl*.

INA GREGORY ▲
Four art students, 'Charterisville', [1890s]
Oil on canvas
29 x 24 cm
Mrs. Robin Kelly, Melbourne

Provenance:
Leonard Joel, Melbourne 1977; Mrs Robin Kelly

INA GREGORY ▲
Girl in the garden, Charterisville, [1890s]
Oil on panel
18 x 21 cm
Signed l.r.: Ina Gregory
Mrs. Robin Kelly, Melbourne

Provenance:
Jessica Lavery until 1975; Mrs Robin Kelly

Ina Gregory was one of the students who attended the summer school at 'Charterisville' run by Fox and Tucker: selected each year from those attending the Melbourne Art School. Fellow students included Violet Teague, Mary Nanson, Bertha Merfield, Henrietta Irving and Ursula Foster. Ina Gregory's rapidly executed small sketches of her contemporaries in the studio and garden show the influence of Fox's and Tucker's teaching, especially in the broad application of a limited range of colours and liberal use of white.

EMANUEL PHILLIPS FOX ▲
Study for 'Art Students', [c.1895]
58.4 x 30 cm
Oil on canvas
Signed l.r.: E.P. Fox
Inscribed l.r.: Miss Baker/a souvenir
Carrick Hill, Adelaide

Provenance:
Cristina Asquith Baker, Melbourne; Sir Edward Hayward

This oil sketch is dedicated to Miss Cristina Asquith Baker, who is depicted standing in the centre in the dotted smock. Following the academic methods he learned in Paris, Fox would complete numerous specific studies before working on a major painting. Although less finished than *Art Students*, it reveals how deliberately he composed the apparently naturalistic and casual view of the young painters at work in the final version.

EMANUEL PHILLIPS FOX ▶
Art Students, 1895
Oil on canvas
182.9 x 114.3 cm
Signed and dated l.l.: E. Phillips Fox/95
Art Gallery of New South Wales
Purchased 1943

Provenance:
The artist's family until 1943

Exhibitions:
Victorian Artists' Society Annual Exhibition Catalogue, Melbourne, September 1895, no.45: 'Art Students – £210'; *Society of Artists Second Spring Exhibition*, Sydney, September 1896, no.6: 'The Art Students – £150'; *Exhibition of Australian Art in London*, Grafton Galleries, London, April 1898, no.71: 'The Art Students'; *Catalogue of the Victorian Artists' Society Exhibition*, National Gallery of Victoria, Melbourne, [July] 1898, no.41: 'Art Students'

Literature:
Age, 20 September 1895, p.7; *Table Talk*, 20 September 1895, p.6; *Argus*, 21 September 1895, p.11; *Times* (London), 4 April 1898; *Daily News* (London), 9 April 1898; *Daily Telegraph* (London), 7 April 1898; *Daily Telegraph* (Sydney), 5 and 12 May 1898, p.6; *Art Journal*, 1898, p.186, illus.; *Herald*, 21 July 1919; Daniel Thomas 1963, p.42; Fox 1969, p.19; McCulloch 1969, p.89; Gleeson 1971, pl.79; Zubans 1980, p.142; Downer & Phipps 1985, no.93

His most important work, Art Students, shows a corner of a studio, with its littered floor and row of easels, before which some girl students are at work, unified by one common inspiration and aim, but possessing each her special individuality. The figures are life size and are seen in profile, the most interesting being that of a girl with luxuriant brown hair, attired in a charming loose, paint stained pinafore, with an intelligent and slightly pathetic expression. Her neighbor, a slender girl, with refined earnest face, has been studied with much sympathetic insight. Good drawing, fine technique and a strong instinct for the harmonious juxtaposition of color distinguish the picture, which, however, is not free from a certain mannerism nor altogether irreproachable as regards aerial perspective. The lighting of the figures is that of the *plein* air rather than of the studio, and they appear slightly flat.
– *The Age*, 20 September 1895

dency to disturb the harmony of the work. The faces of the students wear a most lugubrious expression, as if the master had been administering reprimands all round, [on], say, the growing tendency towards impressionism.
– *Table Talk*, 20 September 1895

Art Students depicts Fox's own students at work in the studio, probably the interior of the Melbourne Art School which he opened in June 1893 with Tudor St George Tucker in the Cromwell Buildings in Bourke Street. According to the prospectus, it was 'founded for the purpose of providing a thorough art Education on similar lines to the best Parisian Schools'. The girl in the dotted smock has been identified as Cristina Asquith Baker, to whom Fox dedicated a study for the painting; the student seated in the centre is Etta Phillips, the artist's cousin, and standing on the extreme right is Ina Gregory. Influences from French Impressionism have been noted in his choice of subject matter and the apparently uncomposed setting with slightly flattened forms and figures cut off by the edge of the canvas. Nevertheless, the low-keyed colour, the wistful mood, the inclusion of details such as discarded tubes of paint on the studio floor or the antique head on a pedestal in the background, together with the naturalism of the figure, reveal the strong influence of English art. One of the London critics wrote, 'The Art Students of Mr Fox is a little pleasantly Whistlerian. There they are in their pinafores busy at their easels. What it wants is composition'.[2] While another said the work was 'a portrait group of a decorative character, rather flat but, in its unconventional way, very cleverly composed'.[3] However in the context of Melbourne in 1895 it had appeared more radical. Such informality in a large-scale figure composition was unprecedented and in marked contrast to the 'national' subjects produced by Roberts, Streeton and McCubbin in the 1890s.

[1] Zubans 1970, p.63.
[2] *Standard*, 4 April 1898.
[3] *Daily Telegraph* (London), 7 April 1898.

Mr E.P. Fox's studio group is one of the most important pictures in the collection. It is not interesting – if interest be considered to centre in the graphic depicting of a story, but it is the cleverest thing in the gallery. The artist has aimed at illustrating an incident in studio life – when several girls are occupied with their work. The amount of figure drawing is tremendous, and for this alone the picture deserves to stand out. The colouring is natural – too natural, for Mr Fox has seen fit to reproduce the ugly realism affected by the young ladies in their painting aprons. So much art muslin, depicted with a naturalness that would delight the heart of the Liberty firm, has a ten-

TUDOR ST GEORGE TUCKER ▶
Springtime, 1890
Oil on canvas
31.5 x 52.5 cm
Signed l.l.: T. St. G. Tucker/ETAPLES/
NOVEMBER 1890
The Joseph Brown Collection
For exhibition in Melbourne only

Exhibitions:
Victorian Artists' Society Exhibition of Paintings, Sculpture and Drawings, Melbourne, April 1893, no.137: 'Springtime – 45 guineas', illus.; probably in the Art Union exhibition to raise funds for the new Victorian Artists' Society building, June 1894 (no catalogue located); *Eighteenth Annual Exhibition of the Art Society of New South Wales, Illustrated Catalogue*, Sydney, September 1897, no.71: 'Springtime – £42.0.0'; *The Exhibition of the Royal Academy of Arts*, London, 1900, no.150: 'Springtime'

Literature:
Table Talk, 26 August 1892, p.6; *Age*, 12 June 1894, p.6; *Daily Telegraph*, 9 September 1897; Daniel Thomas 1980, no. 157

[The painting is] of a young peasant girl, just awakening from a sleep in a grassy glade in an autumn tinted wood. The landscape is unfinished though sketched in with firm, bold touches reproducing the glow and the warmth of the fading summer. The figure of the sleeper is admirably posed, the outline correct and the colouring very pleasing in its complete harmony and the brilliant effect of the light. When finished the picture will be a chef d'oeuvre.
– *Table Talk*, 26 August 1892

Tucker began painting *Springtime* at Etaples, one of the centres for *plein airists* on the Brittany coast, during his stay in France from 1887 to 1892. He brought the uncompleted painting back to Melbourne where it was first exhibited in the Victorian Artists' Society exhibition of 1893.

EDGAR BERTRAM MACKENNAL ▶
Circe, 1892[1]
Bronze statue
Height including base 204.6 cm
Maximum width – rear of base to extended finger tips 92 cm
Diameter of base 56 cm
Inscribed on base: KIPKH/Bertram Mackennal/1893/E. GRUET JNE – FONDEUR.PARIS.
National Gallery of Victoria
Felton Bequest 1910

Provenance:
The original bronze-painted (patinated) plaster version remained in Mackennal's possession until 1901 when *Circe* was purchased by Herr Carl Pinschoff, Melbourne, and cast in bronze; Carl Pinschoff estate, 1910

Exhibitions:
Catalogue illustré de peinture et sculpture, Salon de 1893, Paris, 1893, no.3125: '*Circé statue, plâtre* [plaster]' – awarded *mention honorable*; *The Exhibition of the Royal Academy of Arts*, London, 1894, no.1863: 'Circe, statue'; at the National Gallery of Victoria, in a small exhibition of Mackennal's work; Franco-British Exhibition, 1908, no.1305 (plaster); *Victorian Artists' Society Exhibition*, Melbourne, October 1910, Sculpture no.1: 'Circe – £100' (a cast of the small scale statuette version)

Literature:
Table Talk, 12 May 1893, p.5; 29 June 1894, p.3; *Magazine of Art*, 1895, p.389; *Argus*, 19 February 1901; 13 and 29 March 1901; 1 April 1901 (and numerous other letters); Sir Isidore Spielmann, *Souvenir of the Fine Art Section, Franco-British Exhibition 1908*, no.1305, plaster version illus. opp. p.251; W.K. West, 'The Sculpture of Bertram Mackennal', *Studio* 44, 1908, pp.262ff.; Lionel Lindsay, 'Sir Bertram Mackennal, R.A.', *Art in Australia*, series 3, March 1925; Moore 1934, I, pl. opp. p.202, II, pp.35, 80f.; Cox 1970, pp.50, 425n.31; Noel Hutchinson, *Bertram Mackennal*, Oxford University Press, Melbourne, 1973, pp.9ff.; Sturgeon 1978, pp.63ff.; Scarlett 1980, pp.410ff.

This powerful woman with extended arms and drooping hands, and the serpent-filled tresses of a witch, stands erect, almost rigid in the pride of the consciousness of the irresistible supremacy of her nudity; but form and face are devoid of voluptuousness, and her expression is one of scorn for her victims. It was admirably placed in a central avenue in the Champs Elysées, received an honourable mention... On sending 'Circe' to the Academy last year, a surprise awaited Mr Mackennal. The plinth on which the statue stands is decorated with a flowing series in high relief of small nude figures in animated action and surmounted by a coiled snake. Thus the sculptor indicates the swine, the debased creatures who have drunk of Circe's wine, though he was concerned in the doing of it rather with the greater value these abrupt masses of light and shade were giving to his figure than the allegoric significance of the forms themselves. In Paris, however, his interpretation of the legend was accounted to him as poetry. Not so did it appeal to the Hanging Committee at Burlington House. They were conscious of the merits of the work and anxious to secure its exhibition, but the base appeared to them, to use their own words, 'as not being in accordance with the exigencies of the exhibition'; and courteous negotiations resulted in the diplomatic com-

promise of the retention of the statue in a place of honour, and the covering of the base from public view with a swathing of red baize.
– R. Jope-Slade in *The Magazine of Art*, 1895

Circe was first proposed for acquisition by the National Gallery of Victoria in January 1894 when the Director, Lindsay Bernard Hall, wrote that, judging from photographs and advice received 'it seems to me to be a genuine work of genius – very remarkable and impressive – (without doubt I should say Young Australia's *chef d'ouvre* [*sic*]').[2] Unfortunately the trustees did not agree. The controversy provoked by the statue's exhibition at the Royal Academy later that year made Mackennal famous; and continued when it was first shown in Melbourne in 1901. Once again the work was suggested for the Gallery, but an offer of payment by instalment was not satisfactory to Mackennal. Before returning to Europe he sold the life-sized sculpture privately to Herr Carl Pinschoff, Austro-Hungarian Consul and friend and patron of the Heidelberg School. *The Argus* then announced, 'The plaster cast of "Circe", which the majority of visitors to the gallery accept as veritable bronze, will accordingly be sent to London, where the bronze castings will be made and fitted under the personal direction of the sculptor' (13 March 1901). In fact Mackennal chose a French foundry E. Gruet *Jeune*, to cast this full-scale version. A total of eight small-scale statuette versions were cast, at various dates, from Mackennal's original modello.[3]

[1] Usually dated 1893; but see letter from Mackennal to Dr Felix Meyer, 12 April 1892, in Felix Meyer Papers, University of Melbourne Archive. I am most grateful to Patricia Fullerton and Mary Eagle for this reference.
[2] 22 January 1894. Quoted by Cox 1970, p.50.
[3] Information kindly supplied by Noel Hutchinson.
J.C.

ARTHUR STREETON ▶
Professor Marshall-Hall, 1892
Oil on canvas
76.2 x 50.8 cm
Signed and dated l.l.: Arthur
Streeton-1892.
National Gallery of Victoria
Bequeathed by Miss Lorna Stirling
through the National Gallery Society 1956

Provenance:
Mrs Marshall-Hall until at least 1935; Miss
Lorna Stirling, Hawthorn

Exhibitions:
*Victorian Artists' Society Exhibition of
Paintings, Sculpture and Drawings*,
Melbourne, May 1892, no.193: 'Professor
Marshal [sic] Hall'

Literature:
Streeton 1935, no.59; Croll 1935, pp.190f.;
Croll 1946, pp.59f.; Finemore 1977, p.34,
pl.22; Galbally 1979, no.46, pl.10; Thérèse
Radic, *G.W.L. Marshall-Hall, Portrait of a
Lost Crusader*, Music Monograph 5,
University of Western Australia, Perth,
1982, p.18
Reproduced by courtesy of Mrs Oliver
Streeton

> Marshall-Hall is grand entertainment,
> and his painting is coming on. He looks
> at it and says it is great fun, and gurgles
> far away down in his throat. He says he
> would not like to have a man standing
> and looking out at him as the portrait
> does. He thinks I've caught somewhat
> of his expression – a sardonic sort of
> smile.
> – Streeton to Roberts, 12 April 1892

> He has done a most powerful head of
> myself; very much the reverse of flat-
> tering, but big, big! BIG!
> – Marshall-Hall to Roberts, July 1892

This portrait, one of Streeton's finest, commemorates the close friendship between
the artist and the radical musician George
William Louis Marshall-Hall, first Ormond
Professor of Music at the University of
Melbourne. Marshall-Hall (1862-1915) was
born in London and studied in Berlin and
London before coming to Australia in January 1891 to take up his appointment. He
founded the Melbourne Conservatorium
and conducted orchestral concerts which
were widely acclaimed. His interest in
contemporary music, especially Wagner,
and his outspoken views on most subjects
– which were widely published – outraged
sections of the Melbourne community and
conservative elements within the University. The publication in 1898 of his volume
of verse *Hymns Ancient and Modern*,
described by his detractors as lascivious
and anti-clerical, created a controversy in
the press and at the University which cul-
minated in his dismissal from the Ormond

Chair. He continued to contribute to the
Melbourne music scene through his own
Albert Street Conservatorium and the
Marshall-Hall Orchestra and was ultimately reappointed Professor of Music at
Melbourne University in January 1915,
some six months before his death.
Marshall-Hall enjoyed the support of Melbourne's progressive musical fraternity
and the friendship of many artists including Streeton, Roberts and Fox. There are
two portraits of him by Roberts dated
1899 and 1900. The later 'Charterisville'
artists, Ernest Moffit and Lionel and Norman Lindsay, also knew him well.
Streeton claimed to be the first artist in
Australia to meet the musician[1] and they
both moved in the circle which included
Herr Carl Pinschoff, the Austro-Hun-

garian Consul, and his wife Elise Weider-
mann, a celebrated German singer. Late in
1891 Marshall-Hall joined Streeton at the
Mosman camp and subsequently dedicated his *Hymn to Sydney* to the painter.
They lived together in Melbourne for a
while in 1892, when this portrait was completed.

[1] Letter from Streeton to Henri
Verbrugghen, 28 June 1920.
Marshall-Hall holdings, University of
Melbourne Archives.

TUDOR ST GEORGE TUCKER ▲
Portrait of Tom Humphrey, 1894
Oil on canvas
29 x 22.1 cm
Inscribed l.l.: T StG Tucker/to his friend/
T.H./1894
National Gallery of Victoria
Presented in memory of Dr Mary
Journeaux True (1900-85) by her
daughter Maureen Barden 1985

Provenance:
Tom Humphrey; his daughter, Dr Molly
True, until 1985

Literature:
Topliss 1984, no.8

JOHN LONGSTAFF ▶
Lady in grey (Portrait de Mme L . . .), 1890
Oil on canvas
135 x 90 cm
Signed and dated twice u.l.: J. Longstaff
1890/J. Longstaff 90
National Gallery of Victoria
Presented by John H. Connell 1914
For exhibition in Melbourne only

Provenance:
The artist; John H. Connell, Melbourne

Exhibitions:
Salon of 1890, no.1534: '*Portraite de Mme
L . . .*' (hung on the line); *The Exhibition of
the Royal Academy of Arts*, London, 1891,
no.297: 'Portrait'; Victorian Artists'
Society, Melbourne June 1896 (no
catalogue traced); Old Court Studio,
Swanston Street, Melbourne, August 1898

Literature:
Courrier de l'art, Paris 1890; *Argus*, 14
November 1890; Henry Blackburn (ed.),
The Academy Notes, Chatto and Windus,

London, 1891, no.297, illus.; *Table Talk*, 5
June 1896, p.3; *Tatler*, 13 August 1898,
p.27; *Catalogue of the Connell Collection*,
National Gallery of Victoria, 2nd edn,
1937, no.63; Murdoch 1948, p.115; Timms
1975, no.44

. . . the gem of the collection, a Harmony in Ivory and Grey, otherwise a
very delicate and delicious scheme of
colour in which a painting of an
English lady in Japanese costume is
beautifully rendered. The treatment of
the flesh tones is very refined and the
whole scheme of colour is distinguished by a reserve and yet a quiet
force which is characteristic of the
work in this manner of that marvellous
colourist Whistler, whose good influence is clearly to be seen in this picture.
– *The Tatler*, 13 August 1898

Longstaff's portrait of his wife Rosa – or
'Topsy' as he called her – was painted in
Paris, where he was studying under the
terms of the first National Gallery of Victoria travelling scholarship. The couple had
spent the previous summer with John
Peter Russell and his wife, Marianna, at
their island home Belle-Ile, off the Breton
coast. There, under Russell's influence,
Longstaff had lightened his palette and
temporarily loosened his technique. This
painting also reveals the influence of
Whistler and British Aestheticism, balanced by the more traditional portrait
style of Velasquez. *Lady in grey* evidently
received considerable attention when it
was first exhibited in Paris, 1890, and the
following year at the Royal Academy in
London.

ARTHUR LOUREIRO ▲
An Autumn Morning, 1893
Oil on canvas (laid down on board)
71.1 x 101.6 cm
Signed and dated l.r.: ARTHUR
LOUREIRO/1893
The Joseph Brown Collection
For exhibition in Melbourne only

Provenance:
The artist, until *Catalogue of the whole of
the Oil Paintings, Studies, Models, Carved
Furniture, &c. of Senhor Loureiro*,
Gemmell, Tuckett and Co., Melbourne, 2
August 1907, lot 4: 'An Autumn Morning'
[20 guineas]; Mrs Carrie Templeton, née
Taylor (a former pupil) until 1931; Leonard
Joel, Melbourne, August 1969, lot 40;
Joseph Brown, Melbourne

Exhibitions:
*Victorian Artists' Society Exhibition of
Paintings, Sculpture & Drawings,
Illustrated Catalogue*, Melbourne, April
1893, no.53: 'An Autumn Morning – 21
guineas'; *Victorian Artists' Society
Exhibition of Australian Art Past and
Present*, National Gallery of Victoria,
Melbourne, August 1893, no.35: 'An
Autumn Morning – £21'

Literature:
Argus, 20 April 1893, p.7; *Age*, 21 April
1893, p.6; *Table Talk*, 28 April 1893, p.4;
Daniel Thomas 1980, no.57 (as 'Evening
landscape'); Clark 1985, p.97

An Autumn Morning is an early morning effect. Near the Yarra wreaths of
light mist are lifting from the river,
transparent splashes of shadow lie on
the golden grass, and the magpies hop
gaily about in the early morning sunlight. The effect is truthfully and delicately rendered and communicates to
one something of the exhilaration of
the early morning atmosphere and
light.
– *The Age*, 21 April 1893

J.C.

DAVID DAVIES ▶
Moonrise, 1894
Oil on canvas
119.8 x 150 cm
Signed and dated l.r.: D.DAVIES/94
National Gallery of Victoria
Purchased 1895

Provenance:
The artist

Exhibitions:
*Annual Exhibition of the Victorian Artists'
Society*, Melbourne, October 1894, no.5:
'Moonrise – £75'; *Exhibition of Australian
Art in London*, Grafton Galleries, London,
April 1898, no.58: 'Moonrise – lent by
trustees of National Gallery of Victoria'

Literature:
Table Talk, 27 October 1894, p.4; 8
December 1894, p.9; *Age*, 25 October
1894, p.6; 20 September 1895, p.7; 3
December 1895; *Argus*, 21 September
1895, p.11; *Herald*, 16, 19 and 26
November 1895; *Daily Telegraph*, 5 and
12 May 1898, p.6; Moore 1934, I, p.97; *Art
in Australia*, March 1938, p.47; Smith
1971, p.102; Finemore 1977, p.38, pl.X11;
Hughes 1977, p.77; Sparks 1978, p.69;
Splatt & Bruce 1981, pl.72; Sparks 1984,
no.17; Downer & Phipps 1985, no.85

Mr Davies only exhibits one painting, Moonrise, but he has a great deal to say in it. In its simplicity of composition, the breadth and power of the execution, and in its delicacy of values, it is perhaps the most impressive and original work in the exhibition. While seeing in Mr Davies's technique the value of French influences intelligently accepted and applied, we are also sensible of a tendency which might degenerate into mannerism. This is the thick laying on of color almost in relief on the canvas.

– *The Age*, 25 October 1894

Moonrise was the most spectacular of the series of nocturnes Davies painted between 1893 and 1897 whilst living in the Templestowe area. According to William Moore, it was 'painted close to his studio; being on the spot, he was able to study the effect each evening, the moon rising over the hill in front of him. He managed to make several studies which helped him in carrying out the composition'. As *Table Talk*'s critic remarked, 'Moonrise comes very near being an excellent picture. Every line bears the mark of careful out-door study, and the handling shows a firm, vigorous grasp of the salient points of a landscape'.[1] The painting was generally well received by the contemporary press and was one of a group purchased by the National Gallery of Victoria in 1895. (*Table Talk* noted that these purchases were probably inspired by the Art Gallery of New South Wales, where acquisition of recent Australian art had been more progressive.) Once on view in the Gallery, however, the work created considerable public controversy and a heated exchange of letters took place in *The Herald*. Although some were complimentary – 'The exquisite simplicity of the subject, treated with such masterly technique and artistic feeling, cannot fail to interest those who are sufficiently conversant with art to appreciate it' – the majority were hostile; such as the following comments from an 'Artist': 'perhaps it has been placed there as a lesson in economy, as the whole thing could have been made up with four colours – black, white, Indian red and cadmium – perhaps intermingled . . . with some refuse from the kitchen. If the eyesore is still to be kept there, the state should have the benefit by making a charge for storage or place it in a separate room and allow the public to take in their umbrellas and sticks'.[2]

[1] 27 October 1894, p.4.
[2] *Herald*, 19 and 26 November 1895.

DAVID DAVIES ►
Warm evening, Templestowe, [1890s]
Oil on canvas
38 x 48.2 cm
Signed l.l.: D. DAVIES
National Gallery of Victoria
Purchased by the National Gallery Society
of Victoria with the assistance of a special
grant from the Government of Victoria
1980

Provenance:
Original owner unknown; estate of W.
Oswald Burt, Melbourne 1969; Jack
Manton, Melbourne

Literature:
Radford 1973, no.12; McCaughey 1979,
p.130, pl.58; Splatt & Bruce 1981, pl.71

DAVID DAVIES ▲
Nocturne, Templestowe, [c.1896]
Oil on cedar panel
20.7 x 26.5 cm
Signed l.l.: D. DAVIES
Label verso: 'This was painted by Davies
while residing at Templestowe between
the years 1894-1897 and was given by
him to a personal friend Mr Patterson of
Hawthorn from whom it was purchased'
National Gallery of Victoria
Purchased with the assistance of a special
grant from the Government of Victoria
1979

Provenance:
The artist to Mr W. Patterson, Hawthorn;
W. Oswald Burt, Melbourne; estate of W.O.
Burt 1969; Jack Manton, Melbourne

Exhibitions:
Probably Victorian Artists' Society, June
1896 (no catalogue traced)

Literature:
McCaughey 1979, p.132, pl.59

This may be the painting admired by
Table Talk's critic at the Victorian Artists'
Society in 1896: 'There is more poetry in
the little sketch of pastureland, "Evening",
with its soft purples and pinks and
greys... For sympathy with nature,
there is not a more successful painter' (5
June 1896, pp.3,5).

DAVID DAVIES ▲
Evening, Templestowe, 1897
Oil on canvas
45 x 56 cm
Signed l.r.: D. DAVIES/97
National Gallery of Victoria
Purchased with the assistance of a special
grant from the Government of Victoria
1979

Provenance:
The artist to Professor Walter Baldwin
Spencer; Arthur Norman 1919; Christie's,
Melbourne, March 1973, lot 198; Jack
Manton, Melbourne

Literature:
The Baldwin Spencer Collection, Fine Arts
Society Galleries, Melbourne 1919, no.45:
'Evening', illus.; Radford 1973, no.6;
McCaughey 1979, p.134, pl.62; Splatt &
Bruce 1981, pl.70; Pearce 1983, pl.29

There is a sketch for *Evening, Templestowe* in the Australian National Gallery.

TOM HUMPHREY ▶
Under a Summer Sun, 1895
Oil on canvas
50.5 x 76 cm
Signed and dated l.l.: Tom Humphrey/
1895
Verso: canvas stamp S. Pelletier et Cie/
Paris
National Gallery of Victoria
Purchased with a Government grant 1895

Provenance:
The artist

Exhibitions:
Victorian Artists' Society Annual Exhibition Catalogue, Melbourne, September 1895, no.25: 'Under a Summer Sun – £10'

Literature:
Table Talk, 27 September 1895, p.5; Hall 1979, no.3; Splatt & Bruce 1981, pl.69, p.101

Under a Summer Sun was among the earliest Heidelberg School acquisitions made by the National Gallery of Victoria, in 1895. This group included Withers's *A Bright Winter's Morning* and McCubbin's *Feeding Time*, which were exchanged for other paintings shortly afterwards. Humphrey's slightly more conventional landscape remained in the collection.

WALTER WITHERS ▶
Tranquil Winter, 1895
Oil on canvas
75.7 x 122.6 cm
Signed and dated l.l.: Walter Withers/
1895
National Gallery of Victoria
Purchased with Government funds 1895

Provenance:
The artist

Exhibitions:
Annual Exhibition Catalogue Victorian Artists' Society, Melbourne, September 1895, no.132: 'Tranquil Winter – £52.10.0'; *Exhibition of Australian Art in London*, Grafton Galleries, London, April 1898, no.354: 'Tranquil Winter – lent by trustees National Gallery of Victoria'

Literature:
Table Talk, 20 September 1895, p.6; *Daily Telegraph*, 5 May 1898, p.6; 12 May 1898, p.6; MacDonald 1916, p.87; *The Art of Walter Withers*, pp.21f.; Moore 1934, I, pp.92f.; McCulloch, 1969, pl.93; Finemore 1977, pp.27, 31; Downer & Phipps 1985, p.55, no.224

'Tranquil Winter', a simple subject, with little or no composition, is distinctly Australian, and exactly that kind of picture to bring back the memory of aromatic gum trees, fragrant grass and the dewy freshness of a bright winter day.
– *Table Talk*, 20 September 1895

The more you regard this picture, its tone and colour, the more you will feel the truthfulness and poetry of its interpretation. . . . One feels that in it, nothing has been arranged. Everything is natural and in its place, as though the Artist has come upon some quiet commonplace spot, and, magician like, revealed to you and me its tender beauty.
– Frederick McCubbin, 1916

Tranquil Winter was selected for inclusion in the huge Australian art exhibition of 1898 at the Grafton Galleries in London. The painting was much praised by British critics such as R.A.M. Stevenson:

> This 'Tranquil Winter' is the most beautiful canvas in the show. Rolling downs of green grass, chequered by shadows from white stemmed forest trees, the gently illumined harmony of colour as natural as it is decoratively beautiful.[1]

The work had been acquired by the National Gallery of Victoria in 1895 on the advice of the Director, Lindsay Bernard Hall, in exchange for the artist's *A Bright Winter's Morning*. It is said to depict one of the tenant farmhouses on the 'Banyule' estate at Heidelberg.[2]

---

[1] *Pall Mall Gazette*, May 1898.
[2] The house, identified by the Heidelberg Historical Society, still stands in Walker Court, Viewbank. Downer & Phipps 1985, p.55.

WALTER WITHERS ▲

A Bright Winter's Morning, 1894
Oil on canvas
60.8 x 91.4 cm
Signed and dated l.r.: Walter Withers/
1894
National Gallery of Victoria
Bequeathed by Mrs Nina Sheppard 1956

Provenance:
The artist; purchased by the National
Gallery of Victoria, October 1894;
exchanged for *Tranquil Winter* in 1895;
Mrs Nina Sheppard until November 1956

Exhibitions:
*Annual Exhibition of the Victorian Artists'
Society*, Melbourne, October 1894, no.38:
'A Bright Winter's Morning "When the
sun's warm rays dispel the mist" –
£31.10.0'

Literature:
Argus, 25 October 1894, p.6; *Table Talk*,
27 October 1894, p.4; 8 December 1894,
p.9; McCulloch 1969, pl.93; Gleeson 1969,
pl.27; Gleeson 1971, p.109, pl.74; Radford
1975, no.41; Finemore 1977, pl.XI

His work is characterized by its great
charm of colour and by an increased
suppleness of execution. He brings
before us the evanescent charm of a
passing hour and makes us feel the
'spirit of the season' in the colour and
lighting of his landscape.
– *The Age*, 25 October 1894

Mr Withers exhibits a number of landscapes of varying merit, his best picture being entitled 'A Bright Winter's
Morning'. There is much good work in
this view of a bush township as 'the
sun's warm rays dispel the mist'. The
colour is fresh and true, the grouping
harmonious and there is less smoki-
ness about the light wraiths of mist
than is often the case when an artist
essays to place on canvas such soft
intangible atmospheric effects.
– *Table Talk*, 27 October 1894

JANE SUTHERLAND ▲
Field Naturalists, [c.1896]
Oil on canvas
81.3 x 122 cm
Signed l.r.: J. Sutherland
National Gallery of Victoria
Presented by Mrs E.H. Shackell 1962

Provenance:
Mrs Edward H. Shackell, Melbourne, from
the artist – a family friend

Exhibitions:
Victorian Artists' Society, June 1896, as
'Field Naturalists' (no catalogue traced);
exhibition at Messrs D. Bernard and Co.,
Bourke Street, Melbourne, September
1898, as 'Field Naturalists'

Literature:
Table Talk, 12 June 1896, p.15; *Tatler*, 10
September 1898; Lindsay & Rosewarne
1977, no.11; Burke 1980, pl.80

This painting has previously been titled
'The Pool' and assumed to be one of the
four landscapes exhibited by Jane Sutherland at the Victorian Artists' Society in
1893. Contemporary press reviews of her
picture of that year entitled 'A Riverside
Pool', however, made no mention of the
three figures in the painting. *Table Talk*,
for example, said simply that 'A Riverside
Pool' was 'filled with cool sweet airs; it has
the softened subdued colouring with
which such an atmosphere accords –
there is far more in such a picture than
truthful representation of the place
painted'.[1] The present work is more probably her *Field Naturalists*, exhibited in
1896:

> Field Naturalists, three reckless young
> loiterers, ankle deep in mud and mire
> and wholly absorbed in exploring the
> contents of the swampy paddock.
> Each face is individualised and expres-
> sive and the figures are also made to
> convey the same idea.[2]

◄JANE SUTHERLAND
The Mushroom Gatherers, [c.1895]
Oil on canvas
41.6 x 99.3 cm
Signed l.r.: J. Sutherland
Inscribed on stretcher verso: 'Grosvenor
Chbs.'
National Gallery of Victoria
Presented by Dr Margaret Sutherland
1972

Provenance:
The artist's niece, Dr Margaret Sutherland, Melbourne

Exhibitions:
*Victorian Artists' Society Winter Exhibi-
tion Catalogue of Paintings, Sculpture,
Sketches*, Melbourne, May 1895, no.103:
'The Mushroom Gatherers – £6.6.0'

Literature:
Age, 10 May 1895, p.6; *Table Talk*, 17 May
1895, p.11; Lindsay & Rosewarne 1977,
no.14; Burke 1980, p.30, pl.81

According to Frances Lindsay, Keith Sutherland recalled posing as one of the small
boys in the painting.

[1] *Table Talk*, 12 May 1893, p.5.
[2] *Table Talk*, 12 June 1896, p.15.

CLARA SOUTHERN ▶
An Old Bee Farm, [c.1900]
Oil on canvas
66 x 111.7 cm
Signed l.r.: C. Southern
Inscribed on stretcher verso: Clara
Southern Warrandyte
National Gallery of Victoria
Felton Bequest 1942

Provenance:
Miss Dora Southern until 1942

Exhibitions:
*Victorian Artists' Society Catalogue of
Annual Exhibition*, Melbourne, November 1900, no.45: 'An Old Bee Farm –
£15.0.0'; *Catalogue of Paintings by Clara
Southern (Mrs J. Flinn)*, Athenaeum Hall,
Melbourne, March 1914, no.22: 'The Bee
Farm – 45 guineas'

Literature:
Radford 1974, no.35; Burke 1980, pl.74;
Splatt & Bruce 1981, pl.67

> If you can choose your spot an ideal
> place would be the country, just where
> the cultivation ends and the bush
> begins, so that you will have the wild
> flowers on one side of you and the
> cottage gardens with their wealth of
> fruit blossoms and flowers on the
> other.
> – Mary Gaunt, 'Little Industries for
> Women – Bee Keeping', *The Tatler*, 20
> August 1898

GIROLAMO PIERI BALLATI NERLI ▲
*The beach at Port Melbourne from the
foreshore, St Kilda*, [1890s]
Oil on pulpboard
40.6 x 20.3 cm
Signed l.r.: G.P. [in monogram] Nerli
National Gallery of Victoria
Purchased 1963

Literature:
Gleeson 1971, pl.43; Currie 1978, p.59

> Port Melbourne is fringed by a sandy
> beach a trifle soiled by contact with a
> city and a city's shipping, and from this
> run out two long wooden piers which
> carry their staging a quarter of a mile,
> as it seems, over restless waters. Along
> these piers are moored some scores of
> vessels and others are seen anchored
> off the shore. Here, mingled with the
> brisk sea breezes, are the scents of tar
> and odorous cargoes and by day an
> everlasting rattle resounds from donkey engines and blocks and chains.
> – Alexander Sutherland, *Victoria and
> its Metropolis: Past and Present*, 1888

As Nerli very rarely dated his paintings,
much confusion surrounds the chronology of his *oeuvre* and the extent of his
influence on the Heidelberg painters or,
conversely, their influence on him. *The
beach at Port Melbourne* was most likely
painted on one of his return trips to Melbourne in the early 1890s. (He had moved
to Sydney in 1886.) Nerli's training was
basically academic; and in his Melbourne
studio he exhibited sketches by fairly conservative contemporary Italian painters.
Undoubtedly his bravura style – and his
bohemian character – appealed to fellow
artists in both Melbourne and Sydney.
Streeton wrote to Roberts from Sydney in
1890, 'I like Nerli. He will have some work
for our show next time. Thinks of coming
to stay in Melbourne';[1] and later he
described Nerli as brilliant. The style of
this work, however, suggests possible
influence of Streeton's Sydney harbour
views – long brush strokes, some blue and
gold colouring – and also an awareness of
Conder's beach scenes of the late 1880s.

[1] Croll 1946, p.10.

JOHN FORD PATERSON ▲
Rickett's Point, 1908
Oil on canvas
71 x 144 cm
Signed and dated l.l.: J. Ford Paterson/
1908
David R.C. Waterhouse, Sydney
For exhibition in Melbourne only

Provenance:
By descent in the artist's family to his great
niece; on loan at the McClelland Gallery,
Langwarrin 1980-85; Kathie Robb Fine
Art, Sydney; David R.C. Waterhouse,
Sydney

Although Paterson was evidently popular
and much admired by younger local
painters, especially Streeton, he only
occasionally joined the group at Heidelberg. A jovial personality, bohemian and
careless in dress, he was nevertheless
retiring as an artist. His stated aim was to
paint pictures 'beautiful in form and colour and therefore truly decorative'.[1] He
often claimed that Australian landscape
had 'a new sensation to offer, a new
beauty to explain'. Increasingly, however,
he spoke of art in more metaphysical than
realist terms. 'The romantique is not airt',
he declared, 'Nature is too commonplace,
too near, too brutal. Realism is no airt.
While I think airt is a kind o' suggestive-
ness, a hint, a kind o' promise o' something evanescent. 'Tis a kind of spirituality
o' things I'm after. A dream picture that's
real, an' yet ye canna put your han' to it'.[2]
Here in *Rickett's Point* he revisits and rein-
terprets one of the favourite early painting
grounds of Streeton, Roberts, McCubbin
and Conder. John Mather and Tom Humphrey also continued to paint there for

many years. The water sparkles. Gently
swaying ti-trees frame the composition
with their decorative *'art nouveau'* silhouettes. The colourful figures seem almost
an intrinsic part of the sunlit landscape
itself.

1. *Table Talk*, 25 July 1901, p.16.
2. Quoted by Lionel Lindsay, 'J. Ford
Paterson', *Art in Australia*, no.7, 1917,
p.46.
J.C.

WALTER WITHERS ▲
Breezy day at Point Henry, near Geelong,
[c.1900]
Oil on canvas
25.8 x 51.2 cm
Signed l.l.: Walter Withers
National Gallery of Victoria
Purchased 1958

Provenance:
Original owner unknown;
A.D. McLachlan 1958

Exhibitions:
Perhaps *Victorian Artists' Society Annual
Exhibition*, Melbourne, January 1900,
no.8: 'A Breezy Beach – £4.4.0'

Literature:
Gleeson 1971, pl.75, p.109

EMANUEL PHILLIPS FOX ▲
Sketch for 'A Love Story', [c.1900]
Oil on panel
Verso: detail of skirt
24.8 x 35.4 cm
City of Ballarat Fine Art Gallery
Presented by Mr and Mrs Graham Joel
1982

> Exquisitely decorative composition
> and harmonious combination of blue
> and grey-green tones ... The branch
> of an oak tree overhangs the figure
> which is in soft shadow excepting
> where the sunlight splashes the white
> skirt and garden hat hung to the right
> of the canvas. No sky is visible.
> – *The Age*, 18 January 1900, reviewing
> the full-scale version

A Love Story, for which this is a study, was
shown at the Victorian Artists' Society in
1900, no.18, and a second version exhibited at the Royal Academy in London in
1903. As Fox wrote to McCubbin, 'My
principal picture "A Love Story" is not the
same canvas I exhibited in Melbourne. I
felt a lot of it weak and made a great
number of fresh studies and quite changed
the composition and modified the colour
scheme'.[1] This oil sketch was probably
painted at 'Charterisville'; according to Ina
Gregory another student there, Miss
Ursula Foster, was the model for the girl in
the hammock.[2] She is posed more natural-
istically than the gracefully arranged figure in the finished work. The carefully
restricted range of colours, liberal use of
white and rapid execution of this *plein air*
sketch show the kind of techniques taught
by Fox. As *Table Talk* remarked, 'Messrs
Fox and Tucker will be in the enviable
position of having established a system of
art training in their native city that can
compare with any system in vogue in
Europe'.[3]

[1] 16 May 1903. LaTrobe Collection, State
Library of Victoria. MS 8525 987/2.
McCubbin papers.
[2] Moore 1934, I, p.80. The finished
canvas, *A Love Story*, was purchased by
the National Gallery of Victoria in 1908
but exchanged with Fox for *The Arbour*
in 1911; it is now in the Ballarat Fine Art
Gallery.
[3] 3 January 1896, p.11.

FLORENCE ADA FULLER ▲
Woman in a garden, France, 1895
Oil on canvas
55 x 38.5 cm
Signed and dated l.r.: F.A. Fuller/1895
Larry Patrick Foley

Provenance:
Chris Deutscher, Melbourne 1984; Larry
Patrick Foley, Western Australia

> Of all the lady students who went to
> Europe to gain a greater knowledge of
> their profession, Miss Fuller was the
> most promising.
> – *Table Talk*, 10 January 1896

EMANUEL PHILLIPS FOX ▶
Moonrise, Heidelberg, 1900
Oil on canvas
75.8 x 126.5 cm
Signed and dated l.l.: E.Phillips Fox 1900
Inscribed verso: Mr. E.P. FOX/c/-Mr.
T.St.G. Tucker/12a South Terrace Chelsea
S.W./LONDON/To be sent to London
immediately
National Gallery of Victoria
Purchased 1948

Provenance:
By descent in the artist's family; Mrs
Carrick Fox until 1948

Exhibitions:
Probably *The Exhibition of the Royal
Academy of Arts*, London, 1903, no.169:

'Moonrise, near Melbourne, Australia'; *Société Nationale des Beaux-Arts, Catalogue illustré du Salon de 1910*, Paris, 1910, no.491: *'Lever de la lune Australie'*

Literature:
Souter 1908, pp.88ff.; *Age*, 22 October 1932, p.5; Gleeson 1971, pl.81, p.112; Zubans 1980, p.98

Moonrise, Heidelberg was painted and exhibited in Australia before Fox returned to London in 1901. The work was subsequently sent to London and new studies made from it before Fox completed a second version of the painting which was exhibited at the Royal Academy in 1903. In a letter to McCubbin from London that year Fox described the second version of *Moonrise, Heidelberg* as 'The moonrise painted from an Australian one and much improved'.[1] D.H. Souter, in 1908, contrasted the two versions:

> In his landscape work Mr Fox is equally powerful. Note his 'Moonrise', a natural rendering of a picture exhibited at the Society of Artists some years ago. Now the tones are fuller and richer, the masses broader and stronger and the technique bold in its masterly confidence. Those who remember the first picture, which now must almost be considered but a study for the present work, will note the growth of the painter's art in these few years – the extension of his vision, the

ripening of his fancy and the development of that restraint which marks the work of those who have attained mastery in their art.

In 1932 the Royal Academy version of *Moonrise, Heidelberg* was hanging at the Overseas Club, London. It would appear that the version Fox painted in London for exhibition at the Royal Academy is the painting in the present exhibition, which he commenced in Australia.[2]

Fox's interest in nocturnes extended back to his stay in France and England, where he completed many moonlight scenes which he exhibited on his return to Melbourne in 1892.[3] A critic visiting Fox's studio in May 1894 noted that he was then making 'more than a score of powerful studies or rather notes for a large picture he intends painting of this charming country at the hour when – "Veiled and mystic, like the Host descending, The sun sinks from the hill". In some of these sketches Mr Fox has rendered transitory effects of atmosphere with a science and penetration which gives the spectator the sensation of the hour he has wished to reproduce'.[4] *Moonrise, Heidelberg* is composed of the broken brushwork which he employed consistently in his landscapes at this time. His restricted range of colour and the decorative features of the composition are reminiscent of Whistler. The shadows of the trees and reflection of the moon in the pool are decorative rather

than naturalistic. Yet his choice of emerald and blue tones is certainly in keeping with contemporary accounts of the landscape around 'Charterisville':

> This part of Heidelberg has a double charm in its wealth of English trees and hedges . . . in its wide expanse of bare dome-shaped hills, which offer, in spite of their apparent uniformity, an infinite variety in their ever changing atmosphere.[5]

Other versions of *Moonrise, Heidelberg* include one in the Tasmanian Museum and Art Gallery, Hobart, signed and dated 1900; and one in a private collection in Sydney, signed and dated 1901 and given to the owners of 'Charterisville' before he left.

---

[1] LaTrobe Collection, State Library of Victoria. MS 8525 987/2. McCubbin papers: letter from Fox to McCubbin 16 May 1903.
[2] Presumably also in *Art Exhibition of Paintings by the Late E. Phillips Fox and Ethel Carrick*, Cooling Galleries, London, June 1938, no.1: 'Moonrise in Australia – 100 gns'.
[3] *Catalogue of Pictures and Studies by E. Phillips Fox*, Melbourne, 1892.
[4] *Age*, 19 May 1894.
[5] ibid.

FREDERICK McCUBBIN ▲
A Winter Evening, 1897
Oil on canvas (cotton)
123 x 153 cm
Signed and dated l.r.: F. McCubbin/1897
National Gallery of Victoria
Purchased 1900

Provenance:
The artist; received 20 March 1900 in part exchange for his painting *Feeding Time* which had been purchased in 1894

Exhibitions:
Exhibition of Australian Art in London, Grafton Galleries, London, April 1898, no.66: 'A Winter Evening'; *Catalogue of the Victorian Artists' Society Exhibition*, National Gallery of Victoria, Melbourne, [? July] 1898, no.47: 'A Winter's Evening – £157.10.0': *The Society of Artists' Spring Exhibition*, Sydney, August 1899, no.104: 'A Winter Evening – £150'

Literature:
Table Talk, 10 December 1897, p.9; *Daily Telegraph*, 5 and 12 May 1898, p.6; *Tatler*, 18 June 1898; *Australasian Art Review*, 1 September 1899, p.6; MacDonald 1916, pp.63, 96; David Thomas 1978, p.37; Galbally 1981, p.107, pl.23

Mr Fred McCubbin's new pictures, which are now on their way to Sydney to join the Edith Walker collection for London, are not only the best efforts of the artist, but among the best things that have emanated from an Australian studio. They have neither the impressionism of the French school, nor the hard matter-of-factness of the rival brotherhood. They are pictures in the first sense of the word, well and truly painted as if the artist were happy in his life and surroundings, fully alive and keenly perceptible of the subtle changes of sunshine and air . . . The second picture is a farm study, a flock of geese straggling with mock pomposity to and from a creek. So humourously has Mr McCubbin treated his subject, that again and again one turns in amused attention to watch the birds, for after the manner of their kind they have taken possession of the whole landscape, fence, field and far-off farmyard.
– *Table Talk*, 10 December 1897

In 'A Winter Evening' Mr F. McCubbin reveals a tenderness of treatment suggestive of a water-colour, united with an almost Preraphaelite minuteness in his loving care of every detail, which lends his work irresistable attraction when superadded to its inherent poetry. The bark of the brown tree trunks, and the plumage of the big grey Aylesbury ducks making for the little runnel equally engage his facile brush; while the soft flushing tints of the sky, harmonising with the purple grey of the bare branches, enhance the sense of cheerfulness.
– *The Australasian Art Review*, 1 September 1899

McCubbin's landscapes of the late 90s, for example *A Winter Evening* (included in the Grafton exhibition in London, 1898) reveal an interest shared with many of his contemporaries in the subtlety and mystery of evening light. A comparison with his earlier painting, *Winter evening, Hawthorn* of 1886 shows great development. The influence of the *plein air* style of Bastien-Lepage is still observable in the general adherence to cool grey-green tones and the careful delineation of the tree branches. However, the vibrating pinks and mauves, more broadly applied in the sky and foreground, signal the new direction McCubbin's later work was to take.

FREDERICK McCUBBIN ▲
Autumn Memories, 1899
Oil on canvas
121.9 x 182.9 cm
Signed and dated l.r.: F. McCubbin/1899
The Joseph Brown Collection
For exhibition in Melbourne only

Literature:
Argus, 23 November 1899, p.3; *Table Talk*, 24 November 1899, p.7; MacDonald 1916, p.96; Daniel Thomas 1980, no. 51; Galbally 1981, p.102, pl.20

The nostalgic title and lyrical depiction of a woman in elaborate costume seated in the tangled growth of an untended orchard here combine to form one of McCubbin's most romantic paintings of the late 90s. This woman is his wife Anne, seated on a log in the orchard which formed part of their Brighton property where they moved in 1895. The weatherboard house was frequently visited by artists such as Tucker, Withers, Davies and Longstaff. Both Roberts and Streeton visited on their trips from Sydney. As Streeton wrote:

> I walked over to Prof McCubbin's yesterday and had tea with him in his garden. Mrs Prof in a harmonious yellow gown; all the little Profs buzzing round the garden of fruit trees and the haystack. The Prof is a married man, very happily and securely married.[1]

The painting of the carefully composed figure in a landscape, predominantly in tones of grey, green and brown, continues McCubbin's earlier *plein air* formula. However, his increasing interest in the paint texture itself can be seen in his use of the palette knife and the broad splashes of paint in the foreground foliage. The colours are in a warmer key than those employed in such earlier landscapes as *A Winter Evening*.

[1] Streeton to Roberts, 18 December 1896. Croll 1946, p.62.

TOM ROBERTS ▶
*Sketch for the Opening of Federal
Parliament 1901*, [1901]
Oil on academy board
30.3 x 45.6 cm
Signed l.r. (scratched in the paint): Tom
Roberts
National Library of Australia
Purchased 1920

Provenance:
The artist

Literature:
Croll 1935, pp. 62-77, 94, 137f.; Spate
1978, p.120, pl.33; Downer & Phipps
1985, no.176; Topliss 1985, no.371a

Roberts painted this animated sketch of the light-filled Melbourne Exhibition Building after watching the opening ceremony of the first Parliament of the Commonwealth of Australia on 9 May 1901. He wrote a detailed account for his son, Caleb, of both the occasion and his subsequent work on the vast canvas version:

> When the great day came your mother and I went to the hall of the Exhibition Building, and without getting seats walked quietly at the very back, and climbing up some rails, I was able to see that immense gathering of people from all Australia, and from so many parts of the world. It was very solemn and great. The heads on the floor looked like a landscape stretching away... So I had been a witness of that scene... In the meantime my studio was getting ready, and a day or two later came Mr Jefferson and Mr Milligan, whose idea the whole thing was, to treat with me again; they had given a commission to dear old Waite [James Clarke Waite (1832-1920)] who found himself unable to go on. The result was that the commission came to me, and I made a sketch, then was hurried off to Sydney to do something of their Royal Highnesses, and you can guess, my son, how your father felt. For the first time his work seemed wanted, and things were being done for him, instead of having to bustle himself.[1]

Roberts was invited to paint a full-scale canvas of the ceremony with 'correct representations of the Duke and Duchess of York, the Governor General, the state governors, members of the Federal Parliaments and 250 other distinguished guests'.

He revelled in being selected to execute such a historically important work and in the financial benefits and social contacts that followed from the commission. The painting of the 'Big Picture', as he called it, marked the climax of his Australian historical works and portraits and, in some sense, a *dénoument*. The difficulties of completing a canvas so large – 305 x 510 cm – working from such numerous portrait studies pieced together after the event proved a daunting task and the finished painting captures none of the vitality of the original sketch.[2]

[1] Croll 1935, p.62. Invitations to numerous related functions are in Roberts's papers at the Mitchell Library.
[2] The completed canvas, entitled *'Opening of the First Parliament of the Commonwealth of Australia May 9, 1901, By H.R.H. The Duke of Cornwall and York, Exhibition Buildings'*, now hangs in the High Court, Canberra, on permanent loan from H.M. Queen Elizabeth II. Topliss 1985, no.371.

J.C.

FREDERICK McCUBBIN ▲
Princes Bridge, [1908]
Oil on canvas
61.5 x 92.5 cm
Signed l.l.: F. McCubbin
National Gallery of Victoria
Purchased with the assistance of a special grant from the Government of Victoria 1979

Provenance:
Still in possession of the McCubbin family 1924 (*The Paintings of the Late Frederick McCubbin*, The New Gallery, Melbourne, November 1924, no.37 – 25 guineas); W. Oswald Burt, Melbourne, by at least 1955; estate of W.O. Burt 1969; Jack Manton, Melbourne

Literature:
Hoff 1955, no.14; McCaughey 1979, p.66, pl.25; Splatt & Bruce 1981, pl.65; Downer & Phipps 1985, pl.48, p.56, no.148

The first Australian Federal Parliament was opened by the Duke and Duchess of York on 9 May 1901. As part of the preparation for this momentous event, Princes Bridge was decorated with a colonnade and triumphal arch, designed by Desbrowe Annear, under which the Mayor and the Corporation officially welcomed the royal couple and offered them the freedom of the city.[1] The arch was decorated with symbolic trophies showing:

> the Commonwealth, here typified by the galley named 'Austral', propelled by the labelled oars of the six federated states and won for the people today. Above the arch tower the galley masts, with the Royal Standard of England as the mainsail on which the Commonwealth relies.[2]

McCubbin executed a small oil sketch at the time (now in the Australian National Gallery). This full-scale version of the spectacle was not completed until after he returned from his first and only overseas trip; when he was impressed by Turner's late paintings which, he wrote to his wife, are 'mostly unfinished but they are divine – such dreams of colour – a dozen of them like pearls – no theatrical effect but mist and cloud and sea and land drenched in light – there is no master like him'.[3]

[1] *Cyclopaedia of Victoria*, 1903, I, p.89.
[2] *Argus*, 7 May 1901, p.10 quoted by Downer & Phipps 1985, p.57.
[3] Letter from McCubbin to Anne, 19 July 1907. LaTrobe Library Collection, State Library of Victoria. MS 8525 987/1. McCubbin papers.

BIBLIOGRAPHY

Ashton, Julian. *Now Came Still Evening On.* Angus and Robertson, Sydney and London, 1941.

Astbury, Leigh. 'George Folingsby and Australian Subject Painting'. In Galbally, Ann & Plant, Margaret (eds). *Studies in Australian Art.* Department of Fine Arts, University of Melbourne, 1978a, pp.45ff.

Astbury, Leigh. '"Tom Roberts's Shearing the Rams":The Hidden Tradition'. *Art Bulletin of Victoria* 19, 1978b, pp.68ff.

Astbury, Leigh. 'The Art of Frederick McCubbin and the Impact of the First War'. *LaTrobe Library Journal* 24, October 1979, p.84.

Astbury, Leigh. 'The Heidelberg School and the Popular Image'. *Art and Australia* 17, March 1980a, pp.263ff.

Astbury, Leigh. 'Tom Roberts's "The Breakaway": Myth and History'. *Bulletin of the Art Gallery of South Australia* 38, 1980b, pp.2ff.

Astbury, Leigh. 'Frederick McCubbin: The Spirit of the Pioneers'. *Australia 1888* 7, April 1981, pp.26ff.

Astbury, Leigh. *City Bushmen: the Heidelberg School and rural mythology.* Oxford University Press, Melbourne, 1985, in press.

Astbury, Leigh & Spunner, Suzanne. 'The Heidelberg School of Painters: A Pictorial Exploration of National Identity'. *The Australian City.* Deakin University, Waurn Ponds, 1978.

Baron, Wendy. *Sickert.* Phaidon, London, 1973.

Bate, Weston. *A History of Brighton.* Melbourne University Press, Melbourne, 1962.

Belloli, Andrea P.A. (ed.). *A Day in the Country, Impressionism and the French Landscape.* Los Angeles County Museum of Art, Los Angeles, 1984.

Bénézit, E. *Dictionnaire critique et documentaire des Peintres Sculpteurs, Dessinateurs et Graveurs. . . .* Rev. edn. Libraire Gründ, Paris, 1966.

Boime, Albert. *The Salon and French Painting in the Nineteenth Century.* Phaidon, London, 1971.

Broomfield, Fred. J. 'Art and Artists in Victoria'. *The Centennial Magazine* I, 12, July 1889.

Burke, Janine. *Australian Women Artists 1840-1940.* Greenhouse Publications, Melbourne, 1980.

Burn, Ian. 'Beating About the Bush: The Landscapes of the Heidelberg School'. In Smith, T. & Bradley, A. (eds). *Australian Art and Architecture: Essays Presented to Bernard Smith.* Oxford University Press, Melbourne, 1980, pp.83ff.

Campbell, Julian. *The Irish Impressionists. Irish Artists in France and Belgium.* National Gallery of Ireland, Dublin, 1984.

Cannon, Michael. *The Land Boomers.* Nelson, Melbourne, 1976.

Cantrell, L. (ed.). *The 1890s: Stories, Verse and Essays.* University of Queensland Press, St Lucia, 1977.

Carroll, J. (ed.). *Intruders in the Bush: The Australian Quest for National Identity.* Oxford University Press, Melbourne, 1982.

Chisaburo, Yamada (ed.). *Japonisme in Art. An International Symposium.* The Society for the Study of Japonisme, Committee for the Year 2001 and Kodansha International Ltd, Tokyo, 1980.

Clark, Jane. 'Arthur José de Souza Loureiro 1853-1932'. *Art and Australia* 23, 1, Spring 1985, pp.95ff.

Clausen, George. *Six Lectures on Painting.* Elliot Stock, London, 1904.

Colquhoun, Alexander. '"Old Gallery Days – A Memory", by an Old Student'. *The V.A.S., A Journal of the Arts issued by the Victorian Artists' Society* 5, 1 August 1908, pp.4ff.

Colquhoun, Alexander. *Frederick McCubbin – A Consideration.* Australian Art Books, Melbourne, n.d. [1919].

Cooper, Douglas. *The Courtauld Collection, A catalogue and introduction.* Athlone Press, University of London, 1954.

Cowden, Anthony & Hicks, Emma. *David Davies, The Expatriate Period.* London, 1978.

Cox, Leonard B. *The National Gallery of Victoria 1861-1968, A search for a collection.* National Gallery of Victoria, Melbourne, 1970.

Croll, Robert Henderson. *Tom Roberts: Father of Australian Landscape Painting.* Robertson and Mullens, Sydney, 1935.

Croll, Robert Henderson (ed.). *Smike to Bulldog, Letters from Sir Arthur Streeton to Tom Roberts.* Ure Smith, Sydney, 1946.

Cummins, Cyril R. (ed.). *Heidelberg Since 1836: A Pictorial History.* Heidelberg Historical Society, 1971.

Curnow, Heather. 'William Strutt: Some Problems of a Colonial History Painter in the Nineteenth Century'. In Smith, T. & Bradley, A. (eds). *Australian Art and Architecture: Essays presented to Bernard Smith.* Oxford University Press, Melbourne, 1980, pp.33ff.

Currie, Betty. 'Signor Nerli'. *Art and Australia* 16, 1, September 1978, pp.55ff.

Daplyn, Alfred James. *Landscape Painting from Nature in Australia.* W.C. Penfold and Co., Sydney, 1902.

Davison, Graeme. 'Sydney and the Bush: an urban context for the Australian Legend'. *Historical Studies* 18, 71, October 1978, pp.191ff.

Davison, Graeme. *The Rise and Fall of Marvellous Melbourne.* Melbourne University Press, Melbourne, 1978.

Dickinson, Sidney. *Art Lectures Delivered at the National Art Gallery of New South Wales.* J. Sands, Sydney, 1889.

Dickinson, Sidney. 'What Should Australian Artists Paint?'. *The Australasian Critic,* 1 October 1890; and articles in other issues of this journal.

Downer, Christine & Phipps, Jennifer. *Victorian Vision: 1834 Onwards: Images and Records from the National Gallery of Victoria and the State Library of Victoria.* National Gallery of Victoria, Melbourne, 1985.

Dysart, Dinah. *Julian Ashton 1851-1942.* S.H. Ervin Museum and Art Gallery, Sydney, 1981.

Dysart, Dinah. *The D.R. Sheumack Collection of Australian Paintings.* S.H. Ervin Museum and Art Gallery, Sydney, 1983.

Entwisle, Peter. *William Matthew Hodgkins and his Circle.* An Exhibition to mark the Centenary of the Dunedin Public Art Gallery, Dunedin, October, 1984.

Farr, Dennis. *English Art 1870-1940.* Clarendon, Oxford, 1978.

Feldman, W.C. 'Jules Bastien-Lepage: a New Perspective'. *Art Bulletin of Victoria* 20, 1979.

Finemore, Brian. *Freedom from Prejudice: An Introduction to the Australian Collection in the National Gallery of Victoria.* National Gallery of Victoria, Melbourne, 1977.

Finley, Donald J. 'John Peter Russell and his friends'. *Art and Australia,* June 1965, pp.39ff.

Flint, Kate. *Impressionists in England, The Critical Reception.* Routledge and Kegan Paul, London, 1984.

Fox, Len. *E. Phillips Fox. Notes and Recollections.* Privately printed, Sydney, 1969.

Fox, Caroline & Greenacre, Francis. *Artists of the Newlyn School 1880-1900.* Newlyn Orion Galleries, Newlyn, 1979.

Free, Renée. *Victorian Social Conscience.* Art Gallery of New South Wales, Sydney, 1976.

Galbally, Ann. *The Art of John Peter Russell.* Sun Books, Melbourne, 1977.

Galbally, Ann. 'Australian Artists Abroad 1880-1914'. In Galbally, Ann & Plant, Margaret (eds). *Studies in Australian Art.* Department of Fine Arts, University of Melbourne, 1978, pp.57ff.

Galbally, Ann. 'Mythmaking in Australian Art'. *LaTrobe Library Journal* 6, 24, October 1979, pp.65ff.

Galbally, Ann. *Arthur Streeton.* Lansdowne, Australian Art Library, Melbourne, 1979.

Galbally, Ann (ed.).'Notes by Frederick McCubbin'. *LaTrobe Library Journal* 6, 24, October 1979, pp.69ff. Original in McCubbin papers, LaTrobe Collection, State Library of Victoria.

Galbally, Ann. 'Aestheticism in Australia'. In Smith, T. & Bradley, A. (eds). *Australian Art and Architecture: Essays Presented to Bernard Smith.* Oxford University Press, Melbourne, 1980, pp. 124ff.

Galbally, Ann. *Frederick McCubbin,* Hutchinson, Melbourne, 1981.

Galway, George. *Fifty Years of Australian Art by Members of the Royal Art Society 1879-1929.* Royal Art Society Press, Sydney, 1929.

Garran, Andrew (ed.). *The Picturesque Atlas of Australasia.* 3 vols. Sydney, 1883-89.

Gibson, Frank. *Charles Conder, His Life and Work.* The Bodley Head, London, 1914.